Imitating the Italians

Imitating the Italians

Wyatt, Spenser, Synge, Pound, Joyce

Reed Way Dasenbrock

The John Hopkins University Press · Baltimore and London

© 1991 The Johns Hopkins University Press
All rights reserved
Printed in the United States of America

The Johns Hopkins University Press
701 West 40th Street
Baltimore, Maryland 21211
The Johns Hopkins Press Ltd., London

PR129
I8
D37
1991

Library of Congress Cataloging-in-Publication Data

Dasenbrock, Reed Way.
    Imitating the Italians : Wyatt, Spenser, Synge,
Pound, Joyce / Reed Way Dasenbrock.
        p.   cm.
    Includes bibliographical references and index.
    ISBN 0-8018-4147-X (alk. paper)
    1. English literature—Italian influences.   2. English
poetry—Early modern, 1500–1700—History and criticism.   3. English literature—Irish authors—History
and criticism.   4. Literature, Comparative—English
and Italian.   5. Literature, Comparative—Italian and
English.   6. Pound, Ezra, 1885–1972—Knowledge—
Italy.   7. Italian literature—Appreciation.   8. Imitation (in literature).   9. Italy in literature.   I. Title.
PR129.I8D37   1991
820.9—dc20   90-23519

For Feroza

Hazanghrem baeshzanam

Contents

Acknowledgments

I need to thank an unusually large number of teachers, colleagues, and friends for their help with this book. Three extraordinary teachers need to be thanked first of all: Stanley Fish, Hugh Kenner, and Giuseppe Mazzotta. The origins of this book date back to my graduate education at Johns Hopkins and to the intellectual vitality of an extraordinary department and university. Stanley Fish certainly did not know what he was setting into motion when he suggested one day that I do a presentation on Petrarchism for our class in sixteenth-century poetry; without his shrewd advice and professional generosity, the first part of this book would not exist. Hugh Kenner must be the world's best asker of questions, and I alone know how many of the questions I am trying to answer here, particularly in Part Two, are questions he first asked, in class and in conversation. Finally, when the design of this book was already complete but a good deal of work remained to be done, I had the opportunity to take part in the Yale Petrarch Institute organized by Giuseppe Mazzotta, an experience that immeasurably enriched this book. Every day something was said in the institute that made me rethink or sharpen parts of my argument; my fellow participants in the institute and the outside speakers all contributed as well to the final shape of my argument. One of my teachers I would have liked to have been able to thank is the late Charles Singleton. His coming out of retirement late in his life to teach Dante remains a model for me of true intellectual generosity and commitment. Imitation is at least as important for scholarship and teaching as it is for literature, and I have been fortunate enough to have been given—in Machiavelli's image of imitation—some high targets at which to aim.

Most of the chapters were presented or published separately before being brought together here, and I also need to thank those who helped with the individual chapters. The relation between the published articles and the chapters as they appear here varies: in every case, innumerable small additions, corrections, and revisions were made; in a few places in Part One, duplicated material was dropped; and everywhere material was added to make the connections among the various parts of the argument much clearer. Generally speaking, the chapters of Part I that were previously published are still recognizable in their new surroundings, whereas the chapters of the second part, especially chapters 7 and 8, have been more radically transformed.

An earlier version of Chapter 1 was published in *Comparative Literature* under the title "Wyatt's Transformation of Petrarch." Chapter 2 is based on "The Petrarchan Context of Spenser's *Amoretti*," published in PMLA. Jerry McGann and Stanley Fish made helpful comments on earlier drafts of that essay; I also need to thank the two readers for PMLA who chose not to remain anonymous, Michael West and Janel Mueller, both for some incisive comments and for giving my work a crucial endorsement. Chapter 3 was helped by the comments of Stanley Fish, Kent Hieatt, and Joseph Wittreich and by the editors of SEL, who published it under the title "Escaping the Squires' Double Bind in Books III and IV of *The Faerie Queene*." A very early version of Chapter 4 was presented at the Sixteenth-Century Studies Conference in Tempe, Arizona, in 1987, and I thank William Johnson for inviting me to take part. Chapter 5 was read in detail by Hugh Kenner and was first published in *Modern Philology*.

Chapter 6 profited from the comments of Ernesto Livorni, Bob Spoo, and Hugh Witemeyer, and it was published in ELH under the title "Petrarch, Leopardi and Pound's Apprehension of the Italian Past." Part of Chapter 7 was presented at the Eighth International James Joyce Symposium in Dublin in 1982 and then published in *Eire-Ireland* as "*Ulysses* and Joyce's Discovery of Vico's 'True Homer.'" That article profited from the comments of Louis Berrone, Dominic Manganiello, and Hugh Kenner. A small part of Chapter 8 was presented at the annual meeting of the South Central Society for Eighteenth-Century Studies at El Paso, Texas, in 1986; that was expanded into "Jefferson and/or Adams: A Shifting Mirror for Mussolini in the Middle Cantos," published in ELH, which was expanded again to make Chapter 8. J.G.A. Pocock, Don Pearce, Hugh Kenner,

Hugh Witemeyer, Herb Schneidau, and Ron Bush all had helpful comments along the way. Chapter 9 profited from the comments of Giuseppe Mazzotta, Ernesto Livorni, and Mort Levitt, and was published in the *Journal of Modern Literature*. Chapter 10 was presented at the James Joyce Conference in Philadelphia in 1989 and was published in the *James Joyce Quarterly*.

That is already a long list of people who helped, but even so it is not complete. Others who helped whom I cannot name include members of audiences who asked questions, reviewers and copyeditors for the journals mentioned above, and the readers for the Johns Hopkins University Press. I also thank the staffs of the following libraries: the Branson Library at New Mexico State University, particularly the Interlibrary Loan librarians who have cheerfully put up with my persistent presence over the years; the Library of Congress; the Milton Eisenhower Library at Johns Hopkins; the Sterling Memorial Library and the Beinecke Library at Yale; the Perry-Castenada Library and, above all, the Harry Ransom Humanities Research Center at the University of Texas at Austin, where I need to thank Cathy Henderson and Will Goodwin in particular.

Grateful acknowledgment is given to New Directions Publishing Corporation for permission to quote from the following copyrighted works of Ezra Pound: *The Cantos* (Copyright © 1934, 1937, 1940, 1948, 1956, 1959, 1962, 1963, 1966, 1968 by Ezra Pound); *Personae* (Copyright 1926 by Ezra Pound). Previously unpublished material by Ezra Pound, Copyright © 1991 by the Trustees of the Ezra Pound Literary Property Trust; used by permission of New Directions Publishing Corporation, agents. I also acknowledge and thank the Harry Ransom Humanities Research Center, The University of Texas at Austin and the Collection of American Literature, Beinecke Rare Book and Manuscript Library, Yale University, for permission to quote the previously unpublished material by Pound in their collections; the Harry Ransom Humanities Research Center for the marginalia in Pound's copies of Dante and part of a letter to Ronald Duncan; and the Beinecke for Pound's letters to Oswald Mosley and his letter to Mussolini contained in the appendix. Cathy Henderson at the Harry Ransom Humanities Research Center, Patricia Willis at the Beinecke, and Peggy Fox at New Directions were all most helpful.

Finally, my debts to my family are correspondingly large. Two etchings of Venice were on the wall above my bed when I was a child; they were, I think, a present to my parents from someone I never met, my "crazy Aunt Caroline," a great-aunt who, in the best Henry James tradition, went to Italy as a young woman, married a penniless count and never came home, making a living as a musician in Florence for forty years. I like to imagine that she knew some of the people discussed in this book, but now I will never know. Those Venetian etchings are now in the room of my son, Homi, and I knew a love of Italy had already passed down to the next generation when he, at age four, ordered a meal in Italian after five days among the "bus-boats" of Venice. Finally, I dedicate this book to my wife, Feroza Jussawalla. She has been a constant help and inspiration while this book has taken shape.

A Note on Texts and Translations

Anyone writing about the influence of Italian literature and culture on English-language writers has choices to make that resemble those of the writers being studied: does one use an Italian term or name, assuming familiarity with Italian, or the English equivalent, assuming the opposite? I have tried to steer between Scylla and Charybdis on this issue by generally giving quotations from Italian (or Latin) first in the original and then in an English translation. (The only exceptions are some long quotations from Machiavelli in Chapter 8 and some of the quotations from Dante's *De Monarchia* in Chapter 9, which are given only in English.) This format approximates that of the facing-page translations of the Italian writers that have been so crucial to the appreciation of Italian literature by English-language readers in the modern period, and my translations have generally come from the most recent of these, Singleton's Dante, Durling's Petrarch, and Musa's Machiavelli. *Il traduttore* does not have to be a *traditore*, and Durling's edition of Petrarch's *Canzoniere* has been of especial value and importance for me.

Where a parenthetical translation following the Italian is in quotation marks, I have taken that from the cited source. For untranslated material, I have made my own translations with the exception of three Tasso sonnets discussed in Chapter 2, for which I need to thank Barbara Spackman. I have also made my own translations of the passages I quote from Vico's *Scienza nuova*, although I also cite the appropriate paragraphs of the Bergin and Fisch translation. I have tended to refer to works of Italian literature by their Italian names, Dante's *Commedia* and Petrarch's *Canzoniere*, yet I have also tended to keep the names of cities in their familiar English form, Venice not Venezia, Florence not Firenze, Turin not Torino. Comparably, when referring to the 1500s in England, I have used the English term the *sixteenth century*, but, when referring to the same period in Italy, I have used the Italian term *cinquecento* as the more appropriate. This may seem inconsistent, but the process in which some Italian words have been translated and others brought over into English in an unmodified form is inconsistent. We speak of the *sonnet*, not *il sonetto*, but *terza rima*, *canzone*, and *sestina* retain their unanglicized form just as *opera*, *adagio*, and *sonata* do. Of course, the perfect exemplification of this confusing situation is to be found in the name of the poet who wrote the *Canzoniere*. To call him Francis Petrarch would seem to carry anglicization too far; yet given that familiar anglicized form, calling him Francesco Petrarca seems affected. The solution most critics writing about him in English have adopted is to call him merely Petrarch, and that possibly inconsistent but sensible solution is the one adopted here.

Imitating the Italians

Introduction

The Changing Place of Italy
in English Literature

Eras of greatness in literature in English are almost always eras
in which a strong influence from Italian literature and culture is felt:
the writers one could cite here include Chaucer, virtually all of the
Elizabethans, seventeenth-century poets such as Donne and Milton,
the Romantic poets, particularly Byron and Shelley, Victorian writers
such as Robert Browning, George Eliot, and Henry James, and all the
major modernists. Given that fact, this is clearly not the first and
surely not the last book to explore the complex and fascinating influence of Italy on literature in English. What I hope to do in this introduction is to define the scope of the study that follows, which is not
a microscopic study of a particular writer or period but is also not a
study that pretends to comprehensive coverage. In order to go into
the detail that I have on the writers I cover, I have had to skip over
many writers—indeed, many centuries. The logic organizing the book
is therefore not the familiar chronological building blocks of one period
giving way to the next, although the investigation is ordered generally
according to chronology. I am investigating a conceptual or thematic
thread, not narrating the complete history of the topic.[1]

This should be clear enough from my title, *Imitating the Italians*.
For despite the great influence of Italian culture on English literature,
not every English writer interested in Italy has felt that Italy and Italian
writers were models to be imitated. The first part of this study concerns the sixteenth century, but by the end of the century—for reasons
I explore—the image of Italy in English literature had darkened con-

siderably. By the time of plays such as John Webster's *The White Devil* (1612) and *The Duchess of Malfi* (1614), a representation of Italy as a land populated by wily and dangerous Machiavels had hardened, and this representation was to dominate literature in English about Italy (including that by American writers such as Hawthorne and James) until well into the twentieth century, until the work of the modernist writers discussed in the second part. For three hundred years, then, Italians were not people to be imitated but people seen as profoundly different. The sign of that difference was twofold: Italy was represented as a land of violence and sexuality not stabilized by the institutions of family and marriage. Anarchy and disorder ruled in the bedroom as well as on the streets.

For much of English history, then, Italy was one of the key cultures against which England defined itself, and this differential system of representation is in many ways close to a form of Orientalism as defined by Edward Said. One way of encapsulating the English system of representing Italy that dominated from 1600 to 1900, from Webster to D. H. Lawrence, is that for the English, all of Italy was a land where the English imagined that their identities would be challenged at the most basic level. This representation of Italy contrasts sharply with the attitudes broadly held earlier and later held by the great modernist writers, in which Italy was the home of civilization and the great influence on literature and the arts. So there are two very different ways of thinking about Italy in English-language culture that need to be differentiated: the one is interested in Italy, the other—to use Robert Browning's title—in the Englishman in Italy. Writers in the first tradition imitate Italians; writers in the second define themselves against the Italians.

Imitating the Italians is such a different frame of mind from defining oneself against the Italians that they cannot both be adequately discussed in a single study, and my title indicates which tradition I have chosen. One simple way of explaining this choice and the resulting emphases of this book is that I do not find the Orientalist tradition of representing Italy, with its explicit and xenophobic assumption of English cultural superiority, as interesting, as congenial, or as productive of great literature as the tradition of imitating Italian culture. *The Faerie Queene* is for my taste greater than *The White Devil*, just as *Ulysses* and *The Cantos* seem far more important than Lawrence's *Aaron's Rod* or Forster's *Where Angels Fear to Tread*.

There are, however, at least three ways in which this distinction is not absolute. First, the turn from the Renaissance imitation of Italian culture to the later reaction against it did not take place—as we shall see in Part One—without some blurred edges. Roger Ascham denounced imitations of Italian culture in *The Schoolmaster* as early as 1570, but his was a relatively isolated voice until the decade of the 1590s. It was Spenser, one of the great Italianists of the Elizabethan era, who can be said to have initiated the turn against the imitation of Italian culture that so marked the Elizabethan age. And the anti-Italianism of a Webster establishes itself a good deal earlier on the stage than in poetry: John Donne, Richard Crashaw, and John Milton are seventeenth-century poets oriented toward (different areas) of Italian culture in ways that in some senses carry forward the attitudes of Wyatt, Sidney, and Spenser. However, since these seventeenth-century writers' relation to Italian culture has been extensively studied elsewhere and adds nothing particularly new to the attitudes toward Italy traced in Part One, their work is not something I investigate here.[2]

The second blurred edge is that, although the terms in which Italy is represented remain remarkably stable from Webster to Lawrence, an important change takes place in the romantic period. The lurid Italy of the Revenge tragedies is reborn in the equally lurid Italy of the Gothic novel, and that setting constitutes a potent image for the romantic imagination. Yet the value signs start to switch: the demonic Italy of sex and violence begins—particularly in the work of Byron and Shelley—to become attractive, not repulsive, and by the last gasp of this tradition in the novels of Forster, Lawrence, and Norman Douglas, the English go to Italy precisely to become like the Italians. Forster quotes the Italian proverb first quoted by Ascham, "Inglese italianato è un diavolo incarnato" (Ascham, 66; E. M. Forster, 104), but he and his contemporaries Lawrence and Douglas present this Italianization as a liberation from the straitjacket of English conformity (see Dasenbrock, "Norman Douglas and the Denizens of Siren Land"). Italy is still the land of sex and violence, but this is precisely its attraction. The negative value has become a positive one.

Nonetheless, this inversion of the negative representation of Italy still leaves these writers some distance from the tradition of imitating Italian culture I seek to trace here. They still see Italy and England as worlds opposed to each other. Even if a protagonist or two switches sides, there are still two sides. England and Italy are important thematic counters in all these works, precisely because national identity is an important theme. The tradition I discuss, in contrast, is interested not in a generalized image of Italy as much as in specific Italians and specific works of Italian culture. If there is still a contrast at work, it is not between

England and Italy but between the Italian and the English languages, but that is a permeable barrier for these writers, who write works called the *Amoretti* and the "Vita Vecchia" and *The Cantos* and who (in the cases of Pound and Joyce) write in Italian as well as in English.

This can be put another way, which is that for Wyatt or Spenser or Joyce, Italy is a source of forms; for Webster or Ann Radcliffe or Norman Douglas, Italy is simply a source of content. Italy is a setting for these writers' novels or plays, not a conscious influence on the form and technique of their works. But it must be said that within the Orientalist tradition of representing Italy, traces of the earlier tradition occasionally surface. On occasion in the centuries between 1600 and 1900, Italy is a source of forms to be imitated as well as a source of content or setting. Here one would want to mention the imaginary conversations of Walter Savage Landor, particularly *The Pentameron*, which is an imaginary conversation between Petrarch and Boccaccio clearly based on prose works of Petrarch such as the *Secretum;* Shelley's imitation of Petrarch's *Trionfi* and use of its terza rima in *The Triumph of Life*; Byron's translation of Pulci's *Morgante Maggiore* and his subsequent use of this work's ottava rima in *Don Juan*; and the sonnets and translations of Dante Gabriel Rossetti, particularly *The House of Life* and *The Early Italian Poets*. Italy here, especially among the second generation of romantic poets, regains its earlier status as the primary donor of literary and cultural forms, and it does so in ways that look back to the Italianism of the Renaissance, particularly to Spenser, and anticipates the Italianism of a later figure like Ezra Pound.[3] But *Don Juan* itself shows how this attempt to translate Italian cultural forms uneasily coexists with an acceptance of the Orientalist tradition of representing Italy. And *Don Juan*, Byron's *Beppo*, and Shelley's *The Cenci*—far from breaking with this tradition—help give it another century of life. Browning's *The Ring and the Book* obviously continues this romantic tradition in which Italy is the domain of sex and violence, as do other monuments of Victorian attitudes toward Italy: George Eliot's *Romola* and—across the Atlantic—Nathaniel Hawthorne's "Rappacini's Daughter" and *The Marble Faun*. All of these themes are attenuated in the novels of Henry James, but the old associations of Italy and the Italianized Englishman (or American) with immorality and duplicity resonate through *The Portrait of a Lady*, *The Wings of the Dove*, and *The Golden Bowl*.

One intellectual tradition in English culture less committed to the notion that Italy was irredeemably immoral and un-English is the Victorian scholarship on Italian culture represented by the work of Ruskin, Pater, and Symonds. This tradition is important for Pound, less so for Joyce, but an implicit argument of Part Two is that we have overestimated the importance of the Victorian understanding of Italy for Pound. Seeing his Italianism through Browning and Pater, we have overemphasized the trecento and quattrocento as opposed to later periods; we also have aestheticized his image of Italy, emphasizing his interest in Italian art over his interest in Italian politics and social thought. And this is part of the reason why we have then had so much trouble making sense of his interest in Mussolini and Italian Fascism. I think the same is true for the other writers studied here, Wyatt and Spenser as well as Synge and Joyce. To imitate the Italians means to take Italian society as seriously as Italian art, and this is another impossibility for writers in the Orientalist tradition.

So, although there are some moments at which the two ways of approaching Italy I have delinated here are entangled, my focus in what follows are those moments when they are not, when a straightforward attitude of imitating Italian culture without reservation prevails. My concern here has been the moments that exemplify my theme most completely, not borderline cases. This is, I suppose, a modernist way of proceeding. Pound, theorizing about vorticist art, argued that the artist should put in only the essential, the primary features, and let the beholders fill in the secondary characteristics on their own. But I do not think this modernist mode of proceeding is inappropriate for the earlier writers studied here, Wyatt and Spenser. I hope to show that the Renaissance poets and the modernist writers I discuss have a good deal in common, particularly their Italianism or sympathetic orientation toward Italy and the theory and practice of imitation related to their Italianism. This perception of resemblance has shaped the structure of this book and is congruent with another of Pound's principles, which is that chronological continuity is less important than thematic coherence. In keeping with this principle, I have felt free to move from Part One, primarily about the Renaissance borrowing of Italian forms, to Part Two, which is about the modernist relation to Italy, without trying—except for these brief remarks here— to fill in the intervening periods of time. However, resemblance is not identity; the crucial figure in Italian literature for the English Renaissance is undoubtedly Petrarch, and Petrarch is therefore the key figure of Italian culture for Part One. The corresponding figure for modernism, though a number of other figures are important as well, is Dante, the key figure of Italian culture for Part Two. Wyatt, Spenser, Synge, Pound, and Joyce do not therefore share a set of identical reference points in Italian culture, but they share a common orientation toward Italian culture as a source of forms, as a cultural resource from which to borrow and imitate. Hence my title, *Imitating the Italians*.

But why speak of imitation? Most of us would accept Emerson's dictum in "Self-Reliance": "Insist on yourself; never imitate. Your own gift you can present every moment with the cumulative force of a whole life's cultivation; but of the adopted talent of another, you have only an extemporaneous, half possession. . . . Where is the master who could have taught Shakspeare? . . . Every great man is a unique . . . Shakspeare will never be made by the study of Shakspeare" (*Essays*, 73). And although major romantic poets such as Byron and Shelley did not consider themselves above imitation, Emerson presents here the negative view of imitation generally shared by his century and ours. The received idea of our culture is that imitation and originality are necessarily opposed, and it follows from this that Shakespeares are not taught and are certainly not made by the teaching of Shakespeare.

So why emphasize these writers' imitation of Italian culture? One reason is that they would not have agreed with Emerson. Imitation is a key theme in the work of all these writers, and their work cannot be understood unless we also understand their theory and practice of imitation. Part One examines in some detail Renaissance notions of imitation, but Pound's virtually identical notions—which we will return to in Part Two—serve equally well to introduce the ideal of imitation to be delineated in what follows.

Pound begins his seminal early essay, "The Renaissance," by conceding the customary nineteenth-century case against imitation: "No one wants the native American poet to be *au courant* with the literary affairs of Paris and London in order that he may make imitations of Paris and London models, but precisely in order that he shall not waste his lifetime making unconscious, or semi-conscious, imitations of French and English models thirty or forty or an hundred years old" (214). Pound here seems to accept the conventional opposition between originality and imitation in which originality is valued much more highly than imitation. But the sentence that follows questions this hierarchy: "Chaucer is better than Chestien [*sic*] de Troyes, and the Elizabethan playwrights are more interesting than the Pleiade, because they went beyond their models" (214). Here, the implication is that everyone, including Chaucer and Shakespeare, uses models. The question is not whether to base one's work on a model, but how to do so. Inferior writers, Pound suggests, are unaware that they are imitating: unaware of literary history, they are doomed to repeat it. Chaucer and Shakespeare, in contrast, are aware of their models, and it is this awareness that allows them to go beyond them. As Pound goes on to say, "The first step of a renaissance, or awakening, is the importation of models for painting, sculpture or writing" (214). This only seems to contradict what Pound said first: one needs to know the model in order not to imitate unconsciously, in order to go beyond the model, and one does this precisely by a conscious process of creative imitation.

This passage may not be the best Shakespeare criticism in the world, but it is excellent Pound criticism in the sense that Pound is defining a process crucial to all his work. And the ideal of imitation expressed here runs (with some variations we will examine) through the work of all the writers discussed in this study. For these writers, the dichotomy between imitation and originality is a false one: originality is born out of conscious imitation of the great models of the past, particularly—although not exclusively—out of imitating the great models of Italian literature and culture.

This view of imitation as a desirable and conscious process largely under the writer's control is not a view that has passed without challenge. Harold Bloom has been the critic whose studies of the relation of one writer to another have attracted the most attention over the past generation, and for Bloom the relation of one writer to another is a much less conscious, a much less deliberate, and a much more nerve-wracking affair. And the difference between Bloom's theories and the practice of the writers studied here is instructive in ways that help to define my subject.[4]

The simplest way to put Bloom's position on influence is that, unlike Pound, he accepts as an ideal Emerson's avoidance of imitation but like Pound, he knows this is not possible: "You cannot write or teach or think or even read without imitation, and what you imitate is what another person has done, that person's writing or teaching or thinking or reading" (*A Map of Misreading*, 32). But this inevitable fact is not a happy one for Bloom the way it is for Pound. In Bloom's model, writers feel an imperative to be original, to break from the model, but nonetheless are imitative and depend upon the model, which is what produces the anxiety of influence. One of the things that results from this anxiety is a misreading of the "precursor poet": "If the ephebe [or later poet] is to avoid over-determination, he needs to forsake correct perception of the poems he values most" (*The Anxi-*

ety of Influence, 71). The model is made out to be something he is not, so that there can be something left for the belated poet, the imitator, to do. (And the precursor is always a *he* in Bloom's world; none of Pound's interest in Sappho or support of H.D. here.) The later poet therefore tries to do what the earlier poet has already done, but what enables him to do this is his belief that the earlier poet had done something else. What assuages the anxiety of influence is therefore the fact that each poet misreads his predecessor. But this also never quite works, as each poet is at some level aware of the factitiousness of his misreading: aware therefore of the extent to which his work is a repetition of the model, he is necessarily anxious about its relation to the model, about its originality.

The differences between Pound's theory and practice of poetic imitation and Bloom's theory should be quite clear. According to Bloom, the later poet tries to do what the original did. He cannot be aware of this, which is why he must misread his model and obscure the relation between it and his work; he also cannot succeed in this, so even the greatness of a new or original voice is a kind of failure, a failure of imitation. For Pound, the later poet wants to read the earlier poet correctly to see what he has done, precisely so as to do something different. Imitation is therefore a success, not a failure, when the later poet does not reproduce the model. It is not the failure of imitation that creates the difference between the model and the imitation; such a difference indicates its success and is indeed its point. Nor does the poet have to hide or veil his indebtedness; his sources are "openly declared," as Christopher Beach has written (481), declared to establish both difference from the model and an indebtedness to it.

There are clearly some moments in literary history where Bloom's theory works well, where an anxiety about originality and belatedness prevails. Bloom's great subject is the relation of late eighteenth-century poets and the first generation of romantic poets to Milton, and anxiety is clearly the hallmark of that relation. Moreover, many poets writing after the romantics display anxiety about their relation to the major romantics, and Bloom has written perceptively about this as well. But other writers and other literary periods are characterized not by an anxiety of influence but by a voracious appetite for influence, and here Bloom's model does not work so well. Even within his chosen world of the romantics, Bloom has always had to leave Byron off to one side, and one important reason for this is that Byron's relationship to his predecessors is a more casual and less troubled affair than Bloom's model readily admits. It is significant that, although

Bloom's work has treated the relation of later poets to the model of Milton (and, to a lesser extent, Spenser), he has never had much to say about Milton's and Spenser's relation to their models.[5] It is not difficult to arrive at an explanation for this: the space of imitation for Renaissance poets—as for the later modernists—is a much happier one than for Bloom's chosen romantics.

One of the reasons for this is that Bloom's chain of imitation is caught within the confines of a given national/linguistic tradition: the English poets in his model are always imitating other English poets, never moving across linguistic boundaries to imitate poets working in other traditions and languages. Another student of literary influence, George Bornstein, has seen this limitation to Bloom's model, arguing that Bloom's "anxiety theories seem to posit a postromantic endgame in English poetry deriving from the blocking figure of Milton" ("Pound's Parlayings," 123–24). But Milton is a blocking figure only if one's overly monolingual apprehension of tradition lets him be: "Poets who wrote in a different language can liberate later poets from the intimidations of their own immediate predecessors in their own language" (Bornstein, *Poetic Remaking*, 8).[6]

To know more than one language and one national literature well means to possess more than one tradition with which to establish affiliations, and multilingual writers are therefore much less constrained by (and anxious about) any given national tradition. Byron can go back behind Spenser and read in the Italian romance epics Spenser also read; Shelley can go back behind Milton and read Petrarch's *Trionfi* and Dante's *Commedia*. And the unanxious acts of imitation studied in this book should demonstrate that Bloom's system breaks down in the face of genuine multilingualism. This is why there are aspects of the high romantic achievement of which he can make little sense; it is why he can make no sense of modernism—whose existence he denies[7]— and why he rarely discusses the major achievements of the Renaissance about which his more monolingual poets were so anxious. Spenser and Milton, Byron and Shelley, Pound and Joyce, and even Bloom's favorite living poet, John Ashbery, are all writers who have escaped the anxious relation to the model Bloom assumes because they have access to more than one literary tradition. More specifically, they all consciously and knowledgeably draw on aspects and traditions of Italian literature and culture. And it is the Italian literary tradition and the Italian language that have in all these periods provided the single most important complement to the English literary tradition.

This does not mean that there is an inherent antidote in the Italian literary tradition for the anxiety of influence: as we shall see in a later chapter, Italian writers have been anxious, on good Bloomian lines, about the impressive shadow of Dante for 650 years, and Tasso is an important figure for romanticism at least partially because he had the most severe case of the anxiety of influence ever to strike a major poet. The antidote to anxiety is not being Italian, it is being able to imitate the Italians, it is the ability of English-language writers from Chaucer to contemporary writers to draw on another very rich literary and cultural heritage in addition to their own. And these two heritages are not necessarily in conflict in the work of these writers. Bloom's model suggests that one precursor is all one can have, which would suggest that a turn toward Italian literature as a model would be a turn away from one's own tradition. But this is again a model based on a mono-lingual apprehension of tradition; we will repeatedly see in the chapters that follow that a turn to the Italian tradition enables a rediscovery of one's own. Every writer studied in this book would reverse Emerson and say, "Insist on yourself; always imitate." For it is through the imitation of models—particularly Italian models—that these writers come into possession of their own voices. Shakespeares may not be made by the study of Shakespeare, but the study of Dante and Petrarch seems to help.

Before we turn to an examination of the results of that study, there is a final aspect of my title that needs to be discussed: its emphasis on persons. It is not Italy that is being imitated, but specific figures of Italian culture, specific Italians; and it is a specific set of writers doing the imitating: Wyatt, Spenser, Synge, Pound, and Joyce. This emphasis on persons may seem anachronistic, for surely the dominant trend in literary theory over the past generation has been to speak less and less of writers and more and more of their writing, less and less of the literary work and more and more of the text.[8] In as much as these "texts" have been related to one another, the dominating concept has been that of *intertextuality*, a term implying that the relation existing between texts is one created by a larger generic, literary, or cultural formation, not by the authors involved. The concept of the author is completely unnecessary for an intertextual approach to literature, as Charles Altieri has pointed out critically in *Act and Quality*: "Textualism's insistence on the priority of signifying codes affords no place for describing the nature of human agency or the roles that concept plays in our experience" (99). And of course the late Roland Barthes and Michel Foucault provided theoretical support for this denial of agency in their flamboyant pronouncements about the death of the author and the need to move beyond the "bourgeois" concept of the human individual.[9] In this context, Bloom's insistence on the anxious author worried over his relationship to the past carries with it a sense of the author's presence quite alien to much contemporary literary theory. Yet aspects of Bloom's system place him closer to the impersonalist tradition of structuralist and poststructuralist thought. He insists, for instance, at one point in *The Anxiety of Influence* that the belated author may not even have read the precursor poet he is seeking to displace (70), and this is not the only indication that his system is less a matter of poets responding to other poets than one of poems responding somehow to other poems. As he puts it in *A Map of Misreading*, "Every poem we know begins as an encounter between poems" (70; see also 18, and *Anxiety of Influence*, 70). In places such as this, Bloom moves close to the language of intertextuality just as his emphasis on the inevitability of misreading moves him at times close to the emphasis of Yale-school deconstruction on the linguistic drift essential to all written texts. The affinity here is particularly close to Paul de Man, a critic with a severely impersonalist conception of literature.[10] This wavering on Bloom's part between a personal and impersonal model of literature has been noted before, and Jonathan Culler in fact has criticized Bloom for his "shift from texts to persons" (108), for his retreat from the impersonalism of "his French predecessors."[11] Culler has Bloom's development backward, for Bloom began talking about poets and only later shifted his attention from persons to texts. What Culler criticizes in Bloom's work is precisely what I would praise: its (admittedly inconsistent and wayward) acceptance of the fact that texts are produced by people.

In the study that follows, although I am concerned with the relation between one work of literature and another, I have deliberately avoided the use of the language of intertextuality, even the use of the term *text*. This is not a theoretical work, which is to say that although it is not free of theoretical assumptions, I do not take the time to argue for those theoretical assumptions. But I want to take the time to state them here—if very briefly—partly as a way of indicating to readers that I am not unaware of the theoretical implications of the vocabulary I have chosen. My premise is that literature is made up of works, not texts, created by individual authors working at specific (if not always specifiable) moments in history, and it is too easy to lose sight of this situated aspect of literature when we rely on the concepts of textuality and intertextuality. This is one reason why imitation is an important theme in this book. To speak of one writer imitating the works of another is automatically to assume a world of agents conscious of and deliberating on their actions; to imitate is an intentional act just as to write is an intentional act. This is a sense of the scene of writing very different from that assumed by the language of intertextuality and by many other contemporary literary theories.

Everyone would grant that intentions are complex and often problematic, which is why it seemed for a generation enormously simpler to try to work out a theory of texts freed of authors and the entire problematic world of intentionality. But, just as linguistics and philosophy of language have had to reintroduce the concept of the individual speaker, the individual speech act, and individual intentions to make sense of the complex social scene of language, so too must literary theory reintroduce the concept of the author, the act of writing, and authorial intentions—messy concepts as they are—to make sense of the complex social scene of writing. And, as I have argued elsewhere, it is Anglo-American philosophers of language such as Donald Davidson who can help us with the concepts we need to construct a sophisticated intentionalism that can give us an adequate theory of literature as a social form of life.[12]

Moreover, only such a theory is going to reunite the increasingly divergent worlds of scholarship and interpretation. Over the past generation, our theories of interpretation have repeatedly assured us that authorial intentions and the originating context of a work of art were unrecoverable, while literary scholarship, in complete disregard for these theories, continued to recover contexts and make scholarly reconstructions of probable intentions. This unfortunate rift has been a contributing factor to the incoherence of graduate education in literary studies. I have tried to make this book a contribution to both scholarship and interpretation. Particularly in the chapters on the modern writers, where a good deal of source study remains to be done, I have been concerned with establishing some of the basic data about the acquaintance of these writers with their models and influences. But I have also been concerned with interpretation, with bringing this information to bear on the reading of the literary works involved. But such interpretive use of scholarly work, as not everyone seems to realize, assumes an intentionalist account of literature in which individual authors are agents responsible for their acts. Only in such an account can one speak of imitation, and my argument in what follows is that the "intertextual" resemblance—to use that word for the last time—between the works of English and Italian literature I discuss—

whether partial or complete, whether successful or disastrous—is almost always a matter of deliberate imitation on the part of the English-language writers. These acts of imitation take place and have meaning, of course, only in a larger context or system in the same way that our individual speech acts have meaning only in a larger linguistic and social system. But my focus here is not the system as much as the individual acts of imitation by five writers: Wyatt, Spenser, Synge, Pound, and Joyce.

Part One   *Some Versions of Petrarchism*

Me thought I saw the graue, where Laura lay,
Within that Temple, where the vestall flame
Was wont to burne, and passing by that way,
To see that buried dust of liuing fame,
Whose tombe faire loue, and fairer vertue kept,
All suddenly I saw the Faery Queene:
At whose approch the soule of Petrarke wept,
And from thenceforth those graces were not seene.
For they this Queene attended, in whose steed
Obliuion laid him downe on Lauras herse:

Sir Walter Raleigh, "A Vision upon
this conceipt of the *Faery Queene*"

The essential figure of speech for Petrarchism is the oxymoron, but the essential figure of speech relied on in this first part is synecdoche, the use of a part to represent the whole. The influence of Italian culture on English Renaissance culture, particularly in the Elizabethan era, is so pervasive and multifaceted that a full account of this influence would fill a work of many volumes. What I have chosen to concentrate on is a particular aspect of English poetry that seems to me to capture the Italian influence on the English Renaissance in miniature: Petrarchism. Roger Ascham, writing long before the sonnet sequence craze of the 1590s, wrote that the Italianate Englishmen "have in more reverence the *Triumphs* of Petrarch than the Genesis of Moses" (70), and, although across the sixteenth century Petrarch's *Canzoniere* became more important than his *Trionfi*, there was a good deal of truth to Ascham's comment. For a time it seemed that Petrarch's influence defined English poetic culture, particularly lyric culture. Wherever English poets went, Petrarch was there before them, and this was true even when they began to desire to escape his influence. Sidney complaining in *Astrophel and Stella* about poets who sing of "poore Petrarchs long deceased woes" is simply displaying one more manifestation of Petrarch's influence. For there is nothing more quintessentially Petrarchan than an attempt to go beyond Petrarchism.

One essential mode of English Petrarchism is therefore a struggle with Petrarchism, and it is in keeping with this that more of Part One is devoted to Spenser's struggle with Petrarchism than with the estab-lishment of Petrarchism earlier in the century by Wyatt. The chapter on Synge forms a kind of coda, describing a moment in modern lit-erature when the Petrarchism of the Renaissance makes a brief—if fascinating—return. This serves as a bridge to the Italianism of the modernists, not focused on Petrarch but not without resemblances to the Petrarchism of the Renaissance.

Chapter One

Understanding Renaissance Imitation: The Example of Wyatt

Sir Thomas Wyatt was the first great English Petrarchan. Except for Chaucer's translation of one of Petrarch's sonnets, "S' amor non è" (*Canzoniere* 132), into three stanzas of *Troilus and Criseide*, he was the first translator of Petrarch's lyrics into English and he translated more of Petrarch's lyrics than anyone before the nineteenth century. He introduced the sonnet and the strambotto into English, tried somewhat less successfully to find an English equivalent for the canzone, and translated poems by a number of other Italian Petrarchans, most notably Serafino. Most important, his translations and imitations of Petrarch created a tradition of (and a form and language for) writing love sonnets in English, which later culminated in the great sonnet sequences of Sidney, Spenser, and Shakespeare. Wyatt's interest in and work with Petrarch's poetry, in short, was one of the seeds of the English Renaissance.

All of this is widely known and understood, but our understanding of the seminal role that Wyatt played has not enhanced our opinion of him. Wyatt has a place in literary history for his work in introducing Petrarchism to England, but it is not a highly honored place. Our view of Wyatt as primarily an imitator of Petrarch has prevented us from seeing his verse as anything other than imitative and unoriginal. Wyatt scholarship has tended to categorize his translations according to the degree of faithfulness they bear toward their Petrarchan originals. But this approach fails to make sense either of Wyatt's interest in Petrarch or of the poems that result. Only by considering his versions of Petrarch in his or Petrarch's framework can we avoid the false dichotomy between imitation and originality that has prevented us from understanding this crucial and seminal poetic relationship. And here I also want to present Wyatt as something of a test case: by recovering the positive notion of imitation that Petrarch and Wyatt held in common, we can recover a whole tradition in literature in English of direct imitation of literature in Italian. We need to understand the Italian Renaissance model of imitation in order to understand imitations of Italian Renaissance models.

Many leading Wyatt critics have found his interest in Petrarch utterly inexplicable. This tradition goes back a long way. George Frederick Nott, the editor of the first real edition of Wyatt (published in 1816), wrote that "the sonnets he has selected from Petrarch are for the most part the worst that Petrarch wrote" (quoted in Smith, 333). A century later, Hyder Rollins virtually repeated Nott's judgment: "Wyatt seldom failed to admire the worst features of his Italian masters and by translating their stiff figures and images he set a bad example that helped to deform English poetry" (101). H. A. Mason is perhaps the most eminent contemporary member of this Petrarch-hating school of Wyatt criticism. In his 1959 study, *Humanism and Poetry in the Early Tudor Period*, he makes a number of acute remarks about Wyatt the translator and relates Wyatt's interest in translation to humanism, but he cannot explain Wyatt's choice of Petrarch to translate. "For Wyatt Petrarch was an unfortunate model" (195), Mason comments at one point. Later, he is even more explicit: "Wyatt was bogged down in the habits formed in writing within the [Petrarchan] convention" (198). But he does not think to ask himself why Wyatt disagreed.

Hallett Smith, in 1946, was the first modern critic not to find Wyatt's interest in Petrarch inexplicable, as he recognizes that "Wyatt must have seen something more in these sonnets [of Petrarch] than merely 14-line poems with certain rhyme schemes" (332). But he examines only one of Wyatt's translations, "The longe love that in my thought doeth harbour," and the point of his discussion is simply that Wyatt's translation is a better poem than Surrey's version of the same Petrarch original.

J. W. Lever's discussion of Wyatt in *The Elizabethan Love Sonnet* (1956) is the first detailed discussion of Wyatt's versions of Petrarch, but his discussion is still hampered by an acceptance of a dichotomy between translation and original work, by a distrust of imitation. Lever claims that Wyatt matures as a poet by moving in effect from translation to original composition. In Lever's account, Wyatt began translating Petrarch in a respectful and faithful fashion, but then, repudiating Petrarch's values, he thereafter began to handle his Petrarchan originals in a "cynical and rebellious" fashion (25). His mature, most successful work is so free with the original that Lever calls it original composition, not translation, and this independence for Lever is something to praise. This is an analysis true to our received notions about how a poet achieves an individual voice, but it cannot account for Wyatt's own perspective. If the degree of merit of a Wyatt poem is to be equated with the degree of independence it shows from its Petrarch original, why would Wyatt be interested in translating so many poems of Petrarch? Moreover, our knowledge of the chronology of Wyatt's poems is so sketchy that Lever's construction of a strict temporal sequence for these poems is problematic. Finally, and most tellingly, Lever cannot make his discussion consistent. The next to last sonnet he discusses, "The pillar pearisht is whearto I lent," which he praises highly and justly, is far closer to its Petrarchan source than the poems he presents as representing Wyatt's breakthrough into independence from Petrarch (39). In short, Wyatt's best poems are not necessarily his most original, nor does originality seem to have been his prime concern.

Patricia Thomson's more learned discussion of the same issue in *Sir Thomas Wyatt and His Background* (1964) nonetheless shares Lever's difficulties. At first she stresses the accuracy and faithfulness of Wyatt's renderings, then the liberties he takes with Petrarch. Next, she ascribes much of those apparent liberties to Wyatt's dependence upon later Italian commentaries on Petrarch, particularly Alessandro Vellutello's commentary of 1525. In a final turn, she admits that this does not explain all of "Wyatt's rebelliousness," which she simply ascribes to his originality (200). Thus, none of these prominent Wyatt critics who have concerned themselves with his translations from Petrarch can understand Wyatt's interest in Petrarch. Our concepts of imitation and originality control the terms of their discussion of Wyatt's work with Petrarch, but these concepts do not seem up to the task.

Donald Guss, in a 1965 article, was the first to suggest that what Wyatt was doing with Petrarch was far more coherent and purposeful that these source studies indicate: "Throughout, Wyatt's poems reveal themselves to be his, not Petrarch's" (*John Donne, Petrarchist*, 36). Guss's central intuition was to see that Wyatt transforms his Petrarchan originals in one consistent direction, and that the rationale for this seemingly roundabout method of writing one's own poetry is to be found in Italian Renaissance notions of imitation. Placing Wyatt's translations of Petrarch, in short, in *their* contemporary context makes it far easier to see why Wyatt would imitate Petrarch and how he imitates and transforms him.

Thomas M. Greene included a chapter on Wyatt in his 1982 study of Renaissance notions of imitation, *The Light in Troy*, and his analysis confirms Guss's pioneering notion that we need to recover the Renaissance idea of imitation in order to see why Wyatt would translate so much of Petrarch. A central notion in Italian humanism, stemming largely from Petrarch himself, was that one forms an identity, a personal voice, precisely through the imitation of models. Petrarch's favorite image for good imitation is the way bees make honey: "I quote the authors with credit, or I transform them honorably, as bees imitate by making a single honey from many various nectars" (*Letters From Petrarch*, 183; this is from a letter to Boccaccio of 1359, *Rerum familiarum libri* 22:2). Imitation, hence, is transformation, but a kind that carries over something of the original. Petrarch elsewhere uses a different, perhaps more apposite metaphor:

> A proper imitator should take care that what he writes resembles the original without reproducing it. The resemblance should not be that of a portrait to a sitter—in that case the closer the likeness is the better—but it should be the resemblance of a son to his father. Therein is often a great divergence in particular features, but there is a certain suggestion, what our painters call an "air," most noticeable in the face and eyes, which makes the resemblance. As soon as we see the son, he recalls the father to us, although if we should measure every feature we should find them all different. But there is a mysterious something that has this power.
>
> Thus we writers must look to it that with a basis of similarity there should be many dissimilarities. . . . Thus we may use another man's conceptions and the color of his style, but not use his words. In the first case the resemblance is hidden deep; in the second it is glaring. The first procedure makes poets, the second makes apes. (*Letters from Petrarch*, 198–99; from a letter to Boccaccio of 1366, *Rerum familiarum libri*, 23:19)

Thus, for Petrarch the practice of imitation is internally divided: there are poets who imitate properly but there are also apes who imitate improperly. Correct imitation is creative imitation, the transformation of a model that establishes a relation to that past model yet allows the later writer creative freedom. And in Petrarch's discussions of imitation in his letters, he always criticizes those who simply borrow or translate uncreatively. But how do we tell the difference between a poet and an ape? By Petrarch's stated criterion, a later translator of Petrarch, such as Wyatt, must be an ape, for a translator must use the actual words of his model. But by this criterion, Petrarch himself is an ape: his image of bees making honey is derived from Seneca and Horace, as he admits in the very next sentence of this letter to Boccaccio. Moreover, his own poetry, as he goes on to admit in the letter, borrows from Virgil, and it is in fact full of acknowledged and unacknowledged borrowings from Ovid, Dante, and other poets. This is as true of his poems in the vernacular, the *Canzoniere*, as of the Latin verse discussed in the letter such as his *Bucolicum carmen*.

So there can be no easy, firm criterion to divide the true poet-imitators from the apes. Borrowing the actual words of the model is not enough to disqualify the imitator, so translation is—or can be—a kind of creative imitation. The only criterion is the kind of resemblance that is created: it must be a resemblance with a difference. The original must be transformed and seen in a new light, not merely reproduced.

After Petrarch, this notion of imitation as transformation becomes a central part of the way the Renaissance reads and writes, including the way it reads Petrarch. The poets Petrarch himself imitated were the early Italian poets and above all the Latin classics. But later, Pietro Bembo explicitly presented Petrarch's own verse as a classical model poets should imitate, and a vast body of verse was written in the Renaissance in imitation of Petrarch, called Petrarchan precisely because of that imitation but not necessarily slavishly faithful in its imitation of him.

This quick summary of the Renaissance notion of imitation should provide a context in which Wyatt's (and later poets') imitation of Petrarch can be understood. Wyatt imitates Petrarch partly because he is imitable and partly because he is inimitable. Something of the model can be brought over and that something creates the family resemblance that enables us to call Wyatt's poetry Petrarchan. But the resemblance does not have to be—should not be—exact and in this case it is not: Wyatt also translates Petrarch to establish a difference as well as a kinship. This is all properly part of the process of imitation in the Renaissance, in which one defines one's identity as a poet by engaging in the play of resemblance and difference known as imitation. Originality, in short, is born from imitation. Each poet transforms his model and in that transformation creates his own distinctive and individual style. And for Wyatt, as for a host of writers to follow, the cultural forms to imitate—out of which originality is born—are those of Renaissance Italy.

Donald Guss and Thomas M. Greene have convincingly demonstrated that the category to which Wyatt's work belongs is that of Renaissance imitation. Getting the category right, however, is not the whole story. We also need to see what Wyatt does within the category, and here Guss and Greene are considerably less helpful. If imitation is the way to achieve a proper identity, what identity emerges for Wyatt the poet from this activity? What precisely is Wyatt's relation to Petrarch? And why Petrarch? No answers to these questions emerge from Greene's study, understandably so as it is less concerned with Wyatt than with the larger theme of imitation in the Renaissance. Guss's discussions of Wyatt's individual adaptations are generally perceptive but he sees "Wyatt's Petrarchan lyrics [as] humanistic adaptations of Petrarchan rhetoric to a generally neostoic morality" ("Wyatt's Petrarchism," 13). And although Guss should be credited for establishing the general terms in which Wyatt's translations of Petrarch ought to be seen, his specific thesis about the poetic identity that emerges from these translations seems quite mistaken, as an examination of Wyatt's versions of Petrarch quickly shows.

Wyatt's "O Goodely hand,"[1] based on Petrarch's "O bella man che mi distringi 'l core,"[2] is a typical Wyatt translation, one that has received little attention. Wyatt turns Petrarch's sonnet into a poem of thirty lines, essentially by expanding Petrarch's octave, a description of his Lady's hand. Petrarch goes on in the sestet to make elegant generalizations of the neo-stoic kind that Guss claims Wyatt wishes to make:

> Così avess'io del bel velo altrettanto!
> O inconstanzia de l'umane cose,
> pur questo è furto, et vien chi me ne spoglie.

> ("Would I had again as much of that lovely veil! Oh the inconstancy of human life! Even this is a theft, and one is coming who will deprive me of it.")

Petrarch ends many sonnets with such a final tercet expressing his sense of the general statement embodied in the special situation written about in the octave or the first eleven lines. But Wyatt, ignoring

Petrarch's generalizing move, sticks to the hand, to the concrete situation, and to his own highly personal feelings about it.

Stanzas 1 and 3 are close translations of Petrarch's description of the hand, while the stanza in between develops the description in terms that are consistent with Petrarch's but are Wyatt's own. The last two stanzas, however, represent a characteristic turn by Wyatt, a characteristic modification of his source. In Petrarch, Love consents to the Lady's glove being removed. Wyatt turns this into an imperative: "Consent at last." And the demand he makes is a bigger one than Petrarch ever makes: "reche me love again." This stanza formally corresponds to the *volta*, or turn, of a sonnet, but the turn Wyatt makes is radically different from the turn in Petrarch. Precisely at the point in the sonnet where Petrarch turns from the particular to the general, Wyatt turns back to the personal and turns *on* the Lady. First, he demands his Lady's love in stanza 4 and then in stanza 5, knowing that she is probably not going to consent, he gets his response in first:

> And if not so,
> Then with more woo
> Enforce thiself to strayne
> This simple hert,
> That suffereth smart,
> And rid it owte of payne.

This turn on the Lady can also be seen in "Perdy I sayd hytt nott," which is an abbreviated version of a canzone, "S' i' 'l dissi mai" (*Canzoniere* 206).[3] In Petrarch's poem, the Lady has charged him with unfaithfulness and he is complaining to Love of the injustice of this charge. The poem is therefore not even addressed to the Lady. In concluding, Petrarch testifies to his faithfulness and asks Love to tell his Lady this. Wyatt directs his poem to the Lady, leaving Love out of the poem altogether. The first four stanzas closely follow Petrarch's testimony, but in stanza 5 comes the expected turn on the Lady:

> Yf I be clere from thowght,
> Why do ye then complayn?
> Then ys thys thyng but sowght
> To put me to more payn.
> Then that that ye haue wrowght
> Ye must hyt now redresse.

This sounds like an appeal for justice, but it is actually a demand for personal satisfaction. The Lady's mistake gives Wyatt something he can use: you must redress your wrong, which means, as he goes on to say in the next stanza, "So grant me now my hyer."

The transformations that Wyatt's models undergo in these two quite free translations are remarkably similar. His poems are much more realistic and personal than Petrarch's. Love's presence as a mediating force is sharply reduced or disappears altogether. Petrarch's compensatory abstract conclusions and all mention of the religious or the transcendent also disappear. There is only the poet and the Lady; the poet is dissatisfied with the treatment that he is getting from her and his poem is a complaint about this.

Complaint is a central theme in Wyatt's poetry and we can see Wyatt transforming other poems of Petrarch in which a Lady is not so much as mentioned into similar poems of complaint. Petrarch's sonnet, "Vinse Anibàl, et non seppe usar poi" (*Canzoniere* 103), is a poem addressed to Petrarch's friend and patron, Stefano Colonna. Petrarch alludes to Hannibal's inaction after victory as a way to warn his friend not to do the same thing. He assumes that Colonna will heed his advice and that therefore the comparison will ultimately be a contrast. And he concludes, as usual, by moving away from the situation at hand and by assuring Colonna that his fame will last for thousands of years.

Wyatt turns this poem into an eight-line strambotto about himself, "Off Cartage he that worthie warrier" (Egerton 103), and he assumes a parallel—not a contrast—between himself and Hannibal: Hannibal failed and so did I. And in the conclusion, which introduces two Petrarchan antitheses not in the original, he brings everything back to the situation at hand:

> So hangith in balaunce
> Off warr my pees/ reward of all my payne
> At Mountzon thus I restles rest in spayne.

Petrarch generalizes and praises his friend, whereas Wyatt tells us where he is and how unhappy he is. Thus, although Wyatt is translating quite a different kind of Petrarch poem here than "S' i' 'l dissi mai," he takes it to exactly the same place, another highly personal and specific poem of lament and complaint.

Wyatt proceeds in the same way in "Though I my self be bridilled of my mynde" (Egerton 27). This is a translation of Petrarch's "Orso, al vostro destrier si po ben porre" (*Canzoniere* 98). Petrarch writes to his friend, Orso, who has to be absent from a tournament and who is disappointed because he will miss the opportunity of seeing his Lady there. Wyatt again changes this second-person poem into a first-person poem and writes about his own love situation. He is away from his Lady on duty, and his poem is a fine lament about this.

It is completely characteristic that when Wyatt would have a Lady, he would have to leave her. But this can be put another way: he would not have thought of writing poems about her until he was away from her or unless he had something else about which to complain. Petrarch's love situation was no more satisfactory than Wyatt's, but his poems about Laura are nonetheless almost always in praise of her. Petrarch inherits this tradition of praising the Lady, "lo stilo de la loda," from Dante and more broadly from the traditions of epideictic rhetoric. But epideictic rhetoric can be used to dispraise or to blame as well as to praise (see Aristotle, *Rhetoric*, 1:3 and 1:9).[4] In contrast to Petrarch's praise style, Wyatt's should be called a blame style or a complaint style. There can be an undercurrent of criticism or blame in Petrarch, but Petrarch characteristically—although not always, as we shall see—moves toward a laudatory close, whereas Wyatt just as characteristically moves towards a complaint for which someone specific is to blame. And these freer translations we have been examining are so free because Wyatt must rework Petrarch's poems rather extensively to replace Petrarch's praise and compensations with his own uncompensated blaming and complaints.

What I am suggesting is that the degree of freedom of a Wyatt translation is a function, not of Wyatt's degree of independence or rebelliousness, but of the distance the poem must travel to become a poem by Wyatt. This is quickly confirmed by an examination of some of Wyatt's poems that are based far more closely on their Petrarchan originals. "The piller pearisht is whearto I Lent" (Muir and Thomson 236), for example, is considerably more faithful than the poems we have just examined. Its theme, like that of its model, "Rotta è l'alta colonna e 'l verde lauro" (*Canzoniere* 269), is death. Petrarch has suffered a double loss: Laura is dead and so is his patron, Cardinal Giovanni Colonna. Petrarch names both in the first line through plays on words that specify their importance for him. The Cardinal was his high column (as *colonna* means column in Italian) and Laura was his green laurel, his poetic inspiration and source of fame. Wyatt translates *colonna* as pillar and replaces the half-line on Laura (superfluous for his purposes) with a phrase that emphasizes his relation to that pillar ("whearto I Lent"). His pillar, traditionally, is taken to mean his patron Cromwell, although this identification can never be as close as the play on words in the original.

Thus, typically, Wyatt from the beginning emphasizes the effect of the loss on him rather than the loss itself. Petrarch devotes the octave to describing the loss, the first tercet of the sestet to the effect on him, and the final tercet, as so often, to a generalization about the transience exemplified by these deaths. Wyatt, ignoring the uncongenial final tercet altogether, translates the first six lines of the octave and then completes the sonnet with eight lines about his "wofull hart" and "dolefull state." In place of Petrarch's impersonal aphorism about transience, is, in the final sentence, a question about what he can do, and the final line stresses that death will come to the poet (although, as a relief) just as it has come to his pillar.

Hence, once more, Wyatt faithfully translates the personal lamentation in his model, but he reduces or ignores the public, universal aspects of Petrarch's poem. "The pillar pearisht" is one of the two poems Wyatt based on the more transcendent and spiritual *in morte* part of the *Canzoniere*. The other, "Myne olde dere En'mye" (Egerton 8), based on the canzone "Quel antiquo mio dolce empio signore" (*Canzoniere* 360), is a reasonably literal translation except that it removes the religious implications of the original. In both poems, the poet charges Love at the court of Reason, complaining of his hard treatment. At the end Love says, in effect, "How can he complain? I gave him his Lady." In line 149, Petrarch responds to this, "Ben me la die', ma tosto la ritolse!" ("He gave her to me indeed, but he soon took her back."). Love responds in turn, "Io no, ma chi per sé la volse." ("Not I, but One who desired her for Himself.") *Chi* here must be God, who has taken Laura from Petrarch by taking her to Heaven.

Wyatt accurately translates the poet's complaint as "Thou toke her streight from me" (line 139), but Love answers ambiguously, "Not I (quod he) but price, that is well worthy." God may have taken this Lady, but it may also have been someone more important (or richer, as price and worthy together suggest a financial aspect to this loss).[5] Petrarch's poem of complaint is not that far in tone from a Wyatt poem except for the religious implications of the close. It only needs the suggestion that the Lady or a rival double-crossed Wyatt to sound like Wyatt, and therefore Wyatt translates quite faithfully until the very end.

A poem like "Passa la nave mia colma d'oblio" (*Canzoniere* 189) is a straightforward piece of personal complaint, so Wyatt translates it into English in "My galy charged with forgetfulnes" (Egerton 28) almost without modification. He removes a mythological allusion in line 3 and heightens the sense of despair at the close by changing the original "i' 'ncomincio a desperar" ("I begin to despair") into "I remain dispering." Otherwise this is a faithful translation, but paradoxically *only because* Petrarch writes a poem without his usual compensations in vision, religion, or the possibility of generalizing from and out of his personal experience.[6]

Wyatt, in short, translates Petrarch much more faithfully here because Petrarch is writing a poem more like one of Wyatt's. A quick look at two more of Wyatt's most faithful translations should demonstrate that this is a pattern in Wyatt's translations of Petrarch. "Yf amours faith" (Egerton 12) is a close literal translation of "S' una fede amorosa" (*Canzoniere* 224). Petrarch here uncharacteristically upbraids and attacks his Lady. He describes his situation for twelve lines and then says that if all these things "son le cagion ch' amando i' mi distempre: vostro, Donna, 'l peccato et mio fia 'l danno" ("if these are the causes that I untune myself with Love, yours will be the blame, Lady, mine the loss"). As Petrarch here turns on his Lady in a manner close to that of Wyatt, Wyatt again translates closely except that he strengthens the attack in the final tercet:

> yf burning a farre of and fresing nere
> ar cause that by love my self I distroye,
> yours is the fault & myn the great annoye.

Petrarch will be "untuned" and the Lady blamed; Wyatt will destroy himself and it will be the Lady's fault.

The last translation of Wyatt's that I examine here is his "Cesar, when that the traytor of Egipt" (Egerton 3), which is based on Petrarch's "Cesare, poi che 'l traditor d'Egitto" (*Canzoniere* 102). Petrarch's poem works much like Wyatt's "Off Cartage he": he opens by discussing Caesar and Hannibal in the octave as examples of dissembling. Then the first tercet of the octave generalizes: "l'animo ciascuna sua passion sotto il contrario manto ricopre" ("each soul covers its passion over with the contrary mantle"). Then, the final tercet returns to the situation of the poet:

> Però s'alcuna volta io rido o canto,
> facciol perch' i' non ò se non quest'una
> via da celare io mio angoscioso pianto.

("Therefore if at any time I laugh or sing, I do it because I have no way except this one to hide my anguished weeping.")

Wyatt's translation of this sonnet, a straightforward literal translation that deviates in no significant way from the original, is perhaps the most faithful of all his translations, but he can translate so literally here because Petrarch, in generalizing and then uncharacteristically returning at the close to his own situation, writes a poem that is much more characteristic of Wyatt than of Petrarch. Thus, Wyatt's most faithful translation is nearly identical in spirit and in form to many of his freer translations.

In brief, what Wyatt does to Petrarch's original poems varies because they vary, not because he does. Our division of Wyatt's poems into various groups according to their distance from their Petrarchan models (imitations, free and close translations) obscures their essential similarity. As we have seen in an examination of approximately one-third of Wyatt's translations of Petrarch, his translations are sometimes quite faithful, sometimes quite free, and what determines this is the distance he needs to take the poem in order to transform it into his kind of poem. Petrarch can be addressing friends or Love or Laura; his theme can be politics or love or religion; but Wyatt transforms all of these poems into his own highly personal poems of lament and reproach. The difference in treatment is a function of Petrarch's variety, as Wyatt's poems are all in the style of which Wyatt is the great master, the blame or complaint style. This can be taken as showing that Wyatt's range as a poet is much more restricted than Petrarch's, but within that more restricted register, these poems of Wyatt have great intensity and power. Wyatt is simply not interested in arriving at a faithful—or even at an unfaithful—translation of his model; those categories are not his categories but ours. What he is interested in is writing poems by Wyatt, and what he does with all the poems by Petrarch that he chooses to translate—to put it simply—is to transform them all into poems by Wyatt.

Hence, Wyatt did—according to the Renaissance notion of imitation—find his own identity as a poet through his struggle with his model. And the firmness of that identity is shown when we can say that Petrarch in "Cesare, poi," for example, is proceeding in a way atypical of him, but very typical of Wyatt. Wyatt found this typical manner, in all likelihood, by translating poems such as these in the *Canzoniere*, but his "pervasive transformation" of Petrarch, to use Guss's phrase, allowed him to make that manner his own. Thus, we need to see that our dichotomy of the rebellious and the faithful translation (or translator) is *ours*, and is something that neither Wyatt nor Petrarch would have understood. Wyatt is not necessarily being cynical or rebellious or anti-Petrarchan when he translates Petrarch freely. He is simply transforming his model in accordance with the Italian Renaissance canons of imitation that Petrarch himself established. Moreover, his transformation of Petrarch in a more realistic, personal, and self-centered direction is as important for the later, greater sonneteers of the English Renaissance as is his introduction of the form of the sonnet. The English sonneteers—except for Spenser, as we will see next—lack Petrarch's patience and his consolations in philosophy and religion. Their model in this, the typical English Petrarchan in this divergence from Petrarch, is Sir Thomas Wyatt.

Chapter Two

The Petrarchan Context of
Spenser's Amoretti

*I*t is not only less-recognized poets such as Wyatt who are misunderstood because of our modern distrust of imitation. The achievement even of a great and widely recognized poet such as Edmund Spenser can be misunderstood if we misunderstand the model he is imitating and the relation he is establishing between his work and its model. Spenser's sonnet sequence, the *Amoretti*, has never been fully appreciated precisely because of such a misunderstanding. In the influential judgment of C. S. Lewis, "Spenser was not one of the great sonneteers" (*English Literature*, 372), and most critics have agreed. Perhaps the best reason for the comparative neglect of the *Amoretti* is that they differ radically from the other major Elizabethan sonnet sequences. As G. K. Hunter writes, "the contrast between Sidney and Spenser is one that separates Spenser from all the most successful practitioners of the Petrarchan sonnet in England—Wyatt, Shakespeare, Drayton, as well as Sidney—and shows Spenser running counter to the 'natural genius' of the Elizabethan love sonnet" (132).

I would like to argue here that Spenser's achievement in the *Amoretti* has not been appreciated properly because no one has recognized fully what Spenser was trying to do. Hunter, in his analysis of what he finds wrong with the *Amoretti*, unknowingly comes closest when he speaks of Spenser's "running counter to the 'natural genius' of the Elizabethan love sonnet." The *Amoretti* have seemed unsuccessful because they deviate from the traditionally privileged norm of the English sonnet—the sonnets of Wyatt, Sidney, Shakespeare, and Drayton, to use Hunter's list. But the form of the sonnet used by Sidney or Shakespeare is only that, the form used by these poets. It is a local form, not an immutable and absolute standard. It is my contention that Spenser in the *Amoretti* runs deliberately counter to the established English form of the sonnet and sonnet sequence as exemplified by, say, Sidney's *Astrophel and Stella*. And he does so in order to run deliberately counter to the values expressed in and by that form. This break with Elizabethan conventions is at least partially directed by Spenser's deeper apprehension and more profound imitation of the Italian sources of the sonnet tradition, particularly of Petrarch. But that imitation enabled Spenser to achieve his own powerful and individual achievement in the *Amoretti*. That achievement needs to be judged on its own terms, not—as it always has been—on the terms it wants to criticize.

To see this, we need to look in more detail at the system of love known as Petrarchism, the source of so many aspects of the Elizabethan sonnet sequences. Petrarchism can be defined as the way of writing love poetry derived from (although not, as we shall see, absolutely identified with) Petrarch's poems to Laura, his *Canzoniere*. Perhaps the central legacy of Petrarchism for the Elizabethans is the concept of the self that Petrarch was the first to articulate. Thomas M. Greene defines that concept succinctly:

> The radical stasis of the medieval personality was first explicitly
> challenged by Petrarch who, gazing steadily upon himself, found
> an altogether different state of affairs. The egoism of Petrarch was
> so monumental and so acute that it was an event in European intel-
> lectual history. What troubled Petrarch about himself was precisely
> the *lack* of continuity in his tangled passions, the distractions of
> his cluttered motives, [his] fatal complexity. ("Flexibility of the
> Self," 246)

Petrarch is in this view somewhat unwillingly a new type of personality, flexible, protean, wayward, unstable, and transformable, in contrast to the stable, static, and highly formed ideal of character held by the Middle Ages. Greene labels Petrarch's transformability "horizontal transformation," which he contrasts to the "vertical transformation" believed in by those who, like Pico della Mirandola in his *Oration on the Dignity of Man*, held that human beings could make themselves divine (see "Flexibility of the Self," 242–44, 251–52). Both these kinds of transformation, according to Greene, constitute an important thematic concern of Renaissance literature.

Although Greene does not discuss Petrarchan love poetry (even Petrarch's) in this context, it would have been his best example. The love situations Petrarchan poets describe and the attitudes their poems express are characterized by instability and discontinuity. As Drayton writes in his dedicatory sonnet to his sequence *Idea* (1594), "My Verse is the true image of my Mind, / Ever in Motion, still desiring change" (2:310). Any reader of Renaissance sonnet sequences is familiar with the sense of vertigo induced by the endless shifts in tone, mood, and stance. These shifts occur both between sonnets and within them: the *volta*, or turn, contained in the concluding sestet of the Petrarchan sonnet or in the final couplet of the Shakespearean sonnet may completely reverse the poem's opening position, a reversal often reversed in turn in the next sonnet. The Lady, of course, never changes at all, at least in the sense that she never allows the poet to satisfy his desires. But her inflexibility reinforces the protean and unstable character of Petrarchan love. First, it means that the love situation is never resolved but must go on endlessly, as long as the poet continues to love and to write poems about that love. Second, what he writes about, in the absence of any change in the Lady, is the change in his attitude toward her.

The central stylistic signature of Petrarchan poetry is the Petrarchan antithesis or oxymoron, which further reinforces this tendency toward instability.[1] The Lady is the poet's "sweet enemy," and his love for her is a "living death" or an "icy fire." A living death is obviously not death, yet it is something less than living. The sweet enemy is neither wholly sweet nor wholly an enemy. What then is she? How alive is a living death? The answer depends on how seriously the conceit is used. As one learns from reading Petrarchan poetry, there is an almost infinite number of positions between living and death, between *sweet* and *enemy*. Thus the conceits reinforce the instability and transformability of Petrarchan poetry. It is this common denominator of endless change and transformation that is central to Petrarchism. As Surrey wrote of Wyatt, Petrarchans "quick could never rest" (27).

Petrarch played this game of transformation well. Yet, unlike those who followed him, unlike Wyatt or Sidney, he ultimately sought to go beyond transformation. The Petrarch who is influential for Petrarchism is found in approximately the first half of the *Canzoniere*, in which Petrarch's love situation and his treatment of it are established (although of course even here Petrarch is considerably more complex than Petrarchism makes him). About halfway through, however, the sequence begins to shift. The poet, tiring of the game perhaps or realizing that he is not getting anywhere, begins to think about what lies at the end of all this transience: death. A number of poems in the middle of the *Canzoniere* (such as *Canzoniere* 190, 199, 206) close with anticipations of Laura's death.[2] The tone of these passages is curious: Petrarch is not nearly as upset by the premonitions as one might expect.

In "Una candida cerva" (*Canzoniere* 190), his eyes are tired of looking at the doe, although not sated, when she disappears, taken by her Caesar, God. In the last line of "O bella man che mi distringi 'l core" (*Canzoniere* 199), someone (presumably God) is coming to deprive Petrarch of Laura, and in the conclusion to the canzone "S'i' 'l dissi mai" (*Canzoniere* 206), he imagines Laura going off to Heaven in Elijah's chariot. But instead of saddening Petrarch, these thoughts make him think of his own death, and he begins to perceive death as relieving and resolving his tangled love situation. This idea is made explicit in the sestet of "Anima che diverse cose tante vedi" (*Canzoniere* 204):

> Or con sì chiara luce et con tai segni
> errar non dèsi in quel breve viaggio
> che ne po far d'eterno albergo degni;
> sforzati al cielo, o mio stanco coraggio,
> per la nebbia entro de' suoi dolci sdegni
> sequendo i passi onesti e 'l divo raggio.

> ("Now with so clear a light and such signs, we must not lose our way in that brief journey which can make us worthy of an eternal dwelling; push on toward Heaven, O my tired heart, through the clouds of her sweet disdain following her virtuous steps and divine light.")

It is important to recognize how Petrarch's ideal here has changed from the "Con lei foss' io da che parte il sole" ("Might I be with her from when the sun departs") of "A qualunque animale alberga in terra" (*Canzoniere* 22). No longer looking to consummate his love, he almost seems tired of that love, or at least of the intricacies of his situation. Accordingly, he often closes a sonnet in the middle part of the *Canzoniere* with a final tercet that elevates, generalizes, and escapes

from his personal situation. Two of many examples are the conclusions of the sonnets "Vincitore Alessandro l'ira vinse" (*Canzoniere*
232) and "Rotta è l'alta colonna" (*Canzoniere* 269):

> Ira è breve furore; et chi nol frena,
> è furor lungo che 'l suo possessore
> spesso a vergogna et talor mena a morte.

> ("Anger is a brief madness; for one who does not rein it in, it
> becomes a long madness that often carries its owner to shame and
> sometimes to death.")

> O nostra vita ch'è sì bella in vista,
> com' perde agevolmente in un matino
> quel che'n molti anni a gran pena s'acquista.

> ("Oh our life that is so beautiful to see, how easily it loses in one
> morning what has been acquired with great difficulty over many
> years!")

We have already seen that Wyatt completely ignores this conclusion to
"Rotta è l'alta colonna" in his version of the poem. And this is one
indication that what Petrarch wants to get away from at this point in
the *Canzoniere*, his personal situation, is the very thing that would so
fascinate later poets.

The way in which Petrarch complains in "Rotta è l'alta colonna"
about transformation indicates the only road he sees out of all this.
For Petrarch, all human things, not only his own love situation, are
dominated by change and instability. The way out is the way up, to
the eternal and the divine, and, as we can see from both his verse and
his prose, this is the way Petrarch increasingly desires to take. As he
says in "I' vo piangendo i miei passati tempi," the penultimate poem
of the *Canzoniere*, "Io vissi in guerra et in tempesta" ("I have lived
at war and in storm"); and what he now wishes is to be "in pace et
in porto" ("at peace and in port.")[3] Greene's discussion is again
pertinent:

> The passages in the *Secretum* wherein he complains of that diver-
> sity are too eloquent, frequent, and vivid to be anything but genu-
> ine, and the complaint is repeated again and again in both secular
> and religious contexts, above all in the *Canzoniere* and in the corre-
> spondence. Indeed the most famous of the letters, the account of

the ascent of Mount Ventoux, concludes unforgettably with a prayer for salvation from spiritual instability: "Pray to God," writes Petrarch to Dionigi da Borgo San Sepolcro, "that my thoughts so long restless and fleeting, tossed without purpose about and about, that they turn now to the one good, the true, the secure, the abiding." We note the significant progression of those adjectives as they move from the high to the highest values: "ad unum, bonum, verum, certum, *stabile*." ("Flexibility of the Self," 246)

In the *Canzoniere*, Petrarch turns toward the *stabile*, away from the tempest of life toward the harbor of Heaven. It cannot actually be said that he gets there, that he attains religious transcendence, nor can he, at least inside the *Canzoniere*. For in the terms set by Petrarch in the second part of the *Canzoniere*, only his death, which would end the *Canzoniere* but nonetheless lie outside of it, can put him at peace. This desire for a sacred rest is therefore not one that his poetry can satisfy. This in itself is not a change, for Petrarch never gets what he desires—be his desire earthly or religious—but the object of his desire has changed in the course of the sequence, away from the instability of earthly love. This is not a turn away from Laura, however, as we should already have seen from the conclusion to "Anima che diverse cose tante vedi" (*Canzoniere* 204); instead, his perspective on Laura changes as he changes. In the second half of the *Canzoniere*, even before Laura dies, she is increasingly identified with the stable, divine world for which Petrarch is yearning. One of the closing sonnets of the *Canzoniere* (347) concludes, "prega ch' i' venga tosto a star con voi" ("pray that I may soon come to be with you"); and where she is is given in the opening line of the poem, "Donna che lieta col Principio nostro" ("Lady that gladly [is seated] near our Lord"). This gives Petrarch's *Canzoniere* a shape not unlike that of Dante's *Commedia*, as it begins with Petrarch confessing his errors in the first poem and ends by his hoping to be in Paradise with his Lady, and one way to define the turn in the *Canzoniere* is to say that Laura becomes Petrarch's agent of transcendence, his Beatrice.[4] As he says of Laura in his prose work, the *Secretum*, "It was she who turned my youthful soul away from all that was base, who drew me as it were by a grappling chain, and forced me to look upwards" (121).

Both Petrarch and the poets that followed were aware of this turn. Petrarch formally marks the turn by dividing the *Canzoniere* into two parts. Many Renaissance editions preserved his division, and it became traditional to refer to the two sections as (Laura) *in vita* and *in morte*.[5] These names are not quite accurate, but the inaccuracy is revealing. The poems about Laura's death begin with 267, which creates—at least retrospectively—a nice symmetry, since there are one hundred poems from this poem to the end. However, as Petrarch indicated on his own manuscript of the *Canzoniere*, the second section begins earlier, with "I' vo pensando" (*Canzoniere* 264). "I' vo pensando" is, in Robert Durling's words, "the great canzone of inner debate" (8). In it Petrarch turns decisively from earthly things to heavenly ones, from character transformation to character formation. As he says in line 72, "vorre' 'l ver abbracciar, lassando l'ombre" ("I wish to embrace the truth, to abandon shadows"). That Laura (we might almost say conveniently) dies shortly thereafter puts the seal on this turn. This makes possible the "spiritual transformation of Laura" (Bernardo, 30) after which she can unequivocally be an agent of transcendence. The desire to be with her in Heaven can now be both a religious and a sexual desire. Rather than having to renounce his passion (which might have proved more difficult, even after "I' vo pensando"), Petrarch can sublimate it instead, again after the model of Dante. As Aldo Bernardo has said, "Ultimately it was not necessary for the poet to turn his back to the beloved in order to turn toward God" (157). In this way Petrarch, although still a lover, conforms to the higher spiritual life—for medieval Christianity—of celibacy. But Petrarch maintained his marking of the division between 263 and 264, as if to claim that his internal change was more fundamental for this turn than was Laura's death.[6]

Thus, the conventional titles *in vita* and *in morte* are both appropriate and inappropriate. They are appropriate in the sense that Petrarch's psychological orientation is first *verso vita* and then *verso morte* (toward life and toward death). But to call them *in vita* and *in morte* is to imply that the *Canzoniere* is simply about Laura and about Petrarch's love for her.[7] This view ignores the shift in Petrarch, not away from Laura perhaps, but certainly away from his earlier earthly love for her. Renaissance Petrarchism takes over from Petrarch his love situation, which is so full of twists and turns, but it resolutely ignores his desire to escape his situation, to come to a point of rest outside his self-display and self-delusion. With one exception, "Zefiro torna" (*Canzoniere* 310), poems from *in morte* are rarely translated before the nineteenth century.[8] Wyatt, as we have already seen, translated only two poems from *in morte*, and neither translation respects the transcendent implications of the originals. Analogously, most translations of "Zefiro torna" strip the poem of its sestet of renunciation, leaving only the octave of sensual description that makes it seem conventionally Petrarchan. Surrey, in his translation of "Zefiro torna" ("The soote season"), did keep something of lines 9 and 10 in his concluding couplet: "And thus I see among these pleasant thinges / Eche care decayes, and yet my sorow springes" (2). But in this context a profound religious struggle is changed into something on the order of, "why can't I have fun too?" No Renaissance Petrarchan, in short, can sympathetically and accurately translate poems from *in morte* because none shares Petrarch's desire to transcend Petrarchan love.

Spenser is the first major Renaissance poet to share that desire, to want to imitate Petrarch in his shift away from being a Petrarchan. It is this deeper kinship with Petrarch, as I will now show, that impels Spenser's distinctively non-Petrarchan handling of the sonnet and the sonnet sequence. And this, in turn, is what makes the *Amoretti* so disconcerting to the reader whose expectations are based on *Astrophel and Stella* or any other typical work of Renaissance Petrarchism.

Spenser showed the distinctiveness of his Petrarchism, if we may still call it that, very early in his career. His first work with a Petrarch source is his apprentice translation (through Marot) of Petrarch's "Standomi un giorno" (*Canzoniere* 323), which appeared in *A Theatre for Worldlings* in 1569. He revised this translation later in a form that was published in 1591 as "The Visions of Petrarch," although in fact the 1591 version is further from either Marot's French or Petrarch's Italian.

A translation entitled "The Visions of Petrarch" is obviously not the place to look for self-display by the translator, but that it is so labeled merits some emphasis. Another Petrarchan poet would have claimed as his own even a close translation like this one. "Standomi un giorno" is a canzone with six stanzas and an envoi. Each stanza is a vision of some kind of death and destruction, and each is implicitly—the last, explicitly—an emblematic abstraction of Laura's death. The envoi concludes:

> Canzone, tu puoi ben dire:
> "Queste sei visioni al signor mio
> àn fatto un dolce di morir desio."

> ("Song, you may well say: 'These six visions have given my lord a sweet desire for death.'")

Spenser turns the canzone into a sonnet sequence, his only use of this form before the *Amoretti* except for his *Ruins of Rome: by Bellay* (1591), itself a translation of Joachim Du Bellay's sonnet sequence *Les Antiquitez de Rome*. The version of "Standomi un giorno" that appeared in *A Theatre for Worldlings* contains four douzaines (2,4,5 and 6), two fourteen-line sonnets (1 and 3), and a four-line envoi; in 1591, everything, including the envoi, was expanded to make seven sonnets. It is this padding that is worth examining, since everything else, taken almost verbatim from the 1569 text, is a close translation of the original.

In the 1591 version, Spenser adds lines 10–12 to sonnet 2. Line 10 expands the description of the catastrophe ("And perished past all recourie"), but lines 11–12 expand the reference to the poet in line 10 of the 1569 text: "O how great ruth and sorowfull assay, / Doth vex my spirite with perplexitie."[9] In sonnets 4 and 5, Spenser simply adds a concluding couplet:

> And wounds my soule with rufull memorie,
> To see such pleasures gon so suddenly.

> For ruth a pitie of so haples plight.
> O let mine eyes no more see such a sight.

In these three sonnets, Spenser's additions seem to bring the poet more into the poem but not enough to produce an active personal perspective. The Lady is dead, and the poet can do nothing but perceive unhappily. Spenser's addition to sonnet 6 is an abstract generalizing conclusion very much like one of Petrarch's concluding tercets: "Which make this life wretched and miserable / Tossed with stormes of fortune variable." And finally, he expands the envoi into a full sonnet that continues in the same tone. All the speaker can do is perceive this world of change and unrest and wish to "turne unto my happie rest" (line 6), to get into the peace of Heaven's harbor. The third quatrain addresses a beautiful lady and reminds her of the existence of time and death. But, far from setting up a carpe diem argument, the speaker concludes with these lines: "When ye these rythmes doo read, and vew the rest, / Loath this base world, and thinke of heauens blis."

"The Visions of Petrarch" is admittedly not one of Spenser's masterpieces; we are not even sure it is Spenser's work.[10] But if we accept the consensus that Spenser is the author, we can begin to appreciate the distinctiveness of his interest in Petrarch. He translates comparatively faithfully, but look at what he chooses to translate: not the early restless complaint of an unsatisfied lover but a late complaint of a seeker after "heaven's bliss."[11] And it is significant, I think, that Spenser is the first poet to be able to translate work from *in morte* faithfully. He is the first Petrarchan poet to sympathize with Petrarch's growth away from the instability of the poems *in vita*, the first to share Petrarch's desire to lose the self.

"The Visions of Petrarch" is not Spenser's only translation of Petrarch, since a number of poems in the *Amoretti*, in a fashion typical of Renaissance love poetry, depend on poems by Petrarch. Two of these, *Amoretti* 10 and 67, were also translated by Sir Thomas Wyatt, and a comparison of Spenser's adaptations with Wyatt's typically Petrarchan poems reveals sharp and instructive differences that say much about the kind of poetry Spenser is trying to write in the *Amoretti*.

The source of *Amoretti* 10 and Wyatt's "Behold love thy power how she dispiseth" (Egerton 1) is a nine-line madrigal, "Or vedi, Amor" (*Canzoniere* 121), and the way each poet transforms Petrarch's original is highly characteristic. Although Wyatt expands Petrarch's nine lines into a fifteen-line rondeau, he omits most of Petrarch's matter. Wyatt leaves out Petrarch's description of the Lady and the landscape in lines 4 and 5 altogether and replaces the precise "giovanetta donna" ("young woman") of line 1 with a vaguer "she." Petrarch's poem asserts a parallel between the lover and Love (the Lady scorns both) and reinforces it by the balanced phrasing of lines 2, 6, and 9, each of which refers both to the poet and to Love. Wyatt breaks up this parallel by expanding every reference to himself: "del mio mal non cura" becomes the full line "my great payne how litle she regardeth"; "ver me spietata" is expanded into line 8, "to me spitefull, withoute cause or mesure." In Petrarch, the Lady resists Love, and the poet suggests that Love "revenge" himself by making her fall in love (presumably with the poet) and thus accept Love's reign. Wyatt's Lady is a traitor who has broken a holy oath, and the revenge Wyatt suggests is to break the Lady's heart. The changes Wyatt makes, then, are clear, basic, and utterly characteristic of Wyatt's translations of Petrarch. In Wyatt's more personal poem, the unhappiness of the lover is stressed in place of Petrarch's more abstract equation between the status of the lover and that of Love. Wyatt's is also more self-absorbed in that we learn nothing about the Lady or her surroundings, and it is harsher and darker in that Wyatt seems, unlike Petrarch, to wish to get back at the Lady. Petrarch is concerned with abstractions; Wyatt wants personal satisfaction.

Spenser's poem is quite different from Wyatt's but no closer to Petrarch, since Spenser, like Wyatt, translates faithfully only when his model is completely congenial. Spenser's first line is his own: "Unrighteous Lord of loue, what law is this." He begins with the universal pattern, assumes that Love is reponsible for it, and then descends to the particular situation of Petrarch's poem, the assumption of which is rather that Love has lost control and should regain it. The next three lines follow Petrarch's first stanza closely, although the "lordeth" of line 3 and the "freewill" of line 4, paralleling the "Lord" of line 1, show that mastery remains the subject. Spenser thus continues to emphasize the abstract moral and philosophical issues latent in the love situation.

The next quatrain translates Petrarch's second stanza. Like Wyatt, Spenser removes the description of the landscape and the Lady, but he also removes any description of himself. The Lady expands beyond the cruel fair of Petrarchism to become a "Tyrannesse," like some dreadful figure from *The Faerie Queene*, who massacres people with her eyes. In lines 7–8, Spenser returns to the theme he introduced in lines 1–2, the idea that the Lady and Love are cooperating, taking vengeance against the male sex. Thus, Spenser's analysis of the problem is wider than those of Petrarch and Wyatt: according to them, the Lady is the problem; Spenser suggests rather that love itself is the problem.

The third quatrain is somewhat closer to Petrarch and Wyatt: all urge Love to take some action against the Lady. But Spenser omits the "'i' son pregion" ("I am a prisoner") of the original and urges only a mild action. Bring her down to my level and restore the general balance threatened by her pride and self-will—this seems to be Spenser's plea in line 9, "But her proud hart doe thou a little shake," which is far less severe than Petrarch's "take vengeance" in the sense of "make her fall in love with me," to say nothing of Wyatt's dark-sounding plan of revenge. The concluding couplet refers to the poet for the first time since line 4, but the situation becomes only slightly more concrete. In contrast to Wyatt, then, Spenser translates Petrarch here so as to make the poem less personal and less specific in its depiction of a love situation.

The other poem of the *Amoretti* that closely depends on Petrarch, sonnet 67, is also translated by Wyatt in his "Who so list to hounte I know where is an hynde" (Egerton 7). Petrarch's "Una candida cerva" ("A white doe"; *Canzoniere* 190), their common model, is visionary, pictorial, and religious: the poet has a vision of a white doe, who of course stands for his Lady. She has diamonds and topazes around her neck, emblems respectively of steadfastness and chastity, which say "Nessun mi tocchi, . . . Libera farmi al mio Cesare parve" ("Let no one touch me, . . . It has pleased my Caesar to make me free"). Her Caesar is God, who has made her free to ascend to Heaven, made her free of this world. In the final tercet, the poet reenters the poem, revealing the whole to be his vision, a foreshadowing of Laura's death.

Wyatt's realistic and secular poem is very different. Wyatt turns Petrarch's vision into a chase, but it is a chase that has proved too much for Wyatt. He has withdrawn, figuring that in any case no one is going to win this Lady:

> and graven with Diamonds in letters plain
> There is written her faier neck rounde abowte
> Noli me tangere for Cesars I ame
> And wylde for to hold though I seme tame.
>
> (Lines 11–14)

The symbol for steadfastness, but not the one for chastity, remains. This Lady already belongs to someone, to Caesar, and everyone else must keep his distance. Petrarch's Lady is a bride of Christ; Wyatt's is part of a royal harem. That this "hynde" may be Anne Boleyn and Caesar Henry VIII does not represent a significant change from Petrarch, whose doe can also be read biographically. More significant is the absence of any possibility of transcendence: the sole point in this hunt is to catch the Lady, but Wyatt knows that he is not going to succeed. Moreover, unlike Petrarch's vision, his vision does not compensate him for that loss. In Wyatt's world, there are no comforting abstractions to which the poet can turn; there is only the social world of men and women, which proves highly unsatisfactory. Wyatt thus ends up with nothing, and he makes his poem a personal lament about this state of affairs.

A cursory examination of *Amoretti* 67, Spenser's version of the same poem, would appear to contradict the contrast I have drawn so far. In this poem he seems close to Wyatt in that he transforms Petrarch in a realistic and more personal direction. But at least one other Petrarchan "deer poem" needs to be considered—Tasso's sonnet "Questa fera gentil" ("This gentle beast")—to complete the list of Spenser's models.[12] Although Tasso addresses his poem to a friend, he changes the common Petrarchan model, "Una candida cerva," in a way not unlike the way Wyatt changes it. The deer is a material—not a visionary—young Lady who willingly allows herself to be captured. The octave describes the capture, while in the sestet Tasso imagines for his friend the joys that will be.

Spenser's poem echoes all three of these previous poems. Spenser, like Wyatt, gives up the chase with a note of resignation, but his Lady, like Tasso's, then gives up as well and allows herself to be captured. The rest of the poem follows Tasso, although it goes beyond him in that the poem describes—rather than imagines—what follows the capture:

> There she beholding me with mylder looke,
> sought not to fly, but fearelesse still did bide:
> till I in hand her yet halfe trembling tooke.
>
> (Lines 9–11)

But just at that point, the poem turns and the actual scene dissolves in a way parallel to—although different from—Petrarch's dissolve in "Una candida cerva":

> and with her owne goodwill her fyrmely tyde.
> Strange thing me seemd to see a beast so wyld,
> so goodly woone with her owne will beguyld.
>
> (Lines 12–14)

This is a curious conclusion to a poem that celebrates the actual conquest of the Lady. The love situation loses all its specificity and hence, for many readers, all its interest. Instead of depicting a conquest, it defines the state of mind a Lady must be in to be conquered. Wyatt's deer seems tame but is really wild; Spenser's seems wild but is tame—is tamed in the course of the poem. But she is tamed less by the poet than by her own will. This shows the change in her since *Amoretti* 10, in which she was (or seemed to be) completely hard-hearted and self-willed. In short, to be conquered, she must will her own conquest, while the lover must have no will to conquer. Thus, it cannot be a conquest at all but can only be (as sonnet 65 says) a league "that loyal love hath bound." The poet and the Lady must join together in a relationship utterly different from the Petrarchan dichotomy of the ardent lover and stony Lady.

No other poem in the *Amoretti* is such a direct version of a Petrarchan model.[13] But at least five subsequent sonnets (*Amoretti* 72, 73, 76, 77, and 81) depend on Tasso, whose love lyrics are quite typical of Renaissance Petrarchism in the respects explored here. And in these sonnets we can see Spenser continuing his pattern of adapting Petrarchan poems in a non-Petrarchan direction. Spenser's use of Tasso's sonnets is readily explicable in view of his reliance on Tasso's *Gerusalemme Liberata* in *The Faerie Queene*, but, for reasons that should become clear, Spenser may also have wished to show his distance more from typical Petrarchist poets such as Tasso (or Desportes, another model for a number of sonnets in the *Amoretti*) than from Petrarch.[14]

Amoretti 72 is an interesting transformation of its source in Tasso, "L'alma vaga."[15] Tasso's poem uses an opposition between Heaven and Earth and places the poet's love for the Lady on the terrestrial side, in keeping with Tasso's Platonic frame of reference, in which any consummated love or physical desire is necessarily an earthly or lower form of love.[16] Spenser maintains Tasso's logic, but the reader must pay close attention to discern it. Spenser's first quatrain presents Tasso's distinction between heavenly things and earthly, mortal things. In the second quatrain, the poet's spirit has to turn back to earth to be with the Lady, making her, logically, an earthly thing. The Lady, however, is described as "that souerayne beauty" "resembling heauens glory." The poet's fancy, once it is near her, "ne thinks of other heauen," and the poem concludes: "Hart need not with none other happinesse, / but here on earth to haue such heuens blisse." All the heavenly modifiers he uses describe the supposedly earthly Lady, and the effect is to identify the Lady with Heaven, not with the burden of mortality. The Lady is not, therefore, as in Dante and Petrarch, an agent of transcendence who will aid the poet in his ascent to Heaven or of the Platonic ladder; she is Heaven itself, on earth.[17]

Amoretti 76 and 77, the last adaptations in the *Amoretti* we shall examine, are expansions of a single Tasso sonnet, "Non son sì belli," and their transformations of their source closely parallel those of sonnet 72.[18] Tasso's poem describes his Lady's breasts, principally through two extended conceits. The octave compares them to the rich fruit of autumn, more beautiful by far than the sweet flowers of spring and so beautiful that the poet asks, who could curb his thoughts when they steal their food from such a source? The sestet claims in true Petrarchan hyperbole that these breasts make the golden apples that successfully tempted Atalanta or those that the dragon guarded from Hercules seem vile.

Spenser devoted a sonnet each to the octave and the sestet. This greatly expands Tasso's sensuous poem, but something else happens to it in Spenser's hands. Spenser's subject in sonnet 76 is not so much the Lady's breasts as the poet's thoughts about them, and the poet's thoughts are less physical than theological. Her breasts are "fraught with vertues richest tresure" (line 1). They are "the bowre of blisse, the paradice of pleasure, / the sacred harbour of that heuenly spright" (lines 3–4). The second and third quatrains describe how his thoughts, "whiles diuing deepe through amorous insight" (line 7), saw the breasts (here he hurriedly translates Tasso's main image in lines 9 and 10) and rested on them. The sonnet concludes: "Sweet thoughts I enuy your so happy rest, / which oft I wisht, yet neuer was so blest." The poet wishes to be where his thoughts were, but he implies that it is not yet time, and he playfully chides his thoughts for being where he cannot yet be. When it is time, the poet will have his wish, which is to be *blessed* with *rest*, and I want to stress the conjunction of those rhyme words. The poet does not do anything here, nor does he wish to. His closest approach to action is to construct an image of his desire that conflates sexual and religious desires but does not reduce one to a form of the other.

Spenser continues this image making in sonnet 77, which begins as a vision and by line 6 has again become a vision of her breasts. Following Tasso, Spenser sees them as more precious than the fruit in the myths of Hercules and Atalanta. Spenser then goes beyond Tasso to describe the breasts as:

> Exceeding sweet, yet voyd of sinfull vice,
> That many sought yet none could euer taste,
> sweet fruit of pleasure brought from paradice
> by loue himselfe, and in his garden plaste.
> (Lines 9–12)

Here, as in sonnet 76, the Lady is to be identified with the image of paradise, obviously not in the negative sense explored in Book 2 of *The Faerie Queene*, but in the positive sense explored in Book 3 (see Giamatti, 232–90). And, like the other sonnets we have examined, sonnet 77 shows a remarkable lack of any concreteness and specificity. The poet disappears, as does the Lady, in effect. Nothing particular happens, and, as in sonnets 67 and 72, it seems more as if abstract conditions are being specified than a love situation is being described:

beautiful breasts must be "voyd of sinfull vice" as well as sweet; the Lady must be religious as well as sensuous.

These sonnets are typical: the *Amoretti* are never very descriptive, never tell us anything very specific about the love situation being depicted. This has been noted by G. K. Hunter: "Spenser's sequence is far more concerned with the relationship and far less with the individual. The lover's 'I' or ego is completely ignored and even when mentioned is usually absorbed into a pattern which aborts self-definition" (128). But in that final phrase Hunter reveals his assumption that self-definition is what a sonnet sequence should be about. The self-effacement characteristic of the *Amoretti* stands in sharp contrast to the egotism and self-absorption of typical Petrarchan poets such as Sidney and Wyatt.[19] What would be left of Petrarchism without the self-will and egotism displayed on both sides when the irresistible force of the poet hits the immovable object of the Lady's heart? In specifying the mutual redirection of the will away from egotistical conflict by both poet and Lady as the key condition for the existence of love, as he does explicitly in sonnet 67 and implicitly throughout the *Amoretti*, Spenser is striking at the very heart of Petrarchism. And he does so deliberately: the contrast the *Amoretti* offer to the work of other Petrarchan poets is a deliberate contrast.

This can be seen in two ways. I have already tried to show how individual sonnets transform Petrarchan poems in non–Petrarchan directions, challenging and dissolving the topoi of Petrarchan love. Spenser consciously challenges Petrarchan notions of love when he writes a poem like sonnet 67, which relies on the classic Petrarchan topos of love as a hunt only to conclude that love cannot be a hunt if it be love.

If we look at the shape of the entire sequence, we can see a second way in which Spenser is transforming and challenging the conventions of Petrarchism. What he does to the Petrarchan tradition in sonnet 67 can stand in miniature for what he does to that tradition in the *Amoretti* as a whole. One aspect of the *Amoretti* that has puzzled critics is the presence early in the sequence of a number of sonnets, like sonnet 10 or 30, that are almost parodically Petrarchan in their depiction of the cruel fair and of the instability and restlessness of the love situation (see Lever, 97–103, Martz, and Neely, 372–73). J. W. Lever argues that the *Amoretti* are actually two groups of love poems, one properly Spenserian and the other more conventionally Petrarchan. He identifies eighteen early sonnets as the Petrarchan group, which he says should in fact be removed from the sequence altogether (97–103).[20] Less drastically, Louis Martz also identifies eighteen early sonnets as highly Petrarchan and suggests that their exaggeratedly conventional Petrarchism is a parody (155–62).[21] That Lever's and Martz's lists have only seven sonnets in common suggests that this conventional Petrarchism is more diffused throughout the early sonnets in the sequence than these critics recognize. But there is a group of unabashedly Petrarchan poems early in the *Amoretti* that fits a little oddly with other aspects of the sequence. It is almost as if Spenser had difficulty writing these poems naturally but felt he needed them. He needed to entangle his love situation with the Petrarchan, to make his Lady the cruel fair.

He needed to do so, I would argue, because he was trying to accomplish much more in the *Amoretti* than depict his own courtship. Writing at a time when the accepted and received traditions of love (and of love poetry) were Petrarchan, he begins his sequence of love poems by firmly—even heavy-handedly—situating his own poetry in that tradition. Then, as he continues, he turns that tradition inside out, transforming it in a consistent direction and subjecting it to a searching critique. The problem with his love situation for much of the sequence is that it is caught in the ceaseless transformation and self-absorption of Petrarchan love. The sequence, turning away from that kind of love, turns toward a more stable kind of love in which choices are permanent and involve a fixing and curbing of the self. Spenser is both depicting and advocating a turn toward this kind of love. One achieves such a love by a proper use of the love object, who of course in this view is no object at all. Both poet and Lady must be by their own will beguiled, producing a selfless and mutual concord, not the discord and egotistical self-display of Petrarchism. Other Elizabethan sonnet sequences have a real problem with endings, for the love situations they depict have no satisfactory conclusion. Spenser's does, so the *Amoretti* can lead into his *Epithalamion*, his great poem celebrating his own marriage.

The end of the *Amoretti* gives the sequence a shape many such sequences lack. From the perspective provided by the end, the entire sequence should be seen as a turn away from the restlessness of Petrarchan love and toward the peace and rest Spenser finds in the sacred world of marriage. That desire to turn toward a sacred rest is something we have seen before—in Petrarch—and Spenser, in the way he ends the *Amoretti*, is recovering for the first time since the *Canzoniere*

Petrarch's ideal of a transcendent rest at the end of love and at the end of a cycle of love poems. Both locate that ideal in the Lady and in Heaven, and they seek to fuse the two. The only way Petrarch can fuse them is in death, whereas Spenser fuses them in marriage.

The turn to marriage obviously differs in one vital respect from the turn to death and life after death, but marriage in the *Amoretti* and death in the *Canzoniere* create sacred rest in parallel ways. Both poets wish to lose their selfhood and "'l ver abbracciar, lassando l'ombre." Spenser thus recovers the serious, religious approach to love found in the *volta*, or turn, of the *Canzoniere*, which had been ignored in the intervening two hundred years by the host of Renaissance poets who took their language of love from the first part of the *Canzoniere*. He makes his *Amoretti* trace a parallel turn, away from the instability of Petrarchism toward the stability of a more serious conception of love. In this respect, the *Amoretti* constitutes a turn on the whole Petrarchan tradition, an attempt to transform the tradition in order to redeem its seriousness. (And the adaptations of individual Petrarchan poems we have examined are a crucial part of the attempt.) This explains his choice of what is often felt to be an uncongenial format for his art, the sonnet. Spenser is interested in recovering a use of the sonnet that was once central but has become eccentric. His project in the *Amoretti* is to recenter this use of the sonnet, to recover that balance between spirit and matter lost in the sonnet between Petrarch and himself. He criticizes imitations of Petrarchism but in a way that indicates a more profound imitation of Petrarch.

Moreover, this turn gives the *Amoretti* a shape parallel to that of the *Canzoniere*. In both, love and the Lady are identified with the sacred, are made sacred, *in the course of* the sequence. We have already traced the shift in Petrarch's sequence from an orientation *verso vita* to one *verso morte*, accomplished in poems 264–67 of the *Canzoniere*. First comes the mental change in the poet and then the change in the Lady, her death. The two changes together produce the change in the relationship between the poet and the Lady. The *Amoretti* implicitly divide into two parts also, before and after the two lovers achieve their selfless concord. (These parts might be named profane or Petrarchan love and sacred love.) And, although a division of sonnet sequences into two parts after Petrarch is, as Carol Thomas Neely has shown (368–69), common among Elizabethan sonneteers, only Spenser uses that structure in a comparably serious way.[22] Although the order is slightly different, sonnets 64–67 of the *Amoretti* make the same turn found in poems 264–67 of the *Canzoniere*.[23] Sonnet 64 records the first kiss, but it seems from sonnet 65 as if the Lady quickly has doubts. The poet reassures her in sonnets 65 and 66 by signaling his intention that this is to be a permanent formative relationship, not a restless Petrarchan one:

> There pride dare not approach, nor discord spill
> the league twixt them, that loyal loue hath bound:
> but simple truth and mutuall good will,
> seekes with sweet peace to salue each others wound:
> There fayth doth fearelesse dwell in brasen towre,
> and spotlesse pleasure builds her sacred bowre.
>
> (65.9–14)

This assurance then produces (or at least is followed by) the change in the Lady recorded in sonnet 67, which sets the seal on the turn. As in Petrarch, the Lady changes, the poet changes, and the relationship changes. The rest of the sequence is in fact no more at peace than the concluding poems of Petrarch's, but both poets are preparing that peace, which will be achieved by Petrarch joining his Lady in Heaven and by Spenser joining his in marriage.

Spenser's sequence, of course, transforms as well as imitates Petrarch's. Spenser is truer to Petrarch than any Petrarchan before him, but he, too, has his transformation to make, his original position to take vis-à-vis Petrarch. He replaces Petrarch's passionate but unconsummated love by marriage, presenting that union as the sacred harbor of stability. And, in so doing, he rejects Tasso's Platonic conception of love that would have the lover rise above the realm of the physical just as surely as he rejects Dante's and Petrarch's Pauline and Catholic conception that the truly spiritual life is the celibate one. Spenser's conception of love as sacred when (and only when) it finds expression in a stable, reciprocal, and selfless marriage is peculiarly his own in Spenser's stress on the mutuality and equality necessary for married love. Thus, although he lines up with Petrarch against Petrarchans such as Sidney, Wyatt, and Tasso, he also stands alone as a poet of marriage, articulating in his love sonnets a critique of adulterous love that would consider Petrarch and the Petrarchans alike advocates of a lesser, debased form of love.

The *Amoretti*, of course, is not the only work of Spenser's to articulate that critique. As the next two chapters should show, Books 3 and 4 of *The Faerie Queene* have the same theme and advocate the same conception of love. And if we would grant with C. S. Lewis that the

Spenser of Books 3 and 4 (and, I would add, the *Amoretti*) "is the greatest among the founders of that romantic conception of marriage which is the basis of all our love literature from Shakespeare to Meredith" (*Allegory*, 360),[24] then the *Amoretti* stands as a central work, in this sense at least the most influential of the great Elizabethan sonnet sequences, although also, in this sense, deliberately the least representative.

But we also need to see that Spenser's critique of Petrarch and the Petrarchans as advocates of adulterous love ties this critique to some larger social and political currents. And the discussion of *The Faerie Queene* that follows in the next two chapters should show the social and political implications of Spenser's wrestle with Petrarchism, implications that help end the tradition of imitation of Italian culture in which Spenser is working in the *Amoretti*.

Chapter Three

Escaping the Squires' Double Bind
in The Faerie Queene

Spenser's great epic poem, *The Faerie Queene,* is not as obviously in significant relation to Petrarchism as the *Amoretti,* because the
epic and allegorical narratives of Books 1 and 2 establish a quite different nexus of thematic concerns. But Books 3 and 4 mark a shift in
the poem in that they are as concerned with life in the social world as
with the realm of heroic action. It is for this reason that themes from
the lyric tradition—specifically from the Petrarchan tradition—resonate throughout these books. What results from this combination of
epic and lyric themes is a strange hybrid that Spenser criticism has
never been completely comfortable with. Much less has been written
about these two books than about the others, and the work that has
been done has by and large used critical approaches derived from
and adequate to those less chaotic books that precede and follow. For
example, a standard device of Spenser criticism is to trace the development of an individual figure, and this is perfectly appropriate in
those books structured around the actions of individual figures.[1] But
Books 3 and 4 form much less distinct entities than the first two
books, as most of the narrative elements of Book 3 spill into Book 4.
They also lack the organization around a knight and his quest that
characterizes the other books. Everyone in these books comes in
pairs or in groups; characters are rarely alone and actions of one character or set of characters often parallel those of another. This difference suggests that what is needed to make sense of the plethora of
characters and situations in these books is an approach based on

groups and classes of characters rather than on the individual figure.[2]

One group that has never been seen as such is the group of four squires in Books 3 and 4—Prince Arthur's squire, Timias; the Squire of Dames; the Squire of Low Degree, Amyas; and his friend Placidas. Each of these is involved in a troubled love situation, and most of the trouble results from the fact that these figures are squires. Their social status therefore directly impinges on the narrative. Moreover, in sharp contrast to the micro-narratives in the other books of *The Faerie Queene,* when the narrative takes leave of these squires, their troubled situations have not been resolved, or they have been resolved in a very troubling way. The world of epic action with clear narrative resolutions disappears in the complex social world of these middle books. In order to be properly understood, the squires' individual actions need to be read in relation to each other, as they form a combined narrative that is a perfect example of what Rosemund Tuve calls *entrelacement*.[3] Moreover, this interlaced narrative, in focusing on the problems the squires encounter in their love situations, carries a crucial part of Spenser's larger thematic design in Books 3 and 4. If we look at this interlaced narrative in detail, we can see how the middle books of Spenser's epic move toward a consideration of social virtues and social structures consonant with the turn on the Petrarchan lyric tradition that we have been examining in Chapter 2.

Prince Arthur's squire is the only one of these squires to figure in the narrative prior to Book 3. Although unnamed, he has been in attendance on Arthur in Books 1 and 2 and has assisted Arthur in battle in both books. He is named for the first time in Book 3, canto 1, stanza 18, significantly when he acts independently for the first time. After Florimell rushes by, chased by a "griesly Foster," Arthur and Guyon chase Florimell while Timias, the squire, follows the forester, disappearing only to reappear still in pursuit in canto 5. He manages to kill the forester and his two brothers (stanzas 21–25), but, severely wounded in the fight, is saved only by the care of Belphoebe, the Diana figure already encountered in Book 2.

This is only the beginning, not the end, of his troubles, and these new troubles initiate the narrative I wish to trace. Timias recovers consciousness (35) with Belphoebe at his side, and speaks:

> Angell, or Goddesse do I call thee right?
> What seruice may I do vnto thee meete,
> That hast from darkenesse me returnd to light,

And with thy heauenly salues and med'cines sweete,
Hast drest my sinfull wounds? I kisse they blessed feete.[4]

Timias, who as a squire has already pledged his service to Arthur, his knight, now pledges service to Belphoebe and, in an acknowledgment of his position of servitude, kisses her feet. It does not take long for Timias to fall in love with Belphoebe (42–43), but his awareness of his inferiority prevents him from disclosing his love. The stanzas in which we overhear Timias's internal debate about this (44–47) are crucial, for they outline the bind he is in. Considering Belphoebe's perfections, he is "constrained" to love her, but, considering his mean estate, he is "restrained" from "such hardy boldnesse" as showing any manifestations of his love. It would be disloyal to love her, as it would ill return her care for him.[5] For a "meane squire" to proffer his love to a lady "heauenly borne, and of celestiall hew" (47) would be an insult. But it would also be disloyal not to love her, given that same care. He must love his lady and show that love, as he is in her service and eternal debt.

Timias is therefore caught in a cruel paradox, a paradox that blocks him from any action:

Yet neuer he his hart to her reuealed,
But rather chose to dye for sorrow great,
Then with dishonorable termes her to entreat.

(3.5.49)

But what precisely is dishonorable here? It is not unknown for a squire to love his lady or even to express that love, and no dishonor resulted in courtly love from such a love. Indeed, the love of a squire for his more powerful lady is the essential type of courtly love. But Spenser, although portraying the classic love situation of courtly love, is writing after Petrarch's profound transformation of courtly love. Petrarch, following Dante, made the lady superior in spiritual status rather than in earthly position and incorporated into Petrarchan love a Christian injunction against the consummation of love out of wedlock. The two mottoes in the House of Busyrane that govern much of Book 3 are "Be bold, be bold," "Be not too bold" (3.11.54).[6] But the mottoes that govern Petrarchan love constitute a sharper paradox yet: be bold, do not be bold. Petrarch loves Laura, as any Petrarchan loves his lady, because she is better and purer than he (at least in the fiction of the poetry; I am not making any biographical assumptions about the "real" Laura here). Although he must show his love in order to praise and honor his lady, her perfection makes her unapproachable. So he cannot show his love, yet the perfection represented in that unapproachability redoubles his love and his desire for the unattainable lady.

The bind that Timias finds himself in, therefore, is not one of his own making. It is the bind of Petrarchan love, and we should know that we are in the world of Petrarchan love if only by the oxymorons and antitheses that fill Timias's speeches. As we have seen in Chapter 2, such antitheses are the very signature of Petrarchism, and their paradoxical nature serves to indicate the paradox that lies at the heart of Petrarchan love, the paradox that binds Timias.[7] Petrarchism, of course, dominated the European literature of love for nearly three hundred years and dominated the Elizabethan lyric tradition against which Spenser struggles in the *Amoretti*. As we shall see, the squires are not the only figures in *The Faerie Queene* to adopt Petrarchan poses or to employ the Petrarchan language of love. However, because of their inferior social status, the squires in Books 3 and 4 are the only figures in *The Faerie Queene* truly caught in the Petrarchan bind. The injunction not to be bold doubles in intensity for one of "low degree."

The Petrarchan lover, however, cannot be of too low a degree. In 3.7, two cantos after we take the plight of Timias so seriously, Spenser parodies this plight in the episode of the witch's son and Florimell. When Florimell has come to the witch's house for shelter, the witch's son soon conceives an affection for her. But "Yet had he not the hart, nor hardiment, / As vnto her to vtter his desire; / His caytiue thought durst not so high aspire" (3.7.16). So, thinking as Timias would, he acts as he would as well. He serves his Lady, bringing her flowers and animals and things to eat (17), but never "utters his desire." After she leaves, the "lewd louer" laments her departure so strenuously (20), in characteristic Petrarchan manner, that his mother finally constructs an equivalent for Florimell, False Florimell (3.8.5–9), composed—as Isabel MacCaffrey has written—"out of the materials of Petrarchan convention" (240).[8] And False Florimell, false to the role of the Petrarchan Lady, is more receptive to his advances than Florimell.

The witch's son is a parody of Timias, of the courtly lover (just as False Florimell is a parody of Florimell), because he is so below Florimell in status that the lady's first command, "be bold," show your love, will never be forthcoming. Although a social difference between the lady and the lover binds the lover more fully, too great a class disparity makes it impossible for the lover to be in a bind at all because he cannot be taken seriously as a lady's lover. But this episode is not merely comic, for we shall see something like the witch's son acting out his desire for Florimell with False Florimell several times in Books 3 and 4. Because the double bind of Petrarchism blocks the lover from any action vis-à-vis the lady, he often acts out his desires by finding an equivalent for the lady somewhere else. This is the case in the next story of a squire, a parallel reinforced by its location between Florimell's departure (in canto 6) and the witch's construction of the snowy Florimell.

The first we see of this squire, the Squire of Dames (3.7.37), he is the captive of a mighty Giantess, Argante, a figure of lust, who is carrying the squire off intending to make him "the thrall of her desire" (37). The squire's situation, as he tells his rescuer Satyrane (51–61), is that he loves and serves a "gentle Lady," Columbell. In typical Petrarchan fashion he has served her for a long time without any reward. To test his loyalty to her, she then bound him to a vow that he would spend a year doing "seruice vnto gentle Dames" (54). For a year, then, he acted out the Petrarchan lady's first injunction, to be bold. He is constrained to love as many women as he can, and his total in one year is three hundred. She then binds him to the second half of the Petrarchan bind, to fail in his love quest: she will not see him again until he is refused as many times as he has been accepted. In three years, he had only been rejected three times when he was captured by Argante.

The squire is acting out in sequence the two injunctions that simultaneously bind the squire in his love for Columbell and bind any squire in his love for his lady. He manifests his love on her command, which is part of his service to her, and then is reprimanded for that. He must try to succeed in his quest, but actually fail, just as for Timias to succeed with Belphoebe would be to dishonor her. The only ladies worth loving are those who will not let you love them. It seems never to have occured to the Squire of Dames to disobey his lady, to abandon his foolish quest. He is as clearly the thrall of his desire for her as he is the thrall of Argante's desire. The one thralldom, in fact, represents the other. Thus, the squire fully embodies the domination by the lady inherent in courtly love. He acts according to the options she offers him, and the contradictory nature of these options reinforces her domination. Since any independent action on his part is blocked, he responds cynically by evading and refusing any responsibility for his actions. They are the result of his lady's commands and the nature of women. His identity therefore is her domination. He does not even reveal his name: "as for my name, it mistreth not to tell; / Call me the *Squyre of Dames,* that me beseemeth well" (3.7.51).

The Squire of Dames is a troubling figure because his cynicism undercuts the idealistic assumptions about the nature of women and love so prominent in *The Faerie Queene.* Book 3 celebrates the virtue of chastity, yet in his sample unchaste women outnumber the chaste by at least one hundred to one. And it is entirely appropriate that the last we see of the Squire of Dames is at the tourney for Florimell's girdle, the symbol of chastity he has so much difficulty finding. There he mocks the discrepancy between the ideal and the reality of love:

> Which when that scornefull *Squire of Dames* did vew,
> He lowdly gan to laugh, and thus to iest;
> Alas for pittie that so faire a crew,
> As like can not be seene from East to West,
> Cannot find one this girdle to inuest.
>
> (4.5.18)

But the squire's perspective, finally, is one we must reject. Amoret tries on the girdle and it fits. It would have fitted Amoret's knight, Britomart, and it belongs to and has been worn by Florimell. Consequently, although the squire's vision is true to his own experience of love, there are types of love for which it cannot be adequate. For his experience has been stunting and pathological: his experience of love has been an experience of domination that has deprived him of choice, autonomy, and identity.

Spenser's group of squires is not the only example of how a love situation that puts the weaker party in a double bind leads to a pathological situation and often to a loss of identity. Gregory Bateson's studies of the family context of the schizophrenic child emphasize the role of paradoxical double-bind situations that place the child in a no-win situation in which no response is suitable. According to Bateson's analysis, for a double bind situation to develop, there must be at least two persons, the mother and the child, in a relationship involving dependence and affection. The double bind develops over a period of time as a result of a pattern of repeated experiences, not a single traumatic experience. The pattern in its most elemental form is that the mother issues a strong primary injunction that "may have either of two forms: (a) 'do not do so and so, or I will punish you', or (b) 'If you do not do so and so, I will punish you' " (206).[9] Finally there is a latent tertiary injunction "prohibiting the victim from escaping the field" (207).

Bateson's central example is the manifestation of love: the child's mother is made anxious by and tries to prevent the child's display of affection. But if the child responds to this rebuff and withdraws, the mother punishes that withdrawal or simulates affection for the child. To quote Bateson's summary: "In either case in a relationship, the most important in his life and the model for all others, he is punished if he indicates love and affection and punished if he does not; and his escape routes from the situation, such as gaining support from others, are cut off. This is the basic nature of the double bind relationship between mother and child" (216).

Bateson's theory seems to me a striking parallel to Spenser's depiction of the double bind of Petrarchan love in Books 3 and 4 of *The Faerie Queene*. The crucial point is that Bateson's analysis does not blame the schizophrenic child as much as it does the relationship, the social network or context, in which the child has been raised. In Books 3 and 4 of *The Faerie Queene,* Spenser makes an analogous shift in attention from individuals to the relationships in which individuals are caught. This is true on a number of levels: first, the virtues commended in these books, chastity and friendship, are relational and social, not the property of an isolated individual. Second, protagonists who embody these virtues are therefore seeking to be related: Britomart, the figure of chastity, is seeking her true love, Artegall; Scudamour is seeking Amoret; and so forth. And finally, as already has been noted, characters in these books come in groups, not in isolation. The world of Books 1 and 2, in which an isolated character needed to resist social entanglement in order to be virtuous and to accomplish his quest, is replaced by a more complicated world in which entanglement is inevitable and essential in order to achieve one's quest.

It is important to remember this distinction if only to avoid the problems that can be caused by importing the stark evaluations proper to Books 1 and 2 into Books 3 and 4. As *The Faerie Queene* proceeds, analysis in terms of innate moral characteristics is to a large degree displaced by an analysis devoted to social contexts. Nonetheless, most critical treatments of the Timias-Belphoebe relationship assume that because Belphoebe is both good and chaste, her handling of Timias must in some sense be praiseworthy.[10] Overlooked in this view is the undeniably destructive effect her actions have on Timias. This is not

Belphoebe's fault, and I am not suggesting that we should blame either her or Timias. The problem inheres in a much larger context, a context considered and analyzed at length in Books 3 and 4. The context is the Petrarchan system of love, the system that puts Timias in such a stunting bind.

The reason that critics have not seen Spenser as criticizing the form of love exemplified by the Timias-Belphoebe relationship, I suspect, is that Book 3 celebrates chastity and Belphoebe's handling of Timias is impeccably chaste. But the reappearance of Belphoebe and Timias in Book 4 should enable us to see that Belphoebe is much less persuasive and winning as an embodiment of friendship, the virtue of Book 4, than of chastity. However, just before they reappear in 4.7, another story, that of the Squire of Low Degree, is begun, although it is not ended, as it interlaces meaningfully with that of Timias. Amoret, rescued by Britomart from the House of Busyrane at the end of Book 3, has been carried away by Lust while the weary Britomart was sleeping. Lust throws Amoret into his cave (4.7.4–8), where she meets Aemylia and hears her story (11–18). Aemylia had been "Daughter vnto a Lord of high degree," but she had fallen in love with a "Squire of low degree" (15). As their love was mutual, she did not bind the squire by blocking his love. But her father does. He refuses consent because of the low status of the squire (16), so Aemylia and her squire agree to run away (17). However, when she goes to the meeting place, instead of her squire she finds Lust, whose "wretched thrall" she remains (18).

We later learn (4.8.51) that the squire, too, met a figure of lust at the appointed meeting place. They are trying to consummate a love that, because of their disparity in class, cannot be consummated within their society. They discover that to attempt that consummation in this situation is to drop below society into the realm of the bestial, not to rise above its petty restrictions. This indicates that if the heart of the Petrarchan lady is not stony by nature, it is made stony by her place in society. She cannot *not* be stony without ceasing to be a lady. If she agrees to consummate their love, she and her lover will be Lust's captives, like the Squire of Low Degree and Aemylia in this canto.[11]

After Aemylia tells her story, terrified Amoret runs away (21). (She is always trying to run away from Lust.) Lust chases her (21–24) until they run into Timias, who fights Lust until Belphoebe arrives (29), puts Lust to flight, and kills him (32). When she returns to the place where she left Amoret and Timias,

> There she found him by that new louely mate,
> Who lay the whiles in swoune, full sadly set,
> From her faire eyes wiping the deawy wet,
> Which softly stild, and kissing them atweene,
> And handling soft the hurts, which she did get.
>
> (4.7.35)

Enraged, she thinks of killing them both, but says merely "Is this the faith" (36), turns, and flees.

Timias has broken the injunction not to show one's love. He is, like the Squire of Dames, although in a very different manner, acting out his desire on another object, Belphoebe's twin sister, Amoret. This arouses Belphoebe's anger because Timias is not obeying her commands. Timias had vowed to be her squire, yet he is now making his own choices and acting in a way not subject to her. So she punishes him by showing extreme displeasure and withdrawing from the love situation.

For Timias the loss of this tie to Belphoebe leads to the loss of identity and of any semblance of civility. He lives in the wood like a wild man, takes on the looks and habits of a savage, and even abandons language (38–41). Arthur, coming across him in the wood one day, fails to recognize him, but speaks to him anyway:

> But to his speach he aunswered no whit,
> But stood still mute, as if he had beene dum,
> No signe of sence did shew, ne common wit,
> As one with griefe and anguishe ouercum,
> And vnto euery thing did aunswere mum.
>
> (4.7.44)

His muteness indicates how totally his identity is wrapped up in his servitude. Throughout Book 4, in fact, he is never called Timias, but only the squire. He loses his name as he loses his independence, just as he was only given a name when he acted independently for the first time in chasing the "griesly Foster" in 3.1.

But Timias is not to stay a wild man forever. Canto 8 begins with his rather implausible reconciliation with Belphoebe through the agency of a turtle dove, which coaxes Belphoebe into the forest where Timias lives (9–12). When Timias sees her, he falls at her feet, kisses the ground she stands on, in a repetition of his original act of submission (130), and asks for redress. She then takes pity on him and "him receiu'd againe to former fauours state" (17). Most critics have accepted this as a satisfactory resolution of the story of Timias and Belphoebe, but it is really no resolution at all. Timias recovers Belphoebe's grace, her "former fauours state," but all this means is that he is in the same box as before. What favors did he receive in that state? Timias has recovered the ability to speak, but is still not free to say what he has to say. Belphoebe continues to dominate his field of choice, as is shown when he is said to be "eke all mindlesse of his own deare Lord / The noble Prince" (18). Timias is still in the bind he was in in 3.5, a bind now strengthened by Belphoebe's punishment of his feeble attempt to move outside the bounds she had set up.

This episode comes between the start and the end of the narrative of the Squire of Low Degree, which occupies the rest of canto 8 and the first part of canto 9. It does so, according to the principles of *entrelacement*, to show that to walk out on the Petrarchan bind, as Timias does when he takes to the wood, is no better than to act it out, as the Squire of Dames does. The Squire of Low Degree, as Aemylia has already told Amoret, had also tried to evade the Petrarchan bind, with the result that both he and his lady were captured by figures of lust. Corflambo captures the squire and makes him his thrall (4.8.51). Then Corflambo's daughter, Poeana, sees him in prison and falls in love with him (52), which puts him in exactly the same situation he had been in before with Aemylia. He is, of course, hesitant to act (look where he got the last time), so his good friend and look-alike, Placidas, goes off to help him (55). Placidas acts out the courtly lover role in place of Amyas, the Squire of Low Degree, with Poeana, who plays an identical role to Aemylia (56–60). A measure of doubling and transference and acting out has accompanied the narrative of these squires throughout, but this doubling reaches a peak here as it becomes nearly as difficult for us to keep the characters straight as it is for Poeana.

Placidas is acting out the role of the prisoner of love. His role is one in which he is totally dominated, but this time he is *acting* and he quickly shows his independence. He kidnaps the dwarf of Poeana (61) and runs off. This is a curious gesture, the utility of which is not apparent, but its utility is perhaps simply that it is not a move approved by the lady, that it is a gesture of independence. To withdraw from the love situation in this way is Belphoebe's move, but made this time by the equivalent of Timias. He is chased by Corflambo (62—these squires are chased a lot), but fortunately Arthur, with Amoret and Aemylia in train, appears on the scene (38–41), slays

Corflambo (42–45), and hears the story (47–62) that I have just sum-marized.

Canto 9 begins with praise of the actions of Placidas as an embodi-ment of the highest type of love, Aristotle's highest kind of friendship, that between friends, which is higher than love of kindred or sexual love (1–3). But, although I will argue later that the implicit citation of Aristotle here is extremely important, it would be difficult to argue that the actions of Placidas transcend sexual love when they are so directly connected to it. His actions have led to the inter-vention of Arthur, who, with the help of Placidas, seizes the castle (5–7) and frees Amyas (8). In stanza 9, the freed Amyas embraces Aemylia and Placidas with joy, which makes Poeana jealous and con-fused as to "Which was the captiue Squire she lou'd so deare" (10). Arthur ransackes the castle (12), divides the spoil, and tries to persuade the "trusty Squire" (15) to marry Poeana. He agrees to do so, Arthur gives him lordship of the land, and they live "From that day forth in peace and ioyous blis" (16).

This is not very convincing as narrative, perhaps, because Ar-thur—although a more likely *deus ex machina* than a bird—still wraps things up rather cavalierly. Amyas and Aemylia, the original subjects of the narrative, are alluded to only in passing: "These paires of friends in peace and setled rest" (17). The end of the narrative of these two couples is not really given to us as much as sketched out in the ab-stract, and the resemblance between the two pairs is for Spenser far more significant than their individuality. Placidas has merely acted out Amyas's role, and Poeana is another version of Aemylia. But what Arthur does to resolve Poeana's situation is an abstract sketch of what is necessary for these problematic love situations to be replaced by healthier ones. First, he lowers Poeana's status by seizing her castle and lands; then, he gives those same lands to the squire, which raises his status. These actions, by removing the class disparity between the squire and his lady, make it possible for them to marry and live in "peace and settled rest," precisely Spenser's ideal in the *Amoretti*. And the resolution Arthur forces demonstrates that it is this class disparity that is the source of the problems encountered in the love situations of the squires.

Arthur's forced resolution of the story of the Squire of Low Degree brings the interlaced narrative of the squires we have been tracing to a close. (Timias does reappear in Book 6 but not significantly for our purposes here.) We therefore now need to ask what this narrative is doing in Books 3 and 4 and, more importantly, what it does to Books 3 and 4. For this narrative, as any reader of Spenser knows, does not stand alone but is itself interlaced with many other narrative strands in a web of incredible complexity. Each book of *The Faerie Queene*, as we know from Spenser's letter to Raleigh, is a depiction of a given virtue, and the virtues portrayed in Books 3 and 4 are, of course, the virtues of chastity and friendship. These are both virtues that can be considered forms of love, and C. S. Lewis, more than forty years ago, argued that "we are justified in treating [Books 3 and 4] as a single book on the subject of love" (*Allegory of Love,* 338).[12]

In a consideration of chastity and friendship as virtuous forms of love, Petrarchism—the dominant ideology of love in Spenser's society—would seem to be one's ideal form of love, as it involves the lover in a chaste relationship with the lady. But it would only *seem* to be an exemplary form of love. Petrarchism, far from representing the ideal virtue of love, is for Spenser a negative form of love that needs to be attacked. The love situations of the squires represent no ideal, and the problem with them is that they are Petrarchan love situations.

The problem with Petrarchan love in Spenser's analysis is not—as it may seem from this narrative alone—that it is the women who dominate. The interlaced narrative of the group of squires we have just traced shows that Petrarchan love—if taken seriously—leads to a situation of pathological dominance by the lady. But Spenser also wants to show that Petrarchism—if taken as a game to be played—can lead to a situation of dominance by the lover, a situation equally worthy of condemnation. Consequently, to complement the narrative of the squires, in Books 3 and 4 we also see a number of knights, above the squires in social status, successfully evade the restraining paradoxes of Petrarchan love, only to constrain their ladies in turn.

Paridell is the most obvious example of this. (Blandamour has the values of a Paridell but the success rate of a Timias [4.11.8–11].) The striking thing about Paridell's deduction of Hellenore (3.9–10) is that he uses the Petrarchan language of submission to the lady, but because for him it is an artificial language, he can use it to gain dominance over her. Before he even enters Malbecco's castle, he criticizes Malbecco's thralldom and service to gold in terms that also describe the thralldom of the Petrarchan lover:

> Then is he not more mad (said *Paridell*)
> That hath himselfe vnto such seruice sold,
> In dolefull thraldom all his dayes to dwell?

> For sure a foole I do him firmely hold,
> That loues his fetters, though they were of gold.
>
> (3.9.8)

Paridell wants no fetters, but he can pretend he has them if he needs to. In the first scene between Paridell and Hellenore (3.9.27–31), messages in Petrarchan language go back and forth, but Spenser specifies the falsity of Paridell's:

> But nothing new to him was that same paine,
> Ne paine at all; for he so oft had tryde
> The powre thereof.
>
> (29)

Paridell completes his conquest in canto 10 by feigning being conquered. He acts as if he were a Timias dying from his lady's displeasure:

> But when apart (if euer her apart)
> He found, then his false engins fast he plyde,
> And all the sleights vnbosomd in his hart;
> He sigh'd, he sobd, he swownd, he perdy dyde,
> And cast himselfe on ground her fast besyde.
>
> (3.10.7)

Hellenore, of course, is not one to put up any obstacles: "be not too bold" is one phrase she never uses. But Spenser insists that she is trapped by Paridell (9–11). Not in control of the love situation, she is dumped by Paridell when he wishes. As he says to Malbecco, "I take no keepe of her" (3.10.38).

Paridell sees love as a struggle for power, which he wins by seeming to lose, by seeming to accept the Petrarchan bind. This loss is only a gambit, for he has no intentions of obeying or serving any lady. Paridell cannot be said to be a true Petrarchan; his attitute toward love is Ovidian rather that Petrarchan.[13] But the use he makes of Petrarchism in the seduction of Hellenore shows that the problem with Petrarchism is not simply that it is a system encouraging dominance by the lady. Dominance by the knight leads to a kind of love much further from the ideal. Petrarchism, the hegemonic ideology of love in Spenser's society, is a diseased form of love—according to the critique of Petrarchism developed in Books 3 and 4 of *The Faerie Queene*—because it necessarily involves the dominance of one figure in the relationship. The interlaced narratives involving forms of Petrarchan love in these books concretely demonstrate this time and again.

There are two things wrong with Petrarchan love, an inequality of power and an inequality of desire, and these are really aspects of each other. In both the sincere Petrarchism of Belphoebe and Timias and the false Petrarchism of Paridell and Hellenore, the dominant partner is the one who can live without the other. Chastity thus becomes a weapon in a struggle for power, not a disinterested virtue, and the chastity created by Petrarchism—as we have seen time and again—is simply a form of repression that leads to being enthralled by lust.[14] Moreover, just as the witch's son is a lower-class parody of Timias, there are a number of lower-class rapist parodies of Paridell in Books 3 and 4, grisly foresters, old fishermen, and the like. The open and brutal lust displayed by these figures would seem to be the opposite of Petrarchism, but, although these figures use means that differ from Paridell's, their aim is the same: power and dominion in the love relationship.[15] And Spenser's extended critique of Petrarchism in these books is part of a larger critique of a whole range of types of love dedicated to power. No matter which sex is the dominating figure, they all involve power and dominion, the mastery of one lover, the thralldom and servitude of the other.

These types of love are the negation of virtuous love, and Spenser criticizes them in order to help define the positive ideal of chaste love that he wants to develop in Books 3 and 4. Spenser is thus defining the right kind of chastity by giving us these examples of the wrong kind. The right kind allows for the proper expression of sexuality, which is to be found in a relationship that is the right kind of friendship, one marked by an absence of domination.[16] This has been seen in very general terms by C. S. Lewis, who argued in *The Allegory of Love* that Books 3 and 4 of *The Faerie Queene* tell "the final stages of the history of courtly love," "the final struggle between the romance of marriage and the romance of adultery" (*Allegory*, 338, 340). But the critic who has given us the most precise definition of Spenser's ideal of love is A. Kent Hieatt, in *Chaucer, Spenser, Milton: Mythopoeic Continuities and Transformations*. As the title of this study indicates, Hieatt sees a strong continuity between Chaucer's and Spenser's views of love, and he argues that in Books 3 and 4, Spenser is continuing Chaucer's critique of sexual mastery found in the Marriage Group of the *Canterbury Tales*. (This is one reason why there is so much Chaucerian material in Book 4.) Hieatt sees this Chaucerian critique particularly dominant in the story of Amoret and Scudamour, the two lovers who have such enormous difficulty meeting up with each other in Books 3 and 4.

The root of their problem is that Scudamour is committed to a destructive ideal of sexual mastery. In Hieatt's words, Scudamour "insists on a relation conceived in terms of the jealous domination by which he had won [Amoret] rather than in terms of harmonious trustfulness. He treats her as though she were nothing but the prize which he had initially won the right to woo, and not also as a separate, free ego whose consent must be sought by gentle parley" (125). As Hieatt argues, the only part of the motto in the House of Busyrane that Scudamour understands and follows is "be bold"; (103–13) and Womanhood in the Temple of Venue blames Scudamour precisely

> for being ouer bold;
> Saying it was to Knight vnseemely shame,
> Vpon a recluse Virgin to lay hold,
> That vnto *Venus* seruices was sold.
> (4.10.54)

Paying no attention, he grabs Amoret against her will and carries her out.

Amoret has been imprisoned first in the House of Busyrane, then in the Cave of Lust, and we can now see how these are really versions of her tie with Scudamour: in every case she is the weak prisoner of male sexual desire. But she has no boldness, whereas Scudamour has too much, and for that reason their union is blocked.[17] And we should be able to see that Hieatt's Chaucerian analysis of the problems in this relationship precisely mirrors and complements my own Petrarchan analysis of the problems in relations such as Timias and Belphoebe. For Spenser the two relationships mirrored each other as well: Amoret and Belphoebe are twin sisters. Amoret is the type of the weak or dominated woman denied choice by her lover, the exact opposite of her twin sister, Belphoebe, the type of the strong dominant woman who denies her lover any choice. And the intertwining of the two stories of Amoret's lack of freedom in her relationship with Scudamour and of Timias's lack of freedom in his relationship with Belphoebe demonstrates that the two relationships have the same flaw. In neither case are the two lovers both bold, but not too bold.

There is thus an interlace between Spenser's Chaucerian critique of sexual mastery and his critique of Petrarchan false chastity, and an identical ideal of love emerges from the two. Both Scudamour and Belphoebe have had fairly good press in criticism of *The Faerie Queene,* but both are committed to false and destructive theories of love criticized by Spenser in Books 3 and 4. Apparently positive expressions of love need a much more thorough critique than obviously negative ones, which is why so much more space is devoted to Scudamour and to Belphoebe than to Paridell and to False Florimell. Moreover, as Hieatt has perceptively seen, it is out of such a critique that Spenser's positive ideal of love emerges.

Between Amoret and Belphoebe, Timias and Scudamour, timidity and boldness, thralldom and mastery, lies the ideal kind of love, which is also the ideal kind of friendship and the ideal kind of chastity. This ideal is not merely marriage (Malbecco and Hellenore are married) or even concord in love (Braggadocchio and False Florimell, or Hellenore among the satyrs, offer examples of concord), but a relationship in marriage in which there is reciprocity of desire and dominion.

At the beginning of canto 9 of Book 4, after almost all of the examples of love relationships in Books 3 and 4 have been depicted, Spenser invokes Aristotle's ideal of friendship. The highest type of friendship, in Aristotle's view, is that between two equals in which neither side dominates.[18] Although for Aristotle this ideal is higher than sexual love, Spenser as usual invokes Aristotle only to modify his categories. Spenser's ideal is a sexual love that would be marked by an equality of position *and* an equality of desire. In the ideal love, it is not simply the lover who must find his way between "be bold" and "be not too bold." The lady must also, or, to put it more precisely, the roles of lover and lady must disappear and be replaced by that of two lovers, both bold but not too bold.

Florimell, in contrast to Amoret, swallows her fear and goes off in quest of Marinell, in spite of his indifference to her. This indifference, in blocking any manifestation of her love, had put her in a bind represented by her imprisonment in the Cave of Proteus. Her lament in the Cave, which Marinell overhears in 4.12.6–11, is the lament of Petrarchan thralldom, although in this case spoken by a woman. Overhearing her in turn causes Marinell's love sickness, which puts him in the situation of wanting Florimell and being dependent on her. This mirroring of dominance and dependence, the fact that each has sought the other and each has unknowingly constrained the other, is, I would argue, what enables Marinell and Florimell to achieve union. Each has dominated the other for a period. Each has been bold, but not too bold, and an equality and reciprocity characteristic of the highest type of friendship has been created in the process.

The relationship of Britomart and Artegall displays the same pattern as that of Florimell and Marinell. As psychological types, Britomart is far closer to Belphoebe, and Florimell is far closer to Amoret, but Britomart shares with Florimell the complementary relationship with the mate that enables their union. In fact, Britomart and Artegall's sequence of dependence and domination is in four parts, not simply two, as with Florimell and Marinell. Britomart, like Florimell, begins by questing after Artegall (3.1) because she falls in love with his image, which she sees in Merlin's mirror (3.2). When they finally meet (4.6), Artegall—although the conquerer in battle—is conquered by her beauty and, after service and courtship, he receives her consent to love and marriage. Then Artegall leaves on his quest, which leaves Britomart abandoned, once more the weaker party. However, in Book 5, as we shall see in the next chapter, Britomart rescues Artegall from his thralldom to Radigund (5.7), which puts him in her debt again. Thus, each has sought after or been subject to the other twice, and each has been the more powerful dominating party twice. Each has played the role of the bold warrior, and each has played a more submissive part.

Florimell and Marinell and Britomart and Artegall, therefore, with their very different stories, find a middle way between the kinds of pathological or destructive love situations that Spenser treats in Books 3 and 4. Neither couple finds it easy to achieve this middle way: they shift from one partner dominating (whether deliberately or not) to the other. But that shift establishes a kind of balance, a kind of reciprocity, which shows that there is a way out of the landscape of paradoxical binds and abduction and rape found in these books. The way out is written over the doorways in the House of Busyrane, "be bold, be bold," but "be not too bold." And, although Britomart does not understand these mottoes (3.11.54), she embodies them extremely well.

It would be an easy task to disturb our sense that this Aristotelian mean Spenser is setting forth of equality, reciprocity, and complementariness is a viable one. In Books 3 and 4 we see much more separation than union, much more pathology than health. Florimell and Marinell's wedding celebration is a bust; when last seen, Artegall is a long way from Britomart. But, although these facts show how restricted in availability this ideal is, they do not, I think, affect our sense of it as an ideal. There is only this one road out of pathological forms of love in *The Faerie Queene,* although it is a road increasingly hard to find in Spenser's darkening vision. As we have already seen, the same ideal is expressed in Spenser's sonnet sequence celebrating his own courtship

and marriage, the *Amoretti*; and although the *Amoretti* as lyric remains closer to the terms of the Petrarchan tradition, it contains a parallel critique of Petrarchism. But this ideal may be easier to achieve in the lyric, private world of the *Amoretti* than in the epic, public world of *The Faerie Queene*. The next chapter should help explain why this would be so, why the public world of *The Faerie Queene* contains more pathology than health, in a way that should connect this theme of *The Faerie Queene* to the shift in the place of Italy in English society.

Chapter Four

Queen Elizabeth and the Politics of Petrarchism

Spenser's critique of Petrarchism found in the *Amoretti* and *The Faerie Queene* faults Petrarchism for its reliance on a stunting system of paradoxes, but if the reading of *The Faerie Queene* advanced in the last chapter is at all correct, *The Faerie Queene* and its critique of Petrarchism is caught up in at least two sharp paradoxes as well. As we have seen in the last chapter, the middle books of Spenser's epic present Belphoebe and Britomart as two contrasting types of chaste love. Belphoebe is the type of Petrarchan love, seen by Spenser as false chastity and false love, and Britomart is the type of true chaste love, which finds expression in marriage. But Belphoebe represents a type of chastity widely admired in Spenser's society and embodied in the most powerful person in the realm, Queen Elizabeth. Through his portrait of Belphoebe, Spenser depicts Elizabeth's idealization of herself, and he intended his readers to be aware of this: he says in his letter to Raleigh that Belphoebe is to be taken as a "shadow" of the queen.

A sharp contradiction therefore stands at the very center of *The Faerie Queene*. There can be no doubt that Spenser intended *The Faerie Queene* to be a poem in praise of Queen Elizabeth. The signs of that intention are everywhere, in the poem, in the dedicatory and commendatory apparatus surrounding the 1590 edition of the first three books, and in the letter to Raleigh included in that edition. But it is also a poem with an extended and searching critique of the system of values embodied in the queen. It is thus both directly encomiastic and indirectly critical of the queen at the same time. This has led an in-

creasing number of readers of the poem to doubt whether the poem fully realizes that intention, actually praises Queen Elizabeth in the way Spenser claims. And the material presented in the previous chapter surely supports such doubts. Central to *The Faerie Queene*—as we have seen—is a vision of marriage as the ideal form of chastity and friendship that seems at variance with the praise of the Virgin Queen, who had a rather different sense of the relation between her favorite virtue, chastity, and an institution she dreaded, marriage. And this gives the variance between the poem's moral vision and its epideictic intent a sharper, more political edge. Why does a poem in praise of the Virgin Queen redefine chastity in a way that calls that very praise into question?

The first critic to have opened a space between Spenser's expressed intention of praising Queen Elizabeth and the poem itself is Josephine Waters Bennett in *The Evolution of The Faerie Queene* (1942). The virtue celebrated in Book 3 is chastity, and traditionally this choice has been taken as an intention to praise the Virgin Queen, especially given Belphoebe's prominent place in the book. But Bennett notes that the heroine of the quest who represents chastity, Britomart, is not chaste in the way Belphoebe and (presumably) Queen Elizabeth are, chaste in the sense of maintaining their virginity. Britomart's quest is precisely to lose her virginity: she is in love with the knight Artegall, is searching for him and ultimately marries him in Book 5. Now, it is easy enough to make this narrative outcome coherent with Spenser's moral scheme, as we did in the previous chapter, by seeing Britomart as representing a deeper, more profound chastity, chastity in marriage. But, as Bennett notes, this coherence is achieved at the cost of a lack of fit with the intention of praising Queen Elizabeth, for a vision of chastity intended to praise her must be a fairly unproblematic chastity as virginity. The entire moral plan of the poem, not only the narrative of the squires, seems in conflict with the plan to praise Queen Elizabeth.

Subsequent critics have explored and mapped comparable tensions. Thomas Cain's *Praise in The Faerie Queene* (1978) is perhaps the best testimony to an ambivalence in the poem about the queen, for he desperately wants it not to be there. The theme of his study is that the whole poem is in praise of the queen, but as his discussion continues, he keeps finding impulses the other way he would like not to be there. But as he realizes, the epideictic tradition he focuses on can be a vehicle of blame as well as praise (1–5), and Spenser would seem to be more responsive to the whole tradition than Cain would like to admit. In contrast, Robin Headlam Wells in *Spenser's Faerie Queene and the Cult of Elizabeth* (1983) less perceptively sees none of those impulses, unproblematically presenting a Spenser only praising the queen. She cannot miss the lack of fit between Britomart as the heroine to Book 3 and the praise of Elizabeth: "to address an epideictic poem celebrating the ideal of married love to a virgin queen who is on record as highly commending the single life is nonsensical" (74). But she resolves this discrepancy by first, making the subject of Book 3 courtship, not marriage, and second, arguing that this courtship stands for "Elizabeth's mystical marriage to England" (89). This exclusively allegorical reading makes little sense of the density and specificity of the social relations portrayed in Books 3 and 4. Michael O'Connell's *Mirror and Veil* (1977) offers the most balanced view of this ambivalence in the poem. He focuses on the imagery of mirroring in the poem, and of course mirrors can reflect good and bad, ideal and less than ideal aspects of the subject being mirrored. And O'Connell shows how the negative images of courts and of female rulers that run throughout the poem can be seen as a mirroring of negative aspects of Elizabeth's rule and court in partial contradiction to the idealization of her and the court also running throughout the poem. Judith Anderson has also delineated some of Spenser's ambivalence about the queen in Books 3 and 4, focusing on Belphoebe in ways I shall draw on below.

The issue of the relationship between Spenser's poem and the queen has become quite prominent in recent criticism as new theoretical and feminist perspectives have been brought to bear on the poem. Elizabeth J. Bellamy has argued that Spenser tries but fails to name Elizabeth, less for any contextual reasons than predictably because of a Derridean drift inherent in language. Bruce Thomas Boehrer presents Book 3 as praising the queen and her dynasty "by effacing them, by reconceiving them in the image of their own desires" (569). Less abstractly, Pamela Joseph Benson has argued that the treatment of Britomart (and, implicitly, Queen Elizabeth) in *The Faerie Queene* is, despite appearances, in keeping with Calvinist antifeminist theories about the inappropriateness of female rulers. And Maureen Quilligan comparably sees the comedy involved in the narrative of Belphoebe and Braggadocchio in Book 2 and that of Britomart and Malecasta in Book 3 as revealing Spenser's anxiety about "the already achieved transgression of usual cultural limits that was inherent in Elizabeth's female rulership" (163). Louis Adrian Montrose in a sense unites these two lines of inquiry in "The Elizabethan Subject and the Spenserian Text," a far-ranging article that moves from the figure of Elisa in *The*

Shepheardes Calendar to a consideration of Belphoebe. Montrose concludes that "the stance of *The Faerie Queene* toward what Greenblatt calls 'the autocratic ruler' of the Elizabethan state becomes necessarily ambivalent—alternately or simultaneously adoring and contestatory—because, for the male subject, the authority and the other are now one and the same" (330).

Two issues seem central to the criticism on this issue: first, does Spenser successfully represent Queen Elizabeth in the various characters in his epic who are customarily taken to represent her, particularly Britomart and Belphoebe? Second, assuming he does, what do we make of the contradiction between these successive and partially overlapping representations? But what has been missed in this discussion is how the second question (I take the first as essentially unanswerable) intersects in crucial ways with the themes of imitation and cultural nationalism as sketched in the last two chapters. For the tension Bennett noted between the moral stance of the poem and the praise of Queen Elizabeth—between Britomart and Belphoebe—is also a tension between a Protestant English and an Italianate cultural and political landscape. Belphoebe as the representation of Queen Elizabeth is also a representative of a tradition of Italianate culture to which Spenser is deeply indebted but of which he is increasingly critical. The choice between Britomart and Belphoebe—and I believe Spenser asks us to make such a choice—is a choice between the queen's (and Spenser's own earlier) Italianism and the increasingly Protestant and culturally nationalist English identity Spenser and other English writers articulate.

To see this, we need to back up and trace in some general ways the politics and cultural politics of the cult of virginity. The early Church did not absolutely condemn marriage, for Paul wrote that it was better to marry than to burn. Human sexuality could be spiritually harmful but through the institution of marriage, it could also be channeled in more positive (or at least less negative) ways. But implicit in Paul's formulation is that it would be better not to burn at all; and at least one Church Father, Origen, took some fairly drastic measures to achieve this goal. The Christian ideal quickly became to rise above human sexuality, and this ideal held its place throughout the Middle Ages. The cult of the Virgin Mary that flourished particularly after Saint Francis helped define a role elevated above sexuality for women as well as for men, and the history of love poetry follows a trajectory comparable to the Church's idealization of chastity defined as sexual abstinence. The "romance of adultery," to use C. S. Lewis's term, found in courtly love poetry and Provençal verse was elevated and spiritualized by Dante and Petrarch. Their love for Beatrice and Laura came to represent a higher—because unconsummated—form of love, and it is no accident that the Virgin Mary is prominent at the very end of the *Paradiso* and the *Canzoniere*. The final canto of the *Paradiso* opens with the prayer of Saint Bernard to the Virgin, and Petrarch's *Canzoniere* ends with a prayer to the Virgin Mary, "Vergine bella, che di sol vestita" (*Canzoniere* 366). The close of the *Canzoniere* thus formally imitates the close of the *Paradiso*, and Petrarch refers to Mary in "Vergine bella" as "vera beatrice" ("true bringer of happiness"), manifesting in this conceit as well as in the entire close of the *Canzoniere* both some rivalry with Dante and a perfect awareness of the connections between the love poetry and the Marian tradition.[1]

This complex of attitudes was sharply challenged by the Reformation, for Protestant teaching de-emphasized the importance of the Virgin Mary, criticized the Catholic conflation of chastity and virginity, and argued for a married clergy. In doing so, the Protestants returned to Saint Paul's formulation, with the important additional corollary that one cannot rise above human sexuality: of the two choices remaining, to marry or to burn, marriage was the spiritually higher and more chaste option. This clash of opinions finds one clear expression in the question of clerical marriage, something still controversial in Elizabethan England and disliked by Queen Elizabeth. But exactly the same question resonates throughout love poetry. If one believes that chastity is virginity, then both the clergy and the Lady must be celibate in order to represent a spiritual ideal. Spenser's love poetry in the *Amoretti* and his portrayal of love in *The Faerie Queene* constitute a Protestant and English critique of this Catholic and Italian tradition, replacing the Petrarchan ideal of virginity by a definition of chastity as married love in a way precisely parallel to (and undoubtedly influenced by) the general Protestant redefinition of marriage as the spiritually superior state. Spenser's celebration of marriage obviously would have been unthinkable without the Protestants' repudiation of the position that celibacy was the spiritually superior state and their subsequent "sponsorship of marriage" (George and George, 264).[2] This revaluation of marriage and of the status of women is an absolutely critical moment in the emancipation of women, and Spenser here is part of a broader cultural shift, one found as well in Shakespeare and Milton and more broadly across English culture. But Spenser's ideas were considerably ahead of the general climate of Protestant opinion. One way of putting this is that Spenser could never have written Eve's speech in *Paradise Lost,* "Unargu'd I obey; so God ordained, / God is thy Law, thou Mine" (4.636–37). Milton's insistence on the natural inequality of men and women is fairly typical of mainstream Protestant views;[3] Spenser's stress on the equality of men and women at least in marriage is advanced enough in his time that Spenser's theory of marriage can accurately be called feminist.

This should help to explain the tension between the praise of the queen and the general moral stance of the poem. Petrarchan love was far more than a set of poetic conventions in Spenser's society. For Queen Elizabeth, consciously playing the role of Laura with her court, had brought the forms of Petrarchan love back into the courtly setting from which courtly love originally sprang.[4] Her courtiers were expected to love her and love her alone, yet not to expect any return of that love. They were also expected to write poems in a Petrarchan style praising her for being as chaste, pure, and beautiful as Laura, and they were supposed to be as faithful to her as Petrarch was to Laura. For Spenser's praise of the queen to be recognizable, it had to follow in general terms the scheme in which the queen presented herself, as the Virgin rising above physical love to a spiritualized state, as the English Laura and the English Virgin. Scholars have shown how explicitly and deliberately Elizabeth used the imagery of the Marian and Petrarchan traditions to dignify her refusal to marry (Yates, 78–80, and L. Forster, 122–43).[5] Spenser's Belphoebe follows in this tradition, representing the type of beauty that refuses any physical consummation but demands expressions of love from Timias.

But Spenser follows this line of portraiture only to contrast it to the actions of another woman who is portrayed far more positively. As we have already seen, Belphoebe tyrannizes over Timias in ways that destroy Timias's identity and there is a sharp contrast between these actions and the actions of the true knight of chaste love, Britomart. The chastity of Belphoebe from this perspective is revealed to be a Catholic (and therefore for Spenser, false) view of love, and the chastity of Britomart is the proper, Protestant, indeed English view of true love.[6] Through her name and her role as progenitor of a number of British dynasties, Britomart (however much she depends on Ariostan precedents) is established as a "true Briton," again in contrast to Belphoebe. And her actions, not only in Books 3 and 4 but afterward, show her continuing role as the embodiment of Spenser's ideal of love.

In Book 4, Britomart finally meets up with Artegall, and the two are betrothed in canto 6. Artegall soon leaves, however, to continue on his quest. In Book 5, Artegall encounters an unmarried female ruler, Radigund, and is conquered by her in canto 5. Britomart's response is instructively different from Belphoebe's reaction to Timias's succouring of Amoret in Book 4. Not wrongly condemning her "mate" for his service to another woman, but rightly condemning the woman for her tyranny, Britomart frees Artegall from Radigund's dominance. Britomart defeats Radigund because she alone refuses to accept the conditions "With which she vsed still to tye her fone" (5.7.28). Radigund puts the knights who want to fight her in another double bind, by making the combat an explicit contest for dominance that they have already implicitly lost by accepting those conditions. It is because Britomart is also a woman that she evades Radigund's constraining bind; she has a theory of love that does not confuse love and war and, of the same sex as Radigund, she does not become confused about why she is battling Radigund. Nor does she do this in order to introduce a dominance of her own, as Belphoebe does in Book 4. Artegall is set free so that he is able to complete his quest, but before he goes off again, Britomart shows how a woman should properly rule:

> So there a while they afterwards remained,
> Him to refresh, and her late wounds to heale:
> During which space she there as Princess rained,
> And changing all that forme of common weale,
> The liberty of women did repeale,
> Which they had long vsurpt; and them restoring
> To mens subiection, did true Iustice deale:
> That all they as a Goddesse her adoring,
> Her wisedome did admire, and hearkend to her loring.
>
> (5.7.42)

This stanza sets forth both a theory of governing and a theory of marriage that reflects back on Belphoebe (and the queen) as sharply as it does on Radigund. Thomas Cain has pointed out that Britomart's prompt execution of Radigund (5.7.34) "so little resembles Elizabeth's vacillations in the case of Mary's execution as to insinuate criticism of the queen's behavior. As with his management of the Mercilla episode, Spenser appears here to be undermining the encomiastic statement of Book V" (154). But Radigund may resemble Mary less than she resembles Elizabeth, as Maureen Quilligan has already implied when she notes that "in reinstating masculine rule over Radigund's Amazon empire, Britomart reinstitutes a governing structure that obtains everywhere but in England under Elizabeth" (170). And the language of "mens subiection" may also seem to be undermining what I have earlier called Spenser's feminist position on marriage. But Spenser's position on the proper relation between the sexes is more complex than it might seem. Radigund and her crew of Amazons had upset the proper balance of things by usurping power and ruling over men, but the state Britomart restores is not one of total subjection to men, for it is the woman Britomart who is inaugurating this new realm. Quilligan's summary is a simplification, for it is Britomart who reinstates "masculine rule"—men may rule over women, but one woman at any rate rules over everyone—in an image of how things really were in Elizabethan England. That model of governing would please Queen Elizabeth, but not the model of marriage, for Britomart rules over everyone *but* Artegall. Their relationship is one of equality and concord. And by freeing Artegall, but then letting him go his way to follow his duty (which Belphoebe does not permit Timias to do), Britomart's actions establish that sense of balance between the sexes that is always Spenser's ideal and concern.

So we should be able to see by now that we cannot really let the discrepancy between the praise of the queen and the praise of marriage go by arguing that they lie on two different planes and therefore are not actually in conflict. Each involves a vision of the nature of love (and the nature of society) that finds concrete expression in the narrative, one preeminently in Britomart's quest for Artegall, the other in Belphoebe's treatment of Timias. There is an interlace between the two and we are asked—as always in Spenser—to judge which kind of love is the ideal. That should be easy, if one judges by the results. Belphoebe binds Timias to a position of dependence and servitude, whereas Britomart enables Artegall to achieve his quest as she has achieved hers. The Catholic chastity of Belphoebe is sterile, physically, socially, and spiritually; it pretends to be spiritual but is really an expression of a will to power. Britomart is the central hero or heroine of the central books of Spenser's epic, someone who manages to enable the quests of others and to achieve her own. She—not Belphoebe—embodies Spenser's ideal of love, and in Spenser's world one must choose between them.

Now, if the links between this complex of narratives and Petrarchism are not clear enough, Sir Walter Raleigh made them utterly explicit.[7] (And, as we shall see, it is significant that it was Raleigh who made this connection.) Raleigh drew the connection between Petrarchism and Spenser's portrayal of the queen in the first of the commendatory sonnets published with the first edition of the first three books of *The Faerie Queene* published in 1590, "A Vision upon this conceipt of the *Faery Queene*":[8]

> Me thought I saw the graue, where Laura lay,
> Within that Temple, where the vestall flame
> Was wont to burne, and passing by that way,
> To see that buried dust of liuing fame,
> Whose tombe faire loue, and fairer vertue kept,
> All suddenly I saw the Faery Queene:
> At whose approch the soule of Petrarke wept,
> And from thenceforth those graces were not seene.
> For they this Queene attended, in whose steed
> Obliuion laid him downe on Lauras herse:
> Hereat the hardest stones were seene to bleed,
> And grones of buried ghostes the heauens did perse.
>   Where Homers spright did tremble all for griefe,
>   And curst th'accesse of that celestial theife.
>
> (409)

In this sonnet, we are at Laura's tomb and Petrarch's soul is still worshiping her. Laura's tomb became something of a topos in Renaissance poetry after the French poet Maurice Sceve discovered her tomb in Avignon in the 1540s. Petrarch's love for Laura had been the greatest poetic love before Spenser, and Queen Elizabeth, the Faerie Queene, is an exemplification of Petrarchan love, otherwise the queen would not be at Laura's grave. But Raleigh comes not to praise Laura but to bury her, for he claims that after Spenser's Faery Queene, no one is going to care about Petrarch's Laura any more. According to Raleigh, Queen Elizabeth so surpasses Laura (and Spenser so surpasses Petrarch) that both Laura and Petrarch are sent into oblivion.

This peculiar sonnet establishes a parallel that simply is not much of a parallel. Petrarch loves Laura as a private person and, at least at the start of the *Canzoniere,* wishes to consummate that love. Spenser cannot love the queen in that way at all, for his love, such as it is, can only be addressed to the queen as a public image, not as a private person. He cannot wish for any physical consummation. That is a line that the queen herself loved to blur: to be at her court was often to be cast in the role of Petrarch to her Laura. But it was not so blurred for Spenser, who was never in that kind of proximity nor had that kind of status.

But this sonnet, an English not a Petrarchan or Italian sonnet, was written by Raleigh, and Raleigh was of course one of those who had played Petrarch to the queen's Laura. And in this sonnet it seems for a moment as if Raleigh has written *The Faerie Queene,* that he imagines himself playing Petrarch to the queen's Laura. This seems to be praise yet contrasts oddly with the encomia in the poem itself: Spenser's comparisons of the queen are nearly always with creatures above the queen in status, to goddesses such as Diana and Astraea. Raleigh instead compares her to a common woman, and indirectly expresses his desire for her.

Of course, there is a topical allegory involved here that cements the connection I am trying to draw. The way the queen played the role of Laura at court shapes the portrait of Belphoebe even more directly than we have said so far. For Queen Elizabeth, as for Belphoebe, all her squires had to love her, and she had to have all their love. As this entailed a situation of perpetual chastity, it should occasion no surprise that the queen's "squires" often covertly rebelled against the constraints of their situation. In the early 1590s, after his sonnet and Books 1–3 of *The Faerie Queene* had been published, Sir Walter Raleigh impregnated and then married one of the queen's maids of honor, Elizabeth Throckmorton, but kept insisting, long after it was plausible, that he had done no such thing. But the queen—unlike Laura but like Belphoebe—was in a position to enforce the bind her squires were in. Her anger was not only with Raleigh, for loving another. Elizabeth was always angry when one of her maids of honor married: they had to live up to the role of Laura along with her, in the same way that her squires had to live up to the role of Petrarch. In this case, enraged, she locked Raleigh and his wife in the Tower and never really granted them her full favor again.[9] Violating the Petrarchan bind in Queen Elizabeth's court was dangerous business.

Spenser has traditionally been seen as alluding to these events through the Belphoebe-Timias story (see Adamson and Folland, 182–83 and 203–6; Oakeshott, 89–99; Gilbert, 623–36; and Bednarz). Timias can be identified with Raleigh because of the reference to tobacco (in 3.5.32) and the name Belphoebe—as Spenser himself said— is based on Raleigh's "excellent conceipt of Cynthia, (Phoebe and Cynthia being both names of Diana)" (Spenser, *Poetical Works*, 407).[10]

The interplay here between poem and public world is quite intricate and complex. Before 1590, Spenser writes Book 3 of *The Faerie Queene* in which he portrays the queen as a Petrarchan beloved under the guise of Belphoebe, and Raleigh as her unrequited lover, Timias. Raleigh's poem accompanying the 1590 publication shows that he recognizes the allusion, which in any case is partially taken from Raleigh's own poetry. Subsequently, as if he has also recognized Spenser's point, Raleigh tries in real life to walk out on the Petrarchan double bind, to escape Queen Elizabeth's domination, and Elizabeth reacts with real anger. Then in Book 4, published in 1596, Spenser depicts the new developments; Belphoebe's anger at Timias's succouring of Amoret in Book 4 is traditionally taken to represent the series of events following Raleigh's marriage. This topical allegory clearly shows that Spenser was meditating on forms of love clearly to be found in his society, to be found at the highest level of his society. His critique of those forms of love clearly if subtly constitutes a questioning of the Queen's attitudes toward love that runs throughout *The Faerie Queene*.

But what is the point of this questioning? Discussing the epideictic rhetoric of praise, Aristotle points out that "there is a specific interrelation between praise and advice" (*Rhetoric*, 1.9). Although Aristotle does not mention it, this is true of blame as well, but what advice does Spenser have to give? Spenser cannot be urging the queen to marry: the time was obviously long past for that and Spenser on good Protestant lines had opposed the last real chance for the queen to marry, the proposed marriage to the Duc de Alençon in 1579. But dreading the end of the Elizabethan reign he can see as he writes, a part of him wants to criticize the queen for failing to be Britomart, for failing to create her own successor. In the third canto of Book 3, Merlin tells Britomart about the long line of kings and queens who will spring from her union with Artegall, and the passage builds toward a stanza in praise of "a royall virgin . . . which shall / Stretch her white rod ouer the Belgicke shore" (3.3.49), obviously Queen Elizabeth. But Merlin stops at the end of the stanza, "ouercomen of the spirites powre, / Or other ghastly spectacle dismayd" (50, lines 2–3). Cain has already noted that this passage "articulates the ominous problem of the succession and retrospectively overcasts the whole prophecy" (128). The final books of *The Faerie Queene,* with their critique of the queen's notion of love and corresponding praise of marriage, seem to carry in them, among many other things, a regret that the Queen had not been able to marry, that she could love only inferiors in position

such as Timias instead of true equals like Artegall. And given the co-
lossal mess that the Stuarts made of things after profiting from her
celibacy, one has to credit Spenser with some prophetic insight here.

Sorting out precisely how this critique of the queen fits with the
praise of the queen is a baffling exercise. For here, too, although
fiercely criticizing Petrarchism, Spenser is being highly Petrarchan.
Praise and blame are often inseparable in Petrarch: he seems to praise
yet an undercurrent of blame often results, and we have seen in
Wyatt's reworkings of poems from the *Canzoniere* how easily one can
modulate into the other. This is true to the oxymoronic nature of
Petrarch's verse: the Lady is the sweet enemy, the cruel fair, the dreadful tyrannesse of the early poems of the *Amoretti*. Thus, the very register with which he criticizes the Petrarchism of the queen, an oxymoronic register in which praise and blame coexist and qualify each
other, shows that Spenser is never more Petrarchan than in his mode
of criticizing Petrarch.

This brings us to the second paradox of Spenser's critique of Petrarchism. If Petrarchism is criticized by a Protestant Spenser as Catholic
and therefore in error, how does that fit with Spenser's overwhelming
debt to the Catholic culture of Italy that gave birth to Petrarchism?
Spenser's debt to Italy can be seen everywhere, in the title of the
Amoretti, in the imitations of Petrarch and Tasso already traced, and
in the widely studied and acknowledged imitation of Ariosto's *Orlando
Furioso* and Tasso's *Gerusalemme Liberata* in *The Faerie Queene*. In criticizing Italian literature, he is criticizing the wellsprings of his own art.
And just as Spenser's critique of Petrarchism marks a great fault line
in attitudes toward love and marriage, so too it marks a fault line in
attitudes toward Italy. From the time of Chaucer, and particularly
from the time of Wyatt and Surrey, Italy had been the great cultural
donor in Renaissance England, and Spenser's works are far from the
only examples of the pervasive Italianism of Elizabethan England.
This Italianism culminates in the 1590s, the decade in which nearly
one hundred sonnet sequences were composed in England, but the
Petrarchan love poetry on which we have focused is simply one example of this relationship. Shakespeare's plays of the same decade
from *Two Gentlemen of Verona* and *Romeo and Juliet* to *Twelfth Night*
and *Much Ado about Nothing* represent this moment of Italian influence
most indelibly for the modern reader. Shakespeare does not even need
to depict an Italian setting, does not need to try to naturalize a presumably foreign setting for his English audience. The Italian setting comes

naturally for him (and presumably his audience) in the way that, centuries later, it will still be the assumed norm for operas in England and America to be sung in Italian.

Things changed very quickly, as the difference between these plays and Webster's show. The vogue of sonneteering abruptly ended, so abruptly that Shakespeare's *Sonnets* must have seemed a little dated when they were published in 1609. At the same time—and not simply coincidentally—that the tremendous borrowing of Italian cultural forms that had constituted all the arts in Elizabethan England came to an abrupt end, the representation of Italy darkened sharply. One of the best places to see this shift and to see that this shift is connected with Petrarchism is Thomas Nashe's *The Unfortunate Traveller* (1594). Nashe's picaresque tale is set earlier in the sixteenth century, and his protagonist, Jack Wilton, becomes a servant to the renowned Petrarchan poet, Henry Howard, Earl of Surrey (241–64). At one point in the tale, he and Surrey are thrown in prison in Venice, where they are somewhat improbably joined in prison by a lady by the name of Diamante. Surrey, whose whole voyage to Italy was inspired by his desire to do reverence to the birthplace of his supposedly Italian-born love, Geraldine, imagines Diamante to be Geraldine and spends his time kneeling to her, kissing "the ground [on which she walked] as holy ground" (262), and writing Petrarchan sonnets, one of which Nashe includes in his text (262–63). Wilton comments sardonically, "My master beate the bush and kepte a coyle and a pratling, but I caught the birde" (263). While Surrey casts Diamante in the role of Laura, Wilton gets her pregnant and after their release from prison, travels around Italy with her until further misadventures befall them. Nashe not only makes the attitudes of Petrarchism ridiculous here in a manner far cruder—if also funnier—than Spenser's critique of Petrarchism in his epic; he makes Surrey's respectful imitation of Italian culture equally ridiculous. And this is made perfectly explicit later in the story by another English earl banished from England who has learned through experience to appreciate it. As he tells Jack Wilton after he saves him from a hanging,

> Countriman, tell me, what is the occasion of thy straying so farre out of England to visit this strange Nation? If it bee languages, thou maist learne them at home; nought but lasciuiousnesse is to bee learned here. . . .
>
> *Italy*, the Paradice of the earth and the Epicures heauen, how doth it forme our yong master? It makes him to kis his hand like

an ape, cringe his necke like a starueling, and play at hey passe repasse come aloft, when he salutes a man. From thence he brings the art of atheisme, the art of epicurising, the art of whoring, the art of poysoning, the art of Sodomitrie. (297, 301)

And by the end of *The Unfortunate Traveller,* we should understand that it is not only Jack Wilton who is the unfortunate traveler; all travelers are unfortunate if they at all imitate foreign—and especially Italian—ways. Wilton learns his lesson and at the end of the story returns to England "out of the *Sodom* of Italy" (327).

Spenser's critique of Petrarchism in the *Amoretti* and *The Faerie Queene* surely did not cause this momentous shift, but the way he, as a committed Italianist who perfectly embodies the deep imitation of Renaissance Italy prevalent in Renaissance England, nonetheless begins a serious critique of Italian culture from a culturally nationalistic perspective offers a rich, representative instance of that shift. To put it most simply, England roughly at the turn of the century stops seeing itself as a Renaissance imitator of Renaissance Italy and begins to see itself as a Protestant opponent of Catholic Italy. Such a shift most obviously connects back to the tremendous struggle of Elizabethan England against the leading Catholic power, Spain. Yet this does not explain everything, for the period of most overt Italian influence is in the decade immediately following the Spanish Armada. The death of the Italianate Queen Elizabeth might be another explanation, yet, as we have already seen, Spenser's turn on Petrarchism precedes the Stuart accession to the throne, which in any case he did not live to see. Whatever causes might be considered most prominent, the shift in attitude toward Italy was remarkably quick and uniform, although such a momentous shift obviously does not occur without some blurred edges.

After this shift, imitating the Italians is not the live option for English writers it once was, and the rich, complex process whereby cultural forms of largely Italian origin, such as the sonnet, were given an English identity across the sixteenth century is over. The Jacobean dramatists like Webster who set their plays in Italy have a sense of Italy close to that of Nashe and as different from those of Wyatt, Sidney, and Spenser as possible. And Nashe's depiction of Italy as a lurid land of sex and violence with no authentic relationship to any possibly English cultural ideal sets the terms for the English representation of Italy from his time until the late nineteenth and early twentieth centuries. But precisely at the moment when this tradition receives its final expression in the fiction of E. M. Forster, D. H. Lawrence, and Norman Douglas, the Renaissance sense of Italy as a cultural resource to be imitated is rediscovered, in the work of Synge, Pound, and Joyce. The full terms of this rediscovery will be the concern of Part Two, but a look at Synge's role in that process properly follows, as the last chapter of Part One, because Synge's imitation of Italian literature also took the form of translating and imitating Petrarch, in a body of work that can best be understood in the context of the Renaissance Petrarchism that has concerned us so far.

Chapter Five

Synge's Irish Renaissance Petrarchism

*I*f any part of the small canon of John Millington Synge has been neglected, it has been his translations, the largest group of which are his translations of seventeen sonnets of Petrarch's.[1] This neglect is not difficult to account for: translations tend to receive less attention than original compositions, and the translations that were crucial for the Irish Revival were translations of Irish literature. In the context of the Irish Revival and in the context of Synge's other work, his translations of medieval and Renaissance Italian, French, and German poets have seemed eccentric, peripheral to the main body of his work and to the source of his inspiration. Yeats bears some of the responsibility for this impression, for everyone knows his story of finding Synge in Paris and urging him to go to Aran to "find a life that had never been expressed in literature" (*Autobiographies,* 343). The life in the west of Ireland seems central to Synge's achievement, not his years of wandering and study on the Continent before he went to Aran in 1898.

Nonetheless, this received image of Synge stands in need of some correction. First, although his acquaintance with Petrarch and his knowledge of Italian and the other Continental languages from which he would translate date from the years before Aran, his translations date from the last three years of his life.[2] So Aran did not do away with Synge the scholar of Continental languages and literatures. Moreover, expressing that life on Aran took a great deal of scholarly toil as well, as Declan Kiberd has shown in his *Synge and the Irish Language,* the study that has done the most to change our perception of Synge and his works in recent years. By showing Synge's mastery of Irish and his sophisticated understanding of the work that had been done in translating literature in Irish into English, Kiberd has unquestionably proved his dual contention that Synge's work should be understood as a "bilingual weave" between English and Irish and that "Synge had a genius for translation" (88). All his work, in Kiberd's view, should be seen as a kind of translation.

The focus of Kiberd's study necessarily precluded him from engaging in a close examination of Synge's translations from Continental languages. However, his stress on translation as a key aspect of all Synge's work provides a context in which these translations can be seen as more in keeping with the rest of Synge's work. The focus of this chapter is Synge's translations of Petrarch, and I hope to show that, beyond being interesting works in their own right, they occupy a central place in Synge's canon. Kiberd rightly notes that "Synge was no mere Gaelicist but a man who brought a thorough European sensibility to bear on the native literary tradition" (59). He also brought a thorough Irish sensibility to bear on the Continental literary tradition. And the translations and poems that result from this interaction are worthy of more detailed study. Moreover, a deeper understanding of why Synge would have been interested in translating Petrarch at the very end of his life will give us a deeper understanding of Synge's other late work, not only of these fine translations. Synge's work is yet another case where received notions of translation and imitation have impeded a full understanding of his work and where we have neglected a deep engagement with classic Italian literature.

The act of translating Petrarch, as Synge's "thorough European sensibility" would have informed him, is an act that places one in a rich tradition, for—as we have already seen—poets across Europe during the Renaissance translated and imitated Petrarch endlessly. And it is illuminating to place Synge's Petrarch translations in the context of this Renaissance Petrarchism; Synge's Irish Renaissance Petrarchism in several important respects closely parallels Renaissance Petrarchism. The situation of vernacular poets in the Renaissance writing under the shadow of the classical languages was much like that of Synge. The vernacular had a colloquial vigor that the poet wanted to tap, but it lacked—or had lost—the arsenal of genres, forms, and topoi that constitute a literary language and a literary manner. Analogously, in plays such as *The Playboy of the Western World,* Synge had perfected a style and an idiom that was superbly successful in representing peasants and peasant speech in the west of Ireland. (This was of course not completely his own creation, as Lady Gregory's use of "Kiltartanese" in her re-creations of the ancient Irish sagas in *Cuchulain of Muirthemne* [1902] and *Gods and Fighting Men* [1904] anticipated and influenced Synge.[3]) But that very perfection had created a kind of crisis. Synge saw intuitively, I think, that there were firm limits to what could be done with peasant drama. To stay in that vein would be to exhaust it. Yet, could anything but peasant drama be written in that idiom? Could it be the basis for a genuine literary language?

Poets in the Renaissance such as Wyatt and Surrey in English and Du Bellay and Ronsard in French saw themselves as being in much the same situation: perceiving their own languages as rude and barbaric, as lacking any basis for a literary language, they and a host of other poets in almost every European language set out to construct that new literary language to a large extent by translating Petrarch. As Leonard Forster, discussing a wide range of European literatures, has said: "In each of these cases, therefore, we see that the creation of new poetic diction goes hand in hand with the influence of Petrarch or his followers and with the use of characteristic petrarchistic devices" (71). Why Petrarch? I will again cite Forster: "I would like to return to the suggestion that the attraction of petrarchism to people who were trying to create a new poetic diction was that they needed something to imitate and here was something supremely imitable" (83). Petrarch is highly mannered, almost formulaic, at least in those poems in the *Canzoniere* most frequently imitated in the Renaissance. He wrote on a central human and literary subject, love, and he had the status of a vernacular classic in the Renaissance. So Wyatt and Ronsard, and a host of other poets in a host of other languages, could translate that arsenal of effects into their own language by translating Petrarch, thus expanding the range of effects available to poetry in that language and developing a way of writing about love. These poets, therefore, had no preexisting idiom into which they could translate Petrarch. They translated Petrarch precisely in order to create that idiom, in order to create a poetic diction. These attempts at creating a literary language of love bore fruit, as can be seen in the example of England from the great and highly Petrarchan Elizabethan sonnet sequences of Sidney, Spenser, and Shakespeare.

Moreover, Synge was aware of the work of Renaissance Petrarchans, as well as that of Petrarch, in particular that of the French poet Ronsard. The poems "To Ronsard," "Epitaph: After reading Ronsard's lines from Rabelais," and "On a Birthday" all assert or imply a felt kinship with the French poet. But the names coupled with Ronsard in "On a Birthday" and those in "On an Anniversary," Cervantes and Greene and particularly the repetition of Nashe—as we have seen—are not those of Petrarchans. Except for Petrarch and Ronsard, Synge seems to have felt closest to those whom one could call the "tough guys" of the Renaissance, writers like Villon or Nashe who are characterized by the timbre, strength, and even brutality Synge speaks of in his preface to his poems.

There is some pathos in this identification; when Synge wrote that preface (and much of his poetry), he was weak and dying. This brings us to the second important aspect of Renaissance Petrarchism for a consideration of Synge's translations of Petrarch. One of the reasons why Synge's Petrarch translations have not been accorded much attention is that ever since the Romantics (at least, until recently) translation has not been very highly honored, at least in comparison with the act of writing "original" poetry. Emerson's strictures against imitation are also strictures against translation. Translation and original composition have been seen as two quite distinct activities, and the less imita-tive activity of original composition has been seen as far more signifi-cant. When translating, one was expected to be faithful and invisible; when writing one's own poetry, the opposite was true. Originality was to be praised and imitation discouraged. But Synge's "thorough European sensibility" and historical awareness of Continental litera-ture made him see translation in a different, far more honorable light. As we have already seen, Petrarch held that it was precisely through proper imitation of models that one found an identity, a personal style and voice. Imitation is not the opposite of originality: through the proper kind of imitation, one finds the voice that enables one to be original. This kind of imitation, which sees translation as a way to write original poetry, is central to Petrarch's own poetry and poetics, and it became central for the Renaissance. It is very difficult to draw a line between original composition and translation in the canon of most Renaissance poets, for they freely translated and imitated, creating their own poems out of the poems that had come before.

The Renaissance Petrarchans who imitated Petrarch himself, like Wyatt and Ronsard, "transformed him honorably" according to his principles. We think of Petrarch today primarily as a poet of love, but he is also centrally a poet of death, and he is unsurpassed as a poet in linking these two themes, a fusion that results in the strange last one hundred poems of the *Canzoniere,* fey and erotic at the same time. Of course, Petrarch lived in a society full of death, traumatized by the Black Death, which swept Europe in the 1340s taking the lives of

Laura, Petrarch's patron Cardinal Giovanni Colonna (as we have already seen from "Rotta è l'alta colonna"), and a good deal of the rest of the population. As Petrarch wrote in the *Secretum,* "in truth, I regard this dark shadow of death, not as something afar off, but very nigh and ever at the doors" (40). Writing in a period with a less intense sense of human mortality, Renaissance Petrarchans—as we have already seen in the case of Wyatt—found Petrarch's orientation toward the rest and transcendence of death in the second half of the *Canzoniere* uncongenial. So they translated Petrarch so as to make him more personal and less abstract, more sensual and less ethereal, readier to make demands on the Lady and less willing to wait on her. And that was perfectly in keeping with Petrarch's aesthetic of imitation.

All these aspects of Renaissance Petrarchism, I would like to argue, are relevant to a consideration of Synge's Irish Renaissance Petrarchism. Like the Renaissance Petrarchans, Synge translates Petrarch as an exercise in diction, in an attempt to find new, more elevated uses for a folk diction. He also shared their view of translation as an important mode of composition, and like them he transformed Petrarch as he translated him. The major difference is that he transformed Petrarch in quite a different direction, and we shall later see that in a sense Synge was closer in spirit to Petrarch than were most Renaissance Petrarchans, although he was perhaps no more faithful a translator.

Although no one has previously placed Synge's work in the context of Renaissance Petrarchism, it has been seen that these Petrarch translations were experiments in diction for Synge; that is, in fact, virtually the only thing that is ever said about them. As Alan Price has said, "the translations were mainly exercises made at a time when he was experimenting with the peasant idiom to see if it was adaptable to other purposes" (107). And because they are translations, we can study this process of adaptation in detail by comparing his versions with the original. Let us look at one representative example, Synge's translation of Petrarch's "Quanta invidia io ti porto" (*Canzoniere* 300), which he entitled "He is jealous of the Heavens and the earth":

> Quanta invidia io ti porto, avara terra
> ch' abbracci quella cui veder m'è tolto
> et mi contendi l'aria del bel volto
> dove pace trovai d'ogni mia guerra!
>
> Quanta ne porto al Ciel che chiude et serra
> et si cupidamente à in sé raccolto

lo spirto da le belle membra sciolto,
et per altrui sì rado si diserra!

Quanta invidia a quell'anime che 'n sorte
ànno or sua santa et dolce compagnia,
la qual io cercai sempre con tal brama!

Quant' a la dispietata et dura Morte,
ch'avendo spento in lei la vita mia
stassi ne' suoi begli occhi et me non chiama!

 What a grudge I am bearing the earth that has its arms about
her, and is holding that face away from me, where I was finding
peace from great sadness.
 What a grudge I am bearing the Heavens that are after taking
her, and shutting her in with greediness, the Heavens that do push
their bolt against so many.
 What a grudge I am bearing the blessed saints that have got her
sweet company, that I am always seeking; and what a grudge I am
bearing against Death, that is standing in her two eyes, and will
not call me with a word. (Synge, *Poems,* 91)

The first thing to note is Synge's treatment of the poem's structure.
Petrarch's sonnet is divided into four sentences, each of which record
his envy of something—the earth, Heaven, the saints, and death. He
envies these because they all have more contact with Laura then he
does. Synge keeps the two sentences of the octave intact and gives each
a separate paragraph but links the two concluding tercets with a semi-
colon, making the sestet one slightly longer final paragraph. But the
four are more completely parallel in Synge's version, because he starts
each with the uniform "What a grudge I am bearing," whereas Petrarch varies his expression of envy.

 Much more striking than these changes is the colloquial turn Synge
gives to Petrarch's phrases. The key phrase in Synge's version, "What
a grudge I am bearing," is a fine demotic rendering of "Quanta invidia" ("how much I envy"). In Petrarch the earth embraces Laura; in
Synge it has its arms around her. Synge collapses Petrarch's double
statement "quella cui veder m'è tolto / et mi contendi l'aria del bel
volto" ("her whose sight is taken from me, and keep from me the
breath of that lovely face") into one phrase, "is holding that face away
from me." In line 8, Petrarch says that Heaven "per altrui sì rado si

diserra" ("so rarely unlocks itself for others"). Synge takes this nega-
tively stated phrase and renders it as one concrete action: "that do push
their bolt against so many." Finally, in the last line Synge translates
"stassi ne' suoi begli occhi" ("stays in her lovely eyes") as "that is
standing in her two eyes," a much more concrete and powerful phrase.

Synge handles this poem with considerable syntactic freedom and
verve. His principal innovation lies in the extended use of participials,
a habit taken over from the language of his plays and yet marvelously
appropriate to what he is translating. Petrarch's poems are full of verbs
with unspecified objects or subjects or with only a vaguely specified
duration. Synge often is forced to clarify subject–object relations as he
translates, but through the use of the present progressive tense he generally makes our sense of the poem's duration even vaguer. In this
poem, Synge changes the eleventh line, "la qual io cercai sempre con
tal brama" ("which with what desire I always sought"), to "I am always seeking." This excellent change carries with it the sense of the
entire poem, that Petrarch is always seeking Laura, although he knows
that she is dead. Petrarch is bearing a grudge, the Heavens are "shutting her in," Death "is standing in her two eyes"; these verbs imply
that all this could go on forever, which is certainly the sense found in
Petrarch in general and in this poem in particular.[4]

In this representative sonnet, Synge is a resourceful yet faithful
translator. He quite accurately captures the sense of Petrarch's poem,
yet his translation is also quite fresh and original. The freshness comes,
I think, from the fact that he is not carrying the Petrarch poem over
into an English with a preexisting Petrarchan or Italianate register. He
is putting it in the diction of his earlier peasant plays. This is a radical
experiment inasmuch as there seems to be no very good reason why
nonpeasant speakers would speak in Synge's Anglo-Irish idiom. But
it works: one never feels that Petrarch is lamenting the death of Pegeen
Mike. And the fact that it does work shows (and presumably showed
Synge) that one can do something with the Anglo-Irish idiom perfected in Synge's earlier plays beyond the limits of the peasant drama.
Nonpeasant speakers can express themselves in this idiom without
incongruity or a failure of dramatic decorum. And this expansion of
the range of Synge's manner leads directly to the play Synge left unfinished at his death, *Deirdre of the Sorrows*. A version of an old Irish
legend also dramatized by Yeats and A.E., *Deirdre* was an important
departure or experiment for Synge, for every previous play of his that
reached the stage had been set in contemporary rural Ireland. And it

is an experiment strongly influenced by Synge's slightly anterior Petrarch translations. As Robin Skelton has pointed out, "The speech that Synge constructed for his translations is very similar to that of *Deirdre of the Sorrows*" (*The Writings of J. M. Synge,* 135). In both works, he uses metrical speech, prose paragraphs as equivalents for stanzas, and a restrained version of his idiom spoken by figures very far in origin from the folk in the west of Ireland on whom Synge based this idiom. Synge's Petrarch translations were experiments in diction that served as a trial run for the larger (and tragically unfinished) experiment of *Deirdre*.

Thus, we can see how Synge's work with Petrarch is similar to the work of Renaissance Petrarchans such as Wyatt and Ronsard. Later writers have not built on Synge's work in quite the way the great Elizabethan poets built on Wyatt's, but each is trying to expand a vernacular folk idiom beyond its limits, and each does so by translating Petrarch. Moreover, Synge is also, in keeping with the Renaissance tradition of imitation, imitating Petrarch so as to create his own voice. We have seen this to a degree in the colloquial manner in which he handles his original in "What a grudge I am bearing," but this is much easier to see in some of Synge's other translations, such as "Laura waits for him in Heaven," a translation of "Li angeli eletti et l'anime beate" (*Canzoniere* 346). Here Synge stays faithful to Petrarch's theme of yearning after Laura and Heaven, but with a few modifications that transform our view of Laura, Heaven, and Petrarch's yearning:

Li angeli eletti et l'anime beate
cittadine del Cielo, il primo giorno
che Madonna passò, le fur intorno
piene di meraviglia et di pietate.

"Che luce è questa et qual nova beltate?"
dicean tra lor: "perch' abito sì adorno
dal mondo errante a quest'alto soggiorno
non salì mai in tutta questa etate."

Ella, contenta aver cangiato albergo,
si paragona pur coi più perfetti
et parte ad or ad or si volge a tergo,

mirando s'io la seguo, et par ch'aspetti;
ond'io voglie et pensier tutti al Ciel ergo
perch'i' l'odo pregar pur ch'i' m'affretti.

The first day she passed up and down through the Heavens,
gentle and simple were left standing, and they in great wonder,
saying one to the other:

"What new light is that? What new beauty at all? The like of
herself hasn't risen up these long years from the common world."

And herself, well pleased with the Heavens, was going forward,
matching herself with the most perfect that were before her, yet
one time, and another, waiting a little, and turning her head back
to see if myself was coming after her. It's for that I'm lifting up all
my thoughts and will into the Heavens, because I do hear her
praying that I should be making haste forever. (*Poems*, 97)

Synge's Laura does not simply pass over to Heaven; she passes "up
and down" as if she were taking a promenade "through the Heavens."
Synge usually uses "the Heavens" in these translations, which has a
slight polytheistic flavor to it. This sense that Heaven is not being
treated with Petrarch's reverence is heightened when "Li angeli eletti
et l'anime beate" ("the elect angels and blessed souls") is translated as
"gentle and simple." This is a good example of Synge's direct and
colloquial phrasing, but as a description of Heaven, its directness is
demythologizing. Heaven seems just like earth, with beauties, prome-
nades, and inspections of new arrivals.

The sestet is where Synge's transformation of Petrarch moves beyond nuance. Petrarch in line 10 writes that Laura "si paragona pur
coi più perfetti." This is a passive: she is equal to even the most perfect
in Heaven. Synge interprets (or misunderstands) this as a reflexive
verb and arrives at "matching herself with the most perfect." This has
an altogether different effect, one consonant with Laura passing up
and down. Synge's Laura is rather pushy; she is "well pleased with
the Heavens," as if she had not been sure in advance that she would
like them.

Synge's Laura is therefore altogether more human than Petrarch's,
and she is made to have a more humane attitude toward Petrarch. In
Petrarch it seems that she waits ("par ch'aspetti") and that, being as
humane as she ever is in the *Canzoniere*, she is even praying for Petrarch to hurry to Heaven ("perch'i' l'odo pregar pur ch'i' m'affretti").
Synge drops the *seems* and describes her as "waiting a little." In
the final line she is praying "that I should be making haste forever."
Synge decides that *pur* modifies Petrarch's haste and translates it—
quite oddly—as *forever*.

All these small shifts work together, and together they make Synge's poem quite different in impact from Petrarch's, more personal, more matter-of-fact, more down-to-earth. Some of these changes may stem from misunderstandings of the Italian, but they are nonetheless consonant with the other shifts in syntax and diction toward directness and realism. Synge therefore conforms to the Renaissance canons of imitation in that he transforms his original coherently and pervasively, and he does so in a way remarkably akin to that of Wyatt and Ronsard. Although Synge chooses to translate the seemingly more abstract and less personal sonnets concerned with death and Heaven, his mastery of the colloquial enables him to make even death and the inhabitants of Heaven familiar and concrete.

I am the more confident in relating the liberties Synge takes on occasion with his Petrarch originals to the Renaissance notion of imitation (rather than simply dismissing them as inaccuracies) because a number of Synge's "original" poems use past poets to speak for him in a way that is also part of the Petrarchan heritage of imitation. The naming in "On a Birthday" and "On an Anniversary" works to establish a relationship that revivifies the past author while it enables the modern one. Many of Synge's poems strive to establish such a relationship to a past poet (or poets) and then use that relationship to comment on the present. This comment is authorized by the presence of the past poet, yet it remains Synge's own.

"To Ronsard" is a good example of this:

> Am I alone in Leinster, Meath and Connaught
> In Ulster and the south,
> To trace your spirit, Ronsard, in each song and sonnet
> Shining with wine or drouth?
>
> How you were happy in your old sweet France
> Beside the Bellerie
> Where you heard nymphs and Naiads wheel and dance
> In moon-light jovially.
>
> (*Poems,* 30)

This establishes a relationship that is both an identification and an opposition: Synge identifies himself with Ronsard, but he also establishes a contrast between Renaissance France and modern Ireland, a contrast implicitly in favor of the former. In Ireland, Synge alone invokes Ronsard's spirit, but clearly he wishes that he were not alone in doing so. In this way, Synge invokes Ronsard's voice and spirit (in a number of senses) to make a comment on the lack of wine, nymphs, and joviality in Ireland.

This poem (and there are others like it in Synge's canon) is an imitation in the sense that we have been exploring: Synge reproduces a certain "air" of his model without replicating it. In this sense, it may be more Petrarchan in that it conforms more closely to the canons of creative imitation than do his more faithful versions of Petrarch. But I would claim that these poems and translations accomplish the same task from slightly different directions: both are attempts to recover the Renaissance poetic of imitation found in the poetry of Ronsard and Petrarch. In both, the past poet is revivified and the modern one given a voice. The two voices fuse in the poem at hand.

However, there is a crucial difference between Synge and those Renaissance poets who imitated Petrarch, and the difference is in the voice that emerges from the poetic of imitation. The most obvious difference between Synge and Renaissance Petrarchans such as Wyatt and Ronsard as translators of Petrarch is in the poems of Petrarch's that they choose to translate. As we have seen, Renaissance Petrarchans translate and imitate almost exclusively poems of Petrarch written in Laura's lifetime, poems from *in vita*. Synge translates exclusively from *in morte*. In these last poems, Petrarch is oriented toward death in the sense that he knows death is coming and he is preparing for it. While translating Petrarch in the years 1907 and 1908, Synge also knew that death was coming to him, and it is not too much to say that translating these poems was a preparation for death. This explains Synge's choice of poems from *in morte;* it also shows that they are more than exercises in poetic diction, as the subject matter of these poems was full of thematic resonance for Synge.

Synge was involved in a tumultuous love affair with an actress in the Abbey Theatre, Molly Allgood, and, as the poem "A Question" shows, he was concerned with the fate of their relationship after his death. *Deirdre* is an exploration of these issues, and it is no coincidence that from the beginning Synge intended Molly to play Deirdre. Deirdre's lover, Naisi, dies before her. She laments his death, although she has partially caused it; she refuses to leave his body; and finally she commits suicide rather than live on without him.

I doubt that Synge would have wanted Molly to practice suttee on his grave. But in *Deirdre* he shows anxiety about the depth of her love, hoping that their tie will survive his death yet also claiming, with Deirdre in the second act, that a short intense love may be better than a long life that ends in age and decrepitude: "It may be I will not have Naisi growing an old man in Alban with an old woman at his side, and young girls pointing out and saying 'that is Deirdre and Naisi, had great beauty in their youth.' . . . It may be we do well putting a sharp end to the day is brave and glorious, as our fathers put a sharp end to the days of the kings of Ireland" (*Plays*, 237). The relationship between this theme in *Deirdre* and the poems by Petrarch that Synge chose to translate is both important and complex. Petrarch is, in a sense, a Deirdre who did not commit suicide on his lover's grave. He lives on, but his life seems empty and futile. This paradoxically may have reassured Synge. These final poems of the *Canzoniere* would have shown him that his and Molly's love could survive his death. They also argue that dying first is better than living on in the absence of the beloved, and they portray death as a blessed state.

There are, of course, important differences between Synge's situation and that of Petrarch. Laura was not Petrarch's fiancée and seems never to have paid much attention to Petrarch. Petrarch lived for twenty-six years after Laura's death and clearly did not spend all his time sighing and wishing for death. But the central theme of the poems *in morte* is death and the effect of the early death of a lover on a love relationship. Synge translates primarily those poems of Petrarch's in praise of death, and this completely atypical choice of poems by Petrarch to translate shows that these translations were much more than merely exercises in diction for Synge. These poems are a significant parallel to the preference for death shown by Deirdre in *Deirdre of the Sorrows:* I would say source if the source of both the poems and the play did not lie so obviously in Synge's awareness of (and courageous attempt to come to terms with) his own approaching death. In this way, these translations of Petrarch's love poems about death are at the thematic center of the writings of Synge's final two years.

What I am suggesting, in brief, is that Synge was making his own statement, in effect writing his own poetry, by translating these poems of Petrarch's, which he found to be apposite to his own situation.[5] We should intuit the presence of the translator in these translations: Synge borrows the voice of Petrarch to speak for him. The reason why this has not been seen and why these translations have not been sufficiently appreciated is that the nineteenth-century imperative of originality, which gives such short shrift to translation, has continued to govern our perception of Synge's work. Nonetheless, Synge was not alone in his interest in recovering the Renaissance poetic of imitation. To a considerable extent, this poetic of imitation has been recovered in the seventy-five years since Synge's death. Our notion of what constitutes poetic originality today is far more flexible than it was, both in the sense that we are far better at seeing the originality in translations such as Synge's and, in the wake of recent critical theories about influence, in the sense that we can see the importance of models for all creative work. In these translations, therefore, Synge is (although, again, this has not been recognized) part of a central impulse in modern literature.

Borrowing the voice of a past poet as a speaker, as a persona, was, for instance, the chief aesthetic strategy of the early work of Ezra Pound. The poets he chose, for the most part, were also medieval and early Renaissance lyric poets, mostly Provençal and Italian. Pound developed this poetic of the persona, like Synge, both in translations (of Cavalcanti, Arnaut Daniel, and others) and in original compositions that used poets such as Cino da Pistoia and Bertrans de Born as personae of the poet. Like Synge, his real aim was to break down this distinction between translation and original composition. Furthermore, Pound's recovery of the Renaissance poetic of imitation, so close to that of Synge in these respects, has been tremendously influential, responsible for the interest many contemporary poets have shown in translation.

I would not want to claim for Synge any influence on Pound here. Pound's work in this area was far more prolonged, extensive, and influential than that of Synge. Moreover, although the older poet, Synge is not even the prior in this interest. The poems and translations discussed in this chapter all date from 1906 to 1909, and none was published before Synge's death in 1909. By that time, Pound was writing the poems in *Personae,* also published in 1909, and working on *The Spirit of Romance* (1910). Nevertheless, the similarity in their interests gives us one final, contemporary context for understanding Synge's apparently eccentric interest in Petrarch—not at all eccentric, as I hope I have shown. And in one respect at least, Synge was considerably in advance of Pound. Synge's great achievement in his Petrarch translations was to break through the fake antique quality deemed necessary in the Victorian era for translations of old poems. His diction is fresh, contemporary, and exciting, and he broke through into this diction seemingly without effort.

It took Pound years of effort to get to the same point. As we shall see from one example in the next chapter, his early translations from

Italian literature, the most substantial of which are his translations of Cavalcanti, are stilted, labored, and in thorough need of modernization, as he himself later recognized. It was only when Pound moved away from the early Italian material that Dante Gabriel Rossetti had put his translator's stamp on and began to work with the comparatively unfamiliar material from the Orient that would result in *Cathay* (1915) and *Noh, or Accomplishment* (1917) that he finally achieved a fresh, contemporary idiom for translation.

When he does that, interestingly enough, the one recognizable source for his idiom is Synge. He knew Synge's work—including the Petrarch translations[6]—through his friendship with Yeats, and in fact he was living with Yeats when he translated the Nō plays (see Ellmann, *Eminent Domain,* 70–71 and Longenbach, *Stone Cottage*). Pound's Nō translations of 1917 occasionally slide into something surprisingly reminiscent of Synge's plays: "Times out of mind am I here setting up this bright branch, this silky wood with the charms painted in it as fine as the web you'd get in the grass-cloth of Shinobu, that they'd be still selling you in this mountain" (*Translations,* 286).[7] Where is Shinobu, we wonder for a moment, somewhere in Mayo? And although I do not find this echo of Synge's idiom terribly felicitous in the Japanese context, it can be taken as one final indication of Synge's considerable and still unrecognized achievement in his translations. Synge indeed had a genius for translation, as Declan Kiberd has argued, a genius implicitly manifested in all his work but explicitly manifested in these fascinating translations of Petrarch.

Part Two   *O Patria Mia:*
            Pound and Joyce

Italy is our country; and not ours only, but every man's, wherever may have been his wanderings, wherever may have been his birth, who watches with anxiety the recovery of the Arts, and acknowledges the supremacy of Genius.

Walter Savage Landor, *The Pentameron*

My dear old Ezra. How are you, and what are you doing with yourself? T. S. Eliot sent along your letter and I was rejoiced to see your handwriting again, and receive your messages. I am told you believe yourself to be Napoleon or is it Mussolini? What a pity you did not choose Buddha while you were about it, instead of a politician!

Wyndham Lewis, in his first letter to Pound
after World War II, July 1946

Writing on Vico and Joyce, Northrop Frye has suggested that since the fourteenth century English literature has "been influenced often to the point of domination, by either French or Italian literary traditions" (3). The period of modernism is clearly one of the periods in which the influence of the Italian literary tradition predominated, to the point where an engagement with Italian literature and culture seems one of the constitutive elements of modernism itself. Modernist literature without Dante is almost unthinkable, but one of the points emphasized in the chapters that follow is that the modernist appreciation of Dante does not exist in a vacuum, that it needs to be understood in the broader context of the modernist appreciation of Italian culture as a whole.

We have already seen this deep engagement with Italian literature in the case of Synge, a writer who writes a "Vita Vecchia" at the beginning of his career and goes on to translate Petrarch (and Leopardi) near the end of his life.[1] The chapters that follow focus on Pound and Joyce, the two modernists with the most complex engagement with Italy. Yeats and Beckett, however, with their interest in Dante, Vico, and others, offer further illustration of Italy's impact on the Irish writers, while Eliot's great interest in Dante reinforces that of Pound. Nor does this Italianism stop with the high modernists: a poet like John Ashbery establishes his differences from Pound by choosing a mannerist painting by Parmagianino in *Self-Portrait in a Convex Mirror*, yet his choice of an Italian Renaissance artwork as a mirror for his art and for his situation is deeply Poundian and deeply modernist.

But this list contains no English names. And if one characteristic of international modernist literature in English is a deep and sympathetic engagement with Italian culture, that is simply one more respect in which modernism was un-English. The English writers in this period are still caught up in the older post-Renaissance tradition of seeing Italy as the Other, as a cultural opposite to England. Just as it had been for three hundred years for Protestant English writers since Nashe and Webster, Italy for these writers is a forum in which the Englishman in Italy has his identity challenged. English writers in the modernist period do not succeed in breaking away from this tradition; even D. H. Lawrence does not, despite his interest in Italian futurism and his translations of a number of works by Giovanni Verga.[2] Instead, they give it its last full statement, preeminently in Norman Douglas's *Siren Land* (1911) and *South Wind* (1917), but also in E. M. Forster's *Where Angels Fear to Tread* (1905) and *A Room with a View* (1908) and D. H. Lawrence's *The Lost Girl* (1920) and *Aaron's Rod* (1922). But in the very same years in which this tradition of representing Italy was receiving its last statement, the Irish and American writers who among them define modernism broke away from this cultural problematic, and they did so more easily perhaps because they could see it as an English tradition. Italy was not for them a cultural antagonist full of profoundly dangerous if fascinating—in short, un-English—people; it was a cultural benefactor, the center of the civilized world. These writers could therefore engage much more directly and unproblematically with traditions of Italian culture and literature. And part of what enables them to make such creative use of Italian culture is that their theory about (and practice of) art is deeply bound up with imitation; Pound, in particular, is a theorist of imitation whose theories, as we shall see in more detail, are richly Italianate. And all of this together means that Italy for the modernists is again—as it had not been unproblematically for any English writer since Spenser and Milton—something to be imitated.

It is in these respects that the Italianism of the modernists most clearly resembles the early Italianism of the sixteenth century, of a

Wyatt or a Surrey. Wyatt translates Italian cultural forms in an un-problematic way that writers after Spenser cannot. But Pound, Joyce, and others, cutting through or finding their way around the representation of Italy as a Catholic Other, return to something quite close to the earlier attitude in which Italian culture was something to be imitated. Furthermore, I would argue, the key to the greatness of each writer is that imitation, the process by which a complex identity emerged through the borrowing of Italian cultural forms and voices.

This parallel between the Italianism of the Renaissance and that of the modernists is not exact, however. There are important differences between the Italianism of these two periods that we need to delineate. Of the two crucial differences for our argument here, Synge clearly exhibits one but not the other, showing here, as always, his intermediate, transitional position. The earlier Italianism of the Renaissance and the intervening struggle with Italy had both assumed a bipolar cultural landscape in which England and Italy interacted. With Synge's Irish Renaissance Petrarchism, things had grown more complicated. The modern Ireland he compares to Renaissance Europe is implicitly contrasted to modern England and, in the plays, compared yet again to the ancient Ireland of Deirdre and Cuchulain. So, Italy plays a role in a complex comparative system, not just the role of comparison or contrast to England. And this becomes even clearer—if also a good deal more complex—with Pound and Joyce. Both writers straightforwardly imitate major moments and monuments of Italian culture, but the net result of that imitation is to set those moments in significant relation not only with the present, with Pound's America and Joyce's Ireland, but also with other places and times. This temporal and cultural collage is also—as we shall see—part of the Italian heritage for the modernists, and it shapes how that heritage comes into play.

This is perhaps another way of saying that, for Pound and Joyce, Italy does not represent only the past, a dead cultural monument. Here there is a sharp change in the single generation between Browning and James—as the last great writers in the older tradition—and Pound and Joyce. One cannot imagine Browning or James being influenced by anything in the Italian culture of their time: they lived through the making of modern Italy but never reflected this in their work.[3] Explicitly, for these Victorian writers, the interest of Italy was its great past, not its contemporary culture. And, except for his translation of part of one poem by Leopardi, Synge had continued in the older tradition, finding little to grapple with in Italy since Petrarch. But Pound responded eagerly to futurism, as Joyce did to syndicalism, and both were influenced by contemporary Italian writers such as D'Annunzio. Norman Douglas (1868–1952) was an honorary citizen of the island of Capri at the same time as Benedetto Croce (1866–1952) (see Holloway, 470), but it is impossible to imagine these two almost exact contemporaries having anything else in common. For the latter, Italy was home, for the former, Italy was Siren Land. Pound and Joyce, unlike Douglas, did not live on the same island as Croce, but they did live in the same Italy.

This is, of course, one of the senses in which the Italianism of the modernists resembles that of the Renaissance. Petrarch lived 150 years before Wyatt and 200 before Spenser, but he was still a living force when the English Petrarchans wrote, a classic but a modern one. And the other Italian poets Wyatt and Spenser imitated, Alamanni, Sannazaro, Ariosto, and Tasso, were close contemporaries of the English writers they influenced. The Italianism of the Renaissance, like that of the modernists, was a relation to a living culture. Yet, for the modernists, Italy also represented the past as it did for Browning, Pater, or James: Pound and Joyce appreciated *both* modern Italy and the classics of the *trecento*. For them, Italy was both present and past, both a living force and an emblem of the past. But this does not lead to a bifurcation of their sense of Italian culture. A gap in our sense of their relation to Italy, which I have tried to redress here, is that we have ignored the importance of intermediate periods of Italian culture for both writers: Italy is not only the *trecento* of Dante and the *novecento* of Croce, D'Annunzio, and Marinetti, it is also the *quattrocento* of Valla and Malatesta, the *cinquecento* of Machiavelli and Bruno, the *settecento* of Vico and Goldoni, Metastasio and Vivaldi, and the *ottocento* of Leopardi, Rossini, and Carducci. Pound and Joyce thus have a sense of the full sweep of Italian culture: Italy is not a dead culture because Italian culture never died. And virtually every moment of that cultural tradition had its impact on the works of Pound and Joyce.

If a period of Italian culture influential for Joyce and Pound has been neglected in the chapters that follow, it is the Italy of their own era, the Italy of D'Annunzio, Marinetti, and Mussolini. In the case of Joyce, a discussion of this seemed unnecessary, given the able treatment this relation has already received.[4] In the case of Pound, the relationship is so complex as to require another book, since Pound lived in Italy most of his adult life and participated actively in Italian social, cultural, and political life, most notoriously by actively supporting Italian fascism. This does not mean, however, that I have sought refuge in the Italian past to avoid the controversial topic of Pound's fascism, which is a major theme in the chapters that follow. I have tried to establish the ways in which Pound's appreciation of the Italian past conditioned and led to his commitment to the cause of Mussolini; a detailed study of that commitment, of Pound's relation to the culture and history of fascist Italy, is a subject I hope to treat in a subsequent book. I consider this study the essential groundwork for the other: Pound read and loved Dante before he ever heard of Mussolini.

Dante is of course the supreme figure of Italian culture for both Pound and Joyce, but my emphasis here does not detract from the importance of Dante in their work as much as give us a way to understand it. Dante may be the summit of Italian culture but he is also part of an impressive mountain range. And other key figures in that tradition helped each writer make use of Dante. Vico helped Joyce to his understanding of Dante; Croce and Gentile led him to Vico. Pound's knowledge of Cavalcanti, Cino, and others helped him understand Dante; and Leopardi helped him to make use of that understanding.

This is probably what separates Pound and Joyce most clearly from the other modernists. The focus on Pound and Joyce in the chapters that follow should not be taken as suggesting that the Italianism of the modernists is much broader and richer than the Renaissance, that the Petrarchism of the Renaissance was supplanted not only by the cult of Dante in modernism, but also by the influence of a host of other elements of Italian culture. Pound and Joyce, along with Synge, are really exceptions here, if impressive and influential ones. The Italianism of the other modernists is in fact narrower than that of the Renaissance poets. In place of Wyatt's use of Alamanni, Serafino, and others in addition to Petrarch, his mastery of verse satire, *terza rima*, and the strambotto, in addition to the sonnet; of Spenser's reliance not only on Tasso and Petrarch in his sonnets but also on Ariosto, Trissino, and Tasso in his epic and Sannazaro and Petrarch in his pastorals, we have a narrower if possibly more intense appreciation of Dante in Yeats's *Per Amica Silentiae Lunae*, all of Eliot's major poems, Lewis's *The Hu-*

man Age, and Beckett's fiction, most obviously "Dante among the Lobsters." (There are some exceptions to this generalization, however, most of which will be mentioned in the chapters that follow.) We would need one of Yeats's double-gyres to portray this adequately, with a narrowing gyre of the cult of Dante of the other modernists as opposed to the widening gyre of the Italianism of Pound and Joyce. My primary focus here is not this narrower cult of Dante, widely enough studied by other scholars, as much as the broader Italianism of Pound and Joyce. But the cult of Dante is an important part of my subject, and I will return to the relation of the modernists to Dante in the conclusion.

Chapter Six

Leopardi and Pound's Apprehension of the Italian Past

*I*f one attended solely to Ezra Pound's most prominent statements about Italian literature—statements such as "the best period of Italian poetry ends in the year 1321" ("Cavalcanti," 192)—one might conclude—as Pound criticism by and large has—that Dante and Cavalcanti were the only great Italian writers who significantly influenced Pound's work. Dante's work was obviously not something Pound had to discover on his own. Throughout the nineteenth century, Dante had already been canonized as the great epic poet, particularly in America (among the English-speaking countries), in one of the historical developments without which Pound's work is unthinkable.[1] But Cavalcanti had not been prominent in English-language culture before Pound translated him, and this is one reason why Pound's polemics to establish Cavalcanti's greatness were so extensive and pointed. One of Pound's central strategies for promoting Cavalcanti was denigrating those who came after him, especially Petrarch. Petrarch has customarily been seen as second only to Dante in the Italian poetic pantheon and, as should be clear enough by now, has in fact been a greater influence on poets inside and outside Italy than has Dante. So Pound must have felt it imperative to dislodge "fat faced Frankie" as he called Petrarch in *Guide to Kulchur* (263) from this position in order to lodge Cavalcanti there. Pound put his case with his usual penchant for absolutes: "The Italian of Petrarch and his successors is of no interest to the practising writer or to the student of comparative dynamics in language, the collectors of bric-a-brac are outside our domain" ("Cavalcanti," 199). Or, as he puts it elsewhere in the same essay, "The difference between Guido [Cavalcanti] and Petrarch is not a mere difference in degree, it is a difference in kind" (153).

Pound may not have succeeded in convincing readers and critics of Italian literature about the relative merits of Cavalcanti and Petrarch, but these strong assertions have been successful in shaping our sense of Pound's relation to Italian poetry, to the extent that there is a book on Pound's work on Cavalcanti in addition to one on Dante and Pound and two on the Provençal poets and Pound but not—as far as I am aware—even a single article on Petrarch and Pound.[2] Yet the irony here is that, as Petrarch's translator Robert M. Durling has noted, there are some striking "affinities between Pound and Petrarch—their fascination with Propertius, Ovid, and the Provençal poets, with the broodings of memory, with the fragmentation of experience and of poetic form" (viii).

In at least three key respects, Pound is in fact closer to Petrarch than he is to either Dante or Cavalcanti. First, Pound is a scholarly man of letters in precisely the way Petrarch was. Pound had a scholarly training in languages and literature, and his work as a critic, scholar, and translator took up as much of his time as his own poetry and is not easily separable from it. Likewise, his poetry is dwarfed in extent by his letters, the importance of which we are only now realizing, and by his prose, and in all these respects he is an exemplar of the humanist tradition initiated by Petrarch. Pound's very labor in resurrecting Cavalcanti is something we can easily imagine Petrarch doing, but not Cavalcanti.[3]

This can be put another way, which is that Petrarch and Pound share a feeling of belatedness. To venture what is perhaps an overgeneralization, Dante and Cavalcanti seem to have felt themselves at the beginning of something: they felt that their *dolce stil* was *nuovo*. In contrast, both Petrarch and Pound—despite our later sense of them as crucial innovators—sense that they have come after a period of greatness, that what is called for when they write is a transmitting of that legacy of the past. This leads to a poetics of imitation in addition to scholarly activity, and their list of whom to imitate is remarkably similar: Dante and his contemporaries, Cino da Pistoia and Cavalcanti, the Provençal poets, and finally the Latin classics, Ovid and Propertius, to whom Petrarch would add Virgil, Pound Homer. Despite their parallel strictures against uncreative borrowing, imitation for both poets can seem fairly close to theft: Petrarch's "Lasso me, ch' i' non so in qual parte pieghi" (*Canzoniere* 70) takes opening lines from canzoni by Arnaut Daniel, Cavalcanti, Cino, Dante, and Petrarch himself as closing lines to successive strophes, and it was for this reason that Aldus included these canzoni—including Cavalcanti's "Donna mi prega"—in his 1514 edition of Petrarch's *Rime*. From the beginning of his career, Pound similarly appropriated the work of exactly the same poets. His first book, *A Lume Spento* (with a title taken from Dante's *Purgatorio*), contains the poem "Cino"; phrases from Arnaut, Cavalcanti, and Dante resonate throughout all his work, and he translated poems by all three. Later, Pound will include a translation of all of Cavalcanti's "Donna mi Prega" in Canto 36, and it was to obtain a text of this poem by Cavalcanti that Pound bought his copy of the 1514 Aldine Petrarch.[4]

This poetics of imitation is probably responsible for the third resemblance between their work, the form of their major works, Petrarch's *Canzoniere* and Pound's *Cantos*. Even if Pound's ambition was to write a new *Commedia*, "a perfectly integrated poem" as Robert Durling has described Dante's epic (26), it is generally conceded that he did not succeed in this aim, for reasons that will concern us later and have in fact a good deal to do with his imitation of Dante. What results from this failure is far closer to Petrarch than it is to Dante, creator of a single grand shape in the *Commedia*, or to Cavalcanti, who never essayed any such grand shape. Petrarch wrote his lyrics individually and allowed many of them to be disseminated separately, but he also spent years collecting, revising, and arranging his lyrics into a larger collection. This attempt to create a large-scale structure out of a collection of smaller forms, this attempt to mediate between lyric and epic, between Cavalcanti and the Dante of the *Commedia*, creates something quite like the problematic generic space of *The Cantos*.[5] Nancy Vickers has summarized these aspects of the *Canzoniere* in terms that work perfectly to describe *The Cantos* as well: "Petrarch's poetry is a poetry of tension, of flux, and of alternation between the scattered and the gathered" (277).

Now, if Pound is in all these important ways more like Petrarch than like Dante or Cavalcanti, why did he not see this? Or did he? And if he did, why did he not admit it? The obvious explanation of why he would not readily admit to any resemblance between his work and Petrarch's is that there is a real difference between them. His critique of Petrarch, as expressed in his essay "Cavalcanti" and elsewhere, focuses not on the resemblances we have been exploring but on Petrarch's poetic diction:

In Guido, the "figure," the strong metamorphic or "picturesque" expression is there with purpose to convey or to interpret a definite meaning. In Petrarch it is ornament, the prettiest ornament he could find, but not an irreplaceable ornament, or one that he couldn't have used just about as well somewhere else. In fact he very often does use it, and them, somewhere, and nearly everywhere, else, all over the place. ("Cavalcanti," 154)

This, one has to admit, is perceptive criticism of Petrarch: phrases such as "begli occhi" (beautiful eyes) or "i capei d'oro" (golden tresses) or the numerous references to Laura as "l'aura" (breeze) "lauro" (laurel) or even "l'auro" (gold) are scattered throughout the *Canzoniere*.[6] And critics after Pound have substantiated his perception that Petrarch's vocabulary is much narrower than Dante's.[7] This ornamental or decorative quality of Petrarch's verse had been an aspect of his verse decisively influential for the earlier Italianism of the Renaissance and the English poetic tradition descending to Pound's own time. Pound's reaction against this, toward the spare diction of imagism, was central to his entire poetic project, and his work translating less ornamental poets such as Cavalcanti, as numerous critics have already shown, was an important part of what led to imagism. Anti-Petrarchan in these respects, Pound did not want to consider himself Petrarchan in any respect, particularly in those years when the battle for Pound's imagist style against the decorative verse tradition was still in the balance.

But in these very same years, Pound was far quicker to praise and admit his kinship with another post-Dantescan Italian poet, Giacomo Leopardi (1798–1837). In our general focus on early Italian sources for Pound's aesthetic, Leopardi's influence on Pound has been ignored, but what I hope to show in this chapter is that Leopardi's particular (and rather Petrarchan) apprehension and appropriation of the Italian past, particularly of the classic Italian poets of the *trecento*, is of crucial importance for Pound's mature work.

In order to see this, we need to look at the handful of allusions to Leopardi in Pound's work as well as at his one translation of a poem by Leopardi. Pound generally did not find much to like in Italian poetry after Dante. If we may put the scattered comments of Pound on Italian poetry together, Pound sees Italian poetry after Dante as tending toward a highly literate but unintense ornamental poetry: "Petrarch systematizes a certain ease of verbal expression in Italian" (*The Spirit of Romance*, 166), and unfortunately others continued his work.

Michelangelo is the only vernacular poet after Dante favorably mentioned in *The Spirit of Romance* (1910), mentioned as a poet who preferred Dante to Bembo and was therefore "against the [Petrarchan] spirit of the time" (238). This appreciation of Michelangelo is not particularly original on Pound's part, reflecting John Addington Symonds's 1878 translation of Michelangelo's poems (as well as Pater's chapter on them in *The Renaissance* [85–102]), and in fact Pound described his 1912 Cavalcanti translations to his friend Margaret Cravens as "intend[ing] to be the most important contribution to English-Italian Belles lettres since Symonds translation of Mike. Angelos Sonnets" (Pound and Spoo, 47; also see Spoo, 8–9).

At about the point Pound was finishing *The Spirit of Romance*, however, Leopardi replaced Michelangelo as Pound's exception to the decline of Italian poetry. In 1909–1910 Pound gave a course of lectures on medieval literature generally close to *The Spirit of Romance* in its emphases, and a lecture on Metastasio and Leopardi, the last lecture before the conclusion, was the only one on vernacular Italian poetry after Dante.[8] In 1910, Margaret Cravens tried to transmit her enthusiasm for Giosuè Carducci to Pound. Pound's response, written while Pound was in Sirmione, is revealing:

> P. S. I have been reading or trying to read your friend Carducci.
> I find beauty, & perfect literary culture, but he seems cold or more
> exactly, he lacks intensity, concentration. . . . Leopardi (by the
> way do you know him?) is Leopardi, but after you get rid of the
> culture & the beauty one can't find much Giosuè Carducci . . . he
> seems to me to be as much smaller, proportionately, than Leo-
> pardi, as Petrarch than Dante. (Pound and Spoo, 27)

And later in the correspondence, Pound again found Carducci to be inferior to Leopardi: "[Carducci] is undeniably fine in his management of sound, but Leopardi in his outrageous & splendid parody the 'Paralipomeni' does the same sort of thing with a laugh in his sleeve" (31). Moreover, although the 1910–1915 period is the period of Pound's most profound involvement with Leopardi, this view of Leopardi is not a momentary perception. Pound's remark about the decline of Italian literature after 1321 was made in 1929, but Pound explicitly excepted Leopardi (and D'Annunzio) from his condemnation. Despite his repeated negative comments to Cravens about Carducci, he did translate a sonnet of Carducci's (Pound and Litz, 158; Spoo, 14–17), but he never published it.[9] Translation for Pound was a form of canonization, and Leopardi was the only modern Italian poet he endorsed by translating the poetry and publishing his translation. And this reinforces our sense that for Pound—as for Synge—only Leopardi was worthy of being placed with Dante, Cavalcanti, Cino, the great early Italian lyricists.[10] Hence Pound's translation of "Her Monument, the Image Cut Thereon," subtitled "From the Italian of Leopardi," a poem published in *Canzoni* in 1911 and included by Pound in *Personae*, his collected poems published in 1926, but a poem that has received virtually no critical attention.[11]

Nor is this act of translation an isolated act of homage to Leopardi. In 1912 and 1913, in the middle of the period of deep involvement with Italian poetry we have been discussing, Pound published a series of articles about America called "Patria Mia" in *The New Age*. The significance of using Italian to title a series of articles about his own country is something that will concern us later; what I want to focus on now is that the title is taken from Leopardi. The title comes from the opening of Leopardi's canzone "All'Italia":

> O patria mia, vedo le mura e gli archi
> E le colonne e i simulacri e l'erme
> Torri degli avi nostri,
> Ma la gloria non vedo.

> ("My native land, I do the walls behold,
> The arches, columns, statues and deserted
> Towers by our forbears built,
> But not the glory.")
> (Lines 1–4; Bickersteth, 136, 137)[12]

Pound obviously loved these famous lines, as he also quoted them in *The New Age* some years later (in "American Chaos II" [1915]) and again in a letter to Marinetti written in 1941. "All'Italia" is an early poem of Leopardi's, in which he contrasts the glory of Italy's heritage and the fallen state of the present. This is a political poem, in which Leopardi is lamenting Italy's lack of unity and subjection to foreign powers, but it is also a poem about literary history, as its place in Leopardi's collected verse clearly shows. In the order Leopardi himself established for his poems (followed in all subsequent editions), it comes first, followed by two other poems concerned with Italy's great past and fallen present, "Sopra Il Monumento di Dante che si preparava in Firenze" and "Ad Angelo Mai quand' ebbe trovato i libri di Cicerone *Della Repubblica*." The poems that follow these three—including the poem Pound chose to translate—are in a less overtly historical and political register, but Leopardi had good reasons for keeping these poems in their initial position: they frame and interpret the poems that follow. These poems deplore Italy's lost greatness and urge its resurrection:

> Non fien da' lacci sciolte
> Dell' antico sopor l'itale menti
> S'ai patrii esempi della prisca etade
> Questa terra fatal non si rivolga.
>
> ("Still o'er Italian minds
> The sloth of centuries shall hold dominion,
> Unless of the great deeds done in old days
> This fateful land keen emulation show.")
>   ("Sopra il Monumento di Dante,"
>   lines 3–6; Bickersteth, 144, 145)

But they also achieve—at least in formal terms—some of that resurrection for which Leopardi is calling. They are canzoni and are attempts to imitate and revive the forms of early Italian poetry.[13] For Leopardi would have agreed with Pound's perception of a decline in Italian poetry, although he would probably date the decline not at Dante's death in 1321 but at Petrarch's death in 1374. In fact, he edited Petrarch's *Canzoniere*, as did Carducci, in fine scholarly editions still in print and in use in Italy today.[14] The political and the poetic projects of these canzoni are really one; both attempt to revive Italy's greatness by summoning up the voices of the past, particularly the great early Italian poets:

> Volgiti agli avi tuoi, guasto legnaggio;
> Mira queste ruine
> E le carte e le tele e i marmi e templi;
>
> ("Turn, corrupt stock, turn to your ancestors;
> Mark what these ruins tell,
> These scrolls and paintings, marbles and temple-shrines;")
>   ("Sopra il Monumento di Dante,"
>   lines 191–93; Bickersteth, 154, 155)

The first two canzoni announce the project, but the subsequent more lyrical and more personal poems also carry it forward, for they are deeply embued with the spirit of the *trecento* poets, although Petrarch is generally a greater presence than Dante.[15]

We should be able to see from this very brief and general account of Leopardi's project in these poems why Pound would have found it of compelling interest: in both its poetic and political dimension, this is virtually the same project as Ezra Pound's, particularly in the early period of Pound's career in which he seems to have been most interested in Leopardi. The volume of Pound's in which his translation of Leopardi appeared, *Canzoni* (1911), is perhaps the most extreme example of Pound's attempt to "make it new" by making it old, by the deliberate imitation of older poetic forms. Early Italian poets worked within a number of poetic forms, many inherited from the Provençal poets, but the two most important forms in the *duecento* and *trecento* were the sonnet and the canzone. Pound seems to have felt (as Leopardi must have also) that the sonnet had had its day and had exhausted itself, and his effort, particularly in *Canzoni*, was to resurrect the other important form of early Italian poetry, the canzone.[16] This has long been seen clearly enough by critics who have studied Pound's early poetry such as Hugh Witemeyer: "He also published a volume of poems entitled *Canzoni*. As its name suggests, this volume attempts to capture the spirit and revive the verse forms of Tuscan and Provençal poetry" (88). But we have somehow imagined Pound returning to the forms of early Italian poetry unaided and at a single bound. The importance of Leopardi here was in providing a model for this attempt to resurrect the past. At least one great poet had shared Pound's sense that the lyric tradition needed to be invigorated by a return to its early Italian roots and that the canzone, not the sonnet, was the vehicle for that rebirth.[17] A particular concern of Pound's at this point, I think, was to establish that his interest in historical forms did not make him simply an antiquarian. Leopardi, great scholar that he was, would have provided reassurance on this score as well, and Pound liked to emphasize Leopardi's fire precisely to show that a concern with form and a historical sensibility need not make one bloodless or stilted. As Pound wrote in his important 1915 essay, "The Renaissance": "It is possible that only Cavalcanti and Leopardi can lift rhetoric into the realm of poetry. With them one never knows the border line. In Leopardi there is such sincerity, such fire of sombre pessimism, that one can not carp or much question his manner" (217).

But "Patria Mia" shows that the political side of Leopardi's verse interested Pound as well. Pound's early prose pieces about America, "The Renaissance" as well as "Patria Mia," advance with some seriousness the notion that America was on the verge of a Renaissance: "The thesis I defend is: that America has a chance for Renaissance" ("Patria Mia," 102). Parallels between Renaissance Italy and modern America are drawn again and again in his prose in the 1910–1915 period. But in "Patria Mia," Pound also uses another Italian term, *risorgimento*, to describe his hopes for American culture: "I have declared my belief in the iminence of an American Risorgimento" (111). And according to a reference in a letter of 1911 to Margaret Cravens, Pound considered using "Risorgimento" as a title for this series of articles (Pound and Spoo, 90).

The Risorgimento was, of course, the Italian national awakening and reunification in the middle of the nineteenth century, the answer to Leopardi's call for national renewal and independence in "All'Italia." Leopardi named the movement as well as called for it; his poem, "Risorgimento," although not a political poem, is a source for the term Pound would have known. And Pound's use of Leopardi's term as well as the more familiar one of an American Renaissance in an essay with a title taken from Leopardi suggests a sense of parallelism between Leopardi and Pound: Leopardi called for Italy's cultural and political rebirth based on Renaissance models, and the Risorgimento resulted; I am calling for America's cultural and political rebirth on the same models, and perhaps "Patria Mia" and related texts will some day seem as seminal as Leopardi's call to the *patria* in "All'Italia" and other poems does now. Again a later poet calls for the new to emerge from an imitation of the great Italian past and demonstrates in the process a close relation between individual poetic creation and the creation of a new public culture. Pound's dual project of imitating the early Italians was, as we should be able to see by now, also a project in close imitation of his great predecessor Giacomo Leopardi.

But we should have known this already, for Pound's appropriations of Leopardi clearly indicate this close kinship. For "Patria Mia" is not the only title Pound took from Leopardi. When Leopardi first began to collect his poetry, in a volume published in Rome in 1818 and then in a volume published in Bologna in 1824, the title he chose for both collections was *Canzoni*, and this is the source for Pound's title of his 1911 collection. For it should be understood that although early Italian poets such as Cavalcanti, Dante, and Petrarch wrote canzoni, *Canzoni* is not found as a title for collections of their poems. *Rime* and *Canzoniere* are the customary titles for Dante's, Cino's, Cav-

alcanti's, and Petrarch's verse, since their collections included poems
in several genres and included many more sonnets than they did canzoni. Only later imitators of the early Italians such as Leopardi and
Pound—trying to break away from the sonneteering of the intervening centuries—would gather only canzoni together into a volume.

But as Leopardi moved away from the superficial imitation of his
early canzoni toward a deeper relation with the early Italian masters,
he changed the title of his collected verse. The volume published in
Florence in 1831 (followed by another published in Naples in 1835)
was given the name given to all subsequent editions of Leopardi's poetry, *Canti*. And as Pound moved away from the close imitation of
early Italian forms found in *Canzoni* to write the work on a Dantescan
scale, which he would work on for fifty years, he again took his title
from Leopardi, *The Cantos*. The canto is of course a structural unit in
Italian epics from Dante on, and both titles gesture in Dante's direction, but Dante's cantos were part of a larger whole he confidently
named the *Commedia*. Pound, working on Dante's scale but never utterly assured about achieving Dante's epic form, takes instead the title
that Leopardi uses to describe a series of connected but independent
series of shorter lyrics. The term *Canti* is not quite so purely Leopardi's as is *Canzoni*, but Pound's use of the term unadorned by anything
beyond the definite article is closer to Leopardi's title than to anything
else. Neither *Canzoni* nor *Canti* (or *Cantos*) are terms that *trecento* Italian poets would have used for their collections of poetry; both titles
reflect the fact that Pound is not apprehending the Italian past directly
in some unmediated way, but is apprehending it through an Italian
tradition of which Leopardi is the greatest modern representative.

Seeing this has direct implications for our understanding of Pound's
major poem, *The Cantos*. There has been a close parallel between the
discussion of the form of *The Cantos* and that of the influence of Italian literature on Pound. In both cases, we have attended to remarks
of Pound that establish Dante and the poets of his time as the context relevant to Pound's work. So we have seen the principal formal
model for *The Cantos* as Dante's *Commedia* and have seen Pound's long
poem primarily as an imitation of Dante.[18] Judged in this way against
Dante's *Commedia*, Pound's poem looks rather incoherent. But that
merely puts Pound in the situation faced by every Italian poet since
1321. We have judged the poem as an attempt to be like Dante's, to
rival the *Commedia* in its coherence, a standard by which it is clearly a
failure. But that may be a misunderstanding of the generic ambition

and space of *The Cantos*. *The Cantos* so obviously do not constitute an integrated epic narrative that they may not have been meant to be.

One recent, promising move in Pound criticism has been to argue that *The Cantos* have their source in some of Pound's earlier poetic sequences, less integrated epic shapes than sequences of shorter lyrics compiled and arranged to move toward a larger unity. This is explicitly the argument of Bruce Fogelman, and he presents *Canzoni* as one of the key early volumes in which Pound is exploring the form of the sequence. Fogelman's argument depends upon M. L. Rosenthal and Sally Gall's *The Modern Poetic Sequence*, which argues that *The Cantos* is just such a sequence and that the poetic sequence is the key genre of modern poetry par excellence. But what Rosenthal and Gall miss is that this "modern" form is not new at all. Neither Fogelman nor Rosenthal and Gall mention Leopardi or Pound's interest in him. Rosenthal and Gall trace the modern poetic sequence back only as far as Whitman (16) and briefly try to distinguish Renaissance sonnet sequences from the modern poetic sequence by their lack of generic diversity, their narrative story line, and their "driving emotional pressure toward a balanced resolution" (18). But in each of these respects, Petrarch's *Canzoniere* and Leopardi's *Canti* are on the modern side of the "divide," if indeed there is such a divide. In constructing a long poem made up of free-standing parts, in trying to create a unity of parts, Pound is not the great modernist innovator depicted by so many critics. Fogelman sees this, despite his reliance upon Rosenthal and Gall's work, but he spends only two pages on possible earlier models for Pound's work. Although he mentions Dante's *Vita Nuova* and Petrarch's *Canzoniere*, he does not focus on the Italian tradition I am arguing is crucial. The Italian tradition is crucial because it is made up of poets like Pound who are faced with the massive presence of Dante's *Commedia*. The poets in this tradition evoke Dante without competing with him by combining shorter units into a larger whole in an effort to create a unity of parts.

What I would like to suggest is that the form of *The Cantos* is much more easily grasped and accepted as a form by an understanding of this Italian tradition. Pound criticism has been no more comfortable than Spenser criticism with the melange of lyric and epic elements that constitute *The Faerie Queene* and *The Cantos*, and the Italian lyric tradition is at least as important for Pound's hybrid epic as for Spenser's. Pound never tried to approach or return to the past directly, as the explicitness of his use of Divus's translation of the *Odyssey* in Canto 1 or de Mailla's *Histoire Générale de la Chine* in the Chinese Cantos should show. Pound always wanted to understand the chain of transmission that led from his model to his own time, and he always wanted to attach himself to that chain of transmission. For the Italian lyric tradition in which Pound placed himself, Dante's single great shape, his "perfectly integrated poem," is something of an anomaly. Dante gives his poem a perfectly achieved unity both by architectural design and by the narrative continuity common in the epic tradition, but the lyric poets who follow him—including Pound—work toward architectural unity without narrative continuity: they try to create unity through the devices of lyric, not epic.

Of course, to attempt to create such a "unity of parts" is to move into the classic Petrarchan space of contradiction, of antithesis, of oxymoron, and it is in the nature of things that different poets in this tradition are going to achieve different degrees of unity, different ranges of parts. As we have seen, Renaissance Petrarchans—aside from Spenser—ignored the structure of Petrarch's *Canzoniere* in their focus on the poems *in vita* and in their transformations of individual lyrics. Nonetheless, as we have already seen, Petrarch's *Canzoniere*, beginning with a poet confessing his own errors and ending with a prayer to the Virgin, is a collection of lyrics that closely imitates the *Commedia* in its overall shape. Leopardi's *Canti* is primarily a collection of separate poems, yet the title in its gesture toward Dante suggests, as Bickersteth has claimed, that the *Canti* "are divisions of a large work, just as the *canti* of the *Divine Comedy* are divisions of the cantica they constitute" (88). Yet, the unity Leopardi sought for his collection of lyrics was not that of epic, for Leopardi, despite his great love of Dante, had reservations about the epic genre:

> In fact, the epic poem goes against the nature of poetry: (1) it requires a plan conceived and arranged in all coldness; (2) what can a labor that takes years and years to execute have to do with poetry? Poetry comes essentially from an impulse. And the long poem is against nature in the absolute sense. It is impossible that imagination, the poetic vein and spirit, could last, suffice, and not fail in so long a work on the same theme. The weariness and straining of Virgil are manifest as well as famous in the last six books of *The Aeneid*, written through sheer will rather than impulse or desire. (Casale, 161)

Clearly, the structure of the *Canti* is an attempt to organize his lyrics into a larger unit without betraying this principle. Moreover, Leopardi criticizes Virgil here, not Dante, because he did not consider the *Commedia* an epic in this negative sense. In his commonplace book, the *Zibaldone*, he refers to the *Commedia* as "non è che una lunga lirica" ("nothing but a long lyric"; quoted in Singh, 173), and it is striking that Pound came to exactly the same conclusion: "The *Divina Commedia* must not be considered as an epic; to compare it with epic poems is usually unprofitable. It is in a sense lyric, the tremendous lyric of the subjective Dante" (*The Spirit of Romance*, 153). Thus, both Leopardi and Pound place Dante in the generic space where I have been locating his heirs, Petrarch and Leopardi himself. It is as if both poets accept Leopardi's strictures against the epic but feel that the *Commedia*—because of Dante's lyricism—is not an epic of the kind Leopardi is criticizing. This clearly ignores aspects of Dante's achievement, but it makes sense at least in as much as Dante, too, has a place in that chain of transmission of lyric forms that Leopardi and Pound attach themselves to in their work. If Leopardi and Pound are "misreading" their model here, they do so in a direction diametrically opposed to what Bloom's model would suggest, for they are reducing the space between them and Dante rather than exaggerating it.

For Pound might be describing his own long poem in advance here: clearly *The Cantos* also belongs in this generic space between the isolated lyric and the organized, planned epic. The poem was after all published sequentially and in many cases canto by canto, and each canto stands on its own to a much greater extent than do cantos in the *Commedia*, as they can be read separately in the way individual poems of the *Canzoniere* and *Canti* can be. And although Pound intended his poem to be closer than the *Canzoniere* or the *Canti* to the integrated structure of the *Commedia*, he also tried in *The Cantos* to write an epic not vulnerable to a critique of epic such as that of Leopardi. *The Cantos* are built up from lyric "impulse and desire" more than from a set epic design, and collections such as that of the *Canzoniere* and the *Canti* helped show Pound that this was a possibility. If, by and large, the critical tradition has underestimated the unified design of the *Canzoniere* and the *Canti*, thereby exaggerating their difference from the *Commedia*, we have overestimated the resemblance (or the intention to produce a resemblance) between *The Cantos* and the *Commedia*. *The Cantos* aims for a unity of parts in much the same way the *Canzoniere* and the *Canti* do, and if we understand the tradition and form within which Pound was working, we are less likely to see *The Cantos* simply as a failed imitation of the *Commedia*. Dante is not the only Italian Pound was imitating.

Tracing Pound's references to Leopardi and thinking through their implications as we have done, we have seen two crucial and related debts of Pound to Leopardi: first, as a pioneer in the rediscovery of early Italian poetic forms and second, as a poet interested in using those forms in the service of his nation's aesthetic and political *risorgimento*. But Pound knew Leopardi's work well enough to know that "All'Italia" and the resurrection of the canzone were points of departure for Leopardi, in the same way they were for Pound. For the trajectory of Leopardi's imitative project continues backward beyond the *trecento* canzone to the lyric forms of classical poetry, particularly the idyll.[19] Here, a figure like Sappho becomes central to Leopardi, as we can see from "Ultimo canto di Saffo" (*Canti* 9) in ways that anticipate her importance for Pound. And Pound knew the full range of Leopardi's work: the poem he recommended to Margaret Cravens, *I Paralipomeni*, is a late satiric work not part of the *Canti*; and "Her Monument" is a translation is one of Leopardi's final poems, written in 1834–1835 toward the end of his life and thirty-first of the thirty-six complete poems that constitute the *Canti*. "Sopra il Ritratto," although also a canzone, is a poem very different in spirit from the early patriotic canzoni, and if we are to explain Pound's interest in Leopardi fully, we must explain both his choice of this poem to translate and his transformation of the original in his translation.

To understand this, we need first to understand that there is an important sense in which Leopardi's work on classical subjects was as political as "All'Italia." For Leopardi endorses the "pagan" vision of classical poets such as Sappho at least partially as an angle of attack on Christian orthodoxy.[20] Pound followed Leopardi down this road, of course, and if Leopardi's road to Hellas went through Petrarch's classicism, Pound's went through Leopardi and Cavalcanti—whom Pound presented favorably as more of a free thinker and less of an orthodox Christian than Dante. The crucial essay here is the 1929 essay, "Cavalcanti" (see especially 149–51), in which Pound linked Leopardi and Cavalcanti. And what is crucial here is that Leopardi's return to Italian sources, his "Italianism," was itself part of a broader opening out to other cultures he perceived to be similar, particularly classical Greece, and we shall see a similar process in Pound's (and Joyce's) development in subsequent chapters.

I have deferred a look at "Her Monument" until this point, at least partially because Pound's choice of Leopardi to translate is at least as significant as his choice of which Leopardi poem to translate, but also because we needed first to sketch a context in which "Her Monument" is meaningful. (After all, no one has found it very meaningful without such a context.) Pound's translation is among his most literal and least "creative," as he contents himself with a line-for-line translation with only a few omissions. Stylistically, "Her Monument" has none of the verve or freshness of Synge's translation of part of Leopardi's "Sylvia." Contrast Pound's opening with Synge's:

> Such wast thou,
> Who art now
> But buried dust and rusted skeleton.
> *(Personae,* 41)

Are you bearing in mind that time when there was a fine look out of your eyes, and yourself, pleased and thoughtful, were going up against the boundaries that are set to childhood? (Synge, *Poems,* 81)

And the contrast here is close to the one already drawn in the last chapter between Pound's Cavalcanti translations from the same period and Synge's fine and innovative translations of Petrarch. Although he never subsequently commented on his translation of "Her Monument," Pound himself later recognized the retrograde quality of the diction of his early Cavalcanti translations: "When I 'translated' Guido eighteen years ago I did *not* see Guido at all. . . . What obfuscated me was not the Italian but the crust of dead English, the sediment present in my own available vocabulary—which I, let us hope, got rid of a few years later. . . . I hadn't in 1910 made a language, I don't mean a language to use, but even a language to think in" ("Cavalcanti," 193–94). These terms apply perfectly to "Her Monument" as well, for Pound is still caught up in an archaizing Victorian poetic diction that contrasts sharply with the clarity and vigor of Leopardi's Italian or Synge's English. And these facts account for the little attention paid to "Her Monument" by Pound critics.

But "Her Monument" has some thematic resonance in the context sketched above. It is a sepulchral poem, one of several poems in which Leopardi wrote about gravestones or monuments to the dead. This poetic situation is a way of talking about death but also about art: the actual person commemorated has died and become dust, yet the work of art survives. And this nexus of concerns is central to the classicizing lyrics of Leopardi's final period such as "La ginestra" (*Canti* 34), which is built around a tension between the ruins of classical civilization, Pompeii and Herculaneum, and the flower growing in the desert of lava near the ruins that gives the poem its title. For Leopardi, classical civilization was exemplary because it faced the fact of mortality—the possibility that Vesuvius could erupt at any moment and kill us—without any of the illusions of transcendence or endurance after death that Leopardi found in Christianity. Yet his use of such models from the past implies a kind of endurance potentially at odds with his existential pessimism. And Pound resolves the closely parallel tension of "Her Monument" in one consistent direction, one consistent with Pound's greater historical optimism. The interest of the poem for Pound was not in the theme of the person's death but in what is left behind, what persists across time. This emphasis of Pound's can be seen in the way he leaves out of his translation some of Leopardi's concrete insistence on the physicality of the lady in life and in death. Pound simply omits Leopardi's lines 15–16: "E il seno, onde la gente / Visibilmente di pallor si tinse" (Bickersteth, 314; "That breast which made me visibly turn pale" [Casale 204]). Ruthven says that this omission "betrays an unexpected coyness" (79), but in fact it fits in with Pound's avoidance elsewhere, also noted by Ruthven, of "Leopardi's insistence on the physical decay of the body after death" (79), his rendering of "fango / Ed ossa" ("dirt and bones"; lines 17–18) as "Shameful" and his deletion of "polve ed ombra" ("dust and shadow") of line 52. Pound, in these changes, is trying to shift the focus of the poem from bones to marble, from death to art.

This is seen clearly enough in the title, one place where Pound does make a significant change. Leopardi's full title is "Sopra il Ritratto di una bella donna" ("On the Likeness of a Beautiful Woman"), subtitled "scolpito nel monumento sepolcrale della medesma" ("Carved on her Sepulchral Monument"). Pound changes the order of the title and subtitle, "Her Monument, the Image Cut Thereon," and adds the further subtitle identifying the poem as a translation, "From the Italian of Leopardi." This new title emphasizes the monument over the lady; her "ritratto" becomes "Image," and the change here perfectly expresses the more objective, less personal nature of Pound's poem. This can also be seen in another major change unremarked by Ruthven, Pound's division of the first stanza into two so that the newly created stanza ends with the phrase, "Standeth this image of the beauty sped." Image here translates "simulacra," not "ritratto," and Pound's translation of both words as image reinforces his slight but significant transformation of Leopardi's poem. Leopardi seems to say that the image stands as an emblem of how beauty has sped; his is primarily—although not exclusively—a narrative of loss. Pound tries to turn that loss into gain: beauty may have sped but the image stands. Leopardi moves toward a *ritratto* of the dead woman, Pound toward a celebration of her image, her monument. And this brings with it a sense of the recuperative powers of art, of images, of artistic representation that is one of Pound's central themes.

And across Pound's oeuvre that theme is often linked to representations of Italy and imitations of Italian art. That the image endures across and despite time is for Pound a truth embodied above all in Italy, in the monuments and images of the country, in the power and fame of its writers. He had from an early age been struck by that power, but my claim here is that his discovery of Leopardi—which seems to have come in 1909 or 1910 after the very early phase of Italianism that led to his first book of poems, *A Lume Spento*, and *The Spirit of Romance*—helped Pound make something creative and powerful out of his love for Italy. As long as Pound was interested only in the early Italian poets, particularly Dante, Italy was going to inspire more scholarship in Pound than poetry. Dante staring at a poet across the intervening centuries is an intimidating presence in ways that Bloom's work helps us to understand. But Pound's solution, here as elsewhere, was not to deny influence but to multiply it. What Pound needed to discover was the chain of transmission between himself and Dante, the line of poets who felt Dante's power yet managed to create their own poetic voice. The genre that resulted—the lyric collection that gestures toward a greater unity—is of crucial relevance for Pound's entire work from *Canzoni* to *The Cantos*. The figure in this tradition with whom Pound acknowledged a kinship was Leopardi, but many of the ways in which Pound acknowledged a debt to Leopardi are also ways that indicate an unacknowledged kinship with Petrarch. And later we shall see Lorenzo Valla—another great Italian classicist—filling some of the same role with respect to Petrarch and Italian humanism.

But this is not to say that Leopardi is only a *segnal* or cipher for Petrarch in Pound's work. Leopardi was crucial here both because of his love of past art and because of his concern for the political and cultural questions of the present. He was also crucial because he showed Pound that Italian culture did not die in 1321, that it was still a powerful and living force. Above all, he was crucial because the way he faced the Italian past gave Pound a model for how Pound could face the Italian past. That aid once given, Leopardi declines in importance for Pound: he was the (first) *duca* or guide Pound could leave behind as he explored Italian culture on his own.

But this still does not mean that only Dante's Italy matters for Pound after "Patria Mia." The key text in the next stage of Pound's Italianism is the 1915 essay, "The Renaissance," and it is the Renaissance that is crucial for Pound for the next period of his art. But before we turn to this next period, we need to turn to James Joyce, whose initial apprehension of the Italian past, specifically of Dante, in precisely these same years offers a fascinating parallel—although with important differences—to that of Ezra Pound.

Chapter Seven

Homer Dante Vico Croce Joyce

*W*e have seen in the previous chapter Pound's somewhat indirect path to establishing a creative response to Italian literature in his own mature work. Struck very early by the power of Dante's work, Pound nonetheless needed to find a more modern mediating figure in Italian culture before he could truly see how to make it new by making it old. And the mediating figure he found was Giacomo Leopardi. And we have also already seen—although more of that story remains to be told—how Pound's imitation of Italian culture led him not away from his own culture but toward a sharpened faith in the possibilities for American culture. His interest in the Italian Renaissance led him to look toward an American Renaissance in the same way that his interest in Dante led him to want to write a modern *Commedia*. So we can discern a four-part sequence in Pound's relation to Italy. An initial love of Dante was followed by a greater understanding of Italian culture as a whole, specifically of responses to Dante, which then led to a renewed appreciation of Dante as the greatest glory of that tradition; this was then followed by the use of that apprehension of Dante and Italy to come to a deeper understanding of his own situation, his own country, an understanding expressed in a major work, *The Cantos*.

James Joyce's route to and through Italian culture in the same years immediately preceding 1914 has exactly the same four-part pattern, even though the reference points in later Italian culture, the angle of interest in Dante, and, of course, the situation and country of the writer are all quite different. For Joyce, as surely as for Pound, Dante was the great Italian poet, a poet he discovered in college who shaped and influenced virtually all his subsequent work.[1] For Joyce, as surely as for Pound, Dante was also someone he had to learn how to approach, how to use. However, Joyce's mode of apprehending Dante's achievement had absolutely nothing in common with the lyric tradition descending from the Provençal poets and Cavalcanti, through Dante, to Petrarch and Leopardi that was so important for Pound. Joyce's Dante is not the "lyric Dante" of Pound, for he betrays no awareness of or interest in any of these figures except for Dante. His Dante is the epic and encyclopaedic poet, the architectural master who created the ordered cosmos of the *Commedia*, the great poem of the Italian people. But this Dante is no more of Joyce's own invention than Pound's Dante was of his. In each case, the English-language writer has apprehended the great Italian poet through an Italian tradition: Pound through Petrarch and Leopardi, Joyce through Vico, Croce, and Gentile.

Pound spend a good deal of time in Italy before 1914, visiting Italy almost every year from 1908 on and spending a good deal of time in Venice and in Sirmione, but he was not to live in Italy until 1924. Joyce's trajectory, of course, was the opposite. He lived in Italian-speaking areas from 1904 to 1915 and again briefly after the war in 1919–1920, largely in Trieste although also briefly in Pola and Rome, before moving north to Zurich and then to Paris. This is at once a well-known and insufficiently understood fact about Joyce's life. Because all of his works are set in Dublin, the Irish background of his youth has always loomed large in Joyce criticism, and the years in Paris after 1919 are also prominent, if only because these are the years of Joyce's fame when virtually his every meal or glass of wine was memorialized by someone somewhere. It is the years in between, the years spent mostly in Trieste, that remain the most obscure. Yet the period in which *Dubliners* was finished and published, *A Portrait of the Artist as a Young Man* was written, and *Ulysses* conceived and begun are far more than a "selva oscura" in which "la diritta via era smarrita." Joyce himself always recognized the place of Italy in his intellectual and social formation. One of the most noticeable and remarkable ways was that the Joyce family continued to speak Italian—not English—at home and among themselves even after their moves to Zurich and Paris.

Another way was the intellectual indebtedness he expressed to figures in Italian culture. Central among these is Giambattista Vico, the eighteenth-century Neapolitan thinker, whose importance for Joyce's work, particularly *Finnegans Wake*, Joyce always insisted on in numerous remarks made in conversation and in letters. In the 1928 collection of essays about *Finnegans Wake* that Joyce instigated even before the book's publication (when it was still known as "Work in Progress"), *Our Exagmination Round his Factification for Incamination of Work in Progress*, the first essay, undoubtedly arranged and placed by Joyce, was an essay by Samuel Beckett on "Dante Bruno Vico Joyce." But despite these efforts at explication, Joyce's interest in Vico must have seemed hopelessly arcane to those readers of "Work in Progress" and later *Finnegans Wake* looking for help with the book, for none of Vico's major works had been translated into English in Joyce's lifetime, and Vico was far from a common name among English-speaking intellectuals.[2] Subsequent Joyce scholars have argued over precisely how Joyce came across Vico's work, as if this were a mystery that needed solving. Mary T. Reynolds has suggested that Joyce had read Michelet's translation of Vico's major work, the *Scienza nuova*, into French even before he left Dublin; less speculatively, she has established that Vico was mentioned in Fornaciari's *Disegno storico della letteratura italiana*, a text in one of Joyce's college Italian courses (see "The City in Vico, Dante, and Joyce," 119). But however Joyce made his initial acquaintance with Vico, the general context of Joyce's Vichianism should always have been clear. Vico was no great discovery of James Joyce, even if many readers of Joyce have thought he was. Anyone participating in Italian intellectual life in the period just before the war would have heard a good deal about Vico, for these were precisely the years in which Benedetto Croce and Giovanni Gentile, the two great Italian philosophers of the century, were editing *La Critica* together and discovering and popularizing the thought of their fellow southerner Vico. Croce dedicated a chapter of his *Esthetica* (1902) to Vico, which, according to Richard Ellmann, Joyce knew (*James Joyce*, 340), before writing a separate study on Vico, *La filosofia di Giambattista Vico* (1911). Most of Gentile's studies of Vico date from these same years, and they were collected in his *Studi vichiani* in 1915. Joyce's interest in Vico simply establishes that he was in close contact with central currents of Italian intellectual life.[3] It is no more remarkable or in need of explanation than Wyatt's use of Serafino or Alamanni or Spenser's use of Trissino or Tasso.

One difference between the two eras, however, is that by the twentieth century, the direction of cultural influence and communication was clearly two-way. When an international protest was organized against the piracy of *Ulysses* in the United States in 1927, Croce and Gentile signed the protest. Joyce's reaction was curious: "I feel honoured by many of the signatures and humiliated by some, those of Gentile, Einstein and Croce especially. It is curious about them too on account of Vico" (*Letters*, 1:249). Why humiliated? It has been suggested by H. S. Harris, in one of the few essays on Joyce and Vico with a good sense of the Italian roots of Joyce's Vichianism,[4] that "Joyce's antipathy to the Italian ideal interpretation of Vico, and his assumption that they would regard his use of Vico with disgust, shows in his surprise when both Croce and Gentile signed the International Protest against the pirating of *Ulysses*" ("Mr. Ear-Vico," 79). But this does not quite make sense of Joyce's list: Einstein, Croce, and Gentile. In a letter the previous month, also to Harriet Shaw Weaver, Joyce had said exactly the opposite with regard to Einstein: "I feel greatly honoured by Einstein's signature" (*Letters*, 3:150). And I take the two comments together to mean that it was the signature of these three that most impressed him, most amazed him perhaps, which testifies to his sense of the olympian stature of Croce and Gentile, given how many other eminent writers and thinkers signed the protest.

But surely Harris is right to distinguish Joyce's Vico from theirs. Beckett starts his discussion of Vico in "Dante Bruno Vico Joyce" by citing Croce, one index of the Crocean context in which Joyce saw Vico. And in fact the itinerary of Beckett's crucial essay is precisely the one I am suggesting for Joyce here—for Beckett's discussion of Dante follows and is framed by his discussion of Vico and he introduces his discussion of Vico by means of Croce.[5] But Beckett's reference to Croce is critical:

> Giambattista Vico was a practical roundheaded Neapolitan. It pleases Croce to consider him as a mystic, essentially speculative, 'disdegnoso dell' empirismo'. It is a surprising interpretation, seeing that more than three-fifths of his *Scienza Nuova* is concerned with empirical investigation. Croce opposes him to the reformative materialistic school of Ugo Grozio, and absolves him from the utilitarian preoccupations of Hobbes, Spinoza, Locke, Bayle and Machiavelli. All this cannot be swallowed without protest. (4)[6]

And the point being made by Beckett here, essentially that Croce fails to do justice to the aspects of Vico's thought uncongenial to Croce, has been corroborated by later scholars.[7] So while Croce (and, to a lesser extent, Gentile) performed the function of *duca* or guide, leading

Joyce to Vico, and Joyce knew their discussions of Vico, Joyce makes his own particular use of Vico and is no slavish follower of Croce.

What did Joyce see in Vico and learn from him? Aided by Joyce's hints, readers of Joyce have long found the ideas of Giambattista Vico to be of considerable relevance to Joyce's last work, *Finnegans Wake*, but little has ever been said about the possible relevance of Vico's work to *Ulysses*. This is surprising if only because, as we have seen, Joyce knew of Vico's work when he lived in Trieste, before the writing of *Ulysses* and well before the writing of *Finnegans Wake*. If Vico had such a strong and enduring influence on Joyce, one would expect to find traces of this influence in *Ulysses* as well. The work that has been done on Vico and *Ulysses* has for the most part tried to show that *Ulysses* is influenced by the same Vichian notions that clearly influence *Finnegans Wake*.

Vico's best-known idea is his scheme of the three ages. Each human society follows a certain course or pattern, in Vico's view, from a divine age to a heroic age to a human age, which is followed by a *ricorso* or return to a new divine age. It has long been a staple of *Finnegans Wake* criticism that the organization of *Finnegans Wake*, with its three long books and a short final *ricorso*, which returns to the beginning, is indebted to this notion of Vico. Ellsworth Mason in a 1948 dissertation and, more tentatively, Richard Ellmann in *Ulysses on the Liffey* have argued that similar tripartite Vichian structures are present in *Ulysses*. And Louis Berrone has argued analogously that "Joyce's overall vision in *Ulysses* is largely based on Vico's Three Ages of Man: the Divine, the Heroic, the Human" (85), and he sees *Ulysses* as consciously set in Vico's human age. Another of Vico's ideas is that there are three constants in all human societies: religion, marriage, and burial. William York Tindall and other critics have seen this notion operating in *Finnegans Wake*, and Patrick T. White has argued in an unpublished dissertation that it also provides a key to important themes in *Ulysses*.

However, there is no reason for connecting Vico's work and *Ulysses* only through *Finnegans Wake* and through the idea of the three ages. It has been said by Isaiah Berlin that the idea of the three ages is probably Vico's least plausible and least interesting idea (64). Along the same lines, the most recent major study of Vico and *Finnegans Wake*, John Bishop's *Joyce's Book of the Dark*, criticizes the inherited focus on the three ages theory even in criticism on *Finnegans Wake*: "The critical work on *Finnegans Wake* has failed to account fully for Joyce's passionate interest in Giambattista Vico's *New Science.* . . . Most critics of the *Wake* have remained content to draw on a reading of Vico that had already become gelled, as early as 1950, into a received form destined to be passed on from study to study without much examination or modification" (174). If this is true for criticism of *Finnegans Wake*, it is even more true for criticism of *Ulysses*.

There is a much more direct connection between Vico and *Ulysses* that critics have all but ignored.[8] One of the central themes of Vico's work, in the *Scienza nuova* and elsewhere, is a theory of epic and the relation of epic poems to the societies in which they are written. This is a theory developed at greatest length with respect to Homer, and Homer plays at least as important a role in Vico's work as he does in Joyce's. Vico's first observations on Homer are found in his early juridical work, *Il diritto universale* of 1719–1720, which contains some thoughts on Homer in the context of an investigation into the origin of language. His *Dissertationes* of 1722, essentially a set of detailed annotations to *Il diritto universale*, greatly expand the fragmentary Homeric references in that work. Vico published the first edition of his most important work, the *Scienza nuova*, in 1725 and it contains a substantially modified approach to the Homeric poems. Finally, one of the five chapters of the *Scienza nuova* in its third and final edition of 1744, is entitled "Della discoverta del vero Omero" (Of the Discovery of the True Homer).[9] The analysis of Homer found in that chapter, eccentric as it may be, is, moreover, central to Vico's larger argument in the *New Science*.

Given the importance of Homer in Vico's work and of Vico in Joyce's, it is hardly surprising that Vico's thinking about Homer shaped Joyce's thinking about Homer and, therefore, shaped *Ulysses* in a number of important respects. And in this chapter I hope to show how Joyce's discovery of Vico's "true Homer" had an important effect on *Ulysses*. Moreover, Vico's theories about Homer are not presented as only about Homer, but as theories with a broad range of applicability to other epic poets. The epic poet who according to Vico resembles Homer most closely is Dante, and Vico's applications of this general theory of epic to Dante's *Commedia* is found in the *Scienza nuova* itself—specifically in the chapter "Della discoverta del vero Omero," but also in a briefer piece with the parallel title, "Della discoverta del vero Dante"[10]—and is emphasized in Croce's book on Vico. And what I want to show here is that Vico's theories gave Joyce a way of reading Homer and Dante (and of reading them together) that is absolutely crucial for the design of *Ulysses*. This involves a use of Italian literature close to that we have already seen in Pound, the drawing of parallels between Italy and one's own country. But the introduction of Homer means a further complication, a parallel between Dante's Italy and Homer's Greece as well as back to Ireland or America.

The first step in seeing why Vico's thinking about Homer is important for Joyce is seeing why Homer was important to Vico. Homer offers an unrivaled portrait of the society about which he wrote for Vico, so much so that Vico decides, first, that Homer must have been an ordinary man of the people and, second, that he did not actually exist, but was only the Greek people telling their stories in song (*Opere filosofiche*, 621 [Para. 806]; 633 [Para. 873]). This anticipation of the later Homeric theories of Wolf is less important for Joyce, who insisted upon a distinct identity for the artist, than the prior—and more fundamental—intuition that Homer's works offered a clear portrait of their society. "Homerum in suis fabularum argumentis verum fuisse historicum" (Homer in the content of his fables was a true historian) Vico says in a key passage (*Opere giuridiche*, 851), and although this does not confine Vico to a literal reading of Homer, it does indicate his use of Homer as a historian of his society.[11] That society, in Vico's division of the evolution of societies into three stages, was heroic, or barbaric, strongly contrasting with the rational society of Vico's own day. Homer's greatness as a poet—in another of Vico's anticipations of Romantic critical theory—was intimately connected with this barbaric state of Greek society, for barbaric language is naturally poetic language. The sublimity of Homer's expression stems directly and naturally from the sublimity of the language of the Greek people at that stage of development.[12] And Vico always sees in the Homeric poems indications of the state of civil organization reached by the Greek people at the time the poems were written. Vico's Homer is a social poet whose work narrates a crucial change in his people's history, and this is a crucial aspect of Vico's theory for Joyce.

What makes this relevant to *Ulysses* is that although Homer is "il padre e il principe di tutti i sublimi poeti" (the father and prince of all sublime poets) (*Opere filosofiche*, 626 [Para. 823]), he is not the only sublime or heroic poet whose epics express the state of the societies from which he springs. All sublime or epic poets have a very close connection to the societies from which they spring. This general theme of Vico's work is one of the many aspects of his thought that—as a number of scholars have pointed out[13]—connect his work back to the themes of Renaissance humanism, in particular the work of Valla. Nancy Struever's discussion is apposite:

> Vichian ideas of language relate to the issue of the political nature of Humanist thought, of civic humanism as a dominant or recessive aspect of the Renaissance. Surely the civic Humanists regarded the *polis*, or *civitas*, as the organizing focus of the classical thinkers who were of such authority for them. And surely both Vico and Valla emphasize the social goal as well as the social character of knowledge. . . . both Valla and Vico hypothesize politicality on the deep level of epistemology as well as on the surface level of cultural program. ("Vico, Valla," 184)

Hence, Vico is in the humanist tradition in seeing an intimate connection between—to use Struever's term—politicality and linguisticality. But Vico's unique contribution is to use his typological or paradigmatic perspective to argue that all the sublime poets in his system are also closely comparable. According to Vico's theory that each society runs a course from the divine to the heroic to the human state of society, societies at similar stages of evolution are closely comparable to each other, and so are poets. Vico asserts an equivalence among Homer and two other "poets": Moses, the poet-prophet of the Hebrews; and Dante, "il toscano Omero" (the Tuscan Homer), the Homer of the returned barbarian times (*Opere filosofiche*, 616 [Para. 786]).

The parallel with Dante is quite straightforward and has three major parts. The works of Dante and Homer can be compared "as a history of the period of barbarism in Italy," in terms of their language, and "as an example of sublime poetry" (Vico, "Discovery of the True Dante," 11). Just as the period of barbarism that followed the collapse of the Roman Empire is a replication of the barbarism that preceded classical civilization, so Dante is a replication of Homer. The two poets stand at comparable points in the evolution of their societies:

> By reason of a development which is characteristic of the general mind of nations in the period when barbarism begins to be refined away, the poets of such periods sing truth: for barbarism itself is open and truthful precisely because lacking in that reflective mentality which, ill applied, is the mother of all falsehood. Thus in *The New Science* I called Homer the first historian of gentility; and this I further confirmed in my *Annotations* to his work, where I

showed that he is quite other than the Homer of general acceptance. . . . By the same token our Dante was the first, or among
the first, of Italian historians. (Vico, "Discovery of the True
Dante," 11)

Thus, although their greatness as poets owes much to the barbaric
state of their societies, neither poet wrote in the full depths of the
barbaric period but at the transition point from the heroic to the human age (also see *Opere filosofiche*, 278). Moreover, the character of
their work is intimately shaped by their position as poets of transition.
Both wrote in a composite language—Dante used phrases from all the
Italian dialects, just as Homer used all of the Greek dialects: "come
certamente Dante Alighieri, nel cominciarvisi a mitigar la barbarie,
andò raccogliendo la locuzione della dua *Divina Comedia* da tutti i
dialetti d'Italia" (as Dante, in the start of the lessening of barbarism,
went collecting the locutions of his *Divine Comedy* from all the dialects
of Italy) (*Opere filosofiche*, 278).[14] Samuel Beckett compared Joyce to
Dante on exactly this point in "Dante Bruno Vico Joyce" (18–19),
arguing that the mixed language of *Finnegans Wake* was comparable
to that of the *Commedia*. And this mixed or composite language is
certainly appropriate to the state of their societies' evolution, in which
isolated communities were beginning to trade and communicate.

   And finally, Dante is "a unique example of sublime poetry" (Vico,
"Discovery of the True Dante," 12). "Homer is a sublimer poet than
any who came after him" (12), but Dante is next to Homer in sublimity, and "what was most peculiar to Dante's sublimity resulted
from his having been born with the gift of genius in the era of Italy's
expiring barbarism" (12).

> Onde, come nella Grecia non provenne poeta maggior d'Omero,
> così nell'Italia non nacque poeta più sublime di Dante, perche
> ebbero entrambi la fortuna di sortire incomparabili ingegni nel
> finire l'età poetica d'entrambe le nazioni.
>
> (Hence, as from Greece no greater poet came than Homer, thus in
> Italy no poet was born more sublime than Dante, because they
> both had the fortune of being endowed with incomparable genius
> at the end of the poetic age of both nations.) (*Opere filosofiche*, 278)

And we need to remember that this juxtaposition of Homer and Dante
as the two greatest poets of our civilization—although familiar now—

would be considered startling in Vico's day (when, for example, Dante had not even been translated into English). Where are the Latin poets? Where is Petrarch? Croce praises Vico's revindication of Dante "dopo secoli di gusto antidantesco" (after centuries of anti-Dantescan taste) (*La filosofia di Giambattista Vico*, 207), and Glauco Cambon remarks that Vico praises Dante for "the very qualities that would appear in the new poets of an Italy Vico was never to see: aristocratic, choleric, liberty-minded Alfieri; rebellious, public-spirited, Vichian Foscolo; melancholy, austere Leopardi; earnest, historically minded Manzoni" (21). The only one of these writers influential for Pound or Joyce was Leopardi, and Leopardi also perceived a striking resemblance between Homer and Dante, calling Dante "the second Homer" (quoted in Singh, 33) and presenting the two as closer to each other than to Virgil whom he—like Pound—disliked (see Singh, 40, 66–67).

However, Vico's less explicit comparison between Homer and Moses is more startling yet. The Exodus represents the Hebraic *ricorso*, the revolt against rationalism toward a religious and poetic cast of mind. Moses, too, lived at a transition point and as the leader of his people automatically had that close association with them that Vico sought to establish for Homer and Dante. Moses tells his story and the story of his people in the Pentateuch "con parlari che hanno molto di conformità con quelli di Omero e spesso li vincono nella sublimità dell'expressione" (with expressions that have much in common with those of Homer and often exceed them in sublimity of expression).[15] Elsewhere, Vico extends this comparison to Hebrew as a language: "il popolo di Dio parla una lingua poetica di quella del medesimo Omero vie più sublime" (the people of God speak a poetic language like that of Homer yet even more sublime) (*Opere filosofiche*, 238–239).

Croce in his most extensive and influential work on Vico, *La filosofia di Giambattista Vico*, draws attention in a number of places to the equivalence and quasi-identity for Vico of these three figures, Homer, Moses, and Dante (140–41, 181–82, 206–208). He then, in a passage that is extremely suggestive for *Ulysses*, speculates about whether Vico's patterning mind might not have assimilated Shakespeare into this pattern, had Vico known of him (208). Vico often commented on the natural sublimity of the Germanic languages, speaking of them much as he did of Hebrew. Evidently for Croce, Shakespeare, in his role as national poet, in his historical place at a crucial transition in English history, and in his linguistic energy and range, forms part of the same pattern or paradigm. And, except for Croce's characteristic blurring of genre lines here, this seems an acceptable interpretation or extension of Vico's thought.[16]

What Homer, Moses, Dante, and Shakespeare all have in common in Vico's scheme as amended by Croce is that all are sublime poets who write "epics" richly evocative of a barbaric society in transition—in some cases emerging from barbarism, in the case of Moses reacting against rationalism and moving back to barbarism—which become the central, and in a sense sacred, texts of their culture. Each of these epics and epic writers is central to *Ulysses*. Moses and Shakespeare, of course, each has a chapter largely devoted to him, "Aeolus" and "Scylla and Charybdis," and the division of the novel into three sections with intricate parallels among them owes more to Dante than to Homer. Joyce needed no one's theory to become aware of these figures, obviously, but Vico's theories about epic helps to explain what Joyce does with them. The inclusion of these chapters in a book called *Ulysses* makes much more sense given a perspective that sees Homer, Moses, Dante, and Shakespeare as equivalents. Furthermore, Vico's thinking offers Joyce a reason for establishing these parallels between Homer's narrative and his own in the first place. One question that has never been satisfactorily answered is the simple question, Why use Homer? Even if one is planning to construct a parallel between antiquity and the modern world, or between a classic and a modern text, why use Homer and not someone else?

In Vico's theory, each culture has room for one sublime epic poem that, written at a crucial transition point in that society's evolution, becomes in its centrality and linguistic strength a kind of sacred book, to be endlessly interpreted and mulled over. One such crucial transition is to national independence—political, cultural, and spiritual—and the type of this transition is the rejection of Egyptian rationality by the Jews under the leadership of Moses. The other is the emergence from heroic feudal barbarism into the human age, the world of commerce and peaceful intercourse between nations. Homer, Dante, and Shakespeare all wrote at approximately this point.

Ireland in the period in which *Ulysses* was being written was itself making a crucial transition that involved something of both of these transitions. *Ulysses* is in large measure a portrait of this transition, represented in terms that are often quite close to Vico's. For example, Vico reads Ulysses' encounter with the Cyclops as a representation of the encounter of the new human age of society with the remnants of a more insular barbaric society. Ulysses was a traveler and trader who encountered the hostility of insular clans not interested in peaceful contact or commercial exchange with the outside world (*Opere filoso-fiche*, 501). And this detail shows how Vico translated narrative detail into a social and historical framework. Joyce does this also, although of course the social framework of Dublin is much more densely realized than Vico's portrait of Homeric society.

Joyce's Ulysses, Leopold Bloom, is also an advocate and representative of international commerce and exchange who encounters the hostility of troglodytic nationalists wishing to resurrect an antiquated insular economy with no interaction with forces of international commerce. Vico translates Homer's story out of context and makes it an allegory of social history; Joyce carries over Vico's historical allegory and beautifully translates it into a new, fitting Irish context. Bloom's encounter with the Citizen in the "Cyclops" episode is an encounter of two social systems, two political economies, directly analogous to Ulysses' encounter with the Cyclops as Vico reads it.[17]

This is also a clash between two notions of epic, and again Joyce's notion is Vichian. Joyce's Cyclops, the Citizen, thinks he is an epic hero, as one of the parodies in the chapter shows:

> The figure seated on a large boulder at the foot of a round tower was that of a broadshouldered deepchested stronglimbed frankeyed redhaired freelyfreckled shaggybearded widemouthed largenosed longheaded deepvoiced barekneed brawnyhanded hairylegged ruddyfaced sinewyarmed hero. . . .
>
> He wore a long unsleeved garment of recently flayed oxhide reaching to the knees in a loose kilt and this was bound about his middle by a girdle of plaited straw and rushes. . . . From his girdle hung a row of seastones which jangled at every movement of his portentous frame and on these were graven with rude yet striking art the tribal images of many Irish heroes and heroines of antiquity, Cuchulin, Conn of hundred battles, Niall of nine hostages, Brian of Kincora, the ardri Malachi, . . . [18]

"Rude yet striking": Joyce catches in a phrase a romantic notion of epic that he criticizes at length in *Ulysses*. In this view, true epic is oral epic expressing an utterly "barbaric" ethos, and it is not irrelevant here that many of Joyce's Irish contemporaries held precisely such a view. Lady Gregory had recently translated the Cuchulain cycle of poems in *Cuchulain of Muirthemne* (1902), and she, Yeats, and others were arguing that the salvation of Irish literature lay in a return to such early

Irish models. J. M. Synge, although he had his own cult of things "rude yet striking," anticipated Joyce's critique when he commented privately after seeing one of Yeats's plays, "I do not believe in the possibility of a purely fantastic unmodern ideal breezy spring-dayish Cuchulainoid National Theatre. We had the 'Shadowy Waters' on the stage last week, and it was the most *distressing* failure the mind can imagine" (quoted in O'Tuama, 2). Imitating Cuchulain, according to Synge here and Joyce in "Cyclops," simply would not do.[19]

Moreover, this issue of whether ancient Irish literature could serve as a model for modern Ireland was not simply a literary issue. One of the "Cuchulanoids" was Padraic Pearse, minor poet and later leader of the Easter Rebellion of 1916 and hence presiding spirit over the independent Ireland that resulted from the rebellion. Pearse had almost a religious cult of Cuchulain, and it was in many ways his desire to imitate Cuchulain that led him to the Rebellion.[20] Yeats captured this imitation in "The Statues" in the famous lines, "When Pearse summoned Cuchulain to his side / What stalked through the Post Office?" (337) But Joyce had a more skeptical attitude about such an imitation and the cast of mind that went with it. Pearse was Joyce's Gaelic instructor for a time. However, Joyce did not get very far in his Gaelic studies because Pearse, as Ellmann tells the story, "found it necessary to exalt Irish by denigrating English, and in particular denounced the word 'Thunder'—a favorite of Joyce—as an example of verbal inadequacy" (*James Joyce*, 62; see also Kenner, *A Colder Eye*, 182).

We ought to see how the attitude toward language and toward politics are one and the same: for Pearse, the way to liberate the Irish was to return to the values of the old, to imitate Cuchulain. But Joyce opposes this political and aesthetic atavism in a variety of ways, and his use of Vico is clearly if subtly part of this opposition. The real epic poet, according to Vico, wrote in an era of transition from the barbaric, not in the depths of the barbaric, and he had no Cuchulanoid nostalgia for the barbaric. Thus it is Ulysses, the clever and worldly traveler, who is the real epic hero, not the Cuchulain celebrated by Joyce's fellow Irish writers. Ireland was indeed ripe for an epic poem, according to Vico's scheme, if indeed it was in a period of "expiring barbarism," but the role of the epic poet in this situation was to help usher in the new human age, not revive the barbarism of a Cuchulain or a Cyclops. Joyce is relying upon a program of imitation as much as is Yeats or Pearse, but the model to imitate is Ulysses (and Homer), not the heroes and bards of ancient Ireland.

So, just as the *Odyssey* is the epic of a society in transition, so is *Ulysses*. It announces itself as a new Irish version of Homer and contains discussions about the need for an Irish Moses and Shakespeare. Moreover, the most autobiographical character in the book is obviously preparing himself for these roles. Joyce, aware of the Vichian scheme and of Homer's place in it, designed *Ulysses* to be the new, Irish embodiment of Vico's scheme. There is, of course, no neat, straightforward statement by Joyce to this effect inside or outside *Ulysses*. But Joyce did not need to make any such large, Messianic claims for *Ulysses*. His work had already been done for him. Many other Irish writers and politicians had already made such claims in and for Ireland,[21] and Joyce, as a realist engaged in a detailed portrait of Dublin in 1904, could easily incorporate discussions of these claims into his own text. He therefore did not need to make explicit claims for his own work; instead, he could make this material implicitly register such claims on the behalf of *Ulysses*. In "Aeolus" and "Scylla and Charybdis," in particular, we can see this process; but only from a Vichian perspective can we understand how the discussions in "Aeolus" and "Scylla and Charybdis" contribute to Joyce's larger project of writing a modern *Ulysses*.

"Aeolus" is a portrait of a group of nationalists as fond as Vico of parallels. Professor MacHugh first links the Romans and the English as crass materialists and contrasts them to the spiritual Celts and Greeks who went forth to battle but always fell. He then recites a speech by J. F. Taylor who, with considerably more rhetorical force, compares the modern conflict between the Irish and the English to that between the Jews of the Exodus and their Egyptian overlords. The implicit question in such a scheme is, who is Moses? Who is going to deliver us from the bondage of the Egyptians? Taylor's comparison was a staple of Irish nationalist rhetoric, and Parnell, after he had failed to get the Irish to the Promised Land, or, to be more exact, to get the English out of it, was often assigned the role of Moses. He had been the Prophet, he had set his people on their way, but he had only had a Pisgah sight of Palestine.[22] Parnell assigned himself this role. When about to be voted out as leader of the undivided Irish parliamentary party following the Kitty O'Shea scandal in 1890, he told his rebellious followers: "If I am to leave you tonight, I should like to leave you in security. I should like—and it is not an unfair thing for me to ask—that I should come within sight of the promised land" (quoted in Lyons, 520).

In "Aeolus," Joyce depends upon this familiar nationalist typology of imitation yet he redirects it in Vichian fashion. MacHugh's complaint about the Romans is linguistic as much as it is political: he prefers Greek vowels. J. F. Taylor's linking of Moses to the Gaelic language movement makes the complaint of Moses essentially linguistic as well. His Moses is Vico's Moses: the rejector of Egyptian *sapienza* whose great act is to bring the Tables of the Law, as Taylor says, "graven in the language of the outlaw" (*Ulysses*, 7.869). Hence the Moses of the Irish *ricorso*, according to the characters in "Aeolus," will be a poet, a linguistic innovator. He will do linguistic, not political, battle and free the language from English domination. The nationalism found in "Aeolus" has a special flavor, as is shown by comparison with "Cyclops." J. F. Taylor, unlike the Citizen, grants to the English their sphere of competence; at least, they are good Egyptians. According to the Citizen's absurd glorification of the Irish past, the Irish were at one point both the Jews and the Egyptians, spiritually *and* materially rich. Taylor's much more reasonable position is not at all offensive to Stephen, no ardent nationalist, whereas the constricting nationalism of the Citizen arouses fierce if ineffectual opposition in Bloom, who in his own way is a strong nationalist.

However, Stephen, like Bloom in "Cyclops," moves toward the end of "Aeolus" to deflate the rhetoric of the nationalists. His "A Pisgah Sight of Palestine or the Parable of the Plums" is his example of the kind of art Ireland needs, the kind of thing the Irish Moses needs to say. It makes the essentially Vichian point that this artistic Moses, like Vico's Homer and Dante, will be concerned with Irish reality and not Irish blarney. He will be setting down accurate perceptions in a style in touch with the reality around him, in the same way that Vico says Moses, Homer, and Dante did.

Stephen's parable implies a willingness to take on that role himself, but his new awareness of his own limitations—"Dublin. I have much, much to learn" (*Ulysses*, 7.915)—and the absence here of the exaltation of the artist found in *A Portrait* indicate a Vichian and antiromantic conception of the artist's role. No more flying for Stephen—the author of Vico's epic keeps his feet firmly on the ground. It remains an open question whether Stephen is capable of becoming this figure, for, as we shall see in a later chapter, Stephen still holds onto some of the Wagnerian and non-Vichian notions about art that shaped the end of *A Portrait*. The character in *Ulysses* closest at this point to Vico's ideal of the epic artist is Leopold Bloom who notes everything he sees about him. But whomever might be the best candidate for the Vichian epic artist inside of *Ulysses*, such a writer, Joyce intends us to realize, would be writing a book much like *Ulysses*. And this establishes the political and social dimensions of Joyce's innovations in *Ulysses*: Joyce is a linguistic innovator who—like Vico's Moses—would liberate the language from English control. It is not by imitating Cuchulain but by imitating Vico's epic artist that Ireland is to be freed from English domination. .

If Irish nationalists in 1904 were looking for the Irish Moses, Irish writers were looking for the Irish Shakespeare, a search and an aspiration implicit in the discussion of Shakespeare that takes place in "Scylla and Charybdis." That Shakespeare the Englishman is still the measure of greatness for the Irish Literary Revival is one index of the inadequacy—in Joyce's view—of that movement. It has not yet turned away from English models and standards. (Of course, two Continentally-oriented writers Joyce admired—if on this side of idolatry—who would blunt this portrait, J. M. Synge and George Moore, are kept offstage by Joyce and do not appear in this chapter or elsewhere in *Ulysses*.) This passive and uncreative imitation of English culture is charted unobtrusively in other ways. Both the Hellenism and the theosophy of the Irish Literary Revival were English imports, as the discussion in "Scylla and Charybdis" clearly establishes. Mulligan, who prides himself on his "Hellenism," takes this Hellenism exclusively from English sources—from Swinburne, Pater, and English aestheticism generally. Arnold's opposition of the Hellenic and the Hebraic defines Mulligan's Hellenism and encourages his anti-Semitism. Joyce, with his Jewish Ulysses based on the theories of Victor Bérard, denies Arnold's opposition and repudiates the kind of Hellenism it advocates. And Joyce's orientation toward literatures other than the English is surely at least in part a conscious and analogous gesture of "de-anglicization." Why try to be the Irish Shakespeare when one could be the Irish Dante or the Irish Homer?

But there is more than satire here. "Scylla and Charybdis" is full of double or paradoxical statements that need to be apprehended on two discrete levels—one literally in terms of the immediate context and the other in terms of the context of the whole of *Ulysses*. For example, Mulligan says that Bloom is "Greeker than the Greeks" (9.614–15). In the immediate context, he is calling Bloom a homosexual. What he is saying is untrue and how he says it reveals both the limits and the nature of his Hellenism. But, in a wider sense that is completely discrete, Bloom is "Greeker than the Greeks": he is Ulysses.

Much of what is said about literature in "Scylla and Charybdis" has this paradoxical applicability to *Ulysses* in ways that reinforce the Vichian themes discusses so far. As in "Aeolus," participants in the discussion often make points by means of comparison, and the comparisons follow a familiar pattern:

> —Our young Irish bards, John Eglinton censured, have yet to create a figure which the world will set beside Saxon Shakespeare's Hamlet. (9.43–44)

> —Shakespeare? he said. I seem to know the name. A flying sunny smile rayed in his loose features.
> —To be sure, he said, remembering brightly. The chap that writes like Synge. (9.508–11)[23]

> —The most beautiful book that has come out of our country in my time. One thinks of Homer. (9.1164–65)

Although Joyce is clearly ridiculing the high expectations of the Irish Literary Revival here, he is also sustaining if redirecting those expectations. This Irish bard is not creating a figure to set beside Hamlet; he is borrowing Hamlet himself. One does not tend to think of Homer in connection with Lady Gregory's *Cuchulain of Muirthemne*, despite what Mulligan quotes Yeats as saying; as Vico would have said, her attempt to evoke a barbaric world is very far from Homer's spirit. But one must think of Homer in connection with the book in one's hands, if only to figure out the title.[24]

"Scylla and Charybdis" resembles "Aeolus" in that in both chapters messianic calls are being made for the new Irish Moses and Shakespeare, while Stephen's role in both chapters is to point out how that figure will differ from the other characters' expectations, in the same way that in "Cyclops" Bloom establishes the difference between the true epic hero and the other characters' notion of him. Shakespeare, according to Stephen, was not the "ineffectual angel" of the Dublin aesthetes but an ordinary man in an ordinary situation who made literature out of what was immediately around him. He was Hamlet's father, not Hamlet. Stephen's portrait of Shakespeare is a portrait of the artist as nobody special. That Stephen's Shakespeare resembles the actual Leopold Bloom very closely is an irony that reinforces this point. Morever, as in "Aeolus," Stephen is setting himself the formidable task of imitating the portrait of the ideal artist he has drawn: "Hold to the now, the here," Stephen tells himself (*Ulysses*, 9.89).

Furthermore, we should see that what Stephen aspires to Joyce has achieved: Stephen's Moses writes like Joyce and his Shakespeare leads a life much like that of Joyce. Joyce has held, like Vico's Homer, Dante, and Moses, to the now and the here: the densely realized Dublin of *Ulysses* clashes as strongly as Stephen's ideas with the rhetoric of the windbags of "Aeolus" and the "formless spiritual essences" (9.49) of the parlor Platonists of "Scylla and Charybdis." And the epic he has created portrays a crucial transition in his society's history.

In other words, the theory we hear about in these chapters corresponds to the literary practice we experience in *Ulysses*: the ideal artist is an ordinary man writing about an ordinary situation; what he writes comes immediately, if not necessarily directly, out of his experience—he is a "true historian," at least when read in the right way; and through this precise art, he does, in a scrupulously mean sort of a way, end up creating a conscience—or perhaps a consciousness—for the race. Rather than creepy-crawling "after Blake's buttocks into eternity" (*Ulysses*, 9.88), he holds to the here and the now; but that, paradoxically, gives the artist a much better shot at eternity. By portraying his own society with precision and fidelity he can create his culture's sacred book, Shakespeare for the English, Dante for the Italians, Homer for the Greeks, the Pentateuch for the Jews.

Joyce would, I submit, like us to add his book to that list, *Ulysses* for the Irish, and he has taken a great deal of care to place it in the same relation to Ireland as these books are to their cultures. Placing *Ulysses* in a Vichian perspective enables us to understand two important aspects of Joyce's epic ambitions in *Ulysses*.

First, Joyce's choice of exemplary artists is not at all random: in Vico's typological or paradigmatic thinking, Homer, Moses, Dante, and Shakespeare are themselves equivalent. With this in mind, we can see that when discussing Moses and Shakespeare, Joyce is in a sense discussing Homer and his own work as well. No other set of ideas about Homer creates a pattern of equivalents as close to that found in *Ulysses* as Vico's.

Second, the kind of equivalence asserted by Joyce is Vichian. His Moses and his Shakespeare are Vichian artists and their works are portrayed as Vichian epics, the sacred books of their respective cultures. Of course, *Finnegans Wake*, much more explicitly than *Ulysses*, is a Vichian epic, a single-handed *ricorso* in which an Irish Moses produces tablets "graven in the language of the outlaw." But it is important to realize that this aspiration is also present (and, in my opinion, more successfully realized) in *Ulysses*, and that *Ulysses* is also embued with Vichian ideas. Vico's Homer may not be our idea of the "true Homer," but his Homer, true or false, had a considerable impact on that ambitious writer who set out to be the Irish Homer, James Joyce. And his theories about the relation between epics and the societies in which they are written stands in quite an intimate relation to Joyce's ambitions for his major works of prose fiction.

This is one of the crucial respects in which Italian culture and thought have influenced the work of James Joyce. And we should see both the similarities and one important difference between Joyce's relation to Italy and Pound's, at least in the early period of Pound's career discussed so far. Joyce, like Pound, relied upon an Italian tradition to come to terms with Dante's *Commedia*, and both writers utilize the ideas of this tradition about Dante—essentially generic ideas—in the form of their own works. But Vico's approach to Dante was to place him in a complex comparative framework of equivalence to poets from other societies and times, particularly to Homer and Moses. Croce emphasized this aspect of Vico's work, adding Shakespeare to the paradigmatic network. This means that although Vico bulks a good deal larger in Joyce's work than Leopardi does in Pound's, Dante is a somewhat smaller presence, less *the* great poet than a great poet on a plane with several others.

But this difference is not an absolute one. There is no evidence that Pound paid any attention to Vico or to Joyce's interest in him, even though the fascist interpretation of Vico asserted particularly by Gentile's later work (which came too late for Joyce to have known of it while writing *Ulysses*) was current enough to have been an influence on Yeats.[25] Despite this and despite Pound's expressed contempt for Croce,[26] Joyce's Vichian/Crocean set of equivalences as represented in *Ulysses* seems to have had a strong influence on Pound. Canto I connects Dante and Homer in ways quite consonant with Vico's sense of their relation, and in general Pound moves in *The Cantos* and in his other works away from simple equivalences between Italy and his own situation of the kind expressed in "Patria Mia" toward more complex (and more Joycean) sets of patterns and interrelations. That shift will be traced in the next chapter, which will follow Pound's Italianism from the period of "Patria Mia" and "The Renaissance" to the Middle Cantos. And that itinerary is not without some overlap with the itinerary of Joyce's just traced, as the humanist tradition that helped shape Vico's work is an influence on Pound in these years as well.

Chapter Eight

Pound's Machiavellian Moment

Recently, there has been a move on the part of some Pound critics, particularly James J. Wilhelm in *The American Roots of Ezra Pound* and Wendy Stallard Flory in *The American Ezra Pound*, to emphasize Pound's Americanness, both his American origins and his continuing preoccupation with America. These critics stress Pound's Americanness at least partially to downplay the most notorious aspect of his Italianism, his commitment to Italian fascism and to Mussolini. James Wilhelm gives us a characteristic formulation in his earlier book, *Dante and Pound: The Epic of Judgement*: "Even when Ezra was most caught up in the Mussolini movement, he always followed the lead of Aristotle in keeping open the options for democracy: Jefferson and/or Mussolini. The real political hero of the Cantos is John Adams, not the Boss, and the real center of Pound's blazing interest is America, even if most of his mature years in this country were spent in an asylum. Pound is more liberal than his detractors make him" (158).

As a line of defense, this simply fails to make sense of Pound's cultural commitments. Although it is important to see the ways in which Pound remained an American poet and a writer concerned with American civilization, Italy is not a concern competing for attention with America in Pound's work. Instead it functions as a mirror for America. This can be seen in the way Pound almost always adopts an Italian frame of reference for his discussions of America, both early in his career in the seminal early essay "Patria Mia," his first work with a strong social consciousness, and in later works of prose such as *Jef-*

ferson and/or Mussolini and in *The Cantos*. Pound's pattern-mind identified his "patria mia" with Italy or, to put it another way, he identified
his two "patrie mie" with each other. And it should be clear enough
which country in Pound's view was or should be the pattern for the
other. What America should do is become as much like Italy as possible, and we can see this most clearly in his repeated calls for an
American *risorgimento* or renaissance.

One of the crucial differences between Joyce's situation as an Irish
writer and Pound's is implicit in these repeated calls for a renaissance
on Italian models. Everyone conceded that Ireland in Joyce's lifetime
was in the middle of something important—call it a revival, a renaissance, a *ricorso*—which meant as we have just seen that Joyce did not
have to make such claims but could position himself critically with
respect to them. Pound, in contrast, was writing in a situation comparatively unmarked by such messianic expectations. Albert Gelpi
titled his book on modern American poetry, *A Coherent Splendor: The
American Poetic Renaissance, 1910–1950*, but at the beginning of that
period no one assessing the depressed state of American poetry saw a
renaissance in the offing.

In this context, Pound had both to make claims for American culture and to criticize it. He made some strong claims for a number of
years about the possibilities of an American renaissance, as we have
seen, and this was an analogy he took seriously, both at an abstract
level and at the level of concrete detail. One of his enthusiasms in
"Patria Mia," for example, was for the new skyscrapers rising in New
York, and he sees them as the equivalent to the medieval towers of
Italy: "With the advances of steel construction it has become possible
to build in the proportions of the campanile something large enough
to serve as an office building. This tower is some 700 odd feet high
and dominates New York as the older towers dominate hill towns of
Tuscany" (105–6).

This perception is repeated in "The Renaissance" (219). But to pursue such an analogy is to discover differences as well as similarities.
One key difference was the place of art in the two societies. Both of
the two great surveys that shaped Pound's (and everyone else's) sense
of the Renaissance, Jacob Burckhardt's *The Civilization of the Renaissance in Italy* and Symonds's *Renaissance in Italy*, begin by discussing
the Renaissance princes, or, as they frankly refer to them, the despots
(Burckhardt, 7–29; the entire first part of Symonds [1–331] is entitled
"The Age of the Despots"). Both stress the key role in the Renaissance
played by the great patrons, the princes who subsidized the arts and

competed with each other to gather brilliant artists and intellectuals around them. In Symonds's words, "to be a prince and not to be the patron of scholarship, the pupil of humanists, and the founder of libraries, was an impossibility. In like manner they employed their wealth upon the development of arts and industries. The great age of Florentine painting is indissolubly connected with the memories of Casa Medici. Rome owes her magnificence to the despotic Popes. Even the pottery of Gubbio was a creation of the ducal house of Urbino" (41).

Yeats had already invoked this Renaissance milieu in poems such as "To a Wealthy Man who promised a second Subscription to the Dublin Municipal Gallery if it were proved the People wanted Pictures," in which he contrasts the Renaissance princes with the failure of Ireland to produce any great patrons of the arts:[1]

> And Guidobaldo, when he made
> That grammar school of courtesies
> Where wit and beauty learned their trade
> Upon Urbino's windy hill,
> Had sent no runners to and fro
> That he might learn the shepherd's will.
> And when they drove out Cosimo,
> Indifferent how the rancour ran,
> He gave the hours they had set free
> To Michelozzo's latest plan
> For the San Marco Library,
> Whence turbulent Italy should draw
> Delight in Art whose end is peace
>
> (*Poems*, 107)

Precisely the same aspect of Renaissance Italy is celebrated throughout Pound's prose in the 1910–1915 period. But where Yeats depicts a contrast, Pound hopes for a parallel. He knows that he is writing in a society with real wealth, a great deal of which—as any reader of Henry James knows—has been dedicated to buying up the treasures of the Italian Renaissance. And in "Patria Mia," he explicitly connects the millionaires of the modern era to the Medici: "if the millionaire have by rare chance any acquaintance with history he will remember that the Medici—to use hackneyed example—retain honour among us not for their very able corruption of the city of Florence, but because they housed Ficino and various artists" (126).

Now, all of these invocations of the Medici had a practical component. Pound in these years was a man looking for a patron, looking for a Medici. And in some ways he was reasonable successful, finding in John Quinn a man who—as Timothy Materer has recently argued—exemplified what Pound appreciated about the great Renaissance patrons, their interest in bringing new art into being. Quinn helped finance Pound's activities in ways that immeasurably enriched modern culture. But on a larger scale, Pound's effort was an utter failure, for Quinn remained an exception—if a glorious one. The correspondence with Margaret Anderson, editor of the *Little Review*, provides an illustration of Pound's hopes for patronage and their utterly utopian nature (see *Pound/The Little Review*). Both Pound and Anderson kept hoping that Isabella Stuart Gardner would support the magazine. Gardner was a Boston art collector with whom Henry James had stayed both at the Palazzo Barbaro in Venice (Edel, 324–28) and in Boston and who virtually recreated a Venetian palazzo in Boston, creating what is now the Isabella Stuart Gardner Museum. To have this hope, Pound must have felt that his perception of an analogy between the modernist literature published in the *Little Review* and the work of the Renaissance was shared (or at least could be shared) by people like Mrs. Gardner who might be led to imitate the Medici in supporting contemporary art.

But, as he should have known perfectly well, these modern Medici were Jamesian, not Poundian, in their appreciation of Italy. The Adam Ververs of America wanted to buy the Italian past and install it in their houses and museums, not support a new renaissance in their own time. Anderson received no help from Gardner, and this failure is symptomatic of the larger failure of Pound's project in "Patria Mia" and "The Renaissance." Pound did not manage to reorient the great American collectors toward his ideal of supporting living, working artists.

It is worth pausing for a moment, however, to reflect on Pound's ambition, for it exhibits a very different attitude toward power from that reflected in Joyce's work, a different theory about the relation between art and power. For Joyce, the artist should be indifferent to the crowd's rancour in the way that Yeats's Cosimo and Guidobaldo were. In an early essay, "The Day of the Rabblement," Joyce even criticized Yeats for not being disdainful enough about the crowd: "No man, said the Nolan, can be a lover of the true or the good unless he abhors the multitude; and the artist, though he may employ the crowd, is very careful to isolate himself" (*Critical Writings*, 69). Here the young Joyce was criticizing Yeats's involvement with the Irish Literary Theatre, the forerunner of the Abbey, and this anticipates Joyce's subsequent critique of the Cuchulanoid theater centered around the Abbey. But this critique of the "rabblement" does not commit Joyce to Yeats's and Pound's cult of the patron, of the cultivated man of power, as Joyce's celebration here of a rather different Renaissance figure, the "terribly burned" heretic, Giordano Bruno (of Nola), should show.[2] The artist is not linked to the social elite in Joyce's model; the true artist is as critical of the elite, of the powerful, as he is of the "rabblement." Unlike Joyce, Pound presents no such abstract critique of power; he only wishes to direct what the powerful do with their power. His thesis is a dual one: first, the powerful have a responsibility—whether they recognize it or not—to bring art into being, but the implicit corollary to this is that the artist benefits from a proximity to power, at least to the right kind of power:

> In fostering and hastening a renaissance the millonaire may be, often, very useful. ("Patria Mia," 126)

> Great art does not depend upon comfort, it does not depend upon the support of riches. But a great age is brought about only with the aid of wealth, because a great age means the deliberate fostering of genius, the gathering-in and grouping and encouragement of artists. ("The Renaissance," 221)

In this respect, Pound in his undue respect for power is unfortunately the one truer to the central traditions of Italian culture. From the time of Frederick II to Mussolini rulers of Italy have successfully courted the support of artists and intellectuals. And Pound is surely correct in adducing the example of the Italian Renaissance as an era with a particularly close relation between art and power. His interest in the Renaissance is surely the least original aspect of his Italianism, for Pater's *The Renaissance* and Browning's poems on Renaissance painters were central to the culture of his youth. But even here Pound finds a tack that is peculiarly his own, for he is never as interested in the artists of the period as in the patrons and the scholars who served them.[3] Pound's memoir of his dead sculptor friend, Gaudier-Brzeska, contains an essay, "Affirmations: Analysis of This Decade," that repeatedly compares his fellow modernist artists to figures from the Renaissance, but his Renaissance examples in the essay are Ficino, Pico, Valla, and Machiavelli—humanist scholars and thinkers, not painters and sculptors. Pound's Renaissance is not the Renaissance of Botticelli, Fra Filippo Lippi, and Andrea del Sarto, but the Renaissance of Italian humanism. One reason for this is that the tradition of humanist scholars involved seeking a close proximity to power.

This is an aspect of Italian humanism that goes back to Petrarch who—as Boccaccio told him reproachfully—spent his life with princes. Petrarch never met a prince he didn't like, from the Emperor Charles IV to the Visconti of Milan to Francesco da Carrara of Padua, his patron in his final years. Petrarch's praise of patronage is at least as eloquent as Pound's. As he writes to Francesco da Carrara, "So be generous and kind to scholars, and Padua will be filled with learned men and its university restored to its ancient glory. Nothing entices outstanding men so much as the friendship and patronage of a prince. . . . Where can a talented and intelligent man be happier and lead a better life than under the benevolent gaze of a just and generous prince?" ("How a Ruler Ought to Govern His State," 76). And the spread of humanism across Europe is closely linked to the extension of monarchical power, as we should know in the case of England from the careers of Wyatt and Spenser, royal servants as well as poets and humanist scholars.

This does not mean that humanism is simply to be identified with princely forms of government or with tyranny, for, as Hans Baron has shown in *The Crisis of the Early Italian Renaissance*, there was a strong current of civic humanism in Italy, particularly in the Florentine Republic. Lorenzo Valla showed how humanist philology could serve the cause of liberty by revealing the Donation of Constantine—that bulwark of papal power—to be a fake, and Niccolò Machiavelli gives us the last but most brilliant expression of Florentine civic humanism in his *Discorsi*, one of the great classics of republican political thought.[4] But these two figures nonetheless reveal the opportunism with regard to power so central to humanism; for Valla, eight years after exposing the Donation, went to work in Rome as the Papal Secretary to Pope Nicholas V; more notoriously, while in the middle of writing the *Discorsi*, Machiavelli wrote that handbook for princes, *The Prince*, and dedicated it to one of the Medici. This opportunism is not an utter inconsistency, however, for both Valla and Machiavelli would have said that the princes they chose to work or write for were different from those they criticized. Not all princes were created equal, and their conception of power was personal, not institutional. For the humanists, as well as for Pound, the important question to ask was not to question power itself but to ask what the powerful did with their power. And the question Pound wants to ask of the powerful at this point was this: what were they doing to call art into being? He has an urgent reason for asking, since he believes that unless they help, the Renaissance he hopes for will be stillborn:

> Great art does not depend upon the support of riches, but without such aid it will be individual, separate, and spasmodic; it will not group and become a great period. ("The Renaissance," 221)

> If any great city in America would tether a hundred young artists, chosen for their inventive faculties and not for their capacity to agree with contemporary editorial boards, that city could within two decades become the centre of occidental art. . . . As the American government does not provide any such assistance, there is no reason why the American individual should not. ("Patria Mia," 140)

> If you so endow sculptors and writers you will begin for America an age of awakening which will over-shadow the quattrocento. ("The Renaissance," 224)

This new focus for Pound not on individual writers but on the conditions in which writers work represents the beginning of a crucial shift or expansion in Pound's use of Italy as a model. He began in 1908–1911 by imitating Italian poets and implicitly urging other poets to imitate them, but by 1912–1915, he is also urging that the rich in America imitate their Italian Renaissance counterparts. This is the beginning of a shift in Pound's thought toward urging that America imitate Italian social structures, Italian society, not only Italian art. And as Italy becomes the land of patrons and patronage for Pound, as well as what it represented for the young poet of *A Lume Spento* and *The Spirit of Romance*, the land of poets, the key figures for Pound in the next period in his Italianism are patrons and artists who benefited from their patronage.

Of the figures I have cited, it is Lorenzo Valla who is most important for Pound, particularly in this period. Pound owned Valla's *Elegantiae linguae latinae* in an Aldine edition, and in "Patria Mia," he makes some strong claims for Valla as a writer: "Valla mentions poetry not because he is himself a poet, he wrote the best prose of his day, and no man ever wrote better" (129). But this gives less of a clue to Pound's reason for praising Valla than a later mention of him in "The Renaissance": "The scholars of the quattrocento had just as stiff a stupidity and contentment and ignorance to contend with. It is in the biographies of Erasmus and Lorenzo Valla that we must find consolation. They were willing to work at foundations. They did not give the crowd what it wanted. . . . But the *rinascimento* began when Valla wrote in the preface of the *Elegantiae*" (220). Here I think we can see Pound using Italy as a mirror for his own situation and using Valla as a mirror for himself. "I, too," Pound is implicitly saying, "do not give the crowd what it wants, and I am willing to work on foundations. And perhaps what will follow from my labors will be yet another Renaissance." He had used Leopardi in this way three years earlier in "Patria Mia," but the shift from the romantic, isolated poet to a scholar working for a pope is significant (and offers the sharpest possible contrast to Joyce's celebration of Bruno, burned at the stake 150 years later by the Church for which Valla worked). Pound sees himself in these years not only as a humanist looking for a patron but also as a humanist seeking a society in which patronage would cause art to flourish. His image of this society was Renaissance Italy, and he therefore urges the modern world to imitate the Italians in their systems of patronage.

Valla is admittedly only a fleeting presence in Pound's prose, although he remained a positive image for Pound of the scholar who sought truth. (Pound mentions his exposure of the forgery of the Donation of Constantine in *Guide to Kulchur* [160] and again much later in Canto 89 [615 and 616], and Pope Nicholas's employment of Valla is mentioned again in Canto 104 [753].) But this issue of patronage is an absolutely central theme in *The Cantos*, particularly in the Early Cantos.[5] Despite his calling the comparison to the Medici hackneyed, Pound devotes Canto 21 to the Medici family and their complex machinations aimed at the "able corruption of Florence." But Pound's central figure for the Italian Renaissance prince and patron of the arts is not a Medici. It is the notorious condottiere Sigismundo Malatesta, hero of the Malatesta Cantos (Cantos 8–11). In the midst of Canto 21, the Italian words "affatigandose per suo piacere o non" are included parenthetically (21/97). The alert reader of *The Cantos* will realize that these words have appeared before: they are a verbal repetition of Canto 8, the first Malatesta Canto, from a letter written by Sigismundo Malatesta to Giovanni de' Medici. In Canto 8, Pound renders the letter in idiomatic English, and this phrase is rendered as: "So that he can work as he likes, / Or waste his time as he likes" (8/29). And the original Italian then follows parenthetically, just as in Canto

21. Malatesta here is describing his practice of hiring artists on subsidy, not paying them just for completed work. The letter from which this phrase comes is mostly about a painter from Florence Malatesta would like to hire, and one implication in this passage is that Malatesta was in fact a better patron of the arts than the Medici. And here Malatesta is presented as expressing the ideal stated by Kung in Canto 13: "'When the prince has gathered about him / All the savants and artists, his riches will be fully employed'" (13/59). In Pound's presentation, then, a Renaissance needs both artist and patron, both Valla and Pope Nicholas, both Agostino di Duccio and Sigismundo Malatesta. But not all patrons are created equal. The implicit contrast in Canto 21 suggests Pound's preference for Malatesta over the better-known Medici. The contrast between the Malatesta Cantos and the Venetian Cantos (24–26) delineate a sharper contrast yet, as in Venice, artists like Titian swindled the state and did not paint the paintings they were hired to do. And Pound presents us with this panorama of different modes of Renaissance patronage so that we can pick and choose, perceiving which of the Italian modes of patronage we should imitate. If Italy is to be the model, we in America can learn from the Early Cantos how to imitate it.

But here, as always, Pound does not urge a direct return to the model as much as an understanding of the chain of transmission between us and the model. According to Pound, he is not the first to try to realize an American renaissance on Italian Renaissance models. He is in a chain of imitation here as well, and his great predecessor in his Italianism is Thomas Jefferson. Jefferson first appears in Canto 21, in the middle of the canto devoted to the Medici family, and then is the subject of Cantos 31–34, a series of cantos focusing on the American Revolution.[6] Jefferson's first appearance in *The Cantos* is unforgettable: "'Could you,' wrote Mr. Jefferson, 'find me a gardener / who can play the french horn?'" (21/97) Thus begins the portion of a letter to Giovanni Fabroni that Pound quotes (and rearranges) in Canto 21, and this is a "luminous detail" for Pound, showing Jefferson's dedication to culture and pragmatic approach to obtaining it. He hopes eventually to have a full band of musicians among his domestic servants, and this miraculous combination of gardener and french horn player would presumably be the first step in this direction. Meaning in *The Cantos* is always created by juxtaposition, so Pound's juxtaposition of Jefferson and the Medici in Canto 21 is hardly accidental. The effect of the juxtaposition is to relate Jefferson's particular dedication to the arts to those of the Medici. They are all statesmen dedicated to art, a combination celebrated with reference to the Italian Renaissance throughout the Early Cantos.

But we have already seen that Pound's central figure for the Italian Renaissance prince and patron is Sigismundo Malatesta, not a Medici; and Pound also links Malatesta and Jefferson in a number of ways that strengthen the overall presentation of Jefferson as a "Renaissance man." It is in the middle of the passage quoting from Jefferson's letter that the words "affatigandose per suo piacere o non" are included parenthetically (21/97), and this creates a clear link or subject rhyme between Malatesta's letter and Jefferson's that is underscored by the Medicean context (one historical, the other created by Pound) of both letters (see Kenner, *The Pound Era*, 376, 423–24; D'Epiro, 103).

Malatesta and Jefferson, then, no lazy dilettantes, do not merely appreciate culture. They directly call it into being by their own activity—activity that is here represented by their correspondence. Pound—one of the century's most voluminous correspondents—would have particularly appreciated their correspondence, of course, but that is not the only reason for his focus here on letters. Another link between the two men is that their cultural creativity is ultimately best represented by works of architecture, in Malatesta's Tempio and in Jefferson's Monticello and in the University of Virginia. (And of course these works of architecture stand in a certain relationship, sharing a classicizing impulse.) Pound is being true to his own aesthetic of presentation by presenting their words, which he can do directly, rather than their architecture, which cannot really be represented appropriately through the medium of language. Yet it is noted in Canto 21 that Jefferson's letter was penned at Monticello, and this is Pound's way of indicating the existence of that which he cannot adequately represent.

So in Jefferson's first appearance in *The Cantos*, he is presented as an Italian Renaissance prince in the context of revolutionary America, concerned above all with creating art and culture, the Malatesta or Medici of early America (see Clark Emery, *Ideas into Action*, 34–35; Pearlman, 142; and Kenner, *The Pound Era*, 376, 423–24). Pound may not have found a living American Medici, but he feels that he has found a model patron of the arts in Jefferson, a man who exemplified the imperative of power to create art, the imperative for a ruler to gather the savants and artists around him. But there is a crucial shift between the Early Cantos and the Middle Cantos, between the Jefferson of Canto 21 and the Jefferson of Cantos 31–34 and *Jefferson and/ or Mussolini*.[7] Jefferson and the American Revolution are still being connected to Italy, but the connection grows considerably more complex. In the later period, as the title of the prose work shows, Pound lines Jefferson up not only with Malatesta but also with Mussolini. And we have made better sense of the Malatesta/Jefferson parallel in the Early Cantos than of the Jefferson/Mussolini parallel in Pound's prose and the Middle Cantos.

The first step in understanding that shift in all its implications is to realize that a different notion of imitation is coming into play here. For Pound, as clearly as for Petrarch, the artist-imitator is a transformer of his models. One imitates Dante not to reproduce him but to go beyond him, change him, transform him. But the imitation that Pound advocates in his composite portrait of the Renaissance patron is simply imitation as reproduction, as the creation of resemblance. Pound wants his millionaire to be like the Medici, not to be different from them, even though the art he wants them to buy—works by Wyndham Lewis and Henri Gaudier-Brzeska—was (in keeping with his theory of artistic imitation) utterly unlike the masterpieces of Renaissance art.

This tension or contradiction is also to be found in the Italian tradition Pound is urging us to imitate. The very same Petrarch who insisted upon the creative aspect of literary imitation urged princes to imitate great princes of the past in precisely this uncreative and passive fashion. While visiting the Emperor Charles IV at the emperor's request in Mantua in 1354, Petrarch gave the emperor some ancient coins, "bearing the representations of our oldtime rulers, with very tiny, ancient inscriptions. Among them was the face of Augustus Caesar—a breathing likeness. 'Here,' I said, 'is the Caesar to whom you have succeeded. Here are the men whom you should zealously endeavor to imitate. You should conform your life to their rule, to their model. . . . Your duty is not only to know them but to follow their example'" (*Rerum familiarum libri*, 19.3; *Letters*, 157–58). This notion of imitation is absolutely central to the political program of classicizing humanism: the ruler should try as much as possible to imitate other great rulers of the past, particularly those of Graeco-Roman civilization. And yet the model of imitation that Petrarch advocates here, imitation as conformity to the model, is diametrically opposed to the literary model of imitation he advances elsewhere in his letters.[8]

This ambivalence runs throughout the humanist tradition in the Renaissance, as can be seen clearly enough in the writings of Machiavelli. Imitation is an absolutely essential part of Machiavelli's political thinking. Again and again he insists on the imitation of (or deplores the failure to imitate) great models from the past:

> Since men almost always walk the path made by others and con-
> duct their affairs through imitation, although they are not alto-
> gether able to stay on the path of others nor arrive at the ingenuity
> of those they imitate, a prudent man should always take the path
> trodden by great men and imitate those who have been most out-
> standing; so that, if his own ingenuity does not come up to theirs,
> at least it will have the smell of it [*almeno ne renda qualche odore*];
> and he should act like those prudent archers, who, when the target
> they are aiming at seems too far off, aware of the capacity of their
> bow, set their sight a good deal higher than the desired target, not
> to reach such a height with their arrow but rather to be able, with
> the help of aiming high, to reach their target. (*The Prince*, 41)

> But as for the exercise of the mind, the prince should read history,
> and in it study the actions of distinguished men; to see how they
> comported themselves in war; to examine the causes for their vic-
> tories and defeats in order to be able to avoid the latter and imitate
> the former; and above all he should do as some outstanding man
> before him has done, who decided to imitate someone who has
> been praised and honored before him and always keep in mind his
> deeds and actions; just as it is said that Alexander the Great imi-
> tated Achilles; Caesar Alexander; Scipio Cyrus. (*The Prince*, 125)[9]

The notion of political and social imitation being advanced here for princes is the same ideal of conforming to the model advanced by Petrarch for his prince and by Pound for his modern princes. Yet Machiavelli as a writer does not conform to but rather transforms his model in accordance with the Petrarchan and humanist notion of creative imitation that Pound also approved. The *Discorsi* are based on the first ten books of Livy's history of Rome, but they no more faith-fully reproduce their model than Petrarch ever does. And Machiavelli even turns his transforming power on Petrarch himself, by ending *The Prince* with a quotation from the canzone "Italia mia" (*Canzoniere* 128). This poem is a political poem urging the unification of Italy, as the last chapter of *The Prince* does, and it ends with the word *pace*, in the same way that the very last poem in the *Canzoniere*, "Vergine bella," does. By ending his work with *Canzoniere* 128, not 366, Ma-chiavelli transforms Petrarch as he imitates him, criticizes him as he cites him. There is no prayer to the Virgin to be found here, and this absence indicates Machiavelli's sense that peace is to be achieved only through our own worldly efforts, not through prayer and divine intercession. Salvation does not come from above, but rather from the proper imitation of models of the past. It is up to the writer, the humanist, to articulate those models, but the achievement of peace and order will come only by great men acting on the models from the past.

All of these political themes from Italian Renaissance humanism are sounded again and again in Pound's work; indeed, they inform and virtually describe the project of *The Cantos*. And they enable us to make sense both of Pound's comparison of Jefferson with Malatesta and also of his later comparison of him with Mussolini. His interest in humanism was always part of his interest in the great man or in great men. For instance, Pound headed his *Gaudier-Brzeska: A Memoir* (1916) with a quotation from Machiavelli, "Gli uomini vivono in pochi e gli altri son pecorelle" (men live only in a few [or only a few men are really alive] and the others are little sheep). As early as "The Renaissance," Pound had written that "Democracies have fallen, they have always fallen, because humanity craves the outstanding personality. And hitherto no democracy has provided sufficient place for such an individuality" (224). Pound's cult of the Renaissance patron therefore—like that of Yeats—had political implications from the start. The tone of this passage in "The Renaissance" suggests that Pound is willing to see if democracy can find a place for the "outstanding personality," but the failure of many modern Medici to come forth, the death of his closest approach to a Renaissance patron in John Quinn in 1924, and his move to Italy in the same year suggest that Pound had concluded by then that no democracy can provide a place for the outstanding individual. At least no contemporary democracy, for Pound continues to connect his humanist orientation toward the "outstanding personality" to Jefferson. And this is one reason why, as Jefferson reappears in the Middle Cantos, Pound does not abandon the Italian Renaissance frame already established for him. The cantos on Jefferson and the American Revolution, Cantos 31–34, open in this way:

> Tempus loquendi,
> Tempus tacendi.
> Said Mr Jefferson:
>   (31/153)

Then follows another of Jefferson's letters. The first two lines, "There is a time to speak, there is a time to be silent," were Sigismundo Malatesta's motto, words he put on his wife Isotta's tomb in the Tempio Malatestiana. They are also, of course, the Latin Vulgate rendering of Ecclesiastes 3:7, but with a difference: the Vulgate reads "Tempus tacendi, tempus loquendi," with an emphasis on that time to be silent. Malatesta's emphasis, characteristically for him as for Pound, was on speaking (see Pearlman, 142–51).

So the Italian Renaissance frame remains relevant to Pound's Jeffersonianism as his cultural politics begins to become a full-fledged political theory. And if we seriously examine how Malatesta and Jefferson could be connected in Pound's political thinking, we find that there are ways in which the political thinking of Jefferson can be related to figures like Malatesta. Understanding that allows us to make better sense of the further Jefferson/Mussolini equation, as in essence, the Jefferson/Mussolini parallel is a Malatesta/Jefferson/Mussolini parallel.

What made Pound's portrait of Thomas Jefferson seem so bizarre and anomalous when he advanced it in the 1930s was its radical departure from what has been called the "Lockean paradigm" (Pocock, *The Machiavellian Moment*, 539), the notion that the Declaration of Independence in particular and the American Revolution in general were essentially products of the political thought of Lockean liberalism.[10] That paradigm, having come under attack from a number of directions, no longer holds the unquestioned sway it did fifty years ago, and in this respect Pound's portrait of Jefferson actually anticipated the direction of contemporary scholarship, particularly the work of J.G.A. Pocock. Pocock's central contention that the Italian Renaissance concern with virtue (or *virtù*) and corruption becomes the enduring concern of Anglo-American political thought in the late seventeenth and eighteenth centuries is remarkably parallel to Pound's presentation of Jefferson. I would argue not only that Pocock's and Pound's Jefferson are remarkably akin,[11] but also that Pocock's work goes a long way toward explaining Pound's own Jeffersonianism, his particular version of the larger "dialectic of virtue and corruption," which, according to Pocock, we in America have inherited from the Italian Renaissance. It thus not only provides a richer context for Pound's comparison of Jefferson with Malatesta; in the way it relates Jefferson to the Renaissance, it goes a long way toward explaining Pound's subsequent comparison of Jefferson with Mussolini.

The major thrust of Pocock's study is to argue that there is a line of influence running from the political theoreticians of the Florentine Renaissance, preeminently Machiavelli and Guicciardini, through seventeenth- and eighteenth-century England to the thought of the American Revolution and beyond. This inheritance persists at least partially because the problems to which the Italian thinkers were responding persist. There is a recurring Machiavellian moment because there is a recurring dilemma or problematic: thus, in Pocock's presentation as well as in Pound's, there is a parallel between the Italian Renaissance and the American Revolution as well as a line of influence from one to the other.

The central dilemma that any republic must face is the fact that republics have across history been intermittent anomalies, often destroyed from within rather than from without. How can a republic survive its enemies and last across time? In the Renaissance, the essential enemy is named corruption: republics fail because they grow corrupt, and we have already seen Pound's perception of the Medici as such corruptors. And, to simplify, there are two lines on how to stave off corruption. The first, linked closely to what Pocock calls the Venetian myth and expressed in the work of Guicciardini, argues that one staves off corruption by perfecting the institutions of power, the machinery of government, so that conflicting forces are balanced and brought into order. This line of thought, largely alien to Jefferson (and to Pound at this time), nonetheless runs down to the American Revolution and persists in the thinking of John Adams and in the doctrine of "checks and balances" implicit in the Constitution. The second, associated especially with Machiavelli and his more personal conception of power, argues that *virtù* alone counteracts corruption; no given set of institutions is incorruptible. For Machiavelli, *virtù* means above all activity and innovation:[12] one must avoid depending upon any set of preconceptions and face the newness of any situation newly. This is one reason why Machiavelli can write both the *Discorsi* and *The Prince*, and we can see in Pound precisely the same personal conception of power, which enables him to compare a republican like Jefferson with a *condottiere* like Malatesta or a dictator like Mussolini without a sense of anomaly.

How does Machiavellian *virtù* connect Jefferson and Mussolini for Pound? He admits that differences between Jefferson's and Mussolini's particular actions exist, but he nonetheless insists that Jefferson, faced with Mussolini's situation, would have found the same means:

I don't propose to limit my analysis to what Tom Jefferson recommended *in a particular time and place*. I am concerned with what he actually did, with the way his mind worked both when faced with a particular problem *in* a particular geography and when faced with the unending problem of CHANGE.

If Mussolini had tried to fool himself into finding or into trying to find the identical solution for Italy 1922–1932 that Jefferson found for America 1776–1820, there would have been no fascist decennio. (*Jefferson and/or Mussolini*, 11)

This is pure Machiavelli: as the world changes, so too must the means of a ruler change. And this view enables Pound to argue that much of what has been taken as the political legacy of Jefferson was rather his particular response to a particular situation. The cast of mind revealed by that adaptiveness and quality of innovation is for Pound the true Jeffersonian legacy:

The truth is that Jefferson used verbal formulations as tools. He was not afflicted by fixations. Neither he nor Mussolini has been really interested in governmental machinery. That is not paradox, they have both invented it and used it, but they have both been much more deeply interested in something else.

Jefferson found himself in a condition of things that had no precedent in any remembered world. He saw like a shot that a new system and new mechanisms MUST come into being to meet it.

He was agrarian IN the colonies and in the U.S.A. of HIS TIME, that is to say a time when, and a place where, there was abundance and superabundance of land. (*Jefferson and/or Mussolini*, 62)

Clearly, what Pound is praising in Jefferson in these passages is the spirit of innovation that alone for Machiavelli will stave off a republic's decline.[13] And the connection between this view and Pound's support of Mussolini is not hard to find: according to Pound, those who came after Jefferson lost the animating spirit of virtue that alone made the machinery work: "Jefferson thought the formal features of the American system would work, and they did work till the time of General Grant but the condition of their working was that inside them there should be a *de facto* government composed of sincere men willing the national good" (*Jefferson and/or Mussolini*, 94–95).

The subsequent absence of this "de facto government" led to such corruption that in Pound's day, only radically different means—or so he thought—could restore health to the body politic: "Hence my attention to the NEXT social construction, next in point of time, next SYSTEM of government set up in the AIM that ours was, namely of providing a BETTER system of government than had BEEN BEFORE put in motion anywhere on earth in the occident" ("*Ezra Pound Speaking,*" 112). Thus, what is essential to good government is having the right aim and then acting upon it, and the similarity Pound perceives in this respect between Jefferson and Mussolini is more important than the obvious differences between their methods. Thus, for Pound as well as for Machiavelli, *virtù* in the sense of activity—getting something done—is the key element in the survival of a republic, in good government. And *virtù* in very close to this sense is a key word in Cavalcanti's "Donna mi Prega," a word that Pound leaves untranslated in his rendering of the Cavalcanti poem in Canto 36 (36/177).[14] Analogously, Pound always associated Mussolini with speed and activity, as this brief description in *Guide to Kulchur* shows: "Mussolini, a great man, demonstrably in his effect on event, unadvertisedly so in the swiftness of mind, in the speed with which his real emotion is shown in his face" (105). And the value Pound always places on activity links up with other aspects of his thought, for instance his endorsement in Canto 13 of Confucius taking a cane to the contemplative philosopher Yuan Jang: "You old fool, come out of it, / Get up and do something useful" (13/59).

This focus on action is not at all what most of us mean by virtue, and indeed it has been this kind of Machiavellian functionalism or operationalism that has given the Florentine such a bad name. But in Pocock's analysis, the more common meaning of virtue nonetheless adheres to the Machiavellian tradition as it finds its way to England and America. (Perhaps one way of locating Pound's originality in this tradition is that he does not inherit the tradition as mediated in Anglo-American culture; rather, he takes it from the Renaissance and then applies it once again to the American Revolution.) The familiar conception of America is that as the New World it reacted against the traditionalism of the Old, specifically against monarchy, religious despotism, and feudal land tenure. But Pocock also presents the ideologues of the American Revolution as reacting strongly against a kind of modernity as well, against the complex and often corrupt commercial and financial machinery that ran the British empire. (Hamilton is, of course, the conspicuous exception and, as such, earns Pound's utmost opprobrium as "the Prime snot in ALL American history" [67/

350].) In this, they were inheriting the rhetoric of the eighteenth-century "Old Whig" or "Country" party, and behind that rhetoric—in Pocock's analysis—is Florentine republican thought. Thus, Jefferson's famous celebration of the virtue of the freehold farmer in *Notes on the State of Virginia* and elsewhere involves a critique of the corruption of modern finance as well as a critique of the oppression of feudal patterns of land ownership. In this view, individuals as well as states must stay free of "entangling foreign alliances." Virtue and independence are concomitant terms as are corruption and dependence. To cite Pocock's most succinct formulation of this theme, "The ideal of the patriot or citizen entailed the image of a personality free and virtuous because unspecialized. The function of his property was to give him independence and autonomy as well as the leisure and liberty to engage in public affairs; but his capacity to bear arms in the public cause was an end of his property and the test of his virtue" (*Virtue, Commerce, and History*, 109).

This antimodern stratum of eighteenth-century thought delineated by Pocock sounds again and again remarkably like Pound. Pound's radio speeches repeatedly invoked the related ideal of a free yeomanry, each family with its own "homestead," free of debt. And this is the key respect in which Pound's Jeffersonianism links up with his economics. The primary enemy of country ideologue and Pound alike was finance and international banking, and for both the founding of the Bank of England in 1694 is a key moment. One connection between Pound and the eighteenth century is that, as Pocock points out, this "dialectic of virtue and corruption" runs throughout American culture and history. It certainly informed the settling of the West and the mystique of the frontier: virtue lay in getting west, outside of known and settled ground. In Pound's time, as well as in our own, that populism remained an important part of American culture, particularly in the West, fueling William Jennings Bryan's "cross of gold" rhetoric in Pound's youth and in the very years under study, carrying the Social Credit movement to victory just across the border from Idaho in Alberta.

Paradoxically, although these populist expressions of the Machiavellian moment tend toward antistatist positions, Pound's Jeffersonian concern with corruption quickly led him in the opposite direction. Pound argued that in the years since Jefferson's death, the forces of corruption had grown enormously, and this growth required an enormous growth in power by the state to preserve the freedom of the individual: "The demarcation between public and private affairs shifts with the change in the bases of production. A thousand peasants each growing food on his own fields can exist without trust laws" (*Jefferson and/or Mussolini*, 45). But today we cannot exist without trust laws; we need the virtuously exercized power of the state to protect us against the unvirtuous and corrupt forces of finance. As Pound quoted Adams in Canto 62, "republican jealousy which seeks to cut off all power / from fear of abuses does / quite as much harm as a despotism" (62/344). And this is the paradox of Pound's Jeffersonianism: Pound came to embrace despotism precisely to free us from what he perceived to be a greater despotism.

But the Machiavellian context Pocock's work provides for us gives us a way to understand—if not to accept—that paradox. We should be able to see by now that Pound's portrait of Jefferson was deeply Machiavellian, in precisely the senses Pocock finds the American Revolution in general to be Machiavellian. Malatesta, unmentioned in *The Prince* but mentioned often in Machiavelli's *Istorie fiorentine*, is the perfect Machiavellian innovator, and Pound's portrait of Jefferson as the Malatesta of his era is deeply Machiavellian in its stress on action and innovation. The Early Cantos are more concerned than was Machiavelli with the creation of art as a duty of the Prince; but that theme progressively disappears in the Middle Cantos, and Cantos 31–34 are far more concerned with Jefferson governing than with Jefferson calling art into being.

Jefferson more than Malatesta or Machiavelli is concerned with virtue as well as *virtù*, and in this respect Pound's portrait of Jefferson is in harmony with Pocock's portrait of the Machiavellian tradition in Anglo-American political thought, more concerned with virtuously opposing financial corruption than was the Florentine. Pound's Jefferson is the man opposed to the National Debt, opposed to domestic industries, and committed to the freehold or yeoman tradition of liberty and independence. In all these respects, Pound's Jefferson is a man far closer to contemporary portraits of Jefferson than was the conventional Jefferson of 1935, measured against which Pound's Jefferson has always seemed so bizarre.

Moreover, this context for Jefferson established by Pocock makes more sense both of Pound's comparison of Jefferson to Mussolini and of his subsequent shift in interest from Jefferson to Adams. At this point, Jefferson represented for Pound the possibility of radical transformation, the radical, Machiavellian energy inherent in revolution. This particularly fascinated Pound by the early 1930s, by which time he was looking for a radical alternative to the status quo that he condemned as static and incapable of renovation. He was prepared to look anywhere for this alternative, to Social Credit, to Gesellian economics, to Mussolini, to Marx, later briefly to Roosevelt, to anyone who offered a radical alternative.[15] And it was this free-floating, ideologically eclectic nature of Pound's political thinking that led him to be attracted by the Machiavellian tradition of political thought, with its emphasis on *doing something*. Mussolini, thus, was Jeffersonian and preferable to the other alternatives for Pound in the early 1930s less because of the specific content of his ideas than because of his bias toward action. This was precisely what Wyndham Lewis in *Time and Western Man* criticized about fascism, that with its bias toward action, it was simply "Futurism in practice" (40). Unlike Lewis, Pound praised Mussolini's "bias towards action" in many different ways in these years, through references to Mussolini clearing the Pontine Marshes (see Canto 41/202), increasing the amount of land under cultivation, and so on. And here Pound's line of thinking is close to a line of official fascist thinking, and indeed Pound was not the only supporter of Mussolini to link him to the opportunism of the Italian Renaissance. H. S. Harris quotes "Gentile call[ing] Mussolini 'il Condottiero possente' of whom Machiavelli had dreamed" (*The Social Philosophy of Giovanni Gentile*, 219).

Across the 1930s, however, the plasticity or freewheeling nature of Pound's politics disappears. He became committed to Mussolini as *the* alternative, the possibility for a just society, and not only as a stick with which to beat the status quo over the head. Pound moved, in short, from seeing Mussolini as a figure to oppose to the existing malign order to seeing him as the promulgator of a new, desirable order that needed defense. This corresponds as well—although a full discussion of this would take us too far from our focus here—to a shift in Mussolini's regime, which—until the Abyssinian invasion of 1935—was certainly successfully institutionalizing itself and moving away from the instability of revolutionary politics toward a conservative adaptation to the status quo. And given this shift, Pound needed a new figure to serve as Mussolini's parallel in *The Cantos*. Jefferson's philosophy of energy and innovation would no longer do.

This is the context in which we need to understand Pound's shift in attention from Jefferson to John Adams. The American Revolutionary period remains a major concern of the Middle Cantos, but here, as elsewhere, it is easy to assume a greater degree of continuity than actually obtains. Pound's interests and plans kept changing throughout these cantos. Thomas Jefferson and John Adams are the two figures of the American Revolution Pound portrays at length, and this selectivity might lead us to assume that Pound saw similar virtues in the two men. But arguing against this is the historical fact that Adams and Jefferson were at important moments arrayed against each other in the revolutionary period. They worked together at the time of the Declaration of Independence and they reconciled their differences in the correspondence of their final years, but in between, at the time of their respective presidencies, they were bitter political enemies and held radically different political philosophies. It is true that at times Pound minimized this conflict, emphasizing Jefferson's and Adams's areas of agreement more than their areas of disagreement.[16] But he was clearly aware of those disagreements, clearly aware that Jefferson and Adams stood for quite different aspects of the American Revolution. Although Jefferson was the figure who initially captured Pound's attention, by the time of *Guide to Kulchur* (1938), his interest had shifted and he had begun to see Adams as the more profound figure: "The tragedy of the U.S.A. over 160 years is the decline of Adamses. More and more we cd., if we examined events, see that John Adams had the corrective for Jefferson" (254). Jefferson's ideas are implicitly found wanting by Pound here, and it is Adams who provides the "corrective."

The Middle Cantos begin as if Thomas Jefferson is to be the central figure, the Malatesta of the American Revolution in a way that would point forward to Mussolini as the Malatesta/Jefferson of our time. But after Canto 35, Jefferson largely disappears from *The Cantos*, and Pound's interest shifts to Martin Van Buren, to periods and realms other than the American Revolution, and finally, when he returns to the Revolution in Cantos 62–71, to John Adams, not to Jefferson. Comparably, *Jefferson and/or Mussolini* was written in 1933 and published in 1935; after a brief period of balanced interest in the two men, particularly in their correspondence, the subject of Pound's 1937 essay "The Jefferson/Adams Letters as a Shrine and a Monument," Pound's interest in his prose shifts to Adams as well. By the time of *Guide to Kulchur* (1938), the Adams Cantos (1940), and Pound's broadcasts over Rome Radio during the war, Adams has clearly taken the center-stage position that Jefferson once occupied. In *Jefferson and/or Mussolini*, Adams is usually mentioned simply as one name in a list of major American thinkers and is only once referred to independently; in the radio broadcasts, Jefferson is similarly usually mentioned only in similar lists of names and is almost never examined or discussed separately.

One reason why Adams takes the pride of place that once belonged to Jefferson is that Pound had become concerned about something that had earlier not interested him, the institutions of power. Earlier, in *Jefferson and/or Mussolini*, he argued that government machinery did not matter; what mattered was the will to change and the economic arrangements behind the governmental machinery. But in his radio talks and in the Adams Cantos, he keeps coming back to the need to study systems of government: "I would remind Prof. Beard that Adams studied republics" ("*Ezra Pound Speaking*," 393). As he wrote Sir Oswald Mosley in 1939, "J Adams probably made the MOST serious study of Brit. institutions ever made; before drafting the constitution of Massachusetts and that of the U.S." Pound had begun with a personal conception of power close to Machiavelli's in which Adams's constitutionalism seemed irrelevant. But, perhaps as Mussolini's government became less a personal and more an institutional dictatorship, Pound's conception of power became in turn more institutional than personal. But as Pound shifts from Jefferson to Adams, we are still in the "Machiavellian moment," just in a different aspect of that traditional problematic. To save republics from decline into degeneracy and corruption, Machiavelli had argued that *virtù* was essential; but Guicciardini's contrasting emphasis had been on getting the institutions right. And the "myth of Venice" is a myth of a governmental system so perfectly balanced that degeneracy never set in. Adams, fascinated by constitutions and the author of a substantial if widely criticized contribution to constitutional theory, *A Defence of the Constitutions of Government of the United States of America against the attack of M. Turgot, in his Letter to Dr. Price, Dated the Twenty-Second Day of March, 1778* (1786–1787), is clearly in the Guicciardinian—not the Machiavellian—tradition. And Pound, by the late 1930s, inclined to that side as well, as the cento of quotations from Adams's *Defence* in Cantos 67 and 68 (67-68/393–95) clearly shows. "Johnnie wanted to know what really was the best form of government. And more than any other man, not excludin' Jim Madison and Thomas Jefferson, he got on the trail" ("*Ezra Pound Speaking*," 390).

For Pound, American history showed that the Machiavellian emphasis on opportunistic *virtù* is flawed because it proved incapable of establishing stability. The American Revolution failed to sustain its originating *virtù* past the Civil War, and Pound's sense was that more attention to the "best form of government" might have staved off that failure. The problem with emphasizing men with *virtù* is this: what happens if they are unable to retain power? The history of the Adams family for Pound showed that in America the men with *virtù* were replaced by less capable and less virtuous men. And the consequent need to focus on the institutions of government, not just on the *virtù* of leaders, is a recurrent theme in the Adams Cantos:

> and mankind dare not yet think upon
> CONSTITUTIONS
> (68/395)
>
> how small in
> any nation the number who comprehend ANY
> system of constitution or administration
> and these few do not unite.
> (70/412)

I am for balance

> and know not how it is but mankind have an aversion
> to any study of government
> (70/413)
>
> No people in Europe cares anything
> about constitutions, 1815, whatsoever
> not one of 'em understands or is capable of understanding
> any consti–damn–tution whatever
> (71/418)

So the Adams concerned with constitutional machinery and governmental institutions proved more congenial to Pound than he had earlier. Just as important, the specifics of his constitutional theory proved congenial as well. The traditional problem republics failed to resolve, according to Aristotle, was how to reconcile the conflicting powers and desires of the many, the few, and the one, of the forces of democracy, aristocracy, and monarchy.[17] For Aristotle, each form of government tended to degenerate into its negative mirror image: democracy into anarchy, aristocracy into oligarchy, monarchy into tyranny. Polybius felt that this could be avoided by a mixed form of government that blended elements of all three,[18] and a tradition of English thought praised the English system of the King, the House of Lords, and the House of Commons as achieving the Polybian ideal of a mixed and balanced system. And Adams's constitutional thinking, "classical to the point of archaism," as Pocock has described it (*The Machiavellian Moment*, 531), stays almost entirely within that classical, Aristotelian–Polybian frame of reference. When Pound opens Canto 68 with:

> The philosophers say: one, the few, the many
> Regis   optimatium   populique
>
> (68/395)

he is quoting a passage in Adam's *Defence* in which Adams is quoting Polybius. Adams's concern was always to find a Polybian balance of the one, the few, and the many, and he insisted on the necessity of a strong ruler, a strong "one," to achieve that balance. "'You fear the one, I the few,'" we read in Canto 69 (69/407), Pound's condensation of a letter from Adams to Jefferson, and Adams here encapsulates his and Jefferson's differing positions within this tradition. The entire passage (from a 1787 letter by Adams to Jefferson) reads: "You are afraid of the one, I, of the few. We agree perfectly that the many should have a full, fair, and perfect representation. You are apprehensive of monarchy, I, of aristocracy" (Sanders, *John Adams Speaking*, 426). Adams felt that not having a "one," a single leader, would lead to the few dominating the many, and on these grounds he criticized the radically democratic constitutional thinking of the French Revolution (see Canto 70/412).

Pound felt that events had proven Adams—not Jefferson—correct. He thought that the democratic representation of the "many" was today controlled by the "few," not a traditional aristocracy with responsibility as much as the monied few: "The Democracy that the frog / revoluters and Jefferson theorized about / but that J / did not USE when he became president / means one chamber = manageable by finance" (from a letter to Mosley, 8 February 1939). In Aristotelian terms, aristocracy had degenerated into oligarchy: "Rhetoric about 'our representatives in Parliament' is NOT the point. The point is that your Parliament does NOT represent you" ("*Ezra Pound Speaking*," 134).[19] And Pound felt—with Adams—that a powerful "one" was necessary to enable the many to have that "full, fair, and perfect representation." Adams's position was already a conservative one within eighteenth-century political thought, and his emphasis on the "one" led to his being criticized in his lifetime for his supposed "monarchical" tendencies. And although Adams was no monarchist ("I am a mortal and irreconcilable enemy to monarchy" [Sanders, *John Adams Speaking*, 456]), Pound—turning that criticism into grounds for commendation—approvingly presents an Adams convinced that one must tilt toward the "one" rather than toward the "few" to achieve order and balance: "I am for a balance between the legislative and executive powers, and I am for enabling the executive to be at all times capable of maintaining the balance between the Senate and the House, or in other words, between the aristocratical and democratical interests" (Sanders, *John Adams Speaking*, 456).[20] Thus, although Adams's concern was balance, not innovation, his stress on the importance of leadership establishes a continuity both with Pound's earlier praise of the Renaissance prince and with his praise of *il duce*, the leader.

This theme of leadership is related to another reason why Adams fascinated Pound: the Adams family. Remember that Pound presents "the decline of the Adamses" as the American tragedy. Pound's obvious preference here is for the Adamses to have become in effect an American ruling family, for Charles Francis and his sons to have followed John and John Quincy as Presidents. The Chinese History Cantos that precede the Adams Cantos similarly stress the importance both of dynastic continuity and of having a single strong ruler, and the juxtaposition of the two sets of cantos works to suggest that Adams was (or perhaps should have been) a strong ruler founding a dynasty in the Chinese sense. Pound presents the Adams family as the possible counterweight to the decline of the American revolution that did not work. They were the men with *virtù* who should have arrested the decline of *virtù*, and their failure shows that *virtù* alone without a proper form of goverment is not enough. So the failure of the Adamses paradoxically proves for Pound that Adams was right in his insistence on constitutions and the study of government.

So, in the late 1930s and 1940s, both in his prose and in *The Cantos*, Pound notes real differences between Adams and Jefferson and strongly endorses the position of Adams. As he put it in one of his wartime radio broadcasts, "If Jefferson had stuck by John Adams, instead of making it up when they were both on the retired list, things would have been different" (*"Ezra Pound Speaking,"* 121). Here Pound presents the differences between Adams and Jefferson as the tragic flaw of the American Revolution. Where they differed, Adams was right, and Adams is therefore the crucial figure of the American Revolution, the one whose wisdom can set us straight today: "Johnnie Adams, the first, the real father of his country" ("*Ezra Pound Speaking*," 390).

Now, it should be clear that everything in the Middle Cantos takes on meaning less in itself than in the complex relations Pound sets up between it and other moments in history. In *The Cantos*, Jefferson takes on meaning in relation to the Italian Renaissance, most notably in relation to Sigismundo Malatesta. But by now in Pound's intellectual development, any simple parallel between Italy and America has been complicated—as in Joyce's adaptation of Vico—by the existence of other such parallels and analogies. Adams takes on meaning in relation to Chinese history, because for Pound he is the American equivalent of a Chinese Great Emperor and his concern with balance parallels the Confucian thought that so interested Pound at this point, as is indicated by the appearance of the ideogram *chung* (中), or balance, at various points in the Adams Cantos. These comparisons have their negative side: Adams in particular is subtly reproached for being unable to found a ruling dynasty in the Chinese model; I am not sure Pound thought Monticello quite up to the Tempio Malatestiana either. But it should be understood that this web of relations points forward as well as backward: Jefferson and Adams are also to be compared to Mussolini, the Sigismundo Malatesta and Chinese Great Emperor of our time. The past gives us not information for its own sake, but points of reference for the present, and Pound's portrait of the American Revolution is intended as one crucial point of reference for Italian fascism.

This makes for a relationship between Pound's native and his adopted countries, America and Italy, of dizzying complexity. Contemporary Fascist Italy is related to the American Revolution, yet that revolution is related to the Italian Renaissance. Pound is in the humanist tradition of both describing and prescribing imitation here: he is giving the present models they can imitate, targets of greatness at which they can aim. And if part of Pound's message to Mussolini is that he should take Jefferson and Adams as his great men to imitate, then certainly part of Pound's message to America is that it should take Mussolini as its model. America should imitate the Italians, who should imitate the early Americans, who were in any case imitating the Italians of the Renaissance.

The complexity of this serves to explain why Pound fortunately inspired no one to imitate anyone. But it should also demonstrate clearly enough that Pound's politics cannot be dismissed merely as the ravings of a madman, as both defenders and attackers of Pound have often presented him. His political philosophy kept evolving and changing, but it can be placed in philosophical and political traditions whose importance for our civilization cannot be summarily dismissed. Moreover, as I have tried to show here, the strategy of emphasizing his considerable interest in American history and politics at the expense of his Italianism simply does not work. His portrait of America cannot be understood without reference to his portrait of Italy. But this also means that his love of Italian culture cannot be separated from his politics, and what I hope to show in the next chapter is that the mature or at least fairly stable political theory we have depicted him as moving toward across the 1930s in this chapter, the belief shared by John Adams and Confucius in the order provided by a strong leader, also has deep Italian roots, in the political thinking of Dante.

Chapter Nine

Ezra Pound, the Last Ghibelline

The last chapter traced the evolution of Pound's political think-ing and his use of Italy as a model—two closely related aspects of his work—from 1915 to 1935 through three, partially overlapping stages. In the first, beginning with "Patria Mia" and "The Renaissance" and ending with the Venetian Cantos, Pound's interest in politics was above all in how it affected art, in what political order could bring great art into being. Pound's model here was the Renaissance prince and he presented Thomas Jefferson as just such a prince in an Ameri-can context. This concern modulates into what I have called Pound's Machiavellian moment, a period in which Renaissance princes become Pound's models for more than simply their patronage. But that Ma-chiavellian moment of the early 1930s quickly gave way around 1935 to a critique of the instability of Machiavellian politics, a critique ex-pressed both in Pound's shift in attention from Jefferson to Adams and in Pound's increasing celebration of the Confucian virtue of *chung* or balance.

But what led Pound through this sequence toward the "totalitarian synthesis" of *Guide to Kulchur* (1938), the Chinese History and Adams Cantos (1940), and most notoriously, the wartime broadcasts over Rome Radio? A central piece of the puzzle still escapes us, I think; and it is on that that I wish to focus here. It is clear enough that Pound's admiration for Mussolini was a—perhaps *the*—key catalyst in his evo-lution toward a pro-Fascist position. *Jefferson and/or Mussolini* is evi-dence enough that Pound's admiration was for Mussolini himself, and his idealization of the man always far outstripped his idealization of his regime, culminating in the opening passage of Canto 74, in which the dead Mussolini is represented as a crucified savior whom the world has perversely refused to follow:

> Manes! Manes was tanned and stuffed,
> Thus Ben and la Clara *a milano*
> by the heels at Milano
> That maggots shd/ eat the dead bullock
> DIGONOS, Δίγονος, but the twice crucified
> where in history will you find it?
>
> (439)

But I do not think the question has been asked often enough, why Mussolini? There were plenty of other strong leaders around whom Pound could have idealized, from Lenin to Roosevelt; there were even plenty of other Fascist leaders around, from Eliot's preferred model, Charles Maurras, to Roy Campbell's Franco. The question still remains, why Mussolini?

It is the argument of this chapter that Pound's fixation on Mussolini cannot be understood outside of the larger context of Pound's life-long admiration for Italian culture, in particular, for Italy's greatest poet, Dante. Pound's saturation in Dante begins with his college education, and we know, both from the many references to Dante in his works and from his copies of Dante's works now at the Harry Ransom Humanities Research Center at the University of Texas at Austin, that he read all of Dante carefully and at many different times in his life.[1] But what has not been sufficiently understood is that this interest in Dante was also an interest in Dante's political thinking.[2] From Pound's copies of Dante, we can reconstruct at least four separate times when Pound made a detailed reading of Dante's key text of political theory, *De Monarchia*, annotating the text as he read; two of these readings can be placed in the late 1930s or early 1940s and one other in the 1920s or 1930s.[3] Dante's political philosophy was a shaping influence on Pound's "totalitarian synthesis"; and the fact that Dante held the philosophy he did was part of what crystalized Pound's dissatisfaction with the opportunism of the humanist tradition. To put this another way, Pound's shift from Jefferson back to the more traditionalist John Adams was also a shift from Machiavellianism back to the political thought of Dante. This was of course a return to Pound's first love in Italian culture, as Dante had been an influence on Pound's aesthetic from the beginning, but Pound's politics take on a Dantescan impress only in the 1930s and the 1940s. What I hope to show here is that many of the themes of Pound's politics, particularly his enthusiasm for the figure of Mussolini, can be made explicable by reference to the ideas of *De Monarchia*. Indeed, it is not too much to call Pound the last Ghibelline and to see in his idealization of Mussolini one final belated echo of Dante's perception of Henry VII as the Lamb of God come to take away the sins of the world.

To show this, I first need to sketch the argument of *De Monarchia* and Dante's other political works, using evidence from Pound's annotations when appropriate to show how he received and at times modified Dante's argument. The compact and well-organized *De Monarchia* devotes each of its three books to proving one major point. The first point is that one world requires one government and one ruler; the second, that Rome was divinely appointed as the seat of this ruler's government; and the third, that it is the Empire, not the Church, that was so divinely appointed. Of the three points, only the third establishes Dante's extreme partisanship in the political struggles of the early fourteenth century. The first two could be (and were) used by the Guelfs, those who asserted papal supremacy over all governments;[4] only the third marked Dante as a supporter of the Imperial cause, as a Ghibelline.[5] *De Monarchia* is largely without explicit references to the contemporary political situation, which has made it a difficult text to date, but implicitly in *De Monarchia* and explicitly in a number of political letters, Dante made his stand on the struggles of his time crystal clear.

But before Dante begins to prove his three key points, he spends the first few chapters of *De Monarchia* justifying his own treatise on politics, and this also interested Pound. Marked in both of Pound's copies of *De Monarchia* is this passage in Chapter 2 of Book 1:

> Est ergo sciendum, quod quaedam sunt, quae nostrae potestati minime subiacentia, speculari tantummodo possumus, operari autem non, velut mathematica, physica, et divina. Quaedam vero sunt, quae nostrae potestati subiacentia, non solum speculari, sed etiam operari possumus, et in iis non operatio propter speculationem, sed haec propter illam adsumitur, quoniam in talibus operatio est finis. Quum ergo materia praesens politica sit, imo fons atque principium rectarum politiarum, et omne politicum nostrae potestati subiaceat; manifestum est, quod materia praesens

> non ad speculationem per prius, sed ad operationem ordinatur.
> (Moore, 342)[6]
>
> Now it is to be noted that there are some subjects that are completely outside human control, about which we can only speculate, being unable to affect them by our actions; such are mathematics, physics and revealed truth. There are others, however, that fall within our control; not only can we speculate about them, but also we can do something about them. In these, action is not subordinate to speculation but speculation is for the sake of action, because the aim in such matters is action. Since the present subject is political—indeed, the source and principle of all just governments—and anything political lies within our power, it is obvious that the matter in hand is not primarily directed towards speculation but towards action. (Dante, *Monarchy*, 5)

In other words, the study of politics matters because politics affects every aspect of our lives and because we can do something about it. As Dante says, "Unde Philosophus in suis Politicis ait quod in politia obliqua bonus homo est malus civis; in recta vero, bonus homo et civis bonus convertuntur" (347;[7] "Hence the Philosopher says that 'in the perverted forms [of government] a good man is a bad citizen, whereas in the true form to be a good citizen is the same as being a good man'" [20]).

And this is another passage Pound was sufficiently struck by to mark it in both copies. Nevertheless, the art of politics is not very widely studied, as Dante says in the very first chapter, because there is no profit in it, and here Dante announces a key theme of *De Monarchia*, the pervasiveness and destructiveness of the desire for gain, of *cupiditas*. The rest of Book I is dedicated to Dante's argument that the world needs a single, unified government ruled by one ruler. Dante argues quite straightforwardly for the necessity of hierarchy, of there being a division between the ruler and the ruled. Marked in both copies is a passage in which Dante cites Aristotle's *Politics* (1:2): "Ex quo iam innotescit illud Politicae: intellectu scilicet vigentes aliis naturaliter principari" (343; "From all this one begins to appreciate what is meant in the *Politics* by the sentence: 'Men of superior intellect naturally rule over others'" [8]). But this is not as powerful an argument for there being one ruler as the workings of human *cupiditas*. None of us can desire the good of the whole because we are betrayed by our own cupidity to desire what brings us gain. We therefore need someone above us, free from this cupidity, who can adjudicate the disputes that the body politic is necessarily embroiled in as each of us follows our own self-interest. Anyone responsive to the democratic and egalitarian heritage of the West has a quick comeback to this: what guarantees this ruler's freedom from *cupiditas*? For Dante, it is the fact that the ruler *possesses everything already* that guarantees this. Virtually every appearance of the word *cupiditas* in *De Monarchia* was marked by Pound in one or another of his readings, and Pound seems to have accepted Dante's argument in favor of absolute rule.

I feel more confident in arguing that Pound endorsed Dante's argument about the supreme ruler being the only one able to rise above cupidity because when Pound did not agree with Dante, he expressed this freely. The central idea of Book 2 is that Rome is providentially intended to be the seat of the World Government, and Pound had little sympathy for this hankering on Dante's part for the Roman Empire. In Chapter 3 of Book 2, Dante argues that "Romanus populus fuit nobilissimus; ergo convenit ei aliis omnibus praeferri" (352; "the Roman people were the noblest; therefore it was right for them to be head of all the others" [33]). Pound simply puts a question mark on the side (in Barbi) to register his dissent. In Chapter 9, when Dante argues that it was God who granted victory to the Romans, Pound writes "crude prag[matism]" on the side (in Moore), suggesting, I think, that Dante has it backward, that the victories came first and then the responsibility was assigned retroactively to God. Pound tended to leave blank the chapters extolling the Romans for whom he had no particular sympathy, but one final dissent from Dante is worth recording. In Chapter 5, Dante has a long discussion of various Roman heroes from the time of the Republic and Pound writes on top (in Barbi), "no bearing on monarchy." He is right, here and elsewhere: Dante's focus to a large extent is simply on what makes for good government, not necessarily on monarchy. For Dante, there are two key elements in good government: a sense of the common good and the existence of hierarchy or subjection. Pound heavily marks Chapter 5 of Book 2 in which Dante argues that "impossibile est ius esse, bonum commune non intendens" (354; "It is impossible for right not to be directed towards the common good" [38]). But Pound also marks this passage in Chapter 7 (in Moore):

> Propter quod videmus, quod quidam non solum singulares homines, quin etiam populi, apti nati sunt ad principari, quidam alii ad subici atque ministrare; ut Philosophus adstruit in iis quae de Poli-

ticis; et talibus, ut ipse dicit, not solum regi est expediens, sed
etiam iustum, etiamsi ad hoc cogantur. (357)

Thus we notice that not only individual men but also certain whole
peoples are born to rule, whilst others are born to be ruled and
serve, as the Philosopher argues in his *Politics*; not only is it expe-
dient for the latter to be ruled, it is actually just, even though they
are forced to it. (45)[8]

These dual emphases may seem contradictory to us, but for Pound, as
for Dante, a leader is necessary to delineate the common good. For
our own good, we need to be led.

Book 3 of *De Monarchia* seems the least interesting of all to a modern reader, concerned as it is with establishing that the emperor's right
to rule proceeds directly from God and not through the Church. But
this was a crucial matter in the Middle Ages when advocates of
papal supremacy argued exactly the opposite, and Pound was surprisingly interested in the minutiae of Dante's argument to this effect. In
both copies, Book 3 is marked more heavily and consistently than
is Book 2, although less than is the most general and abstract book
of *De Monarchia*, Book 1. Dante devotes a good deal of the book
to arguing against the Donation of Constantine, that document by
which the Emperor Constantine was supposed to have granted supremacy over the West to the Pope. Valla, in the fifteenth century,
revealed the document to be a forgery, an act celebrated by Pound in
Canto 89. Dante, writing 150 years before Valla, believed the document to be genuine but denied its validity, and Pound endorsed
Dante's Ghibelline position with a real fervor here. During the discussion in Chapter 10 on the Donation, Pound writes in the margin (in
Barbi), "Constantine didn't have the power to give it away!" And he
marks in both copies the passage in Chapter 11 where Dante argues
that "usurpatio enim iuris non facit ius" (372; the "usurpation of a
right does not establish a right" [83]). So I think it fair to say that
Pound accepts both Dante's assessment of the ideal relation between
Church and Empire and his account of how the currently debased
relation of the two developed.

But why does this matter for Pound? To understand that, we have
to understand first why it mattered so much for Dante. It is not simply
a question of the relative power of Church and State, although one of
Dante's concerns in *De Monarchia* and the *Commedia* was to redress
the balance of power between Church and State and to redirect the

Church's attention away from temporal and worldly things. But what is really at stake in the question of whether the Empire has its mandate directly from God or through the Papacy is whether the Empire partakes in the sacred or not.[9] The old joke was that the Holy Roman Empire was neither Holy nor Roman nor an Empire, but for Dante it was essential that it be all three, holy most of all. As Dante states his ideal in the last chapter of *De Monarchia*, providence has designated two goals, "the first is happiness in this life," "the second the happiness of eternal life" (92). From this it follows that: "Two guides have been appointed for man to lead him to his twofold goal: there is the Supreme Pontiff who is to lead mankind to eternal life in accordance with revelation; and there is the Emperor who, in accordance with philosophical teaching, is to lead mankind to temporal happiness" (93). As these two tasks are equally sacred, equally important, so also are the two guides, Pope and Emperor: "If this is so, then God alone elects and confirms the Emperor" (93).

This was heresy for the Church in the fourteenth century, for the Church had a very different sense of these issues. *De Monarchia* was publicly condemned and burned as heretical by the Papal Legate Cardinal Bertrando a few years after Dante's death (Boccaccio, 109), but the Church's condemnation did not manage to suppress the book entirely, for Machiavelli quotes it in the *Discorsi* (303). It was subsequently put on the Papal Index of prohibited books from the time of its first publication in 1554 until 1881. (It did not help, of course, that the first publication was by a Protestant publisher in Basle, who would have been sympathetic to Dante's attacks on the Papacy.) The Church was so agitated by *De Monarchia* because Dante had struck at the heart of the argument for papal supremacy, which was that the Pope is the mediator between God and *all* men. As Kantorowicz summarizes the claims to this effect by Innocent III:

> Innocent's point of departure was that the Pope—though the successor of the prince of the apostles—was not *his* representative on earth, not the representative of any man, but the representative of Christ himself, and through him the representative of God. Direct from God himself he held the *plenitudo potestatis*, the sum total of all power, from which derive all earthly powers: the priest's, the judge's and the king's. (*Frederick the Second*, 41)

Kantorowicz makes the further point that it was the extreme and absolute form of these claims made by the Papacy that caused the supporters of the Empire such as Dante to make their counterclaims so absolute in turn. There is a sense, however, in which both sides to this battle were unknowingly shadowboxing. Although the political landscape in Dante's time was still dominated by these quarrels between Guelf and Ghibelline, pro-papal and pro-imperial forces, these quarrels were increasingly irrelevant. The underlying tendency in all this period was for the major Italian city-states and the national kingdoms outside of Italy to become increasingly powerful and independent of both Pope and Emperor alike. *De Monarchia*, thus, was written in support of a lost cause and, in hindsight, one has to be glad that both the Guelf and Ghibelline causes failed, for it was the failure of either side to achieve a clear victory that preserved the independence of city-states such as Florence. As Hans Baron has shown, there is a close connection between the Florentine resistance—both physical and intellectual—to Ghibelline imperialism, including Dante's, and the subsequent rise of civic humanism and the achievements of *quattrocento* Florence.[10]

However, although Dante's imperialism was a lost cause historically, this insistence on the holiness of Empire was, as both Frances Yates and Ernst Kantorowicz have shown, to have lasting influence on monarchical thinking through the Renaissance (Yates, 1–18; Kantorowicz, *The King's Two Bodies*). Any king—be he Holy Roman Emperor or not—would want to appropriate the argument of *De Monarchia* because, once translated from Dante's Ghibelline frame of reference, it becomes an argument for the sacredness of any form of power. Dante would obviously have objected to such a translation. As his portrayal of the French kings in the *Commedia* and elsewhere would show, he thought that the Empire alone was sacred and he objected to the rising nationalist kings who would later find his ideas so congenial. Yet an even more radical translation is necessary to explain the interest in *De Monarchia* of Ezra Pound, a man who never expressed any interest in any European monarchy, Holy Roman, French, or otherwise. In the key passage from Chapter 15 of Book 3 quoted above, Pound underlined (in Barbi) the passage about happiness in this life but ignored the part about the life everlasting, and this and the comment already quoted about "no bearing on monarchy" are the keys to Pound's particular appropriation of *De Monarchia*. Underscoring Dante's attacks on the Church but ignoring his desire for a purified Church, Pound reads *De Monarchia* as a treatise on good government arguing that a ruler is essential for good government and that the sacred duty of a ruler is to define and will the common good, to lead his people toward that good.[11] There is no moral authority external to the state who can judge it, except perhaps for the poet who can articulate in treatises such as *De Monarchia* and poems such as the *Commedia* the common good toward which the ruler should strive.

But it is also important for Pound's identification with Dante to situate *De Monarchia* back into the immediate context in which it was written. For *De Monarchia* is no abstract piece of theorizing, in the same way that Dante was no abstract political philosopher. Dante followed his own advice about politics being an art where "speculation is for the sake of action," just as surely—and as disastrously—as Pound did. The immediate occasion for *De Monarchia* was the (for Dante, tragically) short-lived revival of imperialist hopes under Henry VII (1308–1313). For all practical purposes, the dream of the Holy Roman Empire had ended with the death of Frederick II in 1250, the last emperor with an effective base in Italy as well as in Germany. Although Dante put Frederick in Hell, his references to him in *De Vulgari Eloquentio* and *Il Convivio* are positive; in an early sketch in *Il Convivio* of the imperialist ideas developed at length in *De Monarchia*, Frederick is called the "last Emperor of the Romans" (Moore, 298), indicating that Dante—writing just before Henry's coronation—does not recognize the emperors who followed as true Roman Emperors.[12]

Pound shared Dante's enthusiasm, even revising his final judgment on him, as Frederick appears as one of the just rulers in the section of *The Cantos* called *Thrones* after Dante's portraits of the just rulers in the *Paradiso*.[13] Following Frederick's death, his Ghibelline supporters transferred their support to Manfred, Frederick's illegitimate son and successor on the Sicilian—although not the Imperial—throne, and Manfred, unlike his father, makes it into Dante's purgatory.[14] Manfred has an important place in Pound's works as well; Pound took the title of his first book of poetry, *A Lume Spento*, from Manfred's speech in *Purgatorio* 3.110–145.[15] But Manfred was killed in the battle of Benevento in 1266, the year after Dante's birth. In the period of confusion that followed the death of Manfred, the municipal independence of many of the cities that would give birth to the Renaissance was more firmly established, but Dante only deplored this trend—the fundamental one of his age—and hailed the crowning of the new Emperor Henry VII as the salvation of Italy. Henry had no Italian possessions of his own the way Frederick had Sicily, but he invaded Italy, and for a moment it seemed to his supporters that he was poised to take command of the Italian peninsula. Dante surely thought so, for he was an eager supporter of Henry, writing the famous letters in praise of Henry:

> Hinc diu super flumina confusionis deflevimus, et patrocinia iusti regis incessanter implorabamus, qui satellitium saevi tyranni disperderet, et nos in nostra iustitia reformaret. Quumque tu, Caesaris et Augusti successor, Apennini iuga transiliens, veneranda signa Tarpeia retulisti, protinus longa substiterunt suspiria, lacrymarumque diluvia desierunt; et, ceu Titan praeoptatus exoriens, nova spes Latio saeculi melioris effulsit. Tunc plerique vota sua praevenientes in iubilo, tam Saturnia regna quam Virginem redeuntem cum Marone cantabant. (409; marked by Pound in Barbi)[16]

> Thus we have long sat by the rivers of confusion, yea, wept our hearts out, and have been ceaselessly entreating the protection of our rightful King, to weep away the minions of the cruel tyrant [Florence] and to restore us to the justice that is ours. And when you, the successor of Caesar and of Augustus, lightly stepped over the range of the Apennine and brought back the venerable standards of the Capitol, at once our long-drawn sighs were stopped, and the floods of our tears dried up, and, as though the Hyperion we longed for were rising, a new hope of better times shone in the eyes of Italy. Then most of us, forestalling our longings in our joy, chanted with Virgil of the Golden Age and the return of the Virgin (Justice). (109–110)

But these apocalyptic hopes (or fears) that Henry would be successful were short-lived. In 1312 he beseiged Florence, probably the chief obstacle to his plans, but failed to take it and died the next year in 1313 near Siena, effectively ending Dante's political dreams.

De Monarchia stands in a close relationship to this series of events, but scholars disagree about its precise relation, dividing on whether it dates from Henry's reign or from immediately afterward.[17] More important than the date of *De Monarchia* for Pound was the fact that Dante acted on his own advice, intervening directly in support of his political ideals by means of his writings. The aftermath is also relevant. Dante, doubly enraged over the Florentine resistance to Henry, wrote a letter to the Florentines in 1311 (Epistola VI in Moore's numbering), addressed to "the arrant scoundrels within the city" (103) and describing them as "the most empty-headed of all the Tuscans, crazy by nature and crazy by corruption" (107), that predicts and delights in the prediction that Henry will utterly destroy Florence:

> To your sorrow you will see your palaces, which you have not raised with prudence to meet your needs but have thoughtlessly enlarged for your pleasures, fallen, since no walls of a revived Troy encircle them, fallen under the battering-ram or consumed by fire. You will see your populace, now a raging mob, disorganized and divided against itself, part for, part against you, soon united against you in howls of fury, since a starving mob can know no fear. (106)

His mother city, equally outraged that Dante would throw in his lot with foreign invaders, sentenced him to death again. Dante had of course been an exile before, but his active support for the Imperial cause put him in a different category from those who had simply chosen the losing side in Florence's internecine strife. In 1311 and again in 1316, amnesties for Florentine political exiles were proclaimed, but in each case Dante was expressly excluded (Toynbee, 94–98).

After Henry's failure, Dante with all concrete political hopes extinguished concentrated on finishing the *Commedia*. But it is important to understand that the *Commedia* in all important respects is true to the political vision expressed in *De Monarchia*.[18] Just as all of the attacks on corrupt popes reinforce Dante's attacks on the Papacy, the figure of the poet Virgil brings with him all of Dante's sense of the importance and providential role of Rome and of Empire. Virgil is also "lo duca mio," Dante's guide, and everything in *De Monarchia* about the importance of hierarchy and leadership finds concrete embodiment in the vision of the *Commedia*.

Now, there is a six-hundred-year gap between Dante's praise of "duca mio" and Pound's cult of *il duce*, between Henry VII and Mussolini, but I hope the foregoing summary of *De Monarchia* and Pound's reading of it has lessened the gap.[19] Pound's economics have long been criticized as an importation of medieval preoccupations with usury, debasement of coinage, and the just price (also found prominently in the *Commedia*) into the modern age, and his support of Mussolini resembles his economics in this respect. The modern world for Pound is as driven by *cupiditas* as Dante's world was for him, and both poets incarnate this *cupiditas* in a given city: Florence for Dante and London for Pound. (And they picked well enough, for the two cities were key economic centers of their time.) But both cities came to represent not only centers of corruption but Hell for the poets,[20] and both poets represented themselves as exiled from these cities because of their opposition to this *cupiditas*. In this view, corrupt man cannot save himself because he follows his own narrow interest, not the good of the whole, and to be saved from this corruption he needs to be ruled, to find a leader. In his poem Dante finds Virgil, the representative of Empire, but in his life he finds Henry VII, the Emperor who is going to set the fractious Italians to order. Pound presents Mussolini in exactly the same terms, as the ruler above cupidity who can see and will the common good. He is the "Boss," the man who by virtue of his superior intellect and virtue is fit to rule:

> Mussolini has steadily refused to be called anything save "Leader" (Duce) or "Head of the Government," the term dictator has been applied by foreign envy, as the Tories were called cattle-stealers. It does not represent the Duce's fundamental conception of his role.
>
> His authority comes, as Eirugina [*sic*] proclaimed authority comes, "from right reason" and from the general fascist conviction that he is more likely to be right than anyone else is. (*Jefferson and/ or Mussolini*, 110)

But, as the humanist tradition always insisted, the role of the poet is to advise as well as to praise the ruler,[21] and, as Aristotle insisted in the *Rhetoric*, advice is often implicit in praise. In the same way that only Dante could fully articulate the mission of Henry VII, so too for Pound no one understands Mussolini's great task as well as he. Hence, Pound needs to speak on Rome Radio, to speak for Mussolini; but he also needs to speak *to* Mussolini, to help articulate Mussolini's mission to Mussolini himself. Mussolini himself is therefore a crucial intended audience of the poem, and this is one reason why Pound kept giving copies of his books, including *The Cantos*, to Mussolini.[22] The beginning of Canto 41 dramatizes Pound's belief in his poem's proper reception by Mussolini by depicting Pound's presentation of a copy of *A Draft of XXX Cantos* to Mussolini in Rome in 1933:

> "Ma qvesto,"
>   said the Boss, "è divertente."
> catching the point before the aesthetes had got there;
> (202; see also Stock, 389–90, and Heymann, 58–59)

And here Pound presents Mussolini's offhand comment ("this is amusing," one thing no one else has ever claimed for *The Cantos*) as if it were a perceptive reading of the poem.

So Pound, like Dante, found his ideal ruler and spoke for him, in fact sacrificed a good deal for him. But this parallel involves a number of ironies.[23] The first is how utterly ineffectual each poet was. Fortunately, Pound's ranting over the radio had no discernible effect on the war; it had no discernible effect on anything except Pound's reputation. Dante's monarchism had its influence over the long term, but in the immediate situation Dante had no effect at all, as Dante's final political epistle (Epistola VII), criticizing Henry's slowness in moving against Florence, shows clearly enough. We have no record of what Henry VII or his supporters thought of Dante and his efforts on behalf of the Imperial cause, but the Fascists entertained serious suspicions about Pound and his pro-Fascist efforts. As early as 1935, Mussolini's officials, commenting on a letter of Pound's, described him as "una mente nebbiosa, sprovvista di ogni senso della realtà" (a cloudy mind, lacking any sense of reality; quoted in Zapponi, 51). Pound had to struggle for permission to broadcast on Rome Radio, and "the Ministry of War advised against accepting Pound's offer of collaboration" (Heymann, 100). According to Camillo Pellizzi, the Italians even thought that Pound might be a double agent, an allied spy broadcasting in code, so widely divergent were Pound's broadcasts from anything else the Italians had encountered (Heymann, 99).

There is no evidence that Mussolini appreciated his Dante; Henry VII probably thought that he had a crazy Ezra Pound on his hands. And there is a certain inevitability in this, for in a sense both Dante and Pound had much more invested in their repective great rulers than the rulers did. Henry VII assuredly did not think of himself as "the Lamb of God, him who taketh away the sins of the world" (Epistola VII; 110); he was simply trying to pacify Italy and control an unruly empire. In a parallel way, although Mussolini undoubtedly thought highly of himself, he would not have been able to recognize himself in Pound's idealization of him as the Great Ruler informed by Dantescan and Confucian wisdom who is worthy of comparison to the great Chinese Emperors of the past as well as to Thomas Jefferson and John Adams.[24] Moreover, although Henry VII and Mussolini were prepared to have poets speak for them, to help popularize their cause, neither was likely to appreciate having a poet speak *to* him as a counselor. Italian rulers from Frederick II to Mussolini tried to enlist writ-

ers as supporters of their cause, but they rarely encouraged those writers' frequent attempts to become counselors as well. Pound wrote
many letters full of praise and advice to Mussolini, but Mussolini neither responded nor paid any attention to Pound's suggestions. And
here Petrarch, Machiavelli, and other humanists join Dante, Pound,
and his contemporaries Gentile and Marinetti as writers and intellectuals who, courted by power or courting power, had nonetheless no
real success in influencing the course of events.

So, all Dante and Pound managed to do by casting in their lots with
their idealized rulers was to make themselves outcasts. The causes they
supported were failures and from our perspective, deservedly so.
They won no supporters by identifying with these lost causes, and in
the process they turned on their own native countries, laying themselves open to charges of treason, although in each case they felt the
treason lay elsewhere. And I wonder—and here we can only wonder—how large an influence Dante was on Pound's dual choice to stay
in Italy after the outbreak of war with the United States in 1941 and
to resume broadcasting over Rome Radio in early 1942. The stance he
adopts—lecturing to the Americans and the British for their failure to
realize Mussolini's greatness and the justice of the axis cause; arguing
that Mussolini is the true leader whom everyone should follow; arguing that the cause of the war was the machinations of London fin-
anciers—is quite reminiscent of Dante's stance in his letter to the "arrant scoundrels" of Florence. Burckhardt perceptively refers to Dante
in his political letters as "one of the earliest publicists" (62), and here
too Pound is following in Dante's steps. Take any of the most repellent
and shocking passages in the radio speeches:

> every sane act you commit is committed in HOMAGE to Mussolini
> and Hitler. Every reform, every lurch toward the just price, to-
> ward the control of the market is an act of HOMAGE to Mussolini
> and Hitler.
>
> They are your leaders, however much you are conducted by
> Roosevelt or sold up by Churchill. You FOLLOW Hitler and Musso-
> lini in EVERY CONSTRUCTIVE act of your governments. (150)

One can hear in this an echo of Dante's frenzied attack on the Florentines:

> you, first and alone in your abhorrence of the discipline of liberty,
> have raged against the majesty of the Roman Emperor, the King

of the world and the lieutenant of God, and, on the plea of pre-
scriptive right, have denied your duty of proper obedience and
preferred to work yourselves into a frenzy of rebellion? . . . You
pitiable offshoot of Fiesole, barbarians now due for a second chas-
tisement (104 and 108).

But more important than any specific parallels is the broad one that
both poets chose the path of apparent treason in the service of what
they felt to be the higher ideals incarnated by their political heroes.
Here it could be said that Pound had a choice whereas Dante did not.
Dante was already an exile and had nothing to lose by supporting the
Henrician cause. But our perception of differences may be less important than Pound's perception of the parallel, and his self-dramatization
of his own exile status was always influenced by the parallel to Dante.[25]

And even if Pound's casting of caution (or sense) to the winds was
not modeled on Dante, it put him in exactly the same place, the place
of the outcast, the exile. Dante was the one the Florentines would not
forgive, Pound was the one we would not let out of the "bughouse."
And although Wyndham Lewis chided Pound in a letter of 1952, "To
take up a strategic position in a lunatic asylum is idiotic" (Materer,
273), Pound in his later years at St. Elizabeths derived a certain enabling energy from his incarceration: he was the one they had to lock
up to keep the truth from getting out, just as Dante had suffered exile
and condemnation. Ronald Duncan reports this conversation with
Pound in St. Elizabeths:

> "Any chance of your getting out of here?" I asked, when a very
> insane old man came and started to look down my ear.
> "No," Ezra replied, "I'm too big to go down the drain. There'd
> be comment if they let me slip away. Maybe after the election
> things may be different . . . but I don't want to get out to be assas-
> sinated." (321)

Pound was wrong here, too, of course, as Duncan immediately points
out: "Clearly this illusion that he was a menace to such power groups
arose as a compensation for being ignored by them. I had never met
any tycoon who'd even heard of Pound, let alone feared his influence"
(321). When he was finally let out, no one assassinated him, and what
comment there was on his release tended to be favorable. He immediately returned to his beloved Italy, dying in an exile that had stopped

seeming like exile, only a few miles from the Verona and Ravenna that had become new homes for Dante in his exile.

A number of critics have found in Dante's *Commedia* a pattern for *The Cantos* and, influenced by remarks of Pound to this effect, have argued that the two poems have a similar shape.[26] But the real similarity is in the shape of the two poets' political commitments, commitments that can be seen explicitly in occasional works such as Dante's letters and Pound's radio speeches and in more abstract or theoretical works such as *De Monarchia* and *Guide to Kulchur*, but which also inform the poets' epics, the *Commedia* and *The Cantos*. Dante is the poet of Ghibellinism, singing of the Empire that he hopes will be restored; Pound is the last Ghibelline, singing less of Empire than of emperors, and thinking that in Mussolini he has found the Great Ruler who would set the world aright.

These connections I am drawing between Dante's and Pound's politics can be seen most clearly in Canto 72, one of two cantos written in Italian during World War II.[27] Canto 72 is a Dantescan vision in which Pound meets the dead spirits of F. T. Marinetti, the founder of futurism who fought on the Russian Front in his sixties before dying in 1944, and then Ezzelino da Romano, whom Dante encountered in Canto 12 of the *Inferno*. Marinetti, who knew Pound for more than thirty years, asks to borrow his body so that he can go on fighting:

> "Be', sono morto,
> Ma non voglio andar in Paradiso, voglio combatter' ancora.
> Voglio il tuo corpo, con cui potrei ancora combattere"
>
> (425)
>
> (Well, I am dead,
> But I do not wish to go to Paradise, I wish to go on fighting.
> I want [to borrow] your body, with which I could fight some
> more.)

Pound tells him to borrow a younger body more suited for fighting, but tells him that he will put him in his poem instead. And this indirectly identifies Pound's poems with Marinetti's fight. Later in the canto, Pound encounters Ezzelino, the son-in-law of Frederick II and leader of the Ghibelline cause in northern Italy.[28] Ezzelino wants to go on fighting too, and his enemies are still the Guelfs, his cause still the Ghibelline:

"Calunnia Guelfa, e sempre la loro arma
Fu la calunnia"

(427)

"E 'l caso ghibellin ben seppe il fiorentino."

(430)

(Guelf calumny, and always their weapon was calumny; and the
Florentine [Dante] knew well the Ghibelline cause.)

Through juxtaposition here, Pound links the representatives of Italian
Fascism and Italian Ghibellinism, Mussolini's Italy and Dante's Italy,
and he links his political cause to Dante's. For Pound, though for almost no one else, these two Italys were one.

But to perceive this parallel and the importance of the parallel for
Pound's oeuvre is to raise new questions in turn. Dante's totalizing
political system was not at all forward-looking in its time, but it was
not six centuries out of date the way it is in ours. Why did Pound
admire Dante's system and attempt to judge the contemporary world
through this medieval instrument? And why, given Pound's acceptance of this system, did he slot Mussolini into the role of the great
ruler? Even if Pound needed a modern counterpart to Henry VII, why
did he not understand that Mussolini was not a great ruler in any sense
of the word?

Appreciating the central place of Dante and Italy in Pound's view
of the world helps us begin to answer these broader questions as well.
I am not sure that we will ever come to a full understanding of why
Pound needed (or thought the world needed) a Great Emperor to
idealize, but an understanding of certain enduring themes of Italian
literature and culture helps us understand his choice of Mussolini. Italy
was the center of civilization for Pound as it was for Dante, but a
civilization weakened then and now, as Dante had argued, in *De Monarchia* and most eloquently in Canto VI of the *Purgatorio*, by its lack
of unity and a strong effective ruler. There was a literary tradition that
Pound knew well descending from Dante through Petrarch, Machiavelli, and Leopardi lamenting the fallen greatness of Italy and calling
for the rebirth and reunification of fallen Italy, and we have already
seen Pound's response to Leopardi's as well as Machiavelli's response
to Petrarch's poems on this subject.[29] In the century between Leopardi
and Pound, Italy had been unified, but the consensus was that reuni-

fication had not led to redemption and renewed greatness. This was precisely what Mussolini claimed to be restoring. So the Ezra Pound predisposed to find his "duca mio" in Italy thought he had found him in the Duce who read Dante as avidly as did Pound and who cast himself as the regenerator of Italy in answer to Dante's and Petrarch's and Machiavelli's and Leopardi's calls. If Mussolini succeeded, moreover, Pound could go one up on Dante, presenting the actual redemption of the fallen world portayed by Dante. Pound's great ruler would not be a deferred hope, an absence in Pound's epic, the way he was in the *Commedia*. But of course Pound's attempt to go one up on Dante led to exactly the opposite: his great ruler's regime collapsed in ignominious failure, and Pound's epic of articulating the great ruler's mission was rendered historically irrelevant and drastically incoherent, a fate that never befell the *Commedia*, as its power over Pound and the other modernists should illustrate.

Moreover, despite Pound's attempt to link his cause with Dante's here, we must realize that this identification with Dante is also a revision of him. Marinetti is explicitly said to be in Paradise, so Ezzelino must be there as well. In contrast, Dante put his political allies (Ezzelino, Frederick, and others) in Hell when he felt they deserved it. Pound's refusal of a moral or ethical code apart from a political one needs to be sharply distinguished from Dante here. Pound's political reading of Dante, in short, is an overly politicized reading of him, one we could fairly call a Machiavellian reading and which recalls Machiavelli's own reading of Petrarch's "Italia mia."

But Pound would have been better off with some of Petrarch's and Machiavelli's opportunism, for then he would not have staked his life, his reputation, and his poem on Mussolini's success. He certainly would have been better off with some of their realism, for both realized that the universal absolutism of Dante's dream was not valid in their time, even though they lived much closer to Dante than did Pound. Yet neither thinker could have helped Pound avoid the two essential and most destructive features of his political commitment to Mussolini: first, the absence of any critical attitude toward power; and second, his belief (shared by Machiavelli and Vico[30]) that, despite historical change, situations did recur in ways that encouraged a direct and unproblematic imitation of past models. Only in conjunction with the first is the second belief disastrous, for without such a belief we would not have a Roman eagle on our currency with all that goes with that symbolic imitation. Pound is certainly correct to ascribe his belief in historical imitation to the Founding Fathers. Yet even so there is a troubling dissonance between the Pound who knew perfectly well that an attempt to replicate the form of the *Commedia* without change would be a disaster and the Pound who thought Dante's political vision could be replicated without modification. The disastrous failure of the political project of Pound's epic shows that the artistic theory of imitation as transformation works better—even in politics—than the alternative humanist theory of imitation as replication. Mussolini was not Dante's Great Emperor who could cleanse the world of its sins; and there was no way he could have been.

Chapter Ten

Understanding Modernist Imitation: *Mozart contra Wagner in* Ulysses

Given the logic organizing the sequence of the previous four chapters, this chapter could have come before any of them. We have been tracing Pound's and Joyce's engagement with Italian culture chronologically from their early involvement with Italian writers and thinkers to Pound's later and more disturbing involvement with Italian politics. This voyage forward through the work of the modernists has been simultaneously a voyage backward through Italian culture. As I have argued, it was later figures in Italian culture (Croce and Vico for Joyce, Leopardi for Pound) who helped them to their particular reading of Dante. And as Pound's political views solidified, his focus in Italian literature and history kept shifting backward, from Leopardi and the Risorgimento to Malatesta and the Renaissance to Dante's Ghibelline imperialism.

The focus of this chapter is some of the ways in which opera—in particular, Italian opera—influenced Joyce's aesthetic and his very different political vision. Opera is comparatively late in the continuum of Italian culture we have been exploring, and the operas crucial for Joyce come from the century between 1775 and 1875. This period is not customarily seen as one of the high points of Italian culture, and in this respect Joyce's use of opera in his major works fits into a pattern we have already seen in both Joyce and Pound, the interest in comparatively neglected or lightly regarded periods of Italian culture, particularly the *settecento* and the early *ottocento*. Pound, moreover, shares Joyce's particular interest in Italian music, although characteristically the composers he celebrates are different from Joyce's. Pound's promoting of the work of Vivaldi, Boccherini, and others, his organizing of concerts in Rapallo in the 1930s, his composing of two operas, and his great interest in the technology of photoreproduction of musical scores are all interests of his that we have not yet fully incorporated into our sense of his work.[1]

However, James Joyce's interest in music and his musical talent both far exceeded Pound's. Joyce was born into a musical Dublin family and like his father was gifted with a beautiful tenor voice. He intermittently considered going into singing—not writing—as a career (see Ellmann, *James Joyce*, 150–52, 168, 199, and 269), and his wife Nora astonished his acolytes later in life by insisting that Joyce made a mistake in choosing literature over music, which she considered his real talent: "Jim should have stuck to singing" (Maddox, 39; see also Ellmann, *James Joyce*, 169 and 561). Joyce's great and abiding love in music was, as we shall see, the Italian operatic tradition, and his first acquaintance with the Italian language would have been through opera. Arguably, it was Joyce's love of opera that led him to study Italian at Belvedere and at University College, to read Dante, to go to Trieste, and to discover all of the aspects of Italian culture that shaped his work.[2]

But there are other, more compelling, reasons to place this chapter after the other discussions of Joyce and Pound. After all, if the previous chapter had been the final chapter, I think the reasonable conclusion to draw from our story would have been that the modernist imitation of the Italians was a big mistake. Pound's project of attempting an imitation of the great achievements of Italian culture led him ultimately to disaster and folly and to thirteen years in a hospital for the criminally insane. The tragedy of this was not simply that Pound was wrong about Mussolini, for it would have been worse if he were right, if Mussolini had been the powerful leader Pound imagined him to be. (Just think how much better off we would all be if Hitler had been an opera buffa dictator like his ally; but his taste in opera was—as we shall see—instructively different.) The problem, as I think the last chapter should have shown, was the project of political/cultural imitation as Pound conceived it. Although Pound knew that poets stood in a different relation to their predecessors, he looked in the world of politics for an exact imitation or repetition of the prior model. *Jefferson and/or Mussolini* should have been called *Jefferson = Mussolini*, but history gives us no equal signs.

Ezra Pound is not the first figure discussed in this book who thought there were such equal signs, whose imitation of Italian culture was based on a desire for repetition without transformation. The Italianism of the Renaissance in a sense culminated in Queen Elizabeth, in her imitation of Laura, in her rigid conformity to the model given by Petrarch and her insistence that the rest of the court conform to that model just as rigidly. This was indeed an aping of Italian cultural forms that understandably led to a Protestant scorning of any such imitation. To have a cult of Laura, a cult of Mussolini, even a cult of Dante places one in the wrong relation to the model; and only bizarre things result from such an attempt to ignore cultural difference, to ignore all that separates one from the model.

But latent in Spenser's highly Petrarchan critique of the queen's Petrarchism was a model of imitation as transformation much more in keeping with Petrarch's stated ideal of literary imitation. And an act of imitation based upon an awareness of difference leads to very different results. Imitation does not in this case lead to a static repetition but to a play of resemblance and difference, to the creation of a new voice different from the model yet enabled by the contact with the model. Petrarchism gave rise to Queen Elizabeth's bizarre court life and quite a few terrible sonnet sequences, but it also led to the mature achievements of Spenser and Shakespeare, to works in which an indebtedness to Italian culture is freely acknowledged yet the models of Italian culture are freely transformed and surpassed. I think Joyce gives us something similar for the modernists. His use of Italian culture, at least as profound as Pound's but not so relentlessly respectful, gives us a critique of Pound's use of Dante and Mussolini and of his whole identification with Italy. Equally important, it gives us a modernist theory (or at least practice) of imitation that is compatible with— although not quite conforming to—the creative notion of imitation we have traced from Petrarch.

One way into this tangle of issues is to back up and ask how Joyce expected us to take the parallels between and among Homer, Moses, Dante, Shakespeare, and himself that we traced in Chapter 7. For although Vico did not present Dante as a conscious imitator of Homer, his system of equivalences nonetheless could set up the same kind of identification (or equal sign) that fascinated Pound. Samuel Beckett begins "Dante Bruno Vico Joyce" criticizing Vico on exactly this point: "The danger is in the neatness of identifications. . . . Giambattista Vico himself could not resist the attractiveness of such coincidence of gesture. He insisted on complete identification between the philosophical abstraction and the empirical illustration, thereby annulling the absolutism of each conception—hoisting the real unjustifiably clear of its dimensional limits, temporalising that which is extratemporal" (3).

And this passage offers a brilliant critique of Pound's theory of history, of his "complete identification between the philosophical abstraction and the empirical illustration."[3] As we have noted, Vico was educated within the humanist tradition of seeing resemblances between antiquity and the present and of urging the present to imitate antiquity, to create more such resemblances. His system of historical repetition can easily be converted into a system for urging historical repetition, historical imitation. This is surely how Pound would have read him, although Pound was temperamentally unsuited to anything quite as tidy as Vico's theory of the three ages.

But this is not how Joyce read Vico or how he would want us to take his work. Questioned later in life about how seriously he took Vico's cycles, he responded with a revealing evasiveness: "I would not pay overmuch attention to these theories beyond using them for all they are worth" (*Letters I*, 241). Joyce, as aware as Beckett of the perils of identification, seems to have tried to do something else, to make connections that nonetheless are not identifications. Leopold Bloom is not Odysseus, *Ulysses* is not the *Odyssey*. Yet they are connected. How? And why?

Curiously, Pound never expressed any interest in this aspect of *Ulysses*, arguing that the "parallels with the *Odyssey* are mere mechanics, any blockhead can go back and trace them" (Read, 250). Nonetheless, the critical tradition that has sought to answer these questions has largely assimilated Joyce's distinctive practice to a Pound-influenced sense of the relation between past and present. That tradition was initiated by T. S. Eliot's famous review of *Ulysses*, "*Ulysses*, Order and Myth." In "*Ulysses*, Order and Myth," Eliot first called attention to an important aspect of *Ulysses*, an aspect he called the "mythical method." Any reader of *Ulysses* notices how the narrated actions represented in *Ulysses* are in important respects parallel to those of other narratives. The *Odyssey* is of course the most obvious such parallel text, made obvious by the title of the book, but *Hamlet, Don Giovanni*, and other works of art are relevant here as well. Eliot considered this "parallel use of the *Odyssey*" of "great importance," having "the importance of a scientific discovery" (270). Since Eliot's seminal essay, his term "the mythical method" (or, more typically, the "mythic method") has passed into general use among Joyce critics, and our sense of the relationship between the *Odyssey* and *Ulysses* has been immeasurably enriched and deepened by the work of many critics. But I think in order to recover Joyce's own sense of his relation to his models, we need to look critically at Eliot's term mythical method, to ask questions about where Joyce may have taken the method and then to see what relation to his models Joyce wants to create for his work.

Eliot's term, "the mythical method," suggests that there is only one such method, but the kinds of parallels employed by Joyce differ in the sense that the characters in *Ulysses* differ in their awareness of them. No one in the book betrays any awareness that he or she is (or is parallel to) a character in the *Odyssey*; this is a parallel entirely imposed from without by the author. Mulligan quotes a Homeric tag and thinks of himself as Greek, but one role he would not have cast himself as is Antinous. There is more internal awareness of *Hamlet*. Haines in "Telemachus" says that "this tower and these cliffs here remind me somehow of Elsinore" (*Ulysses*, 1.566–67), and of course a full chapter, "Scylla and Charybdis," is devoted to Stephen's theory about *Hamlet*. But his theory does not establish a parallel between his situation and *Hamlet*. It writes him out of the play altogether, creating a portrait of Shakespeare remarkably—although Stephen cannot know this—like Leopold Bloom.

The parallel to *Don Giovanni* is quite different in this respect.[4] Leopold Bloom is unaware that he is Ulysses or Hamlet's father but is very much aware—painfully aware—that he is playing a role in *Don Giovanni*. In fact, much of the drama connected with his day is caught up in his reflections on what role from *Don Giovanni* he is playing. Is he Masetto, the cuckolded fiancé/husband of Zerlina, to Molly's Zerlina and Boylan's Don Giovanni? This is suggested by one phrase from *Don Giovanni* that runs through his mind much of the day, "voglio e non vorrei." This is a misquotation of one of Zerlina's lines in "Là ci darem," the seduction duet between Zerlina and Don Giovanni, "vorrei e non vorrei" (I would like [to go with Don Giovanni] and I wouldn't like). She does go willingly with Don Giovanni (although for a variety of reasons the seduction is never consummated), as Molly goes with Boylan, but she also returns to Masetto in the end, and Bloom, thinking of himself as Masetto, may be reciting that line in the hope of a subsequent reconciliation. Or is he the Commendatore, to earn his revenge in a bloody finale, as is suggested by the phrase he repeats nearly as often, "a cenar teco m'invitasti," spoken to Don Giovanni by the Commendatore returned from the grave in the thunderous finale of the opera? Or is he too a Don Giovanni, with Martha Clifford and Gerty McDowell as his conquests? Here, Bloom is in advance of Stephen in their degree of self-knowledge, for Stephen does not realize the extent to which he too has been playing a role from *Don Giovanni*, that of the comic servant Leporello. Just as Leporello begins the opera singing of his desire to serve no longer, "non voglio più servir," in "Telemachus" Stephen reflects to himself and then complains to Haines about his servant-like role.

Robert Martin Adams has argued that Bloom's use of the word *voglio* instead of *vorrei* in the phrase "voglio e non vorrei" is intended to make us think of the opening scene of Mozart's opera (71). He does not relate this to Stephen, however, but to Bloom, seeing Bloom as Leporello-like in his servitude to Molly. But I think Joyce has already directed us to this opening scene of *Don Giovanni*, in the opening scene of his work. In "Telemachus," Stephen first thinks to himself, "I am another now and yet the same. A servant too. A server of a servant" (*Ulysses*, 1.311–12), and then says to Haines, "I am the servant of two masters" (*Ulysses*, 1.638). The second, more frequently quoted phrase is usually taken simply as a reference to Carlo Goldoni's *Il servitore di due padrone*. The reference to Goldoni is clear and helps establish the theatrical and Italianate dimension of *Ulysses* I am exploring here, but Truffaldino, the rogue-servant in Goldoni's comedy, only acquires his two masters across the course of the play; Stephen's complaining about his servitude in the opening scene is far closer in situation to Leporello.

The reason Bloom—unlike Stephen—knows he is in a version of *Don Giovanni* is his wife's citation of it. He suspects that something is afoot between Molly and Boylan at least partially because the two of them are singing "Là ci darem" at home that day. In other words, they are acting out a parallel between their lives and *Don Giovanni*, the kind of parallel that elsewhere obtains between the lives of these characters and the *Odyssey* and *Hamlet*. But they are aware of the parallel: Molly lets Leopold know what is going on with strategic indirection, precisely by citing *Don Giovanni*, by telling him what they are going to sing. Bloom, aware of what they are to sing and what this means, thinks about *Don Giovanni* all day.

There is thus a crucial difference between the relationship between *Ulysses* and *Don Giovanni* and between *Ulysses* and other works. The difference is that Joyce introduces the other parallels into the narrative; the parallel between Mozart's opera and *Ulysses* is built into the texture of the novel largely and consciously by the characters themselves.

Other characters quote Shakespeare and Homer as Molly and Bloom quote *Don Giovanni*, but the difference is that Joyce alone is fully aware of the pertinence of the other works. Molly and Bloom quote *Don Giovanni* precisely because of their awareness of its pertinence.

If this reading is at all correct, it suggests where Joyce took the "mythic method," or method of extended parallelism, so prominent in *Ulysses*. The "mythic method" comes from the normal use of opera arias by Dubliners, at least by musical Dubliners such as the Bloom family and the Joyce family. (And stories from *Dubliners* such as "A Mother" and "The Dead" help specify the milieu I have in mind here.) Opera arias were commonly cited as an indirect way of commenting on the situation at hand in the same way that Molly and Bloom cite *Don Giovanni*. And the very indirectness of this marks this as especially useful in emotionally charged situations such as that faced by the Blooms on 16 June 1904.

That this use of opera is not Joyce's invention is shown clearly enough by two scenes in George Moore's 1898 novel *Evelyn Innes*. Close to the opening of the novel, Evelyn's mother, an opera singer,

> held out her hands and looked at them, striving to read in them the progress of her illness. Evelyn wondered why, just at that moment, her father had turned from the bedside overcome by sudden tears. . . . when father and daughter met in the parlour . . . Evelyn asked why her mother had looked at her hands so significantly.
>
> He said that it was thus her mother foreshadowed Violetta's death [in Verdi's *La Traviata*], when Armand's visit is announced to her. (5)[5]

And later, when Evelyn, who has left her father and also become an opera star, returns home and wants to reconcile herself to her father, she sings and acts out

> the long-expected scene, the scene in the third act of the "Valkyrie" which she had always played while divining the true scene which she would be called upon to play one day. . . . she threw herself at her father's feet, and the celebrated phrase, so plaintive, so full of intercession, broke from her lips, "Was the rebel act so full of shame that her rebellion is so shamefully scourged? . . . Oh tell me, father, look in mine eyes." . . . She knelt at her father's or

at Wotan's feet—she could not distinguish; all limitations had been razed. (212)

But these scenes—although they show the typicality of Molly's citation of *Don Giovanni*—are not Joyce's source. Joyce did not need to read George Moore to portray Molly's use of "Là ci darem." When Joyce's father wanted to be reconciled to his son in 1909, what he did was to sing an appropriate aria:

> The sight of his son and grandson made John Joyce reconsider his old objections to his son's elopement. He took James for a walk into the country, and stopped with him at a village inn for a drink. There was a piano in the corner; John Joyce sat down at it and without comment began to sing. "Did you recognize that?" he asked James, who replied, "Yes, of course, it's the aria sung by Alfredo's father in *Traviata*." John Joyce said nothing more, but his son knew that peace had been made. (Ellmann, *James Joyce*, 276–7)[6]

What I would like to suggest is that it is from this use of opera by the Joyce family that Joyce developed what later became known as the mythic method. Given its origin, the mythic method should probably be known instead as the operatic method.

Now, there is of course a difference betwen singing a single aria and rewriting the *Odyssey*: a difference between parallelism and extended parallelism. But here too opera—or at least a literary use of opera that Joyce knew well—plays a key role. I have already cited George Moore's 1898 novel *Evelyn Innes*, and George Moore, the preeminent Irish novelist in Joyce's youth, is a crucial influence on Joyce's literary development and someone Joyce both borrowed from and reacted against.[7] Moore's book of stories, *The Untilled Field*, provided a model for *Dubliners*, yet Joyce felt, quite rightly, that his apprehension of fact (in particular, Irish fact) was superior to Moore's. He was appalled that Moore has a character in *The Untilled Field* look up the train schedule from Bray to Dublin since anyone living in Bray for three years as the character had would know that the trains run regularly (*Letters II*, 71).[8] And certainly the accuracy of that kind of detail in *Ulysses* far surpasses anything in Moore's "realist" fiction.

A larger but similarly agonistic relationship is established by Joyce in *Ulysses* to the work in which Moore adumbrates—to use Eliot's term—the mythic method, his three volume memoir of the Irish Literary Revival, *Hail and Farewell*. Today, we read *Hail and Farewell*—if we read it at all—for the stories about the Revival, the wickedly funny anecdotes about Yeats and others that made Yeats so furious and made Moore *persona non grata* in Ireland after the 1911 publication of the first volume of *Hail and Farewell*. But Moore had more serious ambitions for the book. He presents himself in *Hail and Farewell* as the figure destined to revive Irish culture, and he attempts to establish this theme precisely by parallels between himself and various mythic figures, derived mostly from Wagner's operas. As William Blissett has said, making precisely the connection I am trying to establish here: "George Moore uses Wagnerian parallels as often as James Joyce was to use Homeric parallels but without Joyce's appearance of system" ("George Moore and Literary Wagnerianism," 57). Toward the end of the third and final volume of *Hail and Farewell, Vale*, Moore makes these parallels explicit:

> And to heighten my inspiration I looked toward the old apple-tree, remembering that many had striven to draw forth the sword that Wotan had struck into the tree about which Hunding had built his hut. Parnell, like Sigmund, had drawn it forth, but Wotan had allowed Hunding to strike him with his spear. And the allegory becoming clearer I asked myself if I were Siegfried, son of Sigmund slain by Hunding, and if it were my fate to reforge the sword that lay broken in halves in Mimi's cave. (210)

As if in answer to his question, he then hears in his garden the music from that part of the *Ring*, and Moore prints the musical phrase from this part of Wagner's score at this point in *Vale*. This is indeed very close to the mythic method as described by Eliot, and in some ways Eliot's language is a more accurate description of *Hail and Farewell* than it is of *Ulysses*, for in place of Joyce's complex interelations among a number of different, mostly non-mythic texts, in Moore we have a relatively straightforward parallel between the present and a single myth, and the relation is established in order to redeem that fallen present.[9]

But Moore's redemptive project is not a triumphal success, and Moore concludes across *Hail and Farewell* that the Irish are not ready for redemption. First, he sees Catholicism as the great barrier to artistic creation in Ireland, so he converts to Protestantism.[10] Then, seeing this as insufficient, he decides that the redemption of the Irish requires his exile as well: "I felt I must leave my native land and my friends for the sake of the book; a work of liberation I divined it to be—liberation from ritual and priests, a book of precept and example, a turning-point in Ireland's destiny" (*Vale*, 257). This reads a lot like the end of *A Portrait*, which was being reworked by Joyce in the years *Hail and Farewell* was being published. Stephen resembles Moore both in his Wagnerian desire to redeem his nation through art and create the un-created conscience of his race and in his sense that this artistic redemp-tion requires an antagonistic relationship between the artist and his people, that "the shortest way to Tara was via Holyhead" (*A Portrait*, 250). Moreover, Stephen's itinerary via Holyhead at the end of *A Por-trait* was clearly modeled on George Moore's. Other Irish writers—Yeats, Wilde, Shaw—had conquered London, but it was Moore, "lec-turer on French letters to the youth of Ireland" (*Ulysses*, 9.1101–2), who had lived in Paris and cultivated a "Latin Quarter" sensibility. And this has a direct connection to his Wagnerianism, for although, as William Blissett has said, "George Moore wore his Wagnerianism like a rash" ("James Joyce in the Smithy of His Soul," 101), it was a French Wagnerianism Moore represented: "what Moore discovered and communicated in his Paris phase was not Wagner himself and his music—that was to come later—but French literary Wagnerianism" (Blissett, "George Moore," 59–60). His good friend Edouard Dujar-din, the same Dujardin who was such an influence on Joyce, was the great French Wagnerian and editor of the *Revue Wagnerienne*.[11]

Moreover, despite the less than absolute success of his trip to Paris between *A Portrait* and *Ulysses*, Stephen is still a thorough young Wagnerian in *Ulysses*. Things are never as simple in *Ulysses* as they are in Moore's straightforward imitation of Wagner in *Hail and Fare-well*, but Joyce deploys Moore's Wagnerian typology in *Ulysses*, letting us know of Moore's ambitions yet deflecting them. In "Scylla and Charybdis," it is noted that "Our national epic has yet to be written, Dr Sigerson says. Moore is the man for it" (*Ulysses*, 9.309–10). One imagines Stephen silently dissenting from this judgment, yet Stephen's epic ambitions are Wagnerian in precisely Moore's fashion.[12]

In "Circe," when Stephen commits his "sin against the light" by smashing the lamp, he yells "*Nothung!*" (*Ulysses*, 15.4242). Nothung is the name of the sword Siegfried reforges in the *Ring*, the sword that Moore thought he was reforging in *Hail and Farewell*. The echo here is too close to be anything but deliberate, and Stephen's actions here align Joyce's *Ulysses* with *Hail and Farewell* or, more precisely, align Stephen and Moore as Wagnerian artists. This helps specify the difference between Stephen and Bloom in some useful ways: Bloom loves Mozart and knows that he is a character in *Don Giovanni* (if he is not quite sure which one); Stephen may be acting like an unheroic character in *Don Giovanni* but he wants to be Siegfried, the heroic revolutionary artist in the *Ring*, taking arms against the world.

Now, how does Joyce ask us to evaluate the Wagnerianism of Stephen and George Moore and the redemptive project of the mythic method? We may begin to answer this by noting that George Moore held Wagner to be supreme and had nothing but contempt for the Italian operatic repertoire. Evelyn Innes shocks her fellow music students in Paris by making fun of Donizetti's *Lucia di Lammermoor* and other standards of the *bel canto* repertoire they and their teacher aspired to sing (149); later when an established opera singer, she confesses that she has sung almost no Mozart, has sung in only one Italian opera, and thinks Verdi's *Il Trovatore* "very common" (442). But of course she has sung almost every one of Wagner's operas,[13] and Rose Leicester, the young woman who goes to Bayreuth in *The Lake* to hear the *Ring*, "knows" that the *Ring* is "the greatest musical work the world has ever known" (174). Moore is broadcasting his own opinions here, as *Hail and Farewell* shows. Moore had made the pilgrimage that Rose Leicester made many times, and a large portion of the first volume of *Hail and Farewell*, *Ave* (127–69), is dedicated to a trip made to Bayreuth with Edward Martyn.

Joyce's taste in opera was precisely the opposite, as any number of remarks in the letters or recorded in memoirs show. As early as 1907, he attended a performance of *Götterdämmerung* in Rome and disliked it (*Letters II*, 214, 217–18; Ellmann, *James Joyce*, 240); in 1909, he sang "at a concert in the quintet from *Die Meistersinger*, an opera he regarded as 'pretentious stuff' " (Ellmann, *James Joyce*, 269). Later, he criticized Wagner to one of his pupils, Oscar Schwarz, and told him he preferred Bellini (Ellmann, *James Joyce*, 382), precisely the kind of composer to whom a Wagnerian such as Moore objected. This is not an isolated remark of Joyce's, as later in Zurich Joyce told the young composer Philipp Jarnach that he was more interested in Donizetti and Bellini than in modern music (Ellmann, *James Joyce*, 409).[14] Finally, he went to see *Tannhäuser* in 1929 when he was beginning his championship of John Sullivan; overwhelmed as he was by Sullivan's singing, he still had nothing but contempt for the opera: "What sort of a fellow is this Tannhäuser who, when he is with Saint Elizabeth, longs for the bordello of Venusberg, and when he is at the bordello longs to be with Saint Elizabeth?" (Ellmann, *James Joyce*, 619). So Stephen Dedalus in his Wagnerianism not only imitates George Moore; he shares his taste—not Joyce's. Joyce's operatic tastes remained—despite his modernist commitments in literature—essentially the Italian repertoire of his youth, from Mozart and Rossini through Bellini to Verdi. Louis Gillet summarizes the musical tastes of his friend Joyce:

> He could not stand modern music and except for *Die Meistersinger* and some arias from *The Flying Dutchman* he had a dislike for Wagner; the Tetralogy irritated him. "Operetta music," he used to say. On the other hand, he doted upon singing, adoring Rossini, Meyerbeer, Verdi, *La Gazza Ladra*, *William Tell*, *Muette*, *La Juive*, *L'Africaine*. He knew how many high-C's there were in all the scores. He took the train for Lyon, Brussels, Milan, any time that one of his favourite operas was performed there. He was mad about *bel canto*. (77)

Wyndham Lewis caught this well in *The Childermass* by naming his James Joyce character Belcanto (178), and if any character in *Ulysses* represents Joyce's musical tastes it is not Stephen but Bloom.

This has larger implications for how we read *Ulysses* that are worth pursuing. I have just argued that Moore's Wagnerianism is an important source for Joyce's mythic method, one more piece of evidence that the mythic method is really the operatic method. But the difference in musical taste between Moore and Joyce is not incidental, for a critique of Wagnerianism lies behind Joyce's use of *Hail and Farewell* and of *Don Giovanni* in *Ulysses*.[15] Critics have seen clearly enough that his use of Wagner and Moore in *Ulysses* was mock heroic, but they have not related Joyce's use of *Don Giovanni* to his critique of Wagnerianism, nor have they seen the full implications of this critique.[16] This network of allusions works together in ways that help us read Stephen's actions (and the politics of those actions) throughout the novel.

Where does Stephen's Wagnerianism get him, after all? All he achieves by his Wagnerian act of revolt is a little damage to the lamp's chimney. "The ruin of all time and space" is surely not achieved here, only one more debt incurred by Stephen and paid by Bloom. In the same way, both the ending and the reception of *Hail and Farewell* shows that Moore's drama of identification with Siegfried was more comic than tragic. Neither Stephen nor Moore quite lives up to the role of Siegfried. They identify with the role of Siegfried, only to fall short of its expectations. The mythic method here does not redeem the present by the past as much as measure the difference between the present and the past. But Joyce does not ask us to criticize Stephen for this failure: the real tragedy would have been his succeeding. For those who identify with their roles are the ones to watch out for in *Ulysses*: the Citizen who thinks he is Cuchulain reborn is the real danger to the body politic. The danger depicted in *Ulysses* is not Stephen's failure to redeem Ireland by myth; the danger is the redemptive project itself.

This is precisely what Nietzsche perceived and criticized in Wagnerianism, in *The Case of Wagner, Nietzsche contra Wagner* (both of which Joyce owned), and his other anatomies of Wagnerianism, and Joyce's critique of Wagner is clearly indebted to Nietzsche's critique.[17] The closing words of *Parsifal* are "redemption for the redeemer"; Nietzsche quotes these words only to plea for "redemption from the redeemer" (*The Case of Wagner*, translated by Kaufmann, 182).[18] Wagnerianism is a system of identification, identification with the role: George Moore understood this well enough in the scene from *Evelyn Innes* we have already quoted from when he writes "all limitations had been razed." Wagner called his son Siegfried, after all, and at Bayreuth, one does not applaud performances of *Parsifal*. To put this another way, although not a way in which Nietzsche would have put it, Wagner's operas are not theater: they do not permit space between the actor and his role, the space of acting, the classical space of mimesis. There is no irony, no play, in the Wagnerian mythic method: only a straightforward identification that "razes" the gap between mythic past and the present in need of redemption. In a phrase that Joyce may have had in mind while writing the chapter in which he has Stephen call out "*Nothung!*," for Nietzsche Wagner uses "Music in the form of Circe" (*The Case of Wagner*, translated by Ludovici, 39). And there is a close relation between this absence of irony and Wagner's desire to resurrect Germanic myths and cultural origins.

Wagner's insistence on the Nordic roots of his art helped shape one of the directions of anti-Wagnerianism, which is to respond to his northern cultural geography with a southern cultural geography. This took shape even before Nietzsche, when Wagner sent Schopenhauer an elaborately bound copy of the *Ring*. In response, as Raymond Furness tells the story, "the philosopher suggested that Wagner should cultivate his poetic, rather than his musical, talents. Preferring Rossini, Schopenhauer had little time for *Zukunftsmusik* and indulged in his ambition to play through all of Rossini's work on the flute" (5).[19] And this is in miniature Nietzsche's critique as well. Nietzsche presents Wagner as all German, all too German. Criticizing young German enthusiasts for Wagner, Nietzsche writes: "Are they not one and all, like Wagner himself, on *quite intimate terms* with such bad weather, with German weather! Wotan is their God: but Wotan is the God of bad weather" (Ludovici, 32). And he straightforwardly links Wagner to the resurgent German state and its dreams of domination and power: "Wagner's stage requires one thing only—Germans! . . . The definition of a German: an obedient man with long legs. . . . There is a deep significance that the arrival of Wagner should have coincided with the rise of the 'Empire' [*Reich*]: both phenomena are proof of one and the same thing—obedience and long legs" (Ludovici, 34). Thus, for Nietzsche the total work of art, the *Gesamtkunstwerk*, is related to the total state; and the system of identification central to Wagnerianism is very dangerous indeed.

Nietzsche's antidote to all this Northern mysticism is southern good sense and good weather: "*Il faut méditerraniser la musique*" (Ludovici, 5). His explicit contrast to Wagner in *The Case of Wagner* is Bizet's *Carmen*. Although it is mentioned in Joyce's play *Exiles, Carmen* is not prominent in *Ulysses*.[20] But Bizet here is a figure for a whole musical tradition and, more important, an attitude toward art that Nietzsche finds generally in Mediterranean and specifically in Italian culture. Mozart is another figure Nietzsche repeatedly opposes to Wagner as is shown by the following passages in which Nietzsche is caricaturing the Wagnerian/Germanic attitude toward music:

> The hunt for low excitement of the senses, for so-called beauty, has enervated the Italians: let us remain German! Even Mozart's attitude to music was—as Wagner said to comfort *us*—at bottom frivolous.
>
> Let us never admit that music "serves recreation"; that it "exhilarates"; that it "gives pleasure." *Let us never give pleasure!* (Kaufmann, 169)

> Mozart's cheerful, enthusiastic, delightful and loving spirit?
> He who fortunately was no German, and whose seriousness is a charming and golden seriousness and not by any means that of a German clodhopper. (Ludovici, 63)

Mozart was Austrian, of course, not German, and this biographical fact, the language of most of his operas, and the spirit of his music leads Nietzsche to identify him with the Italians here. Joyce's aesthetic seems even more opposed to this Germanism of heroic deeds and high seriousness than Nietzsche's, and the use of Mozart's *Don Giovanni* in *Ulysses* functions precisely as an antidote (on Nietzschean lines) to heroic Wagnerianism.

For Joyce, comedy was the greatest form of art, and I think Bloom's description of his own musical taste as "favouring preferably light opera of the *Don Giovanni* description" (*Ulysses*, 16.1752–53) is not Joyce's condescending description of a musical taste inferior to his own but a provocative description of his own taste. Significantly, in the same passage Bloom expresses Joyce's taste exactly by criticizing Wagner as "grand in its way [but] a bit too heavy for Bloom" (1735–36) and praising Mozart, Rossini, and Meyerbeer. The greatest art for Joyce is not the grandest or heaviest, but the lightest and most pleasing. Why can't we, Joyce asks as well as Nietzsche, admit that music serves recreation and gives pleasure? Music is a—possibly the—supreme art for Joyce precisely because of its ability to give pleasure, and for him the great tradition of music was the supposedly "frivolous" music of the Italian tradition, in which he as well as Nietzsche included the music of Mozart. Joyce as a Triestine would have been alive to the Italian-language culture of the Austrian Empire,[21] and I think for him, as well as for Nietzsche, *Don Giovanni* functions as a token of Italianness.

What this overlap between Nietzsche's critique of Wagner and Joyce's use of Mozart suggests is that although the "mythic method" is operatic in origin, one needs to distinguish between two different kinds of operatic methods: the Wagnerian, Germanic drama of identification that seeks in art a mode of redeeming the fallen, modern world; and a less serious (or at least less solemn), more Italianate and Mozartian use of opera in which the only redemption being offered is that redemption from the redeemer asked for by Nietzsche.

For the path of Wagnerianism and heroic, redemptive art is very dangerous, as the history of the twentieth century shows clearly enough. Nietzsche was perfectly correct in seeing a connection between nationalism, state power, and the theater of identification, as can be shown clearly enough by Adolf Hitler's Wagnerianism. Hitler thought he was Siegfried and, unfortunately, the Germans took him more seriously than the Irish took George Moore. And although Pound disliked Wagner as much as Joyce did, his Fascist adaptation of the mythic method is identical in spirit. *The Cantos* depend for their coherence on a precise set of parallelisms between figures in the past and the present, and, as we have seen for Pound, there is always simply an equation between Malatesta or Jefferson and Mussolini, never any play, never any irony in the identification. This shows that Nietzsche's Italianism in itself is no solution, but what Nietzsche was looking for—which I think Joyce gives us—was an appreciation of Italian culture that is not a Wagnerian cult of it.

I think Joyce saw all the dangers of Wagnerian art simply by seeing the use of Irish myth by the Irish nationalists. It is no accident that Padraic Pearse had a "cult of Cuchulain," that his identification with Cuchulain was total in the ways already explored. The Citizen in "Cyclops" provides a handy example of such a local (if unknowing) Wagnerian, someone dedicated to making the ancient myths of his nation come back to life. And it is absolutely essential to an understanding of *Ulysses*, particularly its political dimensions, that we see the difference between Joyce's invocations of the past and this system of identification we can see in the Citizen and in the Irish nationalists from Moore and Yeats to Padraic Pearse. The term *mythic method* obscures this crucial difference, but it is the Citizen—not James Joyce—who seems to embody the mythic method as Eliot defines it.

Joyce does not provide his characters with systems of identification; he provides them with roles they can try on (and take off). Here it is essential that Bloom might be Masetto, the Commendatore, and Don Giovanni—at different times or even at the same time. Because roles are multiple in *Ulysses*, there is always in *Ulysses* an ironic space between the character and the role donned for the occasion. This is one reason why the parallel between *Ulysses* and the *Odyssey* is redoubled by other parallels, particularly to the theatrical texts, *Hamlet, Il servitore di due padrone*, and *Don Giovanni*. For *Hamlet* is a play about someone who does not know what role to take on; *Don Giovanni* is an opera about someone who can take on any role the occasion demands. Both Mozart's opera and Goldoni's play are full of masks, disguises, and characters who take on assumed identities or shift roles with one another. The world of Mozart and Goldoni—the world of eighteenth-century Italian theater—is not a world in which differences are razed, not a world that demands identification with the role; and the way Joyce uses *Don Giovanni* in *Ulysses* is in perfect keeping with this. The world of *Don Giovanni* is a mask the world of *Ulysses* can take on when it is convenient; it is not a system of ideological identifications that rigorously control action in the present.

So, while Joyce took enough of the mythic method from operatic sources that it should be called the "operatic method," Joyce's use of this method needs to be sharply distinguished from the use made by most of his contemporaries, including Eliot and Pound. This is a further reason to call Joyce's method operatic, for surely his sense of play, of masking, of the expanded possibilities of having more than one role, and his critique of the totalitarianism latent in the prescription of a single role, is more characteristic of the world of opera than of the world of myth. That is, as long as one's taste in opera is Joycean: the Italian tradition of opera from Mozart and Rossini to Verdi, not the Germanic tradition from Beethoven to Wagner. Too much Wagner can be hazardous for your health, and this influence of Italian opera on Joyce's work is simply one more of the myriad ways Italy and Italian culture was fundamental in shaping Joyce's mature work.

To speak, then, of imitation in Joyce's work is to speak of a very different kind of imitation from that found in his fellow modernists. Beckett was surely correct when he warned of a danger in overly neat identifications, and this is one reason why Joyce never allows any neat identifications. He does this in several ways. First, on good Vichian lines, he doubles and redoubles the parallels he adduces by overlapping further parallels with *Don Giovanni* and *Hamlet* on top of the parallel with the *Odyssey*. But Pound did this as well, adducing Chinese as well as Italian and American parallels to his *duce*. More importantly, Joyce doubles the parallels within each parallel so that no one-for-one correspondence is ever possible: because Bloom is not only the Commendatore but also Masetto and Don Giovanni, he can never be simply and purely one of these figures. Moreover, and this may come more easily for him as a novelist, Joyce does not allow his characters to slip away into abstractions. Here, the contrast to Pound is clear enough, as despite Pound's love of concrete particulars, his identifications often overpower the individual. He obviously never saw Mussolini for himself, so intent was he on seeing him in terms of someone else. In contrast, Stephen Dedalus may think that he is Siegfried, but we know all too well that he is Stephen Dedalus, B.A. Related to this is the comic nature of Joyce's art. Because Joyce never lost his belief that comedy was the greatest form of art and that literature like music should give pleasure, he simply did not take himself as seriously (or perhaps as solemnly) as Pound did. *Ulysses*, his greatest work and the great masterpiece of twentieth-century literature in English, is the masterpiece it is because it delights as well as instructs. And this is simply another respect in which Joyce is closer to Dante; Dante's masterpiece is a *Commedia*, after all, and Joyce with his love and knowledge of opera and theatre seemed to be able to understand and build on that fact better than his contemporaries. Finally, and most importantly, Joyce's art is theatrical and he has a crucial sense of the importance of theatricality for life as well as art. We all play roles and take on masks, but we can take off these masks and take on new ones. Writers imitate the past in Joyce's world as much as they do in Pound's, for the cultural heritage is our repository of roles, and the cultural heritage they both valued the most was the Italian. Yet the mode of imitation is crucially different, for Joyce never lost sight—as Pound sometimes did—of the difference between the model and himself or between the actor and his role. He was not Prince Hamlet, nor was meant to be.

Conclusion

In Search of the True Dantescan Voice

One of the ways we could describe an aspiration of virtually all the major modernist writers in English is that they were all trying to write the *Commedia* of the twentieth century. Although this study has stressed a range of Italian influences on English literature and is titled *Imitating the Italians*, there is a sense in which Yeats, Wyndham Lewis, Beckett, and Eliot, in addition to Pound and Joyce, were simply imitating *the* Italian, Dante Alighieri. Given that aspiration, I would like to conclude by investigating the extent to which any of them succeeded.

Two aspects of Dante's achievement were widely admired among the modernists, the encyclopaedic scope of his epic, the sense in which a total vision of life is to be found in the *Commedia*, and his architectonic construction, the major form achieved by the *Commedia*. Eliot expressed this double sense when he wrote in *The Sacred Wood*, "Dante's is the most comprehensive, and the most *ordered* presentation of emotions that has ever been made" (168). The modernists were interested in his emotions, the content of his poem, but the emphasis in this passage was given by Eliot and properly so: it was the ordering of those emotions that particularly impressed most modernist readers of Dante. These two are related, of course, for part of his total vision is his ability to place or judge everyone in one of the three realms of Hell, Purgatory, and Paradise, and the division of his poem into three interrelated and densely articulated canticles, one dedicated to each realm, is the best expression of that sense of form. Nonetheless, this division of Dante's achievement into an ideological and a formal dimension is warranted because some modernists successfully imitated one of these dimensions of Dante's achievement but not the other. Pound and Joyce have been the modernist writers whose imitations of Italian culture have occupied our attention here, and what I would like to suggest is that each successfully imitated Dante in one of these respects but not in the other. Pound's Dante and Joyce's Dante are thus interesting mirror images of each other, and the comments of each writer on the other's relation to Dante indicate his awareness of the limits of the other writer's imitation of Dante.

Pound played an important role in seeing *A Portrait of the Artist as a Young Man* and *Ulysses* into print, so as Joyce began writing what was to become *Finnegans Wake*, he was naturally anxious to secure Pound's assistance again. But Pound's reaction to the manuscript sent to him in 1926 was not positive:

> Dear Jim: MS arrived this A.M. All I can do is wish you every possible success.
>
> I will have another go at it, but up to present I make nothing of it whatsoever. Nothing so far as I can make out, nothing short of divine vision or a new cure for the clapp can possibly be worth all the circumambient peripherization.
>
> Doubtless there are patient souls, who will wade through anything for the sake of the possible joke. (Read, 228)

Words for Pound always have a function, and although these remarks are funny, comedy is not one of the functions of language Pound ranked very highly. And here we return to the different conceptions of Dante, at bottom differing generic conceptions, held by Pound and Joyce. Pound always emphasized the lyric and epic aspects of Dante's works, not the dramatic or comic, and although he praised the Flaubertian satire he saw in *Ulysses*, he did not approve of the less didactic comedy that dominates *Finnegans Wake*. The highest function of language for Pound is that of the "divine vision," and clearly Pound is faulting Joyce here for not living up to that task.

Pound is certainly right here in discerning no "divine vision" in *Finnegans Wake*, no attempt to rival the *Paradiso* in sublimity, although whether he is right to condemn the work for that absence is another matter. And this difference of opinion points to an important difference between Joyce's and Pound's sense of Dante. What Pound admired about the *Commedia* was the divine vision, the confidence with which Dante assigns everyone his proper place in the cosmos. What Joyce admired was the intricacies of Dante's forms, Dante's sense of design, not the "epic of judgment" sustained by that design. In *Rude Assignment*, Wyndham Lewis recalls an apposite conversation with Joyce:

> We were talking once, I remember, when I first got to know him about the cathedral at Rouen; its heavily encumbered facade. I had said I did not like it, rather as Indian or Indonesian sacred buildings are a fussy multiplication of accents, demonstrating a belief in the virtue of *quantity*, I said. . . . I continued to talk against Gothic altogether, and its "scholasticism in stone": the dissolving of the solid shell—the spatial intemperance, the nervous multiplication of detail. Joyce listened and then remarked that he, on the contrary, liked this multiplication of detail, adding that he himself, as a matter of fact, in words, did something of that sort. (60; emphasis is Lewis's)

And here they might have been talking about Dante. The Dante who wrote three symmetrical canticles, each ending with the word *stelle*, was not matched in this respect by any of the Italians writers who came after him. But Dante finds his match in the Joyce who begins *Ulysses* with a word starting with *s* and ending with *y*, *stately*, and ends it with a word beginning with *y* and ending in *s*, *yes*. The questions about epic or major form that continue to preoccupy Pound criticism are simply not an issue in the criticism of either *Ulysses* or *Finnegans Wake*. So fully achieved is the form in most respects that readers of Joyce rest content with the belief that every detail of the structure is planned and intended. I can imagine the critics of no other writer of our century accepting the stately/yes chiasmus as anything other than a bizarre coincidence. With Joyce, however, we confidently intuit design even when we perceive no ulterior purpose.[1]

But, as should be crystal clear by now, Joyce had absolutely no interest in the ideological aspects of Dante's work that so attracted Pound. The difference is that Pound secularized Dante's landscape but retains his orientation toward judgment; Joyce humanizes Dante and moves beyond judgment. The world of Joyce's fiction contains many judges and many systems of judgments, but his polyphonic operatic method—as we have just seen—works to subvert any such confident judging. Another way of putting this is that it is simply impossible—as Pound saw—to identify any of Joyce's works with the divisions of the *Commedia*: there is no clear *Inferno*, no clear *Purgatorio*, no clear *Paradiso*. Joyce, in short, simply does not want to imitate the ideological nature of Dante's epic; he takes what he wants from Dante and leaves the rest.

In contrast, although the effort of an earlier chapter was to suggest that Dante's *Commedia* was not the only or the last work of Italian literature relevant to the design of *The Cantos*, clearly Pound's imitation of Dante stands at the center of his project in *The Cantos*. This can be seen in a number of respects, starting with the opening of the poem. Although Canto 1 is a translation of part of Book 11 of the *Odyssey*, placing it first establishes a formal resemblance between Odysseus's voyage to the land of the dead and Dante's. Pound's epic resembles both poems, but both the title and Pound's various remarks about the poem establish Dante as the greater presence.[2] Although the poem as we have it is more than one hundred cantos, for years it was assumed that Pound would stop at one hundred and he encouraged this belief.[3] Various other remarks about the poem indicate that it is modeled on Dante's poem: "For forty years I have schooled myself, not to write an economic history of the U.S. or any other country, but to write an epic poem which begins 'In the Dark Forest' crosses the Purgatory of human error, and ends in the light, and 'fra i maestri di color che sanno'. For this reason I have had to understand the NATURE of error" (*Selected Prose*, 167). And from remarks such as these has developed a critical tradition that sees *The Cantos* as a *Commedia* with an *Inferno, Purgatorio,* and *Paradiso.*

So Pound, in contrast to Joyce, wanted both Dante's epic design and the epic of judgment carried by that design. This was an ambition Joyce saw and parodied mercilessly, in his wonderful parody of *The Cantos* in a 1925 letter:

> Is it dreadfully necessary
> > AND
> (I mean that I pose etc) is it useful, I ask
> this
> > HEAT!?
> We all know Mercury will know *when*
> > he kan!
> > but as Dante saith:
> > 1 Inferno is enough. *Basta*, he said, *un'inferno,*
> *perbacco!*

And that bird—
    Well!
He   oughter know!
≡≡≡   (With apologies to Mr Ezra Pound)
                (*Letters*, 1:228)

This critique is at least as perceptive and as funny as Pound's remarks
about *Finnegans Wake*. Underneath the remarks about the heat, which
is the ostensible subject of the letter, the skillful parody of the appearance of *The Cantos* and of Pound's macaronic shifts in register and
language, and a subtle dig—as Massimo Bacigalupo has observed—at
the inadequacy of Pound's Italian,[4] Joyce is also making a serious point
here. *Un Inferno basta*. Why try for a second? One can respect and
admire Dante's achievement without seeking to duplicate it.

Pound seemed at times as aware as Joyce of the potential incongruity of his ambition, as his references to the *Commedia* often deny
the very parallelism they assert. We have already seen one instance of
this in the passage of Pound's quoted above. "Il maestro di color che
sanno," Aristotle, is not in Paradise but in Limbo, so an epic poem
which "ends in the light" would not in Dante's cosmos end "fra i
maestri di color che sanno." Pound has consciously or unconsciously
changed his model in the very act of asserting its relevance to his
poem. And other remarks indicate an awareness that imitating Dante
was not quite going to do. As he wrote to Hubert Creekmore in 1939,
"I haven't an Aquinas-map; Aquinas *not* valid now" (*Selected Letters*,
323). This implies that Dante's order was given to him by his social
and philosophical context; Pound's epic cannot achieve such an order,
given the disorder of the modern world. And this shows Pound's
awareness that his various remarks about the Dantescan structure,
which cluster in the late 1930s and 1940s, are not really accurate reflections of the poem. What they represent in fact is a replanning of
the poem, a firming-up of the structure of the poem in mid-course,
rather than a plan on which he had always been working.

In this case, why push the parallel? The reason, I think, is ideological. Pound writes in 1944, "I have had to understand the NATURE of
error," and by 1944 he thought he had such an understanding that
could bring the modern world into some kind of order. The parallel
with Dante could have been a frame for the poem which was progressively abandoned as the poem continued (in much the way the brief
comparison to Browning's *Sordello* in Canto 2 works) except for

Pound's increasingly ideological commitment to his vision of fascism and his identification of fascism with Dante, of his vision of error with Dante's analysis of error, of his judgments with Dante's. The passage about "i maestri" comes from the 1944 essay written in Italian, "An Introduction to the Economic Nature of the United States," and this usefully captures his wartime sense of his poem. If the Early Cantos are an *Inferno*, a connection explicit in Cantos 14 and 15, and the Middle Cantos are a *Purgatorio*, Pound in the 1940s is finally ready to write his *Paradiso*, not a vision of a possible just society but a celebration of the just society of fascism. Not only does Pound's love of Dante help explain his fascism, as I have already argued, his commitment to fascism helps explain his use of Dante. Even if Pound's landscape is secularized, he had the ideological closure of Dante—certain people deserved to be in Hell, others in Paradise—and he needed Dante's epic design to reinforce that closure.

Now, as we know by now, Joyce was right, *un inferno basta*, and Pound's imitation of Dante's epic design was a disastrous failure. Cantos 72–73 are the major traces in the poem of the Fascist paradise Pound tried to write, and they have been kept carefully offstage, first by their exclusion from the collected editions of *The Cantos* until 1986 and by their remaining untranslated even after their inclusion in the collected editions of the poem. And as I have shown at length elsewhere, the fall of Mussolini and collapse of his regime led Pound to recast his poem in a direction diametrically opposed to the integrated epic structure on Dante's plan indicated in "An Introduction to the Economic Nature of the United States" (Dasenbrock, *Literary Vorticism*, 213–35). But this does not mean that Dante was far away from Pound's mind as he turned away from Dante's model. The crucial turn toward an acceptance of chaos and fragmentation in his poem is in Canto 74, and the final and most powerful reflection on his failure to attain Dante's integrated design is in Canto 116, and both passages are full of references to Dante.

In Canto 74, the Pound who insisted that "Human wishes are not vain in the least" (*Guide to Kulchur*, 180) surfaces again in his claim that "le paradis n'est pas artificiel" (74/452). But it is *spezzato*, as he goes on to say, fragmented or broken, and here Pound uses the Italian word that Dante uses in the *Inferno* to describe the broken condition of Hell (see my "Dante's Hell and Pound's *Paradiso: tutto spezzato*"). If Paradise is *spezzato*, then there can be "by no means an orderly Dantescan rising," as Canto 74 admits (457), no great orderly division of the world in an imitation of the *Commedia*. Canto 116 returns to a comparable confession of failure:

> Tho' my errors and wrecks lie about me.
> And I am not a demigod,
> I cannot make it cohere.
>
> (116/810)

Here, Pound is again judging his poem as incoherent, judging it by its failure to attain coherence. And Dante is again in his mind, as the passage a few lines later shows,

> chi crescerà i nostri—
> but about that terzo
> third heaven,
> that Venere,
> again is all "paradiso"
>
> (810)

The phrase in Italian, "chi crescerà i nostri," points us to a phrase from the *Paradiso* Pound had quoted earlier, in Cantos 89 and 93. The line in the *Paradiso* (Canto 5:105) is "Ecco chi crescerà li nostri amori" (here is one who will increase our loves). Pound's abbreviation of this here turns it into a question: who will increase our love? In place of Dante's confident cosmology, we have Pound's search for an equivalent. But Pound does not leave it there, with a sense of his difference from Dante:

> i.e. it coheres all right
> even if my notes do not cohere.
> Many errors,
> a little rightness,
> to excuse his hell
> and my paradiso.
> And as to why they go wrong,
> thinking of rightness
> And as to who will copy this palimpsest?
> al poco giorno
> ed al gran cerchio d'ombra
>
> (811)

If this is a confession of failure, it is a breathtakingly ambitious one. "I was thinking of right yet went wrong," Pound is saying, and he identifies his particular failure—as we have done—in his conception of paradise. But he is not the only poet who has made mistakes; "his hell," Dante's *Inferno*, needs excusing as well. Pound here suggests that if his paradise was flawed by ideological rigidity, by lack of compassion, so too was Dante's *Inferno*. So the failure of *The Cantos*, Pound is saying at the poem's end, was not in the failure to achieve an imitation of the *Commedia*; the failure was in the nature of the imitation of the *Commedia*, in Pound's imitation of Dante's ideological closure and rigidity. And this is a perception Joyce (and Beckett) would have shared; in the wrong kind of imitation, in the procrustean bed of identification, the danger is not in failure but in success.

But Pound does not leave it even there, with his disarming and audacious confession, "I'm a failure like Dante." He turns to the reader, asking "who will copy this palimpsest?" Palimpsest is in fact a descriptive term for the crazy weave of voices and languages found in *The Cantos*, and Pound then dramatizes the palimpsestic nature of his poem by making his next line the opening line of Dante's great sestina, "Al poco giorno ed al gran cerchio d'ombra."[5] The citation of the sestina here is startling, as every other Dante reference in this passage is to the *Commedia* and it is clearly of the *Commedia*'s epic structure that Pound is thinking. Is the lyric Dante that Pound had slighted in his quest for epic form the "little rightness," that truer Italian tradition that Pound had abandoned in his quest to build the earthly paradise? Pound had not been concerned with the sestine and canzoni that preoccupied him early for a long time,[6] and in this passage I think he is obliquely regretting this shift of attention. It was the lyric *trecento* with which he should have been more concerned, not just Dante's divine vision. But the content of this sestina is also pertinent here. It is a sestina of desperation and loss, as the line Pound quotes shows: "To the shortened day and the great circle of shade" (Durling, 616). Dante here uses the cold and dark winter season as an objective correlative for his situation, and Pound, in turn, uses Dante's for his. But Dante bounced back from the low point in his life represented by the *rime petrose*, and the inexact resemblance here is inspiriting rather than chastening for Pound. This is shown by what immediately follows:

> But to affirm the gold thread in the pattern
> (Torcello)

al Vicolo d'oro
　　　　　　(Tigullio).
To confess wrong without losing rightness:
Charity I have had sometimes,
　　　　I cannot make it flow thru.
A little light, like a rushlight
　　　　　　　to lead back to splendour.
　　　　　　　　(811)

So despite the wrongness, rightness has not been utterly lost. There is some gold thread in the pattern for both Dante and Pound, enough to "lead back to splendour." That closing splendor is utterly different from the light of Dante's Paradise, yet is impressive in its own way. And this last complete canto suggests that toward the end of his life, Pound came to an awareness of what had been enabling and what had been disabling in his cult of Dante. What he moves toward here, a celebration of the lyric and a critique of the totalizing impulse in Dante, is the best possible commentary on his relation to Dante. As he says in the next fragmentary canto, "I lost my center fighting the world . . . I tried to make a paradiso terrestre" (816), and one needs to blame at least in part his appreciation of Dante for that ambition. But Dante helps him regain his center here, in these poignant and very powerful closing cantos.

This is not the only evidence Pound was thinking about the relation between Dante and the modernists toward the end of his life. The very last piece of prose in *Selected Prose*, and one of the last pieces of prose Pound wrote, is the very brief memorial note, "For T.S.E.," published in the *Sewanee Review* in 1966. It begins, "His was the true Dantescan voice—not honoured enough, and deserving more than I ever gave him" (464). This is a very modernist mode of praise, to praise someone for resembling Dante. But the use of the singular and the definite article suggests more than simply praise for Eliot. According to Eliot, not only was Eliot a true Dantescan voice, he was *the* true Dantescan voice, the one modernist to have achieved that quintessential modernist ambition. At the end of his life Pound knew very well that his imitation of the *Commedia* in *The Cantos* had not been successful, as Cantos 116 and 117 show; this passage shows which modernist Pound felt had successfully imitated Dante.

Moreover, Pound's late sense of Eliot as a more faithful imitator of Dante seems about right. As we have seen, Joyce did not ever aspire to having the true Dantescan voice, as he was too critical of orthodoxies and of settled ideological visions of the world. Pound did so aspire, but he had Dante's ideological vision without Dante's wisdom to cast his vision of paradise in the subjunctive. Of all the major modernists, Eliot does seem closest to Dante in the respects that have concerned us here. He had Dante's confident and totalizing vision of the world and had it without Pound's secularizing of that vision. When Eliot equates Prufrock with Federico da Montefeltro or the world of Part 1 of *The Waste Land* with Dante's *Inferno*, we take those references altogether more seriously than the comparable equations of Cantos 14–16. Moreover, and at least partially because of this, it is a good deal easier to relate Eliot's major works with the three canticles of the *Commedia*: if *The Waste Land* is an *Inferno*, then *Ash-Wednesday* is clearly a *Purgatorio* and *Four Quartets*, particularly "Little Gidding," a *Paradiso*. I am not sure these identifications work perfectly, but they surely work a good deal better than any such identifications with the works of Pound or Joyce, and just as surely the passage in which the poet meets the dead poet in "Little Gidding" is the single best evocation of Dante's dramatic method in modern literature. Finally, what may have enabled this more thoroughly successful imitation of the "dead master" was that Eliot shared Dante's beliefs more completely than any of his contemporaries. Eliot really believed in hell, purgatory, and paradise and did not have to read Dante's worlds as metaphors or internal states of mind the way Pound did. Moreover, Pound and Joyce had no more sympathy for the Marian conception of chastity shared by Dante and Petrarch than had Spenser or Nashe, but as a number of critics have argued, this was a particularly important aspect of Dante's work for Eliot.[7] If modernism has a true "Dantescan voice," that is the voice of Eliot.

Is this an indirect way of saying Eliot is the greatest modernist writer? Only if one thinks it is important to have the true Dantescan voice, which means to have a model of imitation like Petrarch's and Pound's in political matters. Petrarch's model of literary imitation would tell us to "overgo" Dante, not to resemble him, and Pound's failure to achieve Dante's epic form has in fact been more productive, more influential, ironically more imitated by subsequent poets, than Eliot's successful imitation. And here as elsewhere Joyce represents an Aristotelian mean between Scylla and Charybdis. His work is an imitation of Dante that, true to the literary model of imitation prescribed by Petrarch and Pound, transforms Dante as it imitates him: it may be a mediaeval cathedral as Joyce suggested to Lewis, but it has no priests. Joyce is the writer who best understood that there was no Aquinas-map now, that *un inferno basta*, that one paradise *basta* as well, that Italian culture need not be imitated in all respects. Yet, in the terms of creative imitation, this means that he was the best imitator of all.

Appendix

Pound's Map of Italian Literature for Mussolini

Of the many (unanswered) letters written by Ezra Pound to Benito Mussolini in the Ezra Pound Archive at the Beinecke Library, one in particular bears on the subject of this book in fascinating ways. The letter is a proposal for a reform of the literature curriculum of the Italian schools; it is quite a detailed letter and was a carefully considered one, as the crucial page I have reproduced below exists in a draft as well as in the carbon of the actual letter. What precedes and follows this page are plans for the non-Italian literature Pound believed should be taught, a page covering the classics and a few scattered recommendations for modern European literature. But the most interesting page—at least for our purposes here—is reproduced below, as faithfully as possible. One of the things I have been trying to capture is Pound's "map" of Italian literature, his sense of the tradition and his points of emphasis, and what he sent Mussolini was literally his map of Italian literature, a page that graphically represents the whole tradition. The letter is dated 17 November 1933.

La parte strettamente Italiano

(seconda linea)

Guido

    (primi secoli)   Boccaccio

Dante   MichelAngelo

                Lorenzo Medici

                Machiavelli

                Castiglione

		d
Galileo	i leggieri	e
cultura plastica del Quattrocento	Metastasio	c
Leopardi	Goldoni	a
		d
		e
	Manzoni	n
	Verga	z
	(Inferiori a	
	Flaubert, Stendhal	
	Doistoievsky	

RISVEGLIO

bassato sul confronto corragioso
e senza paura, senza vanità locale, con tutti i capolavori
del mondo

EDUCAZIONE NAZIONALE   (Letteratura)

    e Basale

The movement down the page is obviously chronological, moving from the "primi secoli" (first centuries) to the present, but the placement from left to right is a placement according to value, the great figures toward the left, the "seconda linea" (second line) and "leggieri" (the lightweights) on the right. So Cavalcanti and Dante are the only figures placed absolutely at the left margin, and the three others who are put firmly on the left are Galileo, the "cultura plastica del Quattrocento," and Leopardi. Leopardi is no surprise, given the argument of Chapter Six, and Pound's clear placement of him as late as 1933 over all other post-1321 Italian writers shows that his 1910-period appreciation of Leopardi was not an aberration. The "plastic culture of the quattrocento," though not exactly Italian literature, is also a logical inclusion, reflecting the heritage of Pater and Browning in Pound's image of Italy; I expect Pound wrote "cultura plastica" to include sculptors as well as painters and to include their patrons as well. Galileo comes as a bit of a surprise, as his scientific work would seem even further from literature than the "cultura plastica." Pound's emphasis here in fact anticipates modern trends once again, for Galileo is now considered more important as a writer than he was fifty years ago, but I am not sure why Pound has placed him here as one of the five high points of Italian culture.

Although the "seconda linea" is comprised of inferior writers, these writers are still well worth considering, for it is fact a honor even to make it into those ranks. Think of everyone who is not here: where is Petrarch? Ariosto? Tasso? Or in a later period, Foscolo or Alfieri? Pound's attacks on Petrarch we have already detailed, and he considered Ariosto and particularly Tasso to be part of the decadence of "verbalism" also found in Milton ("The Renaissance," 215). Of those who are included in the "seconda linea," we have seen Pound's mention of Michelangelo in *The Spirit of Romance*, and Lorenzo Medici fits in with Pound's emphasis on the princes who were artists in their own right. The presence of Machiavelli here, the only political thinker on the list, is support for my emphases in Chapter Eight; Valla—whom we might also expect here—may be left off because he wrote in Latin and this proposed curriculum focuses on writers who used the *volgare*. Neither Boccaccio nor Castiglione is a major presence in Pound's writings, but Boccaccio was mentioned in the ur-Cantos, possibly—as Ronald Bush has suggested (84–85)—with a sense of the *Decameron* as a possible Ovidian model for *The Cantos*. And the inclusion of Castiglione—mentioned briefly in *Gaudier-Brzeska* (48) and *Guide to Kul-*

chur (146)—helps reinforce the importance of the Renaissance courts for Pound. To move to *i leggieri* (not the term of praise for Pound that it would be for Joyce) and the *decadenza*, Metastasio was long one of Pound's minor interests; Goldoni is more of a surprise, although an interest of Joyce's and someone who fits into Pound's interest in eighteenth-century Italian musical theater and in Venice. Pound's brief mention of Manzoni and Verga as inferior to the French and Russian novelists is acute but not utterly critical; those that Pound really had contempt for do not make it on the list at all.

But the most interesting part of the page might well be the bottom. Although Pound was influenced by and knowledgeable about virtually every phase of Italian culture, he did feel that it had slowly declined since 1321. But in 1933, in the first flush of his enthusiasm for *il duce* (*Jefferson and/or Mussolini* was written in the same year), he sees a "risveglio" in Italy that reverses this decadence. The unnamed "risveglio" must be fascism, and the agent of that awakening must be the addressee of Pound's letter, Mussolini himself. Now, it is interesting that no names appear here, which suggests that Pound does not feel any names are needed, but also that Pound cannot quite bring himself to put any names here to represent this awakening in Italian culture. Who would he put after all? D'Annunzio? Marinetti? Gentile? Pound thought that *he* was the great poet of fascism, so he is not going to put any of his rivals in this place of honor. Yet he cannot quite include himself in his map of Italian literature.

The next point to make about this is the eccentricity of his description of the Fascist "risveglio" that follows: "based on a courageous confrontation, without fear, without local vanity, with all the masterpieces of the world." What is he describing here? This sounds as if he is confusing Italian fascism with an education in comparative literature, specifically with a Poundian education in comparative literature. And I have tried to show, in some ways that is the basis of Pound's misguided commitment to Italian fascism. For it hardly needs saying what a laughably inaccurate description this is of fascism or any fascist writers. Fascism was an extended "vanità locale," full of boasting about the past greatness of Italy that Mussolini was to restore, and I see no signs in D'Annunzio or Marinetti or any other Fascist writer of the "courageous confrontation with the masterpieces of the world" that Pound is claiming here. For him to have made this claim, it is almost as if Pound forgot that the Fascists were Italian, not American like him: he felt that he had moved beyond "vanità locale" to an appreciation of Italian culture, but for Italians to esteem Italian culture as highly as Pound did is emphatically not to move beyond "vanità locale." And the fact that half of Pound's education plan is devoted to Italian literature, that nothing Asian is included, and that, most remarkably, on the previous page "Omero," the first figure mentioned, is described as "geographicamente italiano" shows that the whole plan was an appeal to "vanità locale."

I have reproduced this remarkable document both because of the way it complements and supplements the portrait of Pound's interests in Italian literature and culture we have traced in chapters 6, 8, and 9, but also because it shows how closely Pound's appreciation for Italian literature was linked to his cult of Mussolini. This connection can be drawn both ways: Mussolini was the figure to reawaken Italian literature; but also the first thing it occured to Pound to recommend to Mussolini was a reform of the curriculum in Italian literature. It is as if Pound thought that if the Italians could be weaned from the "poison" of Petrarch and Tasso and read his preferred curriculum instead, they could better appreciate Mussolini's greatness in reawakening Italian literature.

But we should not let the obvious eccentricity of this lull us into considering it utterly harmless. Mussolini's regime, like any dictatorship, relied on the passive consent of the people as well as active force to stay in power, and in fact, until the Nazi alliance of the late 1930s and the consequent Nazification of the regime, Mussolini's regime had that consent in large measure. Antonio Gramsci's attempt to explain this puzzling phenomenon is in large part what led him to his concept of hegemony, and in Gramsci's model intellectuals play a large part in creating hegemony. We have already seen that oppositional intellectuals of the kind desired by Gramsci (and Joyce) were historically few and far between in Italian culture. (Joyce's hero Giordano Bruno, a figure highly praised by anticlerical socialists in Italy in the Trieste years, was a conspicuous exception in this respect, which is precisely why he was so important for Joyce.) And the adherence of many prominent Italian writers and intellectuals to the Fascist regime was an important aspect of that regime's claim to respectability. The effect of all this was far from innocuous, as can be seen from the reaction of one literate twenty-two-year old to a lecture on Italian culture in Brussels in 1941:

> On aura donc la occasion d'acquerir une vue d'ensemble sur la poésie italienne contemporaine et de constater comment, dans le climat fasciste, une tres belle et originale poesie a pu s'épanouir.

(Here one will have the chance to acquire an overview of contemporary Italian poetry and to observe that, in the climate of fascism, a beautiful and original poetry has been able to bloom.)

The young man was Paul de Man writing in the Nazi-controlled paper *Le Soir* on 11 February 1941 (*Wartime Journalism, 1939–1943*).[1] And we should never let the sheer eccentricity of Pound's vision of fascism obscure the fact that the support of intellectuals was actively sought by fascism and that this support was not without its effect on the course of events.

Notes

Introduction

1. A number of good chronological surveys of aspects of the relation between Italy and literature in English have already been written. A. Lytton Sells's 1955 study, *The Italian Influence in English Poetry: From Chaucer to Southwell* and Mario Praz's *The Flaming Heart* (1958) concentrate on the Renaissance, although Praz does include a discussion of Eliot. Kenneth Churchill's *Italy and English Literature, 1764–1930* is a competent although necessarily very general survey of its period. Steve Ellis's *Dante and English Poetry: Shelley to T. S. Eliot* fills an important gap in Churchill's treatment. And Nathalia Wright's *American Novelists in Italy* complements these studies of English literature.

2. For a full-length study of Milton's debt to Italian literature, see Prince, *The Italian Element in Milton's Verse*; for a study of Donne's, see Donald Guss, *John Donne, Petrarchist*. Crashaw died in Italy in the sanctuary of the Casa Santa at Loreto; as a Catholic, he was clearly removed from the anti-Italian traditions of Protestant English culture. His relation to Italian literature has been studied by Schaar, Barbato, Gibaldi, and others.

3. The Romantics are Spenserian above all in their interest in the Italian romance epic poets—in Tasso, a great influence on both Spenser and Milton, as well as in Ariosto and Pulci. They look forward to Pound above all in their interest in Dante, and it must be remembered that, for English literature, Dante was a discovery of the Romantic period. Corrigan's "Introduction" to *Italian Poets and English Critics, 1755–1859* has a good discussion of this discovery (9–17), although her discussion focuses on critical essays and not the prior use of Dante in the creative work of Shelley and others. The early chapters of Ellis's *Dante and English Poetry* redress this imbalance.

4. Bloom's writings on influence are scattered throughout a dozen books, but his general theory is articulated most clearly in *The Anxiety of Influence* and *A Map of Misreading*. Pound's and Bloom's respective theories of influence have recently

been expertly contrasted by Christopher Beach in his "Ezra Pound and Harold Bloom: Influences, Canons, Traditions, and the Making of Modern Poetry." My discussion is indebted to his, although he does not make the distinction between Pound's multilingual model and Bloom's monolingual one that seems crucial to me. This is probably because his area of interest is Pound's influence on contemporary American poetry, not earlier writers' influence on Pound.

5. One exception is an essay in *A Map of Misreading*, "Milton and His Precursors" (125–43). In keeping with his monolingual orientation, here Bloom presents Spenser as the essential precursor of Milton. But this is a maneuver that obviously cannot be repeated with Spenser, as Bloom admits in a quick reference to "Spenser's resourceful and bewildering (even Joycean) way of subsuming his precursors, particularly Virgil, through his labyrinthine syncretism" (128). I find this an attractive admission on Bloom's part, suggesting that he is aware that there are indeed great writers unanxious about influence, and his linkage of Spenser and Joyce as two such writers anticipates some of my argument in Part Two. The High Renaissance and high modernism are presented here as expressing a different notion of imitation from that found in romanticism, and this seems largely correct. Elsewhere, however, Bloom makes these two kinds of imitation an historical sequence, the age of anxiety following the more generous notions of imitation that ruled from Homer to Shakespeare (*Anxiety of Influence*, 122), and this is unfortunately more consistent with his refusal to admit that any post-Renaissance poets escape his model.

6. Bornstein's entire discussion in his "Introduction: Four Gaps in Postromantic Influence Study," in *Poetic Remaking* (1–12) is valuable, as is his earlier "Pound's Parlayings with Robert Browning," in which he specifies Pound as an example of a poet using his multilinguality to escape Bloom's anxiety of influence: "Pound's firmly comparative stance pulls him outside his own language" (123).

7. One characteristic formulation: "Modernism in literature has not passed; rather, it has been exposed as never having been there" (*A Map of Misreading*, 28). Bloom's own model offers a possible explanation of these bizarre statements, as Bloom can be seen as misreading his critical precursors. Pound and Eliot are probably the modern critics who have theorized most about imitation and tradition, and Bloom must feel a need to pretend that their work—which has helped to make his own possible—does not exist.

8. Roland Barthes's "From Work to Text," in *Image, Music, Text* (155–64) is a representative and influential instance of this shift.

9. Barthes's classic statement is in his "The Death of the Author," in *Image, Music, Text* (142–48). One characteristic formulation: "Writing is the destruction of every voice, of every point of origin. Writing is that neutral, composite, oblique space where our subject slips away, the negative where all identity is lost, starting with the very identity of the body writing" (142). Comparable pronouncements by Foucault are everywhere in his work; see, for instance, the closing passage of *The Order of Things* (384–87).

10. Stanley Corngold's "On Paul de Man's Collaborationist Writings" relates de Man's later theoretical indifference to the person behind the text to his earlier politics in a provocative and compelling way.

11. The essay from which this comes, "Presupposition and Intertextuality," offers a clear discussion of contemporary theories of intertextuality.

12. On the contribution of analytic philosophy, see my *Redrawing the Lines*; for

a more specific discusion of the contribution Davidson can make to literary theory, see my "Do We Write the Text We Read?" I perhaps need to make it clear that Davidsonian intentionalism does not entail the belief that the only valid interpretation of a literary work is the reconstruction of the author's intentions, which is how I would characterize "naive intentionalism." A sophisticated intentionalism recognizes the appropriateness and validity of other modes of interpretation but insists that we must recognize that writing shares with all other forms of social action the property of being an intentional act.

Chapter One: *Understanding Renaissance Imitation: The Example of Wyatt*

1. My text for the poems of Wyatt available in his study is Richard Harrier, who includes a transcription of the Egerton Manuscript. All subsequent citations from Harrier's transcription will be parenthetical and will use his numbering. This is Egerton 89.

2. All citations from and translations of Petrarch's *Canzoniere* are from Robert M. Durling. All subsequent citations will be parenthetical by number. This is *Canzoniere* 199.

3. My text for the poems of Wyatt not found in Harrier is that edited by Kenneth Muir and Patricia Thomson. All subsequent references to such poems will be parenthetical and will use the Muir and Thomson numbering. This is Muir and Thomson 86. The Muir and Thomson edition has been seriously criticized (for a book-length critique see H. A. Mason, *Editing Wyatt*), but it is still the most recent unmodernized text of Wyatt's entire oeuvre.

4. For good general discussions of how epideictic rhetoric influenced the practice and theory of poetry in the Renaissance, see Cain, 1–14, Hardison, Brian Vickers, and Kallendorf.

5. See the commentary in Muir and Thomson (276–77) for the debate on this point.

6. This sonnet was the last poem in the *in vita* section at the stage in the evolution of the *Canzoniere* represented by the Chigi Manuscript (see Wilkins, 160–63, and Bernardo, 32–35). Michelangelo Picone has argued that the poem was placed there because it depicts the absolute nadir of the *Canzoniere*, that point at which none of Petrarch's usual consolations consoles him. It is worth noting that quite a large proportion of Wyatt's translations from Petrarch come from this section of the *Canzoniere*, the later part of *in vita*, the section that anachronistically we could call the most Wyatt-like of the sequence.

Chapter Two: *The Petrarchan Context of Spenser's* Amoretti

1. For a fine study of the Petrarchan antithesis, see Leonard Forster.

2. These poems may actually have been written after Laura's death, and they were certainly placed in the *Canzoniere* after her death (see Wilkins, 167–74, and Bernardo, 37 and 39–41). But my concern here is the achieved shape of Petrarch's relation to Laura as expressed in the *Canzoniere*, not how that shape reflects Petrarch's real relation with the real woman. For Petrarch's own editing and arranging of the *Canzoniere*, see E. H. Wilkins, particularly his essay "The Making of the *Canzoniere*," 145–94, Bernardo, 26–63, and Durling, 7–11.

3. For further discussion of this key metaphor of Petrarch, see Greene, "Petrarch *Viator*," and Picone.

4. This is not a claim that all critics of Petrarch would accept. Clearly, there is a

difference between Beatrice and Laura, between Dante and Petrarch: Dante depicts himself brought to Paradise by Beatrice, whereas Petrarch only longs for it. Thus, Petrarch's imitation of Dante, in accordance with his own principles of imitation, creates a resemblance that is also a difference, and some readers are going to be more struck by the resemblance, others by the difference. The worldliness of Petrarch's love for Laura—how long it takes him to turn towards the Divine—strikes the reader looking at Petrarch from Dante's perspective, but the unworldliness of that love—the fact that he at least wants to turn toward the Divine—will strike any reader coming to Petrarch from the perspective of later Petrarchism. Petrarch's rather defensive remarks about Dante in a letter to Boccaccio (*Rerum familiarum libri*, 21:15; Bishop, 176–82) can support either reading, either Petrarch's difference from Dante or his indirect (and somewhat anxious) imitation of him. Freccero's "The Fig Tree and the Laurel" expresses a great Dante scholar's sense of these matters, which is sharply at odds with the view expressed here.

5. See E. H. Wilkins, "The Quattrocento Editions of the *Canzoniere* and the *Triumphs*," 379–401, for details on the division of the *Canzoniere* into two parts in the early printed editions.

6. Petrarch in fact divided the *Canzoniere* into two parts with "I' vo pensando" opening the second section before Laura's death (see Wilkins, 152–53 and 190–93, and Bernardo, 27). Hans Baron also discusses the date of "I' vo pensando" briefly (*Petrarch's* Secretum, 51–52 and 57) in the context of a discussion (47–57) of how the poem relates to Petrarch's *Secretum* and thus to Petrarch's spiritual turmoil of the 1340s.

7. The Renaissance commentaries on Petrarch, such as Vellutello's, show this implication quite readily. See Patricia Thomson, 191–96. Many early printed editions—such as the 1514 Aldine edition owned by Pound—in fact make the division between 266 and 267.

8. For information on translations and imitations of Petrarch in the Renaissance, see George Watson, Anthony Mortimer, Jack D'Amico, and Stephen Minta.

9. All quotations from Spenser are from *Poetical Works*, ed. J. C. Smith and E. de Selincourt.

10. For the most complete discussion of this question, see *The Works of Edmund Spenser*, 8:611–24.

11. J. W. Lever has only contempt for this work and sees no connection between it and the Renaissance love sonnet: "Yet for close on 25 years he was content to use this form for little more than pious exhortations and homiletic laments on the mutability of worldly things" (93). Although Lever is the only critic who has previously discussed *The Visions of Petrarch* and the *Amoretti* together, his dismissal of the earlier work is typical of *Amoretti* criticism in that it sees Petrarchism as a context for the *Amoretti* but does not see the *Canzoniere* in all its complexity as relevant to the *Amoretti*. Petrarch uses the sonnet for "pious exhortations and homiletic laments" as well.

12. The text of Tasso's previously untranslated sonnet:

> Questa fera gentil ch'in sì crucciosa
> Fronte fuggía pur dianzi i vostri passi
> Tra spini e sterpi e dirupati sassi
> Strada ad ogn'or prendendo erta e dubbiosa;
> Or, cangiato voler, d'onesta posa

Vaga, discende a i sentier piani e bassi,
E, quasi ogni durezza indietro lassi,
Incontro vi si fa lieta e vezzosa.
Vedete omai come 'l celeste riso
Benigna v'apre, e come dolcemente
I rai de' suoi begli occhi in voi raggira.
Pavesi, s'or tal gioia al cor v'inspira,
Che sarà poi quando più volte il viso
D'amor vi baci di pietate ardente?

(This gentle beast that, till moments ago, fled with angry countenance before you between thorns and brush and steep and jagged rocks, always taking the steep and tortuous path,

Now, having changed her will and longing for dignified repose, descends to level and low paths. And, as if leaving behind all harshness, she comes to meet you merry and alluring.

You can see now how, well disposed, she opens her celestial smile to you, and how sweetly the rays of her beautiful eyes envelop you.

Pavesi, if now she gives such joy to your heart, what will happen later when, burning with compassion, she will often and lovingly kiss your face?) (2:1; trans. Barbara Spackman)

13. Watson lists several other poems in the *Amoretti* as imitations of poems in the *Canzoniere*, but I fail to see any resemblance.

14. Lever discusses Spenser's use of Desportes (104–7) and of Tasso (107–13); the pioneering source studies on which both Lever's discussion and my own rely are Janet Scott, "Spenser's *Amoretti*" and *Les Sonnets Élisabéthains*. For a discussion of the Petrarchan elements in Tasso's lyrics, see C. P. Brand, "Petrarch and Petrarchism"; and for a discussion of Tasso's influence on the *Amoretti*, see Brand, *Torquato Tasso*, 290–94.

15. L'alma vaga di luce e di bellezza
Ardite spiega al ciel l'ale amorose;
Ma sì le fa l'umanitá gravose
Che le dechina a quel ch'in terra apprezza;
E de' piaceri alla dolce esca avvezza
Ove in sereno volto Amor la pose
Tra bianche perle e mattutine rose,
Par che non trovi altra maggior dolcezza;
E fa quasi augellin, ch'in alto s'erga,
E pio discenda al fin ov' altri il cibi,
E quasi volontario s'imprigioni;
E fra tanti del ciel graditi doni
Sì gran diletto par che in voi delibi
Ch'in voi solo si pasce e solo alberga.

(The soul desirous of light and beauty spreads her wings, loving and bold, to the heavens; but the human burden weighs them down and bends them to that which the soul values.

And, being accustomed to the sweet bait of pleasures, it seems that she finds no greater sweetness than that which she finds there, where Love has placed her among white pearls and morning roses.

And she does as the bird who aims toward the heights and then, finally, descends to where others feed it, and almost of its own free will, imprisons itself.

And among so many pleasing gifts from the heavens, it seems as if she tastes such great delight in you that in you alone does she draw nourishment and dwell.) (2:98; trans. Barbara Spackman)

16. How seriously one should take Tasso's Neoplatonism in his love poetry is a matter of debate. Brand considers the Neoplatonic elements in Tasso's lyrics to be "formal and rarely convincing" ("Petrarch," 259), whereas V. Kostic finds Tasso quite serious in his Neoplatonism. But both see a split in Tasso between sensual and Neoplatonic conceptions of love, whereas Spenser, as Kostic rightly observes (72), is seeking to reconcile the two. The classic Renaissance exposition of the Neoplatonic conception of love, of course, is Pietro Bembo's discourse on love in Book 4 of Baldassare Castiglione's *The Book of the Courtier*.

17. In contrast, Edwin Casady writes about the *Amoretti* that "the sequence [is] a consistent study of a lover climbing the Neo-Platonic Ladder" (295). In my opinion, there is no warrant for such a reading. Although the influence of Neoplatonism on Spenser's *Fowre Hymnes* cannot be denied, one does not, in the *Amoretti*, rise above physical love to a spiritual love; the proper kind of physical love is spiritual.

18. Non son sì belli i fiori onde natura
Nel dolce april de'vaghi anni sereno
Sparge un bel volto, come in real seno
È bel quel ch'a l'autunno Amor matura.
Maraviglioso grembo, orto e cultura
D'Amore e paradiso mio terreno!
Il mio audace pensier chi tiene a freno
Se quello onde si nutre a te sol fura?
Quel che i passi fugaci d'Atalanta
Volser dal corso, o che guardò il dragone,
Son vili al mio desir ch'in te si pasce:
Né coglie Amor da peregrina pianta
Pomo ch'in pregio di beltà ti done,
Che nel tuo sen sol di te degno ei nasce.

(The flowers with which nature adorns a beautiful face in the sweet, serene April of youth are not as beautiful as that which Love ripens in a royal breast in autumnal years.

Marvelous womb, garden and cultivation of Love and my earthly paradise! Who holds the reins of my bold thought if it robs only from you that by which is it nourished?

He whom Atalanta's swift steps turned from the path, or he who looked at the dragon, is miniscule compared to my desire that draws its nourishment from you.

Nor does Love need gather a pome from an exotic plant so that it can award you a prize for your beauty, because the only pomes worthy of you grow in your bosom.) (3:133–34; trans. Barbara Spackman)

19. The critique of the will found here is Spenser's own, I think, but Petrarch's love poetry was not very descriptive or self-revealing either, as we have already seen from examining Wyatt's transformation of Petrarch in a more realistic direction.

20. Lever's list of sonnets: 10, 11, 12, 18, 20, 23, 25, 31, 32, 37, 38, 41, 47, 48, 49, 53, 54, 56.

21. Martz's list: 10, 12, 16, 18, 20, 24, 26, 28, 29, 30, 32, 33, 37, 43, 46, 48, 50, 57. Lever and Martz list sonnets 10, 12, 18, 20, 32, 37, and 48 in common.

22. My discussion of the two-part structure of the *Amoretti* is indebted to Neely's perceptive article, but she does not characterize the turn the *Amoretti* take as distinctive among Renaissance sonnet sequences or as a turn on the Petrarchan tradition or as a turn parallel to that found in the *Canzoniere*. According to Neely, the second part of the *Amoretti* "departs still further from the Italian model than did that of Sidney" (372).

23. Neely sees the turn occurring in sonnets 68–70 (367), after which "debts to Petrarch and the use of Petrarchan motifs diminish" (373). G. K. Hunter also sees a turn in the sequence around this point (125), which for him starts in sonnet 62, but he does not relate this turn to anything else.

24. Lewis's mention of Shakespeare as following in Spenser's tradition should remind us that the comedies and romances are based on a conception of love that is quite close to the one found in the *Amoretti* and *The Faerie Queene*. Moreover, Rosalie Colie in *Shakespeare's Living Art* (135–67) has shown how a number of Shakespeare's plays, *Romeo and Juliet* and *Othello* among them, also reshape— although in a rather different way—Petrarchan conventions in applying them to marriage.

Chapter Three: Escaping the Squires' Double Bind in The Faerie Queene

1. The only full-length study of Books 3 and 4 together, Thomas P. Roche's *The Kindly Flame* perfectly exemplifies this approach, organizing its discussion of these two books around individual figures such as Britomart and Amoret. So do other studies of these books, such as Isabel G. MacCaffrey, *Spenser's Allegory* and Kathleen Williams, *Spenser's World of Glass*, 79–150.

2. The critic who has done the most along these lines is A. Kent Hieatt, in *Chaucer, Spenser, Milton*, 75–94, who studies a number of "four-groups" of lovers in Book 4. Another study that has employed an approach similar to what I am recommending here is Jonathan Goldberg, *"Endlesse Worke,"* the one full-length study of Book 4. Both Hieatt and Goldberg situate Book 4 in relation to "The Squire's Tale" of Chaucer, which complements my stress on the group of squires here.

3. Rosemond Tuve, *Allegorical Imagery*, 362–63, 367, and throughout chapter 5. See also Eugene Vinaver, *The Rise of Romance*, especially chapter 5, "The Poetry of Interlace" (68–98), although Vinaver does not explicitly discuss *The Faerie Queene* as Tuve does.

4. Edmund Spenser, *Poetical Works*, ed. J. C. Smith and E. de Selincourt, *The Faerie Queene*, Book 3, canto 5, stanza 35. All subsequent citations to *The Faerie Queene* will be to this text and will be parenthetical in this form: (3.5.35).

5. Ironically, her cure of his physical wounds gives him new emotional or meta-phoric "wounds" instead, as A. Leigh DeNeef has observed in "Spenser's *Amor Fuggitivo* and the Transfixed Heart" (8–9). DeNeef's study relates a whole series of such literal and metaphorical wounds in Book 3.

6. For a study of the source of these mottoes and of how they help us understand Britomart's quest, see Iris Tillman Hill, "Britomart and *Be Bold, Be Not Too Bold*," 173–87.

7. The best study of the Petrarchan antithesis is Leonard Forster's *The Icy Fire*; Rosalie L. Colie's *Paradoxica Epidemica*, although it says less than it might about the paradoxes of Petrarchism, is also quite pertinent.

8. James Nohrnberg has acutely characterized False Florimell as representing "a dead Petrarchanism" (575).

9. I am quoting from "Towards a Theory of Schizophrenia" (1956), reprinted in *Steps to an Ecology of Mind*, 201–27, but all of "Form and Pathology in Relationship," Part 3 of *Steps* (159–339), is pertinent.

10. Roche, for example, says that Belphoebe "can do no wrong" (147), and Williams says that "there is, of course, no question of Belphoebe's nobility" (100). Both Williams and MacCaffrey characterize the Timias-Belphoebe relation as Platonic (109 and 267–68), and Williams epitomizes the traditional view—which I think completely wrong—when she concludes: "Spenser does not, I think, intend particularly to condemn 'Petrarchan' love or 'courtly' love, any more than he means to condemn the 'Platonic' aspect of Petrarchism in Timias and Belphoebe" (109). See both Roche's entire discussion of Timias and Belphoebe (136–48) and Gilbert (629–34), for extended treatments of this relationship that find no fault with Belphoebe and adopt her perspective as the only acceptable one. Anderson is probably the first critic to break with the long tradition of finding no fault with Belphoebe here (58–60).

11. Hieatt points out, however, that "Aemylia's role in subjection to lust had not been simply passive. Her own description of her prospective lover is suspect in Spenserian terms" (79).

12. MacCaffrey has made much the same point: "Between Book II and Book V, Spenser explores, with unmatched subtlety and inventiveness, the whole great subject of love" (237).

13. But it is worth noting that at least one poem in the *Canzoniere*, "Geri, quando talor meco s'adira" (179), presents Petrarch's own posture of humility toward Laura as something he assumes in essence to manage her. And this use of Petrarchan language as a pose is something often highlighted in sixteenth-century commentaries on the *Canzoniere* that present it as a kind of *ars amatoria*.

14. Nohrnberg has made the relevant point that the figure of Busyrane shows that Petrarchan love "is mixed with lust" (474); discussing False Florimell, he points out that "if the lady's virtue is specious, then Spenser's treatment implies that a good deal of the sentiment expressed in Petrarchan form is only superficially chaste" (575). I would go beyond Nohrnberg to argue that even with virtuous ladies and with more noble lovers than Busyrane, the sentiment of Petrarchan love is "only superficially chaste."

15. Hieatt makes the following apposite comment: "Nothing is more despicable in the inglorious career of the unstable four-group led by Blandamour in Book 4 than its members' fighting for, and exchanging, females as booty" (92).

16. This redefinition on Spenser's part is, of course, part of a general Protestant tendency to define chastity not as virginity but as the proper expression of conjugal love. See George and George, 265–75; Haller; and Halkett.

17. This helps to explain one of the mysteries in the narrative in Book 4, in A. Kent Hieatt's phrase, "probably the most scandalous loose end in the whole

Faerie Queene" (85). Twice, Amoret should be present when Scudamour arrives but she mysteriously disappears both times: in canto 5, she is traveling with Britomart; Britomart explains her disappearance in stanza 36 and the narrative finds Amoret again in canto 7. Arthur finds her in canto 8 and takes her under his care. Arthur and Scudamour meet in canto 9, so Amoret should be reunited with him at that point, but Amoret does not seem to be present, although her absence is neither noted nor explained. Spenser goes to a good deal of trouble to prevent Amoret and Scudamour from reuniting; he also replaced the original ending of Book 3, in which they were united, with the ending we now have in which Scudamour does not wait to meet Amoret after Britomart frees her from the House of Busyrane.

18. Aristotle's treatment of friendship is in Books 8 and 9 of the *Nicomachean Ethics*.

Chapter Four: Queen Elizabeth and the Politics of Petrarchism

1. Aldo S. Bernardo has pointed out that "many of the attributes given to Mary by the poet are reminiscent of Laura" (157). Franco Suitner's discussion is also relevant:

> Le qualificazioni attribuite alla Vergine nella canzone non sono cioè soltanto quelle stesse di Laura ma, direttamente o indirettamente, quelle delle donna dello Stil Nuovo, intesa in tutta la ricchezza delle sue connotazioni. (159–60)

> (The qualities attributed to the Virgin in the canzone [366] are not only those of Laura but, directly or indirectly, those of the woman of the Stil Nuovo, taken in all the richness of her connotations.)

The entire chapter from which this quotation is taken, " 'Vergine bella' " (157–65), is apposite. Wilkins has shown that Petrarch had established "Vergine bella" as the last poem of the *Canzoniere* long before the collection was complete or the order of the poems immediately preceding it had been settled (179).

2. This is not an unproblematic issue, and George and George concisely summarize the debate over the Protestant conception of marriage: "Concerning the Protestant sponsorship of marriage, and especially the sponsorship of the marriage of the clergy, the question has been raised whether the logical mechanism involved is the Protestants' more emphatically positive view of marriage or more emphatically and generally negative view of human nature" (264). Luther's more negative view is that marriage is a "Temporal, worldly thing" that "does not concern the Church" (quoted by George Elliott Howard, 1:388). In contrast, William Haller sees the Puritan clergy in England "teaching, in other words, how marital relationships might be suffused with religious and hence with greater emotional significance" (83). Protestants, in short, had a range of opinions on the sacredness of marriage; so Spenser, although clearly influenced by Protestant teaching on marriage, is not simply applying a preestablished Protestant doctrine on marriage as much as working out his own doctrine.

3. On Milton's attitudes toward marriage, see—in addition to the works already cited—Louis B. Wright, 204, and John Halkett, 39–47, 103–7 and passim.

4. See Leonard Forster, *The Icy Fire*, in particular "The Political Petrarchism of

the Virgin Queen," 122–43; Frances Yates, *Astraea: The Imperial Theme in the Six-teenth Century*, especially 112–16; and Montrose, 325–26.

5. Robin Headlam Wells is also informative on how Marian imagery was used by Elizabethan apologists (16 ff.), although she includes Spenser in that category.

6. Anthea Hume seems to point in this direction when she says that "his Prot-estant epic contains a distinctively Protestant mythologisation of marriage" (126), but ironically, given her focus on Spenser's Protestantism, she misses the polemical anti-Catholic thrust of his portrait of love: "Spenser's inclusive art celebrates both virginity and marriage, friendship and sexual love" (126).

7. This connection between Belphoebe and Petrarch is one Judith Anderson has also made (57–58), although she sees "a significant distance between this vision of Laura's living successor and Spenser's fully idealized Belphoebe, whose rose opens fully only in death" (58). Kathleen Williams makes the relevant point that "Bel-phoebe has her connections, clearly, with that exaggerated adoration and idealiza-tion which was one aspect of the literary tradition which has come to be called Petrarchan" (102).

8. For Raleigh's authorship, see Adamson and Folland, 185. Montrose briefly relates the sonnet to the Petrarchism of Elizabeth's court (325).

9. For discussions of Raleigh's complex relationship to Queen Elizabeth, see Walter Oakeshott, *The Queen and the Poet* and J. H. Adamson and H. F. Folland, *The Shepherd of the Ocean*, 85–103, 178–216, and passim.

10. Subsequently, Raleigh returned the compliment, as he refers to the queen as Belphoebe in his *Ocean to Cynthia*.

Chapter Five: Synge's Irish Renaissance Petrarchism

1. Some information about these translations and their neglect: Synge com-pleted seventeen translations, all done in 1906–9. Eight of these were published in the Cuala Press edition of Synge's poems in 1909, four more were included in the Maunsel edition of 1910, and five more were published for the first time in the 1961 Dolmen Press edition of Synge's translations. There have been four discus-sions of these translations more extended than a brief remark. T. R. Henn, in *The Plays and Poems of J. M. Synge* (1963), compares Petrarch's poem "Zefiro torna" (*Canzoniere* 310), Synge's version, and Surrey's famous translation of the same poem, "The soote season." He also makes some favorable remarks about Synge's diction in these translations. Robin Skelton, in the *The Writings of J. M. Synge* (1971), discusses Synge's experiments in poetic prose in the translations in relation to *Deirdre of the Sorrows*, and I summarize his points below. Skelton also, in his beautiful bilingual edition of Synge's Petrarch translations (*Some Sonnets from "Laura in Death" after the Italian of Francesco Petrarch* [1971]), gives an account of the history of Synge's interest in Petrarch and suggests that Synge depended on various other translations for help with the Italian. Most recently, Toni O'Brien Johnson, in *Synge: The Medieval and the Grotesque* (1982), has made a number of remarks about Synge's translations in the context of a study of Synge's "medieval-ism," but as medievalism is her focus, she concentrates on the translations from Villon, Walter, and others, not on the translations from Petrarch. It should be clear from the rest of this essay that I consider the Renaissance a more useful context for Synge's work than "medievalism." Thus Synge's Petrarch translations have not been extensively studied or appreciated by critics of Synge. The highest praise these translations have received, ironically, came from C. S. Lewis, who, in the

midst of a discussion of Renaissance Petrarchism, the thrust of which was to distinguish Petrarch from his later imitators, made this telling aside: "Readers who do not know Italian will, by the way, learn much more of that strange, great work [Petrarch's *Canzoniere*] from Synge's prose version than from all the Elizabethans and all the Pleiade put together" (*English Literature in the Sixteenth Century excluding Drama*, 229). I think Synge's translations are more influenced by Renaissance Petrarchism than Lewis implies here, but Lewis's assessment of the faithfulness of Synge's translations is high praise indeed, coming from a great medieval and Renaissance scholar.

2. Synge traveled in Italy in 1896 and while there bought and started to read the poems of Petrarch (see Andrew Carpenter, ed., *My Uncle John: Edward Stephen's Life of J. M. Synge*, 96). He began his Petrarch translations in 1906, when Agnes Tobin, an American poet who had translated Petrarch, visited him in Ireland (see Robin Skelton, *J. M. Synge and His World*, 103–4).

3. Hugh Kenner (in *A Colder Eye*, 62–81) has an excellent discussion of the Gaelic basis of Lady Gregory's and other Irish writers' style that complements Kiberd's study of Synge.

4. Thomas M. Greene (*The Light in Troy*, 119) has made the related point that Petrarch makes frequent use of iterative present tense verbs; Synge's use of participials is an appropriate equivalent.

5. Robin Skelton has touched on this, although he has not explored his insight: "All the sonnets that Synge chose to translate are from *Laura in Death* and express moods which he himself was feeling at this time" (Skelton, ed., *Some Sonnets from "Laura in Death" after the Italian of Francesco Petrarch*, 16).

6. Dorothy Shakespear, his future wife, wrote him on 20 April 1911, "I have been reading Petrarch sonnets and J. M. Synge's translations, which are really exquisite" (Pound and Litz, *Ezra Pound and Dorothy Shakespear: Their Letters 1909–1914*, 31).

7. Kenner, in his introduction to *The Translations of Ezra Pound* (13), sees an echo of Yeats rather than of Synge in Pound's Nō translations; Ellmann notes a generally Irish tone (*Eminent Domain*, 71); but it is unmistakably Synge's voice that comes across in phrases like "Times out of mind am I here setting up this bright branch."

Introduction to Part Two

1. Synge's "Vita Vecchia," written between 1895 and 1897 and printed in his *Prose* (16–24), is a sequence of poems connected and framed by a prose narrative that is obviously based on Dante's *Vita Nuova*. In *Synge and the Irish Language* (97–101), Declan Kiberd argues that Synge is trying to "recreate a romance of the Gaelic mode in modern English" (100), and, although the Irish tradition might well be relevant here, for Irish romances did combine verse and prose, his failure even to mention Dante is one measure of how even the best critics of Synge have gone astray in ignoring the Continental sources of Synge's art.

2. Lawrence's interest in futurism can best be seen in his letters to A. W. McLeod and Edward Garnett of 2 June and 5 June 1914 (*Letters 1*, 279–83); the letter to Garnett is often quoted, for Lawrence's reflections on Marinetti lead him into one of the best definitions of his own fiction. The interest in Verga comes later and is stronger; in 1921 he calls him "the only Italian who does interest me" (*Letters 2*, 670). His translations of Verga led to three books, *Mastro-don Gesualdo* (1923),

Little Novels of Sicily (1925), and *Cavalleria Rusticana and Other Stories* (1928). His interest in Verga is discussed in the chapter, "Translations of Verga," in Jeffrey Meyers's *D. H. Lawrence and the Experience of Italy* (50–71) and in Armin Arnold, "D. H. Lawrence, the Russians, and Giovanni Verga."

3. Elizabeth Barrett Browning offers an interesting contrast in this respect, as her poems on the Italian Risorgimento in *Casa Guidi Windows* (1851) and *Poems Before Congress* (1860) show. See Churchill (99–104).

4. Joyce's interest in D'Annunzio has just received its fullest study in Corinna del Greco Lobner's *James Joyce's Italian Connection*, a study that focuses on Joyce's interest in D'Annunzio and Marinetti and on Joyce's play with the Italian language in *Finnegans Wake* and elsewhere.

Chapter Six: Leopardi and Pound's Apprehension of the Italian Past

1. Hugh Kenner has briefly pointed this out in *The Pound Era*: "in New England they decided the culture needed an epic and elected Dante's" (320). He goes on to connect Eliot—not Pound—to this Harvard tradition of Dante studies, but it lies behind Pound's interest in Dante as well, even if Pound was more thoroughly trained in Dante scholarship than Eliot.

2. The works referred to here are David Anderson, *Pound's Cavalcanti*; James J. Wilhelm, *Dante and Pound: The Epic of Judgement*; Stuart Y. McDougal, *Ezra Pound and the Troubadour Tradition*; Peter Makin, *Provence and Pound*.

3. For Petrarch's indebtedness to and interest in Cavalcanti, see Franco Suitner's chapter "Cavalcanti in Petrarca" (45–63). As we shall see in a later chapter, Pound was willing to admit his indebtedness to later humanists such as Lorenzo Valla, whose *Elegantiae linguae latinae* he owned in an Aldine edition.

4. Pound's Aldine Petrarch is now in the collection of the Harry Ransom Humanities Research Center at the University of Texas in Austin. In the "Cavalcanti" essay of 1929, Pound tells of acquiring this text: "Thanks to Mr Adrian Stokes I have been able to locate the Aldine text: not of Guido's complete poems but of this canzone. Aldus printed it at the end of his second or third edition of Petrarch with the canzoni of Dante and Cino cited by Petrarch in 'Lasso me, ch'io non so in qual parte pieghi' " ("Cavalcanti," 190).

5. Earlier poets had collected their shorter verse, of course, but no one before Petrarch combined works in different forms together into a whole. The discussion of E. H. Wilkins is relevant:

> Of the 366 poems of the *Canzoniere* of Petrarch, 29 are *canzoni*, nine are *sestine*, seven are *ballate*, four are *madrigali*, and 317 are sonnets. In the *Canzoniere* these forms are not kept separate, but are so mingled as to afford a pleasing variety. In view of the consistent practice of the separation of canzoni and sonnets in MS collections of pre-Petrarchan lyrics, Petrarch's procedure in mingling canzoni and sonnets is clearly seen to constitute a notable poetic innovation. (266)

6. These references would have been closer yet in Petrarch's manuscripts since the apostrophe was not in use and Petrarch simply elided words together (Durling, 27).

7. See Gianfranco Contini, "Preliminari sulla lingua del Petrarca," 169–92. Contini's distinction between what he calls Dante's "plurilinguismo" and "plurità di toni" (171) as opposed to Petrarch's "unilinguismo" and "l'unità di tono"

(173–74) is crucial for understanding Joyce's interest in Dante as well as Pound's. See in particular Samuel Beckett's discussion in "Dante Bruno Vico Joyce" (17–19).

8. The plan of lectures is reprinted in Pound and Litz, 21. Although, like Pound, Leopardi "had a relatively high opinion of Metastasio" (Carsaniga, 86), this juxtaposition of the librettist and poet Pietro Metastasio (1698–1782) and Leopardi is probably only a matter of chronological proximity. Metastasio, however, is a presence in Pound's work elsewhere (see Bush, 136 and Stock, 119), quoted in the first ur-canto (reprinted in Bush, 306) and mentioned in "A Retrospect" (*Literary Essays*, 8), in *Guide to Kulchur* (180), and in *The Pisan Cantos* (78/492).

9. Robert Spoo has identified the sonnet as "Peregrino del ciel, garrulo a volo"; see "Pound's Cavalcanti and Cravens's Carducci," 14–17. Beckett's character Belacqua in "Dante among the Lobsters" memorably expresses a similar frustration with Carducci: "the nineteenth century in Italy was full of old hens trying to cluck like Pindar. Carducci was another" (17).

10. The only Italian poet translated by Synge after Petrarch is also Leopardi. He translated part of one poem, "Silvia" (*Poems*, 81). Pound's translations of Saturno Montanari in *The Translations* come much later, in 1951.

11. None of the four books focusing on Pound's early verse (Nagy, Witemeyer, Jackson, or Fogelman) even mentions "Her Monument." The only criticism of "Her Monument" is found in Ruthven, who discusses every poem in *Personae*. Ruthven's discussion (78–81) is helpful, providing the Italian text of Leopardi's poem and pointing out some of the citations of Leopardi elsewhere in Pound discussed here.

12. Bickersteth's bilingual facing-page edition of 1923 is the best scholarly edition of Leopardi's poems available in English, with thorough notes and a detailed introduction. His sense of diction, however, is Victorian enough to get between contemporary readers and Leopardi's poetry. Casale's excellent contemporary translation of a selection of Leopardi's work is therefore cited here for those poems he translates, although he follows modern taste in not selecting either "All'Italia" or "Sopra Il Monumento di Dante."

13. See Bickersteth's discussion, 61–67 and 74–78.

14. Carducci also wrote a study of Leopardi, *Degli spiriti e delle forme nella poesia di Giacomo Leopardi*.

15. See Bickersteth's discussion of the influence of Petrarch on Leopardi (53–60) and Bigi.

16. The canzone in fact is more important than the sonnet for both Dante and Petrarch. In both the *Vita nuova* and the *Canzoniere*, "canzoni and groups of canzoni [work] as structural nodes or pillars at varying intervals among the short poems" (Durling, 11). Pound was also interested in the sestina, of course, as "Sestina: Altaforte" shows.

17. This is perhaps what most sharply aligns Pound's interest in the early Italians with Leopardi's and differentiates it from Rossetti's. Rossetti's translations from *duecento* and *trecento* Italian poetry, collected in *The Early Italian Poets*, were obviously crucial for the development of Pound's awareness of figures such as Cavalcanti. Pound's copy of Rossetti, a 1908 edition matching the Temple Classics Dante, which is now at the Humanities Research Center, shows this clearly enough. Pound annotated his copy twice, first in pen at the time he was preparing the Cavalcanti translations and then much later in pencil (for these annotations

include ideograms). The substantial Cavalcanti section is the only one marked extensively in pen. But the difference between Rossetti's and Pound's sense of Cavalcanti can best be shown by Rossetti's dismissive comments on Cavalcanti's "Donna Mi Prega," the poem that Pound—and, on the evidence of *Canzoniere* 70, Petrarch—considered Cavalcanti's masterpiece: "on examination, it proves to be a poem beside the purpose of poetry, filled with metaphysical jargon, and perhaps the very worst of Guido's productions. . . . I have not translated it, as being of little true interest" (Purcell, 137). Moreover, Rossetti's work, Petrarchan in the senses Pound wanted to get away from and centered on the *Vita Nuova*, made no polemical distinctions among the Italian poets or in favor of the canzone as opposed to the sonnet, so in these crucial respects his apprehension of the Italian past was less helpful a model for Pound than Leopardi's was.

18. Pearlman's *The Barb of Time* and Wilhelm's *Dante and Pound* are the two studies that elaborate this perspective most fully, but its centrality to the tradition of Pound criticism is best seen in the way Hugh Kenner, in his extremely influential study, *The Poetry of Ezra Pound*, takes as a given that *The Cantos* are a poem of one hundred cantos based on the *Commedia* (41, 302, 327).

19. Bickersteth again has a good discussion of Leopardi's turn to the idyll (63–67).

20. See the discussion of Timpanaro, who refers to "la polemica apertamente anticristiana dell'ultimo Leopardi" (137; the openly anti-Christian polemic of Leopardi's final years). Timpanaro's discussion of how Leopardi uses classicism as the basis of a critique of Christian orthodoxy makes him closely parallel to Pound.

Chapter Seven: Homer   Dante   Vico   Croce   Joyce

1. For the fullest study of this relationship, see Mary T. Reynolds, *Joyce and Dante*.

2. Max Harold Fisch and Thomas Goddard Bergin begin the translation of Vico's important works into English with the *Autobiography* in 1944 and the third edition of *The New Science* in 1948. However, Croce's study of Vico was translated by R. G. Collingwood into English in 1913. Mooney has a complete list of translations of Vico into English (274–75), and the most thorough study in English of the spread of Vico's ideas is in Fisch and Bergin's Introduction to *The Autobiography of Giambattista Vico* (61–107).

3. The best study of Joyce's relation to prewar Italian intellectual life is Manganiello, *Joyce's Politics*, particularly 43–66, although of course Ellmann's *James Joyce* also presents a good deal of information in passing.

4. H. R. Harris is the author of a full-length study of Gentile, *The Social Philosophy of Giovanni Gentile*, and the translator of Gentile's *Genesis and Structure of Society*. His introduction to Gentile's work has a thorough introduction which is a good general survey of Gentile's life and work (1–63), though Harris doesn't focus on Gentile's interest in Vico.

5. The one figure in Beckett's essay not discussed here is Giordano Bruno, whose influence on Joyce is obviously also part of the influence of Italy on Joyce's work in ways that will be important in subsequent chapters. The tradition of criticism relating Bruno to *Finnegans Wake* initiated by Beckett here is similar to the tradition concerning Vico in that it has stayed with only one idea, that *Finnegans Wake* is indebted to Bruno's notion of the coincidence of opposites also found in Nicholas de Cusa. And Richard Ellmann has argued in *Ulysses on the Liffey* (53–56)

that this has influenced *Ulysses* in the way Stephen and Bloom as opposites connect toward the end of *Ulysses*. More recent explorations of Bruno's influence on Joyce include Theoharis (39–87) and Rabaté.

Joyce's interest in Bruno does connect the Italianism of the modernists with the Italianism of the Elizabethans, for of course Bruno was a friend of Sidney's and spent the years 1583 to 1585 in close contact with Sidney in England (see Imerti, 9–12). Bruno's critique of Petrarchism in *De gli eroici furori* (see *The Heroic Frenzies*, 64), a work published while Bruno was in England and dedicated to Sidney, is therefore a possible influence on Spenser's critique, although Spenser was in Ireland while Bruno was in England and it is unlikely that the two met. Spenser would seem, however, to have taken little from Bruno beyond the information that Italians were criticizing Petrarchism also, for Bruno's work is deeply Neoplatonic (see John Charles Nelson, particularly 168–90) and does not break with the cult of virginity associated with Dante and Petrarch (see particularly the conclusion of Bruno's work [267]). *Degli eroici furori* is interestingly the one work by Bruno in Joyce's Trieste library, in an edition now at the Humanities Research Center.

6. Croce calls Vico "disdegnoso dell'empirismo" in *La filosofia de Giambattista Vico* (66) in a passage that distinguishes him from the other figures Beckett mentions in this passage. Beckett therefore read Croce's book on Vico, not just the more readily available chapter in the *Esthetica*, and he read it in Italian, although it had been translated into English. This shows that figures close to Joyce were reading Croce's work on Vico, possibly by Joyce's prompting.

7. Hayden White's discussion of this question is pertinent and detailed; according to White, although Croce "worked mightily to establish Vico's reputation in the twentieth century, [his] conception of his achievement was both biased and restricted" (379). Nicola Badaloni in the "Introduzione" to Vico's *Opere filosofiche*, edited by Cristofolini, is even more abrupt. After praising one point Croce made about Vico, Badaloni comments, "È questo forse l'unico punto in cui Croce mostra apprezzamento per i contenuti della ricerca vichiana" (this is perhaps the only point in which Croce shows an appreciation for the tenor of Vico's project) (xi).

8. There have been some brief remarks suggesting the connection I am going to argue for here, but no sustained development of the idea. A. Walton Litz, in "Vico and Joyce," did mention Vico's work on Homer and suggested that here "he would have found strong support for his plan to reincarnate Homer's hero in modern Dublin" (246). He did not, however, relate Vico's specific ideas on Homer to *Ulysses*. Donald Phillip Verene suggested briefly in "Vico as Reader of Joyce" that "*Ulysses* itself may have been inspired by the fascinating third book of Vico's *Scienza Nuova*, the search for and discovery of the true Homer" (221–22). Most recently, after the publication of the initial version of this chapter, John Bishop has continued in this one-liner tradition, referring to the way in which Vico's work "richly illuminate[s] *Ulysses*" (178).

9. Of these works, only the third edition of the *Scienza nuova* has been translated into English in its entirety, which helps to account for the neglect of Vico's work on Homer by Joyceans, although, ironically, the very first work of Vico translated into English was "The Third Book of Vico's *Scienza Nuova* [1744]: On the Discovery of the True Homer," translated probably from Michelet's French translation by Henry Nelson Coleridge and included in the second edition published in 1834 of his *Introductions to the Study of the Greek Classic Poets: Designed Principally for the Use of Young Persons at School and College* (see Mooney, 274). *Il*

diritto universale and the *Dissertationes* were written in Latin but are available with facing-page translation into Italian in Giambattista Vico, *Opere giuridiche*, edited by Paolo Cristofolini. The first and third editions of the *Scienza nuova*, both written in Italian, are available in Giambattista Vico, *Opere filosofiche*, edited by Paolo Cristofolini. I will be citing from these two editions throughout; all translations from the Italian will be my own. Any citations from the third edition of the *Scienza nuova* will be followed by the number of the paragraph the passage appears in the Fisch and Bergin translation.

10. The separate discussion of Dante has been translated into English and is available in *Discussions of the Divine Comedy*, edited by Irma Brandeis (1961). Glauco Cambon's "Vico and Dante" is one of the few discussions of Vico to emphasize Dante's place in his thought.

11. He goes on to say that it is because of the change in the meaning of the words that Homer no longer seems true; thus, it takes philogogical skill to recover the true history in Homer.

12. It must be understood that barbaric has no negative connotations for Vico; his work is a defense of the "barbaric wisdom" of earlier stages of society.

13. In addition to Struever's essay quoted below, see Michael Mooney, *Vico in the Tradition of Rhetoric* and Donald R. Kelley, "Vico's Road: From Philology to Jurisprudence and Back." Gentile always emphasized this connection in his work on Vico, but he focused not on the political humanism of Valla but on the neoplatonism of Pico, Ficino, and Bruno (see *Studi vichiani*, 30–37, 49–54, 109–10, passim). Gentile's interest in Bruno led to a full-length study of Bruno, *Giordano Bruno e il pensiero del renascimento* (1920), which also stresses Bruno's indebtedness to the Florentine Platonists of the *quattrocento* (see especially 140–49).

14. This is one point (the only point) on which Vico changed his mind between the first (1725) *Scienza nuova* and the later "Della discoverta del vero Omero," which Brandeis dates between 1728 and 1730 (see Cambon's discussion, 18–21). In the later work, Vico explicitly repudiates his own theory in these terms:

> it is still commonly supposed that Dante gathered together the speech of all the various Italian dialects. Which false notion must have taken root in the sixteenth century when learned men . . . observed in Dante a great number of locutions they had not found in other Tuscan writers, and, recognizing that many of these were, by good fortune, still current in other parts of Italy, concluded that Dante had gathered them thence into his *Comedy*. ("Discovery of the True Dante," 11)

However, given Beckett's echoing of the *Scienza nuova* on precisely this point in "Dante Bruno Vico Joyce" and the parallel to Joyce's own practice, it seems reasonable to assume Joyce's agreement with the position in the far more important and widely accessible *Scienza nuova*. In all other respects, the two discussions of Dante agree.

15. Quoted without a reference by Benedetto Croce in *La filosofia di Giambattista Vico*, 181.

16. Croce in his study, *Ariosto, Shakespeare, Corneille*, went even further, identifying Shakespeare and Vico in this way: "Giambattista Vico, a mighty spirit who resembles Shakespeare, both in his full, keen sense of life and in the adventures of his life and his fame" (290).

17. Mary T. Reynolds has already briefly identified the Citizen as a Vichian giant (114).

18. All citations from *Ulysses* will be from the 1986 Gabler edition, using the chapter and line numbering established in that edition. This is from "Cyclops" (12.151–77).

19. I have argued elsewhere that Joyce's critical parody of the nationalist appropriation of the early Irish epics is anticipated by Synge, particularly in *The Playboy of the Western World* (see my "J. M. Synge and Irish Mythology," 141–43), and Synge's critique is in some ways more authoritative, given his first-hand knowledge of the Irish material.

20. For Pearse's imitation of Cuchulain, see William Irwin Thompson, *The Imagination of an Insurrection*, 75–77 and passim; for a less reverential discussion that focuses on how Joyce shapes "Cyclops" around this, see Kenner, *A Colder Eye*, 176–79 and 202.

21. For discussions of the Irish Revival's quest for a sacred book, see Herbert Howarth, *The Irish Writers, 1880–1940*, 16–20, and passim; and Hugh Kenner, *A Colder Eye*, 198.

22. On the Irish-Hebrew and Parnell-Moses parallel, see Howarth, 24–25, Kenner, *A Colder Eye*, 198, and Thompson, *The Imagination of an Insurrection*, 49–51, 231–47.

23. According to Weldon Thornton (*Allusions in Ulysses*, 184), Yeats compared Synge to Aeschylus and Buck Mulligan is presumably poking fun at this comparison here.

24. Mulligan is again deliberately misquoting, one presumes: Yeats did call *Cuchulain of Muirthemne* "the best book that has come out of Ireland in my time" (*Explorations*, 3), but according to Thornton (218) he never compared Lady Gregory to Homer.

25. Yeats admired Gentile and linked Gentile's interpretation of Vico to Italian Fascism: "Students of contemporary Italy, where Vico's thought is current through its influence on Croce and Gentile, think it created, or in part created, the present government of one man surrounded by just such able assistants as Vico foresaw" (*Explorations*, 354). This reflects Gentile's pro-Fascist interpretation of Vico, something with which both Croce (whose book on Vico Yeats had read) and Joyce (whose enthusiasm for Vico is mentioned in the passage [353]) would have disagreed.

26. A representative comment on Croce can be found in a letter to Ronald Duncan written on 27 March 1938: "Croce is PLOP / not worth mention, unless he has done something utterly unknown to me / He has poisoned a whole generation of Italian near-minds, with abstractness." (unpublished letter in Harry Ransom Humanities Research Center, University of Texas at Austin). The one study that has linked Pound and Croce is Longenbach's *Modernist Poetics of History*, which asserts a general parallel between Croce's theory of history and Pound's. Longenbach does not argue for an influence of Croce on Pound, nor does he discuss Pound's expressed contempt for Croce.

The interesting lacuna in Pound's works is the absence of any discussion of Gentile, whose quasireligious conception of the state (see Harris, *The Social Philosophy of Giovanni Gentile*, 64–70) and whose intense interest in pedagogy (see Harris, 51–98) is reminiscent of Pound. Pound's dislike of Croce may have a political basis given Croce's opposition to Mussolini, but Gentile became Mussolini's Minister of

Education and remained an ardent Fascist until his assassination (precisely for that reason) in 1944. (For an early study of fascism with a number of parallels to Pound's later arguments for fascism, see Aline Lion's *The Pedigree of Fascism*, [1927], which presents Vico, Bruno, and Machiavelli as intellectual precursors of fascism, virtually identified by Lion with Gentile's philosophy.) Nonetheless, although mentioned once in Canto 89 (613) in a list of assassinated fascist leaders whom Pound is mourning, Gentile is not a major presence in Pound's writings. Lawrence Rainey, in a review of Longenbach's book, has criticized Longenbach's failure to mention Gentile, whom Rainey claims was a major influence on Pound as well as on Yeats (109–10). But in the limited amount of space at his disposal in a review, Rainey presents more evidence for Gentile's influence on Yeats than on Pound.

Chapter Eight: Pound's Machiavellian Moment

1. Yeats came to his appreciation of the Italian Renaissance independently of Pound, although I expect Pound reinforced it. Yeats first traveled in Northern Italy in 1907 with Lady Gregory, who also read Castiglione's *The Book of the Courtier* to him, which helps explain Yeats's choice of Urbino as a model here and elsewhere. Corinna Salvadori's *Yeats and Castiglione* explores the relation at length.

2. In a conversation found both in *Stephen Hero* (170) and in *A Portrait* (249), Stephen's Italian professor describes Bruno as a "terrible heretic" to which Stephen responds that he was "terribly burned." It's unclear how Joyce came to his early and abiding enthusiasm for Bruno whom—as this conversation indicates—he would not have been reading in his Italian classes in Catholic educational institutions. "The Day of the Rabblement," written in 1901 when he was nineteen, indicates a knowledge of Frith's 1887 *Life of Giordano Bruno*, and two years later Joyce reviewed J. Lewis McIntyre's *Giordano Bruno* (*Critical Writings*, 132–34). I think what Joyce admired about Bruno was precisely the fact that he was "terribly burned," his uncompromising opposition to the Church. And the Dante he admired was the Dante who in his fierce criticism of Florence and the Church and in his exile resembled Bruno in this respect.

3. Pound's relation to Pater's work is the subject of a revealing passage in *Guide to Kulchur*: "Every critic however anti-paterine ought to want to accomplish something of the sort that Pater indubitably did with his *Renaissance*. Pater made his limited circle of readers want to know much of a period. I think I owe him Valla, I can pardon his inflation of Pico della Mirandola" (207). But here Pound is defining a difference as well as admitting to a line of influence, for Pater's chapter on Pico (54–68) is the only chapter on a humanist in *The Renaissance* and is followed by a half-dozen chapters on Renaissance artists. One way of distinguishing Pound's interest in the Renaissance from the received nineteenth-century one is that Pound was more interested in Valla than in Raphael or Leonardo.

4. Pound himself has connected these figures in a suggestive way: "The finest force of the age, I think, came early—came from Lorenzo Valla. He had a great passion for exactness, and he valued the Roman vortex. By philology, by the 'harmless' study of language, he dissipated the donation of Constantine. . . . As Valla had come to exactness, it was possible for Machiavelli to write with clarity. . . . In Machiavelli's prose we have a realism born perhaps from Valla's exactness and the realism of Homer" (*Gaudier-Brzeska*, 113).

5. *The Cantos* are customarily divided by critics into the Early Cantos (1–30),

the Middle Cantos (31–71), and the Later Cantos (85–117), and this conventional terminology will be followed here, although the thrust of my argument here will be to make distinctions that weaken any sense of the Middle Cantos as a static entity. *The Pisan Cantos* (74–84) are usually not incorporated into any of these groups, and Cantos 72–73 form a whole problem unto themselves, as we shall see in the next chapter. All quotations from *The Cantos* will be cited parenthetically by canto number and page number: 21/97. I will be citing the most recent New Directions printing.

6. Nothing comparable to Frederick K. Sanders's *John Adams Speaking: Pound's Sources for the Adams Cantos*, which collects Pound's sources for the Adams Cantos in one place, has been done for Jefferson, although Philip Furia in *Pound's Cantos Declassified* (51–63) discusses the documents that make their way into this section of *The Cantos*. Pound's interest in Thomas Jefferson has received considerably less attention than many of his more recondite interests. This might seem surprising and a confirmation of Pound's point about the sad neglect of the writings of the Founding Fathers if it did not have a simpler explanation. Pound's interest in Jefferson is inextricably bound up with the scandal of Pound's politics, inextricably bound up by Pound himself, whose central work on Jefferson (aside from the cantos on Jefferson we shall examine) he titled *Jefferson and/or Mussolini*. And one index of the scandal represented by this book is the difficulty it has had getting (and staying) published: written in 1933, it was turned down—in Pound's account—by forty publishers and only published in 1935 (iv). Pound himself then tried to suppress it later in life when Horace Liveright put it back into print in 1970. The reprinted volume states on the back: "This book is being reissued under a contract which was executed in 1935 and does not necessarily reflect Ezra Pound's later views." It is possible to depoliticize Pound's interest in Confucius or Dante and focus on the aesthetic or cultural aspect of his interest in their work. But faced with *Jefferson and/or Mussolini*, one can do no such thing with Pound's interest in Jefferson. As a result, Pound's portrait of Jefferson (and his portrait of Revolutionary America) has received little serious attention.

7. *Jefferson and/or Mussolini* was written in 1933 and published in 1935. Canto 21 was first published as part of *A Draft of the Cantos 17–27* in 1928, and these were then incorporated in *A Draft of XXX Cantos* in 1930. Cantos 31–33 were published in *Pagany* in 1931, and then were published as part of *Eleven New Cantos* in 1934.

Pound's knowledge of the American Revolution comes almost entirely from primary sources, above all from the Memorial edition of Jefferson's works given him by Eliot in the early 1920s (Andrew A. Lipscomb, ed., *The Writings of Thomas Jefferson*) and *The Works of John Adams* he began to work through later. (For Eliot's gift, see Noel Stock, *The Life of Ezra Pound*, 294; and William M. Chace, *The Political Identities of Ezra Pound and T. S. Eliot*, 49.) "The Jefferson-Adams Letters as a Shrine and a Monument" contains his clearest statement of the importance he ascribed to the correspondence of these two men. The only secondary work on the American Revolution that Pound refers to in *Jefferson and/or Mussolini* is W. E. Woodward's *George Washington, The Image and the Man*, which he refers to twice, and Woodward's rather breezy study seems only to have reinforced Pound's perception of Washington as rather a lightweight in contrast to Jefferson and Adams, who for him are the only figures of importance in the American Revolution. (Garry Wills's *Cincinnatus: George Washington and the Enlightenment* makes Washington altogether more interesting and much closer to Pound's concerns about virtue and independence.) Pound corresponded with Woodward, and three letters of Pound's to Woodward have recently been published ("Letters to Woodward"). In the collection of Pound's library now at the Harry Ransom Humanities Research Center at the University of Texas at Austin, the only other secondary studies of the American Revolutionary period are two books by Charles A. Beard, *An Economic Interpretation of the Constitution of the United States* and *Economic Origins of Jeffersonian Democracy*, with notations by Pound throughout. Woodward refers admiringly to Beard's work and may have directed Pound's attention to him. Beard's general stress on the economic basis of the politics surrounding the debates over the Constitution and his focus on the key role played by debt in the period would certainly have been grist for Pound's mill, although Beard's defense of the necessity of Hamilton's "pro-debt" politics and his discussion of the opposition between Adams and Jefferson would not have been congenial to Pound. However, as Pound's copies are 1935 and 1936 editions, they could not have played a formative role in Pound's portrait of Jefferson; he does refer to Beard in some of his World War II radio speeches and in Canto 84. Neither his editions of Adams or Jefferson are in the Texas collection, only a single volume published in 1825 of Jefferson's *Notes on the State of Virginia*, and I have not been able to consult these.

8. Petrarch's prose work, *De Vita Solitaria* (translated as *The Life of Solitude*), also advanced the same vision of imitation as conformity to the classic model. This is a work in praise of the solitary life, and the second book is entirely devoted to the adducing by Petrarch of various examples from antiquity of a preference for the *vita solitaria*.

9. Imitation is an important theme in the *Discorsi* as well, but in the *Discorsi* Machiavelli more often criticizes republics for their failure to learn from and imitate the past: "Nonetheless, in setting up states, in maintaining governments, in ruling kingdoms, in organizing armies and managing war, in executing laws among subjects, in expanding an empire, not a single prince or republic now resorts to the examples of the ancients" (191; from the Preface to the First Book). Clearly, the *Discorsi* represent Machiavelli's attempt to facilitate such resorting to "the examples of the ancients," and given a broader definition of antiquity than Machiavelli's, that is a good summary of the project of *The Cantos* as well.

10. For the central statement of the Lockean paradigm, see Carl Becker, *The Declaration of Independence*, 24–79. Pocock implicitly criticizes this view throughout *The Machiavellian Moment*; for an explicit critique, see Garry Wills, *Inventing America*, 168–75 and passim.

11. It should be noted that Pocock spends very little time actually discussing Jefferson, so it is perhaps a bit misleading to speak of his "portrait of Jefferson." One should say instead, his portrait of revolutionary America which establishes a context for Jefferson.

12. How to translate *virtù* is a major dilemma for English translators of Machiavelli. Mark Musa devotes one third of his Introduction to the problem, listing the fifty-nine times the word appears in *The Prince*. He uses twelve different words to translate *virtù*, using virtue only three times. See Mark Musa, trans. and ed., *Machiavelli's* The Prince: *A Bilingual Edition*, x–xv. For Hanna Pitkin's sense of the meaning of *virtù*, see n. 15 below.

13. I should specify here that I am arguing less for the direct influence of Machiavelli on Pound than that Machiavelli theorizes about a political practice Pound already knew directly through his knowledge of the Italian Renaissance. It is not

that Pound saw Malatesta through Machiavelli's eyes as much as that Machiavelli usefully summarizes for us what Pound saw in a figure like Malatesta. But Pound owned and used Machiavelli's *Istorie fiorentine*, as it was his source for Canto 21 and a copy of it annotated by Pound is in the Pound library at the University of Texas. His edition of Machiavelli's *Istorie* was published in 1921, and Pound seems to have bought and read it shortly after its publication while researching the Malatesta Cantos, as every reference to Malatesta in the fifth and sixth books is marked. Burckhardt and Symonds both draw on Machiavelli's *Istorie* and may have drawn Pound's attention to it; in fact, their two works offer a thorough introduction to Machiavelli's life and work. Pound also owned and annotated an extraordinarily detailed history of Florence from 1527 to 1538, full of references to Machiavelli, the *Storia fiorentina* of Benedetto Varchi (1503–1565). And the references to and quotations from Machiavelli in *Gaudier-Brzeska* indicate familiarity earlier with his works. It is also relevant that Pound's two closest literary friends and allies in the 1920s, Wyndham Lewis and T. S. Eliot, were both writing about Machiavelli at this time. See T. S. Eliot, "Niccolò Machiavelli," in *For Lancelot Andrewes: Essays on Style and Order*, 49–66; Eliot, "Niccolò Machiavelli," *Times Literary Supplement*, 413–14; and Wyndham Lewis, *The Lion and the Fox: The Role of the Hero in the Plays of Shakespeare*. So Pound knew his Machiavelli.

14. Also see Ezra Pound, "Cavalcanti," 152, 155–56. Virtue or *virtù* was a key word for Pound for many years: for a rather different, earlier Poundian use of the word, see "On Virtue," in "I Gather the Limbs of Osiris," 28–31; and James Longenbach's discussion in *Modernist Poetics of History*, 55–61. Hanna Pitkin's contention that the fundamental meaning of *virtù* is "manliness" is relevant here, for Pound's conception of energy was always, as one says today, "phallocentric," and his appreciation of the "manly" energy in the Italian Renaissance from Cavalcanti to Malatesta was an important part of his cult of the Italian Renaissance. See Hanna Fenichel Pitkin, *Fortune Is a Woman*, 25.

15. Peter Nicholls has a good discussion of Pound's brief dialogue with Marxism in the 1920s; see his *Ezra Pound: Politics, Economics and Writing*, 47–59. The various prefaces to *Jefferson and/or Mussolini* record Pound's brief interest in and subsequent disillusionment with Roosevelt.

16. See "The Jefferson-Adams Letters." One can also see this process at work in his annotations of Beard's volumes at the HRC. The chapter in *Economic Origins of Jeffersonian Democracy* dealing with "The Great Battle of 1800" between Adams and Jefferson (353–414) is almost completely unmarked in Pound's copy, except for a few references to banks, whereas the previous chapter, "The Politics of Agrarianism" (322–52), with its emphasis on the Jeffersonian critique of the banking interests, is heavily marked and annotated.

17. For Aristotle on the one, the few, and the many, see the *Politics*, 3:1ff; see also Pocock, *The Machiavellian Moment*, 66–80 and passim. Pound's well-marked copy of Aristotle's *Politics* is at the University of Texas.

18. The second chapter of Machiavelli's *Discorsi* (196–201) has an excellent summary of the Aristotelian theory of government and also endorses a Polybian theory of mixed government:

> I say, then, that all the said types are pestiferous, by reason of the short life of the three good and the viciousness of the three bad. Hence, since those who have been prudent in establishing laws have recognized this defect, they have

avoided each one of these kinds by itself alone and chosen one that partakes of them all, judging it more solid and more stable, because one keeps watch over the other, if in the city there are princedom, aristocracy, and popular government. (199)

Machiavelli's positive recommendations here are very close to the Polybian tradition that helped shape Adams's thinking and the American Constitution; what is particularly his own here is the stress on the fragility of all such arrangements, his focus on the problem of time and mutability.

19. This comes from a speech broadcast to England, not to the United States, which accounts for the reference to Parliament. Pound also applied his Polybian analysis to British politics, arguing in a series of unpublished letters to Sir Oswald Mosley, leader of the British Union of Fascists, that England's political system had been thrown out of balance by the transformation of the monarchy into a figurehead: "As to the CONST/ its basis is a BALANCE between executive, legislative (or representative) and judicial. . . . At the start of the 19th. century & progressively the LEGAL executive (crown etc.) in ENG/ was knocked to bits / weakened ending with Eddie's exit" (Edward VIII's abdication in 1937) (unpublished letter to Mosley of 8 February 1939).

20. This passage is the source for a passage on 70/413.

Chapter Nine: Ezra Pound, the Last Ghibelline

1. Pound's admiration for Dante can be seen in his published works in the chapter on Dante in *The Spirit of Romance* (118–65); in "Hell," a review of Laurence Binyon's translation of the *Inferno*; in the numerous quotations from Dante in *The Cantos*, and virtually passim in his prose works and letters. The one book-length study of Pound's relation to Dante is Wilhelm, *Dante and Pound*; Pearlman argues at length for the structural indebtedness of *The Cantos* to the *Commedia*. Pound began to read Dante at Hamilton College in 1903 or 1904 under the tutelage of William Pierce Shepherd (Tytell, 22), and in 1905 he wrote to his mother: "Find me a phenomenon of any importance in the lives of men and nations that you cannot measure with the rod of Dante's allegory . . . I shall continue to study Dante and the Hebrew prophets" (Stock, 26). This is a somewhat ironic conjunction in view of Pound's later anti-Semitism, but also a sign that his interest in Dante was an interest in his content. His first copy of Dante was probably the three volumes of the Temple Classics *Commedia*, compact bilingual, facing-page editions; his copies of these, now at the University of Texas, are dated and signed March 1904. But he quickly supplemented this edition with the Oxford Dante, *Le Opere di Dante Alighieri*, edited by Edward Moore (Oxford, 1897); Pound probably bought this during graduate school at the University of Pennsylvania, at any rate before leaving the United States for Venice in 1908, for he wrote his father in 1909 asking that it be sent to him in England (Stock, 89). Although published in England, this presents the works only in their original languages, Italian and Latin; even the prefatory material is in Italian. Finally, probably in Italy in the 1920s, he purchased the 1921 critical edition of the Società Dantesca Italiana, *Le Opere di Dante: Testo critico della Società Dantesca Italiana*, edited by a team of editors led by Michele Barbi. Both of these *Opere di Dante* are at the University of Texas. Thus after buying an accessible bilingual edition, Pound successively bought the best contemporary scholarly editions available to him. Redman also lists an 1869 edi-

tion of *La Divina Commedia* (Florence: G. Barbera) as being in Pound's possession (219), but this is at Brunnenberg in the collection of Pound's daughter, Mary de Rachewiltz, not at Texas.

2. A number of scholars who might have been expected to touch on this do not. Neither Pearlman, studying the relevance of Dante to *The Cantos*, nor Nicholls, studying Pound's politics, connect the two. Wilhelm's *Dante and Pound* has only two pages on *De Monarchia* (87–89). He draws a number of parallels between Dante's monarchical theories and Pound's support of Mussolini but does not argue for a direct influence. Wilhelm's treatment of Pound's politics is in any case vitiated by his explicit assumption discussed in the previous chapter that Pound was not antidemocratic. Finally and most recently, Robert Casillo spends only a sentence on the topic: "His notions of political authority owe something to Dante's *De Monarchia*, which envisions European unification under a benevolent Catholic king. But by the late 1930s and early 1940s Pound's medievalism has more sinister implications" (50). Casillo heavily criticizes those (like Wilhelm) who aestheticize Pound by separating his poetry from the more unpleasant aspects of his thought, but we can see here a similar sanitizing of Dante, who is firmly—and incorrectly, I think—separated from the "more sinister" aspects of Pound's thought.

3. *De Monarchia* is the only work aside from the *Paradiso* that is annotated in both of Pound's complete Dantes, and each copy shows evidence of having been read and annotated twice. Moore's edition of *De Monarchia* was gone through twice, once in pencil and then again in red pencil. The first reading dates from the 1910s most probably, because "Fenollosa" is marked once on the side; the second in red pencil has to date from the 1930s or 1940s for some of Pound's marginalia include Chinese ideograms. The Barbi edition has also been read and marked twice, and obviously, given the date of publication, both readings are after 1921. The first is in ink and if I had to venture a date, it would be the 1920s, the most logical time for Pound to have bought the book. The second reading is in pencil and includes ideograms, so it is from the 1930s or 1940s.

4. The terms Guelf and Ghibelline are, of course, a translation of the German terms, Welf and Weiblingen. See Kantorowicz, *Frederick the Second* (67–68 and passim) for the derivation of the term and the historical background. For a good survey of these events that Pound knew early on, see Toynbee (1–35), which is cited in *The Spirit of Romance* (118–19). Toynbee begins his life of Dante with three chapters on this political background, grouped together as "Part I Guelfs and Ghibellines," one index of how important Dante scholars who were prominent during Pound's education thought this political background was.

5. Dante, it must be remembered, began his political involvements in Florence as a White Guelf, but his political ideology as he developed it after his exile in 1302 was clearly Ghibelline. Moreover, the actions that led to his exile could be called "proto-Ghibelline," as they involved opposition to Florentine support for the Pope and Charles of Valois (see Toynbee, 82–85).

6. My citations from *De Monarchia* and the *Epistolae* come from Moore's edition, which in any case is virtually identical to Barbi's. I cite the original Latin whenever Pound has specifically marked the passage I have quoted; otherwise, I only give the passage in an English translation.

7. The "Philosopher" is, of course, Aristotle, "il maestro di color che sanno," and the reference here is to his *Politics*, 3:4. The numerous citations from the *Politics* in *De Monarchia* may well have directed Pound's attention to the *Politics*; in

any case, the two influences are congruent, as we have already seen in the influence of Aristotle on Pound's presentation of John Adams.

8. The reference is to 1:5.

9. These questions are not original with Dante, of course; in a 1931 book that Pound read and annotated and is now at the University of Texas, Kantorowicz treats in great detail Frederick II's imperial theory, presenting him as the initiator of political themes inherited and carried forward by Dante (*Frederick the Second*, 228–261 and 668). My only reservation about Kantorowicz's study is that he seems altogether too enthusiastic about Frederick's all-embracing, sacred state, but this was clearly what recommended the book to Pound. His later, more famous study, *The King's Two Bodies*, has a chapter on Dante focusing on his political thought and *De Monarchia* (451–95) that is also relevant, although it comes too late to influence Pound.

10. Hans Baron also discusses how the later civic humanism led to a reinterpretation of Roman history at odds with Dante's (48–54). To later Florentines, "Dante appeared to be wrong in his appraisal of Caesar and his enemies; the view of the ancient and mediaeval Empire enshrined in the *Divina Commedia* became alien to Florentine readers" (445). Pound, in contrast, always stressed the continuity between Dante and the *quattrocento*; for instance, he marked on the side a passage in *Frederick the Second* in which Kantorowicz wrote that "in the thirteenth century the Ghibelline spirit stood for that secular and intellectual light that often bordered on heresy" (67).

11. There are obviously a number of parallels here to the Confucian classics, and one of the problems in delineating any one influence on Pound is that his syncretic cast of mind never restricts itself to only one influence. As mentioned in n.3 above, Pound's marginalia to *De Monarchia* (and other works of Dante) included Chinese characters at places where he found a resemblance between Dante and Chinese ideas, in much the way *The Cantos* juxtapose ideograms and text in Western languages. (This is more startling in Pound's marginalia, however, as one realizes that this habit and syncretic cast of mind were perfectly natural to Pound, not at all worked up for poetic effects in *The Cantos*.) One passage in the radio speeches should show the close resemblance between what Pound drew out of Dante and his reading of the Confucian classics:

> When Mencius went to see King Huei of Liang, the King said, have you got something that will bring PROFIT? Profit motive, already known, two thousand five hundred years before Blast; 2,400 years before Marx half swallowed Hegel. And Mencius said, why use that word, what I got is my sense of EQUITY. If you can't use that in your Kingdom, good morning, I have mistaken the address.
>
> Well, now the sense of EQUITY, sense of justice, was what England had lost or mislaid. *Ben dell'intelletto* Dante called it, or something not very far from it. Homely English would get that down to "use of your wits," but I reckon Dante meant something nearer to Mencius's meaning. (*Ezra Pound Speaking*, 109)

12. For Dante's discussions of Frederick, see *Il Convivio*, Book 4:3–6 (Moore, 298–303), *De Vulgari Eloquentia* 1:12 (37–41) and *Inferno*, 10.119; a good discussion of Dante's attitude toward Frederick is found in Davis, 11–14. Kantorowicz claims a strong influence of Frederick on Dante (*Frederick the Second*, 247–61 and passim).

13. Pound had earlier praised Frederick in *Guide to Kulchur*: "The attempt of Frederic II of Sicily to enlighten Europe both culturally and economically was a MAJOR event" (261). One of Frederick's poems was included in Rossetti's *Early Italian Poets*; although unmarked by Pound in his first reading of Rossetti, it was marked in a later reading. Frederick is mentioned in Cantos 97, 98 and 105, and Pound in his 1962 *Paris Review* interview with Donald Hall specifically linked this section of *The Cantos* to Dante: "The thrones in Dante's *Paradiso* are for the spirits of the people who have been responsible for good government. The thrones in the *Cantos* are an attempt to move out from egoism and to establish some definition of an order possible or at any rate conceivable on earth" (quoted in Kearns, 225). Dante's *Convivio* was also a potent influence on the Late Cantos, as Canto 93 in *Rock Drill* is a virtual cento of passages from it; see Wilhelm, *The Later Cantos* (46–63), *Dante and Pound* (145), Nicholls (206–11), and Ellis (204–6).

14. Manfred is praised along with his father in *De Vulgari Eloquentia* 1:12 (37–41); see Ferrante (209–12) for a discussion of why Manfred—unlike his father—is in Purgatory.

15. It seems improbable that Pound would have had Manfred's politics in mind when naming *A Lume Spento* in 1908. According to Wilhelm's interpretation: "The dedication suggests that, like Manfred, [William Brooke] Smith [to whom *A Lume Spento* was posthumously dedicated] (as well as Pound) was an artist who was considered an outcast by the rest of society" (*American Roots*, 100). And this use of Dante to suggest the theme of exile and alienation continues throughout Pound's life and work just as it does through Joyce's.

16. Pound did not go through the *Epistolae* as carefully as he did *De Monarchia*, but they are marked throughout in Barbi, the edition he bought later (only the "Letter to Can Grande" about the *Commedia* is marked in Moore). Although this passage equating Henry VII with Justice is marked, the sixth letter chastising the Florentines is generally marked more heavily than the fifth and seventh, which are in praise of Henry.

17. Boccaccio dates *De Monarchia* during Henry's reign (108). Some scholars have interpreted the absence of specific references as indicating either an earlier or a later date, but I think that shows a misunderstanding of the genre of *De Monarchia*, which is abstract and not concrete. The strongest argument for a late date is the reference to the *Paradiso* in Chapter 12 of Book 1 (see Mancusi-Ungaro, 14–15).

18. Bergin puts it well when he says that "the *Comedy* contains, broadly speaking, everything we find in the *De Monarchia* and the *Convivio*" (96). Ferrante echoes Bergin, arguing that the views of Church and State in the *Commedia* "are quite consistent with Dante's positions in the *Monarchy*" (126). Kantorowicz also stresses the continuity between Dante's political writings and the *Commedia* (*Frederick the Second*, 259). Others have disagreed, however; see Ferrante (3–9) for a summary of the opposing views. Mancusi-Ungaro summarizes the debate (13–17) before arguing that "the only difference between the *Monarchia* and the *Commedia* is one of genre" (23).

19. Dante's *duca* and Mussolini's *duce* are two different words, guide and leader, although with a common Latin root in *dux*, so my collocation of them here is somewhat adventitious. Nonetheless, the verbal echo is not unimportant for Pound, I think, who, as a non-native speaker of Italian, would have been more alive to the resemblance between the words than the difference.

20. Pound's Hell in Cantos 14–15 is closely modeled on—although vastly inferior in power to—Dante's (see Wilhelm, *Dante and Pound*, 108–9). Canto 14 begins: "Io venni in luogo d'ogni luce muto" (*Inferno*, 5.28). And what Ferrante says about Dante's reasons for using Florence also apply to Pound and London: "There are also personal reasons for Dante to model Hell on Florence; what better way to avenge himself on the city that exiled him than to cast it as Hell" (61).

21. Petrarch's "How a Ruler Ought to Govern His State" is a good, early statement of this humanist position from which we have already quoted. Although Pound showed absolutely no awareness of Petrarch's political thinking, Petrarch's series of stances resembles Pound's. His early support of Cola di Rienzo is a forerunner of republican humanism, just as this late political letter addressed to Francesco da Carrara is a forerunner of the humanism of the courtier. In between, Petrarch moved close for a time to the Ghibelline position of *De Monarchia* in his support for Charles IV (see *Rerum familiarum libri*, 23:2, a letter to Charles as well as the letter about his visit to Charles already quoted in the last chapter, *Rerum familiarum libri*, 19:3). And the whole panorama shows how Petrarch begins the opportunism characteristic of humanism.

22. According to references in Pound's extensive correspondence with (or rather to) Mussolini at the Beinecke Library at Yale, Pound sent Mussolini copies of *Eleven New Cantos, Cantos 52–71, ABC of Economics*, and *Make It New* in addition to *A Draft of XXX Cantos* and the manuscript of *Jefferson and/or Mussolini* before its publication.

23. Wilhelm has briefly linked Henry VII and Mussolini but in a way that distances the poets from their rulers: "Dante had undoubtedly lost a great deal of faith in the Swabian [Henry VII] even before that time [his death], just as Pound foresaw the end of Mussolini long before he was hanging by the heels in the square at Milan" (*Dante and Pound*, 9). But this seems quite misleading to me. Wilhelm goes on to quote the opening line of *The Pisan Cantos*, "The enormous tragedy of the dream in the peasant's bent shoulders," but this line expresses no distance from Mussolini even after his death. As late as 1957, Pound is arranging to have writings by Mussolini translated and published in *Edge* ("In Captivity"). I see no evidence that he ever reconsidered his belief in Mussolini's wisdom; I think he reconsidered the wisdom of his support of Mussolini, but that is not quite the same thing.

24. This raises the question of whether Pound's application of *De Monarchia* to Mussolini and the situation of contemporary Italy was at all influenced by Fascist thinking or whether it was his own idiosyncratic reading. I have found no evidence of any contemporary official use of *De Monarchia* to bolster Mussolini's regime; Mussolini, of course, made many references to the Roman Empire as did Dante, but this is the aspect of Dante's thought and the Fascist regime that least interested the author of the "Homage to Sextus Propertius."

However, Aline Lion's 1927 *The Pedigree of Fascism* does compare Mussolini at length to Dante (211–13) and briefly mentions *De Monarchia* as a foreshadowing of Vico's "Immanentist doctrine of history and society" (80), which, following Gentile, she sees as anticipatory of fascism. Gentile's *Giordano Bruno* goes into a good deal of detail about this Immanentism, which Gentile finds the key theme in the Italian philosophical tradition.

25. Bacigalupo has a good discussion of Pound's life-long sense of exile (*The Forméd Trace*, 53–58); Wilhelm compares Pound to Dante in this respect (*Dante*

and Pound, 24). The lives of other poets are relevant here as well: Hugh Kenner relates that Pound, after his release in 1958, "told the press that Ovid had it worse, in the long years at Pontus, a statement the press was unprepared to evaluate" (*The Pound Era*, 536).

26. Pearlman has argued quite straightforwardly that the Early, Middle, and Pisan Cantos represent an Inferno, Purgatorio, and Paradiso. Wilhelm tends to make similar claims but retract them at the same time. Two representative instances from *Dante and Pound*:

> The rhythm of the *Cantos* is, in other words, genuinely the rhythm of the *Comedy*, but we still cannot approach the two works as if they showed a complete resemblance. (96)

> I will not say that the Later Cantos form an exact parallel with Dante's *Paradiso*, but I will frankly admit that there is a strong heavenly cast to much of the rhetoric. (136)

27. These two cantos were published in part in Italy in 1945 but were not included in English-language editions of *The Cantos* until the tenth New Directions printing of 1986. For a good summary and discussion of these cantos with some translations, see Bacigalupo, "The Poet at War."

28. Pound's awareness of Ezzelino was undoubtedly prompted by his friend Manlio Torquato Dazzi's translation (into Italian) of Albertino Mussato's 1315 Latin tragedy, *L'eccerinide*, a copy of which Dazzi gave him in 1927 (which is now at the Humanities Research Center). Dazzi—though still alive in 1945—appears in Canto 72 in between Marinetti and Ezzelino. As late as 1958, Pound was still trying to have Mussato's work translated into English by Peter Whigham; for Pound's interest in Mussato and Dazzi, see Bacigalupo's "The Poet at War," 75–78. But Mussato presents the traditional portrait of Ezzelino as a monster, and Ezzelino in fact complains to Pound in the canto about the portrayal of him as a "fiol d'Orco" (son of a monster) in the poem that "il tuo amico ha tradotto" (your friend translated). Pound wants to reverse the traditional judgment on Ezzelino in the same way he reversed the received view of Malatesta, and Pound links the two in this canto for he at first thinks Ezzelino is Malatesta. Kantorowicz may have prompted this identification, as he says, in a passage marked by Pound, that "through his son-in-law Eccelino of Romano, the Devil of Treviso, [Frederick] became the ancestor of Sigismundo Malatesta and of Cesare Borgia" (612). Pound follows Kantorowicz in seeing the despots of the *quattrocento* as descended from the Ghibellines of the *duecento*, and the often brutal exercize of power by all these figures does not seem to have bothered him. Also marked in Kantorowicz by Pound is this celebration of the Great Ruler: "The history of Frederick II demonstrates how much a law-giver can accomplish by force and compulsion, so long as he knows what his aims are, and so long as those aims are just." (292). And Pound—like Dante—sees his role as defining the just aims toward which the Great Ruler should work.

29. The key text of Petrarch for this tradition is the canzone "Italia mia," *Canzoniere* 128 (Durling, 256–63), which, as we have seen, Machiavelli quotes in the last chapter of *The Prince* (which urges Italian independence and unification). The closing words of *The Prince* are in fact the quotation from "Italia mia." The key

text of Leopardi is "All'Italia," *Canti* 1 (Bickersteth, 136–43), which is clearly based on Petrarch's canzone, and we have already discussed Pound's use of Leopardi and of "All'Italia" in Chapter 6.

30. Vico's paradigmatic or cyclical theories of history might well have been inspired by Machiavelli, as any number of passages in Machiavelli could show:

> He who considers present affairs and ancient ones readily understands that all cities and all peoples have the same desires and the same traits and that they always have had them. He who diligently examines past events easily foresees future ones in every country and can apply to them the remedies used by the ancients or, not finding any that have been used, can devise new ones because of the similarity of the events. But because these considerations are neglected or are not understood by those who read or, if they are understood, are not known to rulers, the same dissensions appear in every age. (*Discourses*, 278)

Chapter 2 of Book 1, the chapter summarizing the Aristotelian theory of government already cited in Chapter 8, refers even more explicitly to "the circle in which all states revolve" (199). This connection has already been made by Croce, in his essay "Machiavelli and Vico" (1924): "the veritable and worthy successor of Machiavelli whose powerful mind brought together and fruitfully married the immortal thought of the Florentine Secretary and the scattered wisdom of his critics was another Italian, Vico, . . . The two great Italians can truly stand together as a symbol of the whole philosophy of politics in its basic idea" (658).

Chapter Ten: Understanding Modernist Imitation:
Mozart contra Wagner in Ulysses

1. *Ezra Pound and Music: The Complete Criticism*, ably edited by R. Murray Schafer, presents most of the essential documents. And Pound's and Joyce's interests in music are closer than they might seem at first glance. For both, the supreme musical tradition is the Italian, not the German, and although Pound intensely disliked most nineteenth-century music (of any nationality), he did admire the early part of the operatic repertoire beloved by Joyce. See Pound's admiring discussion of a 1917 production of *Le Nozze de Figaro* (61–65), in which he draws a contrast between Mozart and Wagner (64–65), and his 1938 *Townsman* article, "Musicians; God Help 'Em" (437–40), in which he praises Rossini, in addition to other, more fleeting references (see *Ezra Pound and Music*, passim). Another musical interest they had in common was Elizabethan English songs and the rediscovery of early music by Arnold Dolmetsch, although Pound as usual carried this a good deal further than Joyce (on Pound's interest in Dolmetsch, see *Ezra Pound and Music*, 35–50; on Joyce's in him and in Elizabethan music, see Ellmann, *James Joyce*, 154–55, and *A Portrait*, 176, 219). Schafer's introduction to *Ezra Pound and Music* also contains a spirited defense of Pound's musical culture as opposed to Joyce's (16–22).

2. Corinna del Greco Lobner's recent *James Joyce's Italian Connection* has a good survey of Joyce's training and command of Italian (1–4 and 15–25).

3. I do not suspect Beckett had Pound in mind here, but he could have. Kenner tells us of Pound jeering at one of Joyce's disciples in Paris: "Of one slim youth he enquired, in withering tones, whether he might be writing an *Iliad*, or would it be a *Divina Commedia*. One should not say such a humiliating thing to anyone, cer-

tainly not to anyone who has done no harm, but it is especially regrettable that he should have said it to Sam Beckett" (*The Pound Era*, 396). "Dante Bruno Vico Joyce" suggests that Beckett might have been perplexed, not humiliated: why rewrite the *Commedia* instead of writing a new one?

4. The pioneering and still most thorough exploration of the echoes of *Don Giovanni* in *Ulysses* is Vernon Hall, Jr., "Joyce's use of Da Ponte and Mozart's *Don Giovanni.*"

5. Joyce had this edition of this novel (as well as a Tauchnitz edition of 1901) in his library, as well as every other book by Moore mentioned in this chapter and six other books by Moore; these are all now in the collection of Joyce's library at the Humanities Research Center.

6. Ellmann's source for this anecdote is Louis Gillet, *Claybook for James Joyce*, 103.

7. Dominic Manganiello has a good discussion of Joyce's "literary rivalry" with Moore in *Joyce's Politics*, 212–15.

8. Hugh Kenner discusses the broader implications of this criticism of Moore in *Ulysses*, 31.

9. This is probably no accident, as *The Waste Land* shows that Eliot is more of a Wagnerian than Joyce, more interested in the redemptive project of the mythic method. It is perhaps also relevant to note that Jessie L. Weston was a fervent Wagnerian, writing *The Legends of the Wagner Drama* (1896), a book in which many of the themes of the later *From Ritual to Romance* are developed. See the discussion of Herbert Knust (22–24), who is generally informative on Eliot's use of Wagner in *The Waste Land*.

10. Dominic Manganiello has argued that Joyce alludes critically to Moore's conversion in *A Portrait* when Stephen dismisses Protestantism as "illogical and incoherent" (213).

11. Dujardin is mentioned often in the section of the first volume of *Hail and Farewell, Ave*, that narrates one trip made by Moore to Bayreuth. A. G. Lehmann discusses the influence of "Wagner in France" in *The Symbolist Aesthetic in France, 1885–1895*, 194–206, although his central point is to distinguish Wagner from French Wagnerianism. Dujardin's influence on Joyce has been studied by a number of critics, including, most recently, R. B. Kershner, Jr., in "Joyce and Dujardin's 'L'Initiation au péché et à l'amour'."

12. Critics who have studied Joyce's use of Wagner in *Ulysses* include Blissett, "James Joyce in the Smithy in His Soul"; Raymond Furness, *Wagner and Literature*, 124–27; John Louis Di Gaetani, *Richard Wagner and the Modern British Novel*, especially "Comic Uses of Myth: Richard Wagner and James Joyce," pp. 130–57; and Manganiello, *Joyce's Politics*, 210–12.

13. The one Wagner role she has not sung is that of Kundry in *Parsifal*, and even in this detail, Moore is reflecting his own taste, as he tells in *Ave* of running into Siegfried Wagner one evening when he is not at the opera and confessing to him that he does not particularly care for *Parsifal* (168).

14. Here it may also be relevant to note that the song "Arrayed for the Bridal" sung in "The Dead" is an adaptation of an aria from Bellini's *I Puritani*.

15. Vicky Mahaffey has recently argued (in "Wagner, Joyce and Revolution") just the opposite, that despite the parody of Wagner's operas which she admits are there, that there is a serious use of Wagner's essays on revolutionary art and music. I would agree only to the extent that one takes someone seriously by disagreeing with him. The anecdote about Joyce walking out of a performance of *Die Walküre*

because Ottocaro Weiss would not admit the superiority of "Sirens" to Wagner (Ellmann, *James Joyce*, 460) does show, however, a sense of rivalry with Wagner on Joyce's part.

16. The phrase "mock-heroic" comes from Blissett, "James Joyce," 102, who compares Stephen's sword-play to Moore's reflections in *Vale* and sees both as Wagnerian. Di Gaetani makes the parallel point that Stephen's subsequent flight from the brothel is "comic and deflating rather than heroic" (142–43). And both critics see one of the functions of this identification of Stephen with a parody of Wagner as establishing Bloom as the real hero.

17. Joyce owned *The Birth of Tragedy, The Joyful Wisdom*, and a volume including *The Case of Wagner, Nietzsche Contra Wagner*, and *Selected Aphorisms*; these are all at the Humanities Research Center. John MacNicholas clearly took the title of his article on Joyce's use of Wagner in *Exiles*, "Joyce contra Wagner," from Nietzsche, but he does not relate Joyce's parody of Wagner there—which he sees as rather more sympathetic than the critique of Wagner I am sketching in *Ulysses*—to Nietzsche.

18. The Ludovici translation Joyce owned uses *Saviour* and *salvation* here instead of *redeemer* and *redemption*. Kaufmann's translation is more accurate, but I have generally cited Ludovici's here since it was the copy Joyce owned.

19. Another expression of precisely the same dichotomy, although of course not one Joyce could have known, is the marvelous conversation in Pynchon's *Gravity's Rainbow* about whether Beethoven or Rossini is the better composer: "a person feels good listening to Rossini. All you feel like listening to Beethoven is going out and invading Poland. Ode to Joy indeed" (Thomas Pynchon, *Gravity's Rainbow*, 440) In this passage, Beethoven is explicitly identified with "the German dialectic" that culminates in dodecaphonic music, and (the pro-Nazi) Webern's death at the hands of an American soldier is mentioned as well (441). Pynchon's character goes on to relate his taste precisely to a generic preference for comedy in a way quite close to Joyce: "With Rossini, the whole point is that lovers always get together, isolation is overcome, and like it or not that is the one great centripetal movement of the World. Through the machineries of greed, pettiness, and the abuse of power, love occurs."

20. Joseph Kestner, in "Joyce, Wagner, and Bizet: *Exiles, Tannhäuser*, and *Carmen*," discusses Joyce's use of the operas by Wagner and Bizet in his play *Exiles*, but does not mention Nietzsche's use of *Carmen*, which would seem to me to be Joyce's source for this juxtaposition. *Carmen* would actually have worked nicely in *Ulysses* to reinforce Molly's Spanish associations, but these are reinforced just as well by the Spanish setting of *Don Giovanni* and Joyce has other, more powerful reasons for using the Italian resonances of *Don Giovanni*.

21. In another parallel between Joyce's and Pound's interests, Pound was also interested in the extensions of Italian-language culture into Austria in this period. He preferred Mozart's Italian operas to his German ones (*Ezra Pound and Music*, 64). We have already seen that Metastasio, the court poet for Maria Theresa's court in Vienna, was one of Pound's *settecento* Italian enthusiasms; and Pound in fact mentions Metastasio's libretti (and his own early citation of him) in the 1938 *Townsman* article on Rossini cited in n.1 (439). Joyce had no great enthusiasm for Metastasio, however, who was one of the writers he was tested on in his second year of Italian (Lobner, 2); in "Drama and Life," Joyce refers in passing to the "starchglaze of [Metastasio's] godliness" (*Critical Writings*, 40).

Conclusion

1. Kenner points out the stately/yes chiasmus in *Ulysses* (155) but does not commit himself to seeing it as designed.

2. Stephen Sicari has recently established Dante's relevance even to those sections of the poem that use Odysseus as a personae by arguing that Dante's Ulysses is integral to Pound's conception of him.

3. Kenner's 1951 study *The Poetry of Ezra Pound* assumes even at that late date that the poem was to have one hundred cantos (302, 327), and he cites Pound in a way that suggests both that Pound encouraged him in this belief and that Pound was still working on a Dante-based plan and hoped to end with a *Paradiso*. A note in the book reads: "According to Pound, Cantos 72 and 73 loop forward to the unwritten 85–100, and have been held in reserve at this time to obviate confusion" (327).

4. Bacigalupo argues that "Pound's lack of Italian is subtly suggested by the superfluous apostrophe in '*un'inferno*'—a mistake which is in fact found in Canto 72, line 49 ('un'altro tono')" ("The Poet at War," 71). Bacigalupo elsewhere contrasts Pound's and Joyce's use of Italian a little differently. In "Pound/Joyce: Style, Politics and Language," although again he insists justly on Joyce's much greater formal mastery of the language, he also praises Pound's willingness to experiment with the language. For Bacigalupo, Cantos 72–73 "are no mean performance, repulsive though their out-and-out pro-Fascism may be, and in fact are more original and take more chances than anything Joyce ever did with his excellent command of Italian" (169). Lobner does not cite Bacigalupo but she could be answering his point in her work. Her chapter on "Joyce and *Scioglilinguagnolo*" (15–44) establishes Joyce's expert command of Italian but also argues that his exposure to Triestine dialect, his interest in *parole alterate* (altered words), and his own playing with Italian as illustrated in his letters lead directly to the innovations of *Finnegans Wake*. So, although Joyce's Italian is a good deal more correct than Pound's, Pound is not the only one to play with the language.

5. This sestina is one of a group of poems known as the *rime petrose* or stony rhymes for the stony or harsh nature of the Lady being addressed in the poems. They are important enough for Petrarch's work that Durling reprints and translates them in his edition of Petrarch's *Canzoniere* (612–29). His translation is altogether more idiomatic than that by Foster and Boyde in their edition of *Dante's Lyric Poetry* (text and translation in vol. 1, 162–65; commentary in 2, 265–68).

6. Pound had cited the same opening line in Canto 5, but with the exception of Canto 93, full of echoes of the *Convivio*, the references to Dante that follow tend not to be to the lyric Dante, the Dante of *The Spirit of Romance*.

7. On this point, see Lyndall Gordon's recent biographical study, *Eliot's New Life*, and the discussion of "Ash-Wednesday" in Ellis's *Dante and English Poetry*, (210–19).

Appendix

1. I have discussed Paul de Man's enthusiasm for Italian fascism and related this to Pound's politics in "Paul de Man, the Modernist as Fascist."

Bibliography

Adams, John. *The Works of John Adams*. Boston: Little, Brown and Co., 1850.

Adams, Robert Martin. *Surface and Symbol: The Consistency of James Joyce's Ulysses*. New York: Oxford University Press, 1967.

Adamson, J. H., and H. F. Folland. *The Shepherd of the Ocean: An Account of Sir Walter Ralegh*. London: Bodley Head, 1969.

Altieri, Charles. *Act and Quality: A Theory of Literary Meaning and Humanistic Understanding*. Amherst: University of Massachusetts Press, 1981.

Anderson, David, ed. *Pound's Cavalcanti: An Edition of the Translations, Notes, and Essays*. Princeton, N.J.: Princeton University Press, 1983.

Anderson, Judith H. "'In liuing colours and right hew': The Queen of Spenser's Central Books." In *Poetic Traditions of the English Renaissance*, edited by Maynard Mack and George deForest Lord, pp. 47–66. New Haven, Conn.: Yale University Press, 1982.

Aristotle. *Politics*. Translated by H. Rackham. Loeb Classical Library. London: Heinemann, 1932.

———. *The Rhetoric of Aristotle*. Translated by Lane Cooper. New York: Appleton-Century-Crofts, 1932.

Arnold, Armin. "D. H. Lawrence, the Russians, and Giovanni Verga." *Comparative Literature Studies* 2 (1965): 249–57.

Ascham, Roger. *The Schoolmaster*. 1570. Edited by Lawrence V. Ryan. Ithaca, N.Y.: Cornell University Press, 1967.

Babbitt, Irving. *Democracy and Leadership*. 1924. Cambridge: Riverside, 1962.

Bacigalupo, Massimo. *The Forméd Trace: The Later Poetry of Ezra Pound*. New York: Columbia University Press, 1980.

———. "The Poet at War: Ezra Pound's Suppressed Italian Cantos." *South Atlantic Quarterly* 83, no. 1 (1984): 69–79.

———. "Pound/Joyce: Style, Politics, and Language." In *Joyce Studies in Italy* 2, edited by Carla de Petris, pp. 161–70. Rome: Bulzoni, 1988.

Barbato, Louis R. "Marino, Crashaw, and *Sospetto d'Herode.*" *Philological Quarterly* 54 (1975): 522–27.

Barbi, M. et al., eds. *Le Opere di Dante: testo critico della Società Dantesca Italiana.* Florence: R. Bemporad, 1921.

Baron, Hans. *The Crisis of the Early Italian Renaissance: Civic Humanism and Republican Liberty in an Age of Classicism and Tyranny.* Revised edition. Princeton, N.J.: Princeton University Press, 1966.

―――. *Petrarch's* Secretum: *Its Making and Its Meaning.* Cambridge, Mass.: Medieval Academy of America, 1985.

Barthes, Roland. *Image, Music, Text.* Translated by Stephen Heath. New York: Hill and Wang, 1977.

Bateson, Gregory. "Towards a Theory of Schizophrenia." In *Steps to an Ecology of Mind,* pp. 201–27. New York: Ballantine, 1972.

Beach, Christopher. "Ezra Pound and Harold Bloom: Confluence, Canon, Tradition, and the Making of Modern Poetry." *ELH* 56, no. 2 (1989): 463–83.

Beard, Charles A. *An Economic Interpretation of the Constitution of the United States.* 1913. New York: Macmillan, 1935.

―――. *Economic Origins of Jeffersonian Democracy.* 1915. New York: Macmillan, 1936.

Becker, Carl. *The Declaration of Independence: A Study in the History of Political Ideas.* 1922. New York: Vintage, 1958.

Beckett, Samuel. "Dante among the Lobsters." In *More Pricks Than Kicks,* pp. 9–22. 1934. New York: Grove Press, 1972.

―――. "Dante . . . Bruno. Vico . . . Joyce." In *Our Exagmination Round His Factification for Incamination of Work in Progress,* pp. 3–22. 1928. New York: New Directions, 1972.

Bednarz, James P. "Ralegh in Spenser's Historical Allegory." *Spenser Studies* 4 (1984): 49–70.

Bellamy, Elizabeth J. "The Vocative and the Vocational: The Unreadability of Elizabeth in *The Faerie Queene.*" *ELH* 54, no. 1 (1987): 1–30.

Bennett, Josephine Waters. *The Evolution of* The Faerie Queene. 1942. New York: Burt Franklin, 1960.

Bergin, Thomas G. *Perspectives on the* Divine Comedy. New Brunswick, N.J.: Rutgers University Press, 1967.

Berlin, Isaiah. *Vico and Herder: Two Studies in the History of Ideas.* New York: Viking, 1976.

Bernardo, Aldo S. *Petrarch, Laura, and the* Triumphs. Albany, N.Y.: State University of New York Press, 1974.

Berrone, Louis, ed. and trans. *James Joyce in Padua.* New York: Random House, 1977.

Bickersteth, Geoffrey L., ed. and trans. *The Poems of Leopardi.* Cambridge: Cambridge University Press, 1923.

Bigi, Emilio. *Dal Petrarca al Leopardi: Studi in stilistica storica.* Milan-Naples: Riccardo Ricciardi Editore, 1954.

Bishop, John. *Joyce's Book of the Dark:* Finnegans Wake. Madison: University of Wisconsin Press, 1986.

Blissett, William. "James Joyce in the Smithy of His Soul." In *James Joyce Today,* edited by Thomas F. Staley, pp. 96–134. Bloomington: Indiana University Press, 1966.

————. "George Moore's Literary Wagnerianism." In *George Moore's Mind and Art*, edited by Graham Owens, pp. 53–76. Edinburgh: Oliver and Boyd, 1968.

Bloom, Harold. *The Anxiety of Influence: A Theory of Poetry.* New York: Oxford University Press, 1973.

————. *A Map of Misreading.* New York: Oxford University Press, 1975.

Boccaccio. "Vita di Dante." Translated by James Robinson Smith. In *Aids to the Study of Dante*, edited by Charles Allen Dinsmore, pp. 64–111. Boston: Houghton Mifflin, 1903.

Boehrer, Bruce Thomas. "'Carelesse Modestee': Chastity as Politics in Book 3 of *The Faerie Queene.*" *ELH* 55, no. 2 (1988): 555–73.

Bornstein, George. *Poetic Remaking: The Art of Browning, Yeats, and Pound.* University Park: Pennsylvania State University Press, 1988.

————. "Pound's Parlayings with Robert Browning." In *Ezra Pound among the Poets*, edited by George Bornstein, pp. 106–27. Chicago: University of Chicago Press, 1985.

Brand, C. P. "Petrarch and Petrarchism in Torquato Tasso's Lyric Poetry." *Modern Language Review* 62 (1967): 256–67.

————. *Torquato Tasso.* Cambridge: Cambridge University Press, 1965.

Bruno, Giordano. *Degli eroici furori.* Milan: Società Editrice Sonzogno, 1906.

————. *The Heroic Frenzies.* Translated by Paul Eugene Memmo, Jr. Chapel Hill: University of North Carolina Press, 1964.

Burckhardt, Jacob. *The Civilization of the Renaissance in Italy.* Translated by S. G. C. Middlemore. 1929. New York: Modern Library, 1958.

Bush, Ronald. *The Genesis of Ezra Pound's Cantos.* Princeton, N.J.: Princeton University Press, 1976.

Cain, Thomas H. *Praise in* The Faerie Queene. Lincoln: University of Nebraska Press, 1978.

Cambon, Glauco. "Vico and Dante." In *Giambattista Vico: An International Symposium*, edited by Giorgio Tagliacozzo and Hayden V. White, pp. 15–28. Baltimore: Johns Hopkins University Press, 1969.

Carducci, Giosuè. *Degli spiriti e delle forme nella poesia di Giacomo Leopardi.* Bologna: Nicola Zanichella, 1898.

Carducci, Giosuè, and S. Ferrari, eds. *Le rime di Francesco Petrarca.* 1899. Florence: Sansoni, 1957.

Carpenter, Andrew, ed. *My Uncle John: Edward Stephen's Life of J. M. Synge.* London: Oxford University Press, 1974.

Carsaniga, Giovanni. *Giacomo Leopardi: The Unheeded Voice.* Edinburgh: Edinburgh University Press, 1977.

Casady, Edwin. "The Neo-Platonic Ladder in Spenser's *Amoretti.*" *Philological Quarterly* 20 (1941): 284–95.

Casale, Ottavio M., ed. and trans. *A Leopardi Reader.* Urbana: University of Illinois Press, 1981.

Casillo, Robert. *The Genealogy of Demons: Anti-Semitism, Fascism, and the Myths of Ezra Pound.* Evanston, Ill.: Northwestern University Press, 1988.

Chace, William M. *The Political Identities of Ezra Pound and T. S. Eliot.* Stanford, Calif.: Stanford University Press, 1973.

Churchill, Kenneth. *Italy and English Literature, 1764–1930.* Totowa, N.J.: Barnes and Noble, 1980.

Colie, Rosalie L. *Paradoxica Epidemica*. Princeton, N.J.: Princeton University Press, 1966.

———. *Shakespeare's Living Art*. Princeton, N.J.: Princeton University Press, 1974.

Contini, Gianfranco. *Varianti e altra linguistica: Una raccolta di saggi (1938–1968)*. Turin: Giulio Einaudi Editore, 1970.

Corngold, Stanley. "On Paul de Man's Collaborationist Writings." In *Responses: On Paul de Man's Wartime Journalism*, edited by Werner Hamacher, Neil Hertz, and Thomas Keenan, pp. 80–84. Lincoln: University of Nebraska Press, 1989.

Corrigan, Beatrice, ed. *Italian Poets and English Critics, 1755–1859*. Chicago: University of Chicago Press, 1969.

Croce, Benedetto. *Aesthetic: As Science of Expression and General Linguistic*. Translated by Douglas Ainslie. 1909. London: Peter Owen, 1953.

———. *Ariosto, Shakespeare, and Corneille*. Translated by Douglas Ainslie. 1920. New York: Russell and Russell, 1966.

———. *La filosofia di Giambattista Vico*. 1911. Bari: Laterza, 1973.

———. "Machiavelli and Vico." 1924. In *Philosophy Poetry History: An Anthology of Essays*. Translated by Cecil Sprigge, pp. 655–60. London: Oxford University Press, 1966.

Culler, Jonathan. "Presupposition and Intertextuality." In *The Pursuit of Signs: Semiotics, Literature, Deconstruction*, pp. 100–18. Ithaca, N.Y.: Cornell University Press, 1981.

D'Amico, Jack, ed. *Petrarch in England: An Anthology of Parallel Texts*. Ravenna: Longo Editore, 1979.

Dante Alighieri. *Dante's Lyric Poetry*. 2 vols. Edited by Kenelm Foster and Patrick Boyde. Oxford: Oxford University Press, 1967.

———. *De Vulgari Eloquentia*. Translated by A.G.F.H. In *A Translation of the Latin Works of Dante Alighieri*, pp. 3–124. 1904. New York: Greenwood Press, 1969.

———. *The Divine Comedy*. With translation and commentary by Charles S. Singleton. Bollingen Series 80. Princeton, N.J.: Princeton University Press, 1970–1975.

———. *Monarchy and Three Political Letters*. Translated by Donald Nichol and Colin Hardie. London: Weidenfeld and Nicholson, 1954.

Dasenbrock, Reed Way. "Dante's Hell and Pound's *Paradiso*: '*tutto spezzato*.'" *Paideuma* 9, no. 3 (1980): 501–4.

———. "Do We Write the Text We Read?" *College English* 53, no. 1 (1991): 7–19.

———. "J. M. Synge and Irish Mythology." In *A J. M. Synge Literary Companion*, edited by Edward A. Kopper, Jr., pp. 135–44. Westport, Conn.: Greenwood Press, 1988.

———. *The Literary Vorticism of Ezra Pound and Wyndham Lewis: Towards the Condition of Painting*. Baltimore: Johns Hopkins University Press, 1985.

———. "Norman Douglas and the Denizens of Siren Land." *Deus Loci* 5, no. 4 (1982): 1–9.

———. "Paul de Man, the Modernist as Fascist." *South Central Review* 6, no. 2 (1989): 6–18.

———, ed. *Redrawing the Lines: Analytic Philosophy, Deconstruction, and Literary Theory*. Minneapolis: University of Minnesota Press, 1989.

Davis, Charles T. *Dante's Italy and Other Essays*. Philadelphia: University of Pennsylvania Press, 1984.

D'Epiro, Peter. *A Touch of Rhetoric: Ezra Pound's Malatesta Cantos.* Ann Arbor: UMI, 1983.

De Man, Paul. *Wartime Journalism, 1939–1943.* Edited by Werner Hamacher, Neil Hertz, and Thomas Keenan. Lincoln: University of Nebraska Press, 1988.

DeNeef, Leigh A. "Spenser's *Amor Fuggitivo* and the Transfixed Heart." *ELH* 46 (1979): 1–20.

DiGaetani, John Louis. *Richard Wagner and the Modern British Novel.* Rutherford, N.J.: Fairleigh Dickinson University Press, 1978.

Drayton, Michael. *The Works of Michael Drayton.* 5 vols. Edited by J. William Hedel. Oxford: Blackwell, 1961.

Duncan, Ronald. *How to Make Enemies.* London: Rupert Hart-Davis, 1968.

Durling, Robert M., ed. and trans. *Petrarch's Lyric Poems: The* Rime Sparse *and Other Lyrics.* Cambridge, Mass.: Harvard University Press, 1976.

Edel, Leon. *Henry James: The Middle Years, 1882–1895.* Philadelphia: J. P. Lippincott, 1962.

Eliot, T. S. "Niccolò Machiavelli." In *For Lancelot Andrewes: Essays on Style and Order.* London: Faber and Gwyer, 1928.

———. "Niccolò Machiavelli." *Times Literary Supplement.* 16 June 1927, pp. 413–14.

———. *The Sacred Wood.* 1920. London: Methuen, 1960.

———. "*Ulysses*, Order and Myth." 1923. Reprinted in *James Joyce: The Critical Heritage, Volume One, 1902–1927,* edited by Robert H. Deming, pp. 268–71. London: Routledge and Kegan Paul, 1970.

Ellis, Steve. *Dante and English Poetry: Shelley to T. S. Eliot.* Cambridge: Cambridge University Press, 1983.

Ellmann, Richard. *The Consciousness of Joyce.* London: Faber and Faber, 1977.

———. *Eminent Domain: Yeats among Wilde, Joyce, Pound, Eliot, and Auden.* New York: Oxford University Press, 1967.

———. *James Joyce.* Revised ed. New York: Oxford University Press, 1982.

———. *Ulysses on the Liffey.* New York: Oxford University Press, 1972.

———. *Yeats: The Man and the Masks.* London: Macmillan, 1949.

Emerson, R. W. *Essays.* Boston: Fields, Osgood, and Co., 1869.

Emery, Clark. *Ideas into Action: A Study of Pound's Cantos.* Coral Gables, Fla.: University of Miami Press, 1958.

Ferrante, Joan M. *The Political Vision of the Divine Comedy.* Princeton, N.J.: Princeton University Press, 1984.

Flory, Wendy Stallard. *The American Ezra Pound.* New Haven, Conn.: Yale University Press, 1989.

Fogelman, Bruce. *Shapes of Power: The Development of Ezra Pound's Poetic Sequences.* Ann Arbor: UMI, 1988.

Forster, E. M. *A Room with a View.* 1908. Harmondsworth: Penguin, 1955.

Forster, Leonard. *The Icy Fire: Five Studies in European Petrarchism.* Cambridge: Cambridge University Press, 1969.

Foucault, Michel. *The Order of Things: An Archaeology of the Human Sciences.* New York: Vintage, 1973.

Freccero, John. "The Fig Tree and the Laurel: Petrarch's Poetics." 1975. In *Literary Theory/Renaissance Texts,* edited by Patricia Parker and David Quint, pp. 20–32. Baltimore: Johns Hopkins University Press, 1986.

Frye, Northrop. "Cycle and Apocalypse in *Finnegans Wake.*" In *Vico and Joyce,* edited by Donald Phillip Verene, pp. 3–19. Albany, N.Y.: State University of New York Press, 1987.

Furia, Philip. *Pound's* Cantos *Declassified*. University Park: Pennsylvania State University Press, 1984.

Furness, Raymond. *Wagner and Literature*. Manchester: Manchester University Press, 1982.

Gelpi, Albert. *A Coherent Splendor: The American Poetic Renaissance, 1910–1950*. Cambridge: Cambridge University Press, 1987.

Gentile, Giovanni. *Genesis and Structure of Society*. Translated by H. S. Harris. Urbana: University of Illinois Press, 1966.

———. *Giordano Bruno e il pensiero del renascimento*. Florence: Vallechi Editore, 1920.

———. *Studi vichiani*. 2d ed. Florence: Le Monnier, 1927.

George, Charles H., and Katharine George. *The Protestant Mind of the English Reformation, 1570–1640*. Princeton, N.J.: Princeton University Press, 1961.

Giamatti, A. Bartlett. *The Earthly Paradise and the Renaissance Epic*. Princeton, N.J.: Princeton University Press, 1966.

Gibaldi, Joseph. "Petrarch and Baroque Magdalene Tradition." *Hebrew University Studies in Literature* 3 (1975): 1–19.

Gilbert, Allan H. "Belphoebe's Misdeeming of Timias." *PMLA* 62 (1947): 623–36.

Gillet, Louis. *Claybook for James Joyce*. Translated by Georges Markow-Totevy. London: Abelard-Schuman, 1958.

Goldberg, Jonathan. *"Endlesse Worke": Spenser and the Structures of Discourse*. Baltimore: Johns Hopkins University Press, 1981.

Greene, Thomas M. "The Flexibility of the Self in Renaissance Literature." In *The Disciplines of Criticism*, edited by Peter Demetz, Thomas M. Greene, and Lowry Nelson, Jr., pp. 241–64. New Haven, Conn.: Yale University Press, 1968.

———. *The Light in Troy: Imitation and Discovery in Renaissance Poetry*. New Haven, Conn.: Yale University Press, 1982.

———. "Petrarch *Viator*." In *The Vulnerable Text: Essays on Renaissance Literature*, pp. 18–45. New York: Columbia University Press, 1986.

Guss, Donald L. *John Donne, Petrarchist: Italianate Conceits and Love Theory in the Songs and Sonets*. Detroit: Wayne State University Press, 1966.

———. "Wyatt's Petrarchism: An Instance of Creative Imitation in the Renaissance." *Huntington Library Quarterly* 29 (1965): 1–15.

Halkett, John. *Milton and the Idea of Matrimony: A Study of the Divorce Tracts and Paradise Lost*. New Haven, Conn.: Yale University Press, 1970.

Hall, Vernon, Jr. "Joyce's Use of Da Ponte and Mozart's *Don Giovanni*." *PMLA* 66 (1951): 78–84.

Haller, William. "Hail Wedded Love." *ELH* 13 (1946): 79–97.

Hardison, O. B., Jr. *The Enduring Monument: A Study of the Idea of Praise in Renaissance Literary Theory and Practice*. Chapel Hill: University of North Carolina Press, 1962.

Harrier, Richard. *The Canon of Sir Thomas Wyatt's Poetry*. Cambridge, Mass.: Harvard University Press, 1975.

Harris, H. S. *The Social Philosophy of Giovanni Gentile*. Urbana: University of Illinois Press, 1960.

———. "What is Mr. Ear-Vico Supposed to Be 'Earing?" In *Vico and Joyce*, edited by Donald Phillip Verene, pp. 68–82. Albany: State University of New York Press, 1987.

Henn, T. R. *The Plays and Poems of J. M. Synge.* London: Methuen, 1963.

Heymann, C. David. *Ezra Pound: The Last Rower.* New York: Viking, 1976.

Hieatt, A. Kent. *Chaucer, Spenser, Milton: Mythopoeic Continuities and Transformations.* Montreal: McGill-Queen's University Press, 1975.

Hill, Iris Tillman. "Britomart and *Be Bold, Be Not Too Bold.*" *ELH* 38 (1971): 173–87.

Holloway, Mark. *Norman Douglas: A Life.* London: Secker and Warburg, 1976.

Howard, George Elliott. *A History of Matrimonial Institutions.* 3 vols. 1904. New York: Humanities, 1964.

Howarth, Herbert. *The Irish Writers, 1880–1940: Literature under Parnell's Star.* London: Rockliff, 1958.

Hume, Anthea. *Edmund Spenser: Protestant Poet.* Cambridge: Cambridge University Press, 1984.

Hunter, G. K. "Spenser's *Amoretti* and the English Tradition." In *A Theater for Spenserians,* edited by Judith M. Kennedy and James A. Reither, pp. 124–44. Toronto: University of Toronto Press, 1973.

Imerti, Arthur D., ed. and trans. "Introduction." In *The Expulsion of the Triumphant Beast,* by Giordano Bruno, pp. 3–65. New Brunswick, N.J.: Rutgers University Press, 1964.

Jackson, Thomas H. *The Early Poetry of Ezra Pound.* Cambridge, Mass.: Harvard University Press, 1968.

Jefferson, Thomas. *Notes on the State of Virginia.* Philadelphia: J. C. Carey and I. Lea, 1925.

Johnson, Toni O'Brien. *Synge: The Medieval and the Grotesque.* Gerrards Cross: Colin Smythe, 1982.

Joyce, James. *The Critical Writings.* Edited by Ellsworth Mason and Richard Ellmann. New York: Viking, 1959.

———. *Letters of James Joyce.* Volume 1. Edited by Stuart Gilbert. 1957. New York: Viking, 1966.

———. *Letters of James Joyce.* Volume 3. Edited by Richard Ellmann. New York: Viking, 1966.

———. *A Portrait of the Artist as a Young Man.* 1916. New York: Viking, 1969.

———. *Stephen Hero.* Edited by Theodore Spencer. New York: New Directions, 1944.

———. *Ulysses.* Edited by Hans Walter Gabler. New York: Random House, 1986.

Kallendorf, Craig. *In Praise of Aeneas: Virgil and Epideictic Rhetoric in the Early Italian Renaissance.* Hanover, N.H.: University Press of New England, 1989.

Kantorowicz, Ernst H. *Frederick the Second, 1194–1250.* Translated by E. O. Lorimer. London: Constable, 1931.

———. *The King's Two Bodies: A Study in Mediaeval Political Theology.* Princeton, N.J.: Princeton University Press, 1957.

Kearns, George. *Guide to Ezra Pound's Selected Cantos.* New Brunswick, N.J.: Rutgers University Press, 1980.

Kelley, Donald R. "Vico's Road: From Philology to Jurisprudence and Back." In *Giambattista Vico's Science of Humanity,* edited by Giorgio Tagliacozzo and Donald Phillip Verene, pp. 15–29. Baltimore: Johns Hopkins University Press, 1976.

Kenner, Hugh. *A Colder Eye: The Modern Irish Writers*. New York: Knopf, 1983.
———. *The Poetry of Ezra Pound*. 1951. Lincoln: University of Nebraska Press, 1985.
———. *The Pound Era*. Berkeley: University of California Press, 1971.
———. *Ulysses*. London: Allen and Unwin, 1980.
Kershner, R. B., Jr. "Joyce and Dujardin's 'L'Initiation au péché et à l'amour.'" *James Joyce Quarterly* 26 (1989): 213–25.
Kestner, Joseph. "Joyce, Wagner, and Bizet: *Exiles, Tannhäuser*, and *Carmen*." *Modern British Literature* 5 (1980): 53–63.
Kiberd, Declan. *Synge and the Irish Language*. London: Macmillan, 1979.
Knust, Herbert. *Wagner, The King, and* The Waste Land. University Park: Pennsylvania State University, 1967.
Kostic, V. "Spenser's *Amoretti* and Tasso's Lyric Poetry." *Renaissance and Modern Studies* 3 (1959): 51–77.
Landor, Walter Savage. *Imaginary Conversations*. London: Walter Scott, n.d.
———. *The Pentameron*. Boston: Roberts, 1888.
Lawrence, D. H. *The Collected Letters of D. H. Lawrence*. Edited by Harry T. Moore. 2 vols. New York: Viking, 1962.
Lehmann, A. G. *The Symbolist Aesthetic in France, 1885–1895*. 2d ed. Oxford: Basil Blackwell, 1968.
Lever, J. W. *The Elizabethan Love Sonnet*. 1956. London: Methuen, 1966.
Lewis, C. S. *The Allegory of Love: A Study in Mediaeval Tradition*. 1936. Oxford: Oxford University Press, 1958.
———. *English Literature in the Sixteenth Century excluding Drama*. Oxford: Oxford University Press, 1944.
Lewis, Wyndham. *The Childermass*. 1928. London: John Calder, 1965.
———. *The Lion and the Fox: The Role of the Hero in the Plays of Shakespeare*. 1927. London: Methuen, 1966.
———. *Rude Assignment*. Edited by Toby Foshay. Santa Barbara, Calif.: Black Sparrow, 1984.
———. *Time and Western Man*. 1927. Boston: Beacon Press, 1957.
Lion, Aline. *The Pedigree of Fascism: A Popular Essay on the Western Philosophy of Politics*. London: Sheed and Ward, 1927.
Lipscomb, Andrew A., ed. *The Writings of Thomas Jefferson*. Washington, D.C.: Thomas Jefferson Memorial Association, 1905.
Litz, Walton A. "Vico and Joyce." In *Giambattista Vico: An International Symposium*, edited by Giorgio Tagliacozzo and Hayden V. White. Baltimore: Johns Hopkins University Press, 1969.
Lobner, Corinna del Greco. *James Joyce's Italian Connection*. Iowa City: University of Iowa Press, 1989.
Longenbach, James. "Ezra Pound and the Vicissitudes of Post-Romantic Ambition." *Southern Review* 24 (1988): 481–501.
———. *Modernist Poetics of History: Pound, Eliot, and the Sense of the Past*. Princeton, N.J.: Princeton University Press, 1987.
———. *Stone Cottage: Pound, Yeats, and Modernism*. New York: Oxford University Press, 1988.
Lyons, F.S.L. *Charles Stewart Parnell*. New York: Oxford University Press, 1977.
MacCaffrey, Isabel. *Spenser's Allegory: The Anatomy of Imagination*. Princeton, N.J.: Princeton University Press, 1976.

McDougal, Stuart Y. *Ezra Pound and the Troubadour Tradition*. Princeton, N.J.: Princeton University Press, 1972.

Machiavelli, Niccolò. *Discourses on the First Decade of Titus Livius*. In *The Chief Works and Others*. translated by Allan Gilbert, pp. 175–529. Volume 1. Durham, N.C.: Duke University Press, 1965.

———. *Istorie fiorentine*. 1532. Turin: G. B. Paravia, 1921.

———. *Machiavelli's* The Prince: *A Bilingual Edition*. Edited and translated by Mark Musa. New York: St. Martin's, 1964.

McIntyre, J. Lewis. *Giordano Bruno*. London: Macmillan, 1903.

MacNicholas, John. "Joyce contra Wagner." *Comparative Drama* 9 (1975): 29–43.

Maddox, Brenda. *Nora: The Real Life of Molly Bloom*. Boston: Houghton Mifflin, 1988.

Mahaffey, Vicki. "Wagner, Joyce, and Revolution." *James Joyce Quarterly* 25 (1988): 237–47.

Makin, Peter. *Provence and Pound*. Berkeley: University of California Press, 1978.

Mancusi-Ungaro, Donna. *Dante and the Empire*. New York: Peter Lang, 1987.

Manganiello, Dominic. *Joyce's Politics*. London: Routledge and Kegan Paul, 1980.

Martz, Louis L. "The *Amoretti*: 'Most Goodly Temperature.' " In *Form and Convention in the Poetry of Edmund Spenser*, edited by William Nelson, pp. 146–68. New York: Columbia University Press, 1961.

Mason, Ellsworth. "James Joyce's *Ulysses* and Vico's Cycles." Ph.D. diss., Yale University, 1948.

Mason, H. A. *Editing Wyatt: An Examination of* Collected Poems of Sir Thomas Wyatt *together with Suggestions for an Improved Edition*. Cambridge: Cambridge Quarterly, 1972.

———. *Humanism and Poetry in the Early Tudor Period: An Essay*. London: Routledge and Kegan Paul, 1959.

Materer, Timothy. "From Henry James to Ezra Pound: John Quinn and the Art of Patronage." *Paideuma* 17, nos. 2 and 3 (1988): 47–68.

———, ed. *Pound/Lewis: The Letters of Ezra Pound and Wyndham Lewis*. New York: New Directions, 1985.

Meyers, Jeffrey. *D. H. Lawrence and the Experience of Italy*. Philadelphia: University of Pennsylvania Press, 1982.

Minta, Stephen. *Petrarch and Petrarchism: The English and the French Traditions*. Manchester: Manchester University Press, 1980.

Montrose, Louis Adrian. "The Elizabethan Subject and the Renaissance Text." In *Literary Theory/Renaissance Texts*, edited by Patricia Parker and David Quint, pp. 303–40. Baltimore: Johns Hopkins University Press, 1986.

Mooney, Michael. *Vico in the Tradition of Rhetoric*. Princeton, N.J.: Princeton University Press, 1985.

Moore, E., ed. *Le Opere di Dante Alighieri*. Oxford: Oxford University Press, 1897.

Moore, George. *Evelyn Innes*. London: T. Fisher Unwin, 1898.

———. *Hail and Farewell*. 3 vols. 1911–14. London: Heinemann, 1947.

———. *The Lake*. London: D. Appleton, 1906.

Mortimer, Anthony. *Petrarch's* Canzoniere *in the English Renaissance*. Bergamo: Minerva Italica, 1975.

Muir, Kenneth, and Patricia Thomson, eds. *Collected Poems of Sir Thomas Wyatt*. Liverpool: Liverpool University Press, 1969.

Mussato, Albertino. *L'ecerinide*. Translated by Manlio Torquato Dazzi. Città di Castello: S. Lapi, 1914.

Mussolini, Benito. "In Captivity: Notebook of Thoughts in Ponza and La Maddalena." *Edge* 4 (March 1957): 10–26.

Nagy, N. Christoph de. *The Poetry of Ezra Pound: The Pre-Imagist Stage*. 1960. Bern: Francke Verlag, 1968.

Nashe, Thomas. *The Unfortunate Traveller*. 1594. In *Works of Thomas Nashe*, vol. 2, edited by Ronald B. McKerrow, pp. 187–328. London: A. H. Bullen, 1904.

Neely, Carol Thomas. "The Structure of English Renaissance Sonnet Sequences." *ELH* 45 (1978): 359–89.

Nelson, John Charles. *Renaissance Theory of Love: The Context of Giordano Bruno's* Eroici furori. New York: Columbia University Press, 1958.

Nicholls, Peter. *Ezra Pound: Politics, Economics, and Writing: A Study of* The Cantos. Atlantic Highlands, N.J.: Humanities, 1984.

Nietzsche. Friedrich. *The Birth of Tragedy and The Case of Wagner*. Translated by Walter Kaufmann. New York: Viking, 1967.

———. *The Case of Wagner: Nietzsche contra Wagner, Selected Aphorisms*. Translated by Anthony M. Ludovici. Volume 8 of *The Complete Works of Friedrich Nietzsche*, edited by Oscar Levy. 2d ed. Edinburgh: T. N. Foulis, 1911.

———. "Nietzsche contra Wagner." In *The Portable Nietzsche*, edited and translated by Walter Kaufmann, pp. 661–83. 1954. New York: Viking, 1971.

Nohrnberg, James. *The Analogy of* The Faerie Queene. Princeton, N.J.: Princeton University Press, 1976.

Oakeshott, Walter. *The Queen and the Poet*. New York: Barnes and Noble, 1961.

O'Connell, Michael. *Mirror and Veil: The Historical Dimension of Spenser's* Faerie Queene. Chapel Hill: University of North Carolina Press, 1977.

O'Tuama, Sean. "Synge and the Idea of a National Literature." In *J. M. Synge: Centenary Papers, 1971*, edited by Maurice Harmon, pp. 1–17. Dublin: Dolmen, 1972.

Pater, Walter. *The Renaissance*. Cleveland: Meridian, 1961.

Pearlman, Daniel D. *The Barb of Time: On the Unity of Ezra Pound's* Cantos. New York: Oxford University Press, 1969.

Petrarca, Francesco. *Canzoniere*. Commentary by Giacomo Leopardi. Edited by Ugo Dotti. Milan: Feltrinelli, 1979.

———. "How a Ruler Ought to Govern His State." Translated by Benjamin G. Kohl. In *The Earthly Republic: Italian Humanists on Government and Society*, edited by Benjamin G. Kohl and Ronald G. Witt, pp. 35–78. Philadelphia: University of Pennsylvania Press, 1978.

———. *Il Petrarca*. Venice: Aldo Romano, 1514.

———. *Letters from Petrarch*. Edited and translated by Morris Bishop. Bloomington: Indiana University Press, 1966.

———. *The Life of Solitude*. Translated by Jacob Zeitlin. Urbana: University of Illinois Press, 1924.

———. *Petrarch's Secret or The Soul's Contest with Passion*. Translated by William H. Draper. 1911. Westport, Conn.: Hyperion, 1978.

———. *Rerum familiarum libri—Letters on Familiar Matters*. 3 vols. Translated by Aldo S. Bernardo. Baltimore: Johns Hopkins University Press, 1975–85.

Picone, Michelangelo. "Petrarch's Navigational Metaphor in the *Canzoniere*." Lecture at Yale Petrarch Institute, 5 July 1989.

Pitkin, Hanna Fenichel. *Fortune Is a Woman: Gender and Politics in the Thought of Niccolò Machiavelli*. Berkeley: University of California Press, 1984.

Pocock, J.G.A. *The Machiavellian Moment: Florentine Political Thought and the Atlantic Republican Tradition*. Princeton, N.J.: Princeton University Press, 1975.

———. *Virtue, Commerce, and History: Essays on Political Thought and History, Chiefly in the Eighteenth Century*. Cambridge: Cambridge University Press, 1985.

Pound, Ezra. "American Chaos II." *New Age* (16 September 1915): 471.

———. *The Cantos*. New York: New Directions, 1989.

———. "Cavalcanti," pp. 149–200. 1934. In Pound, Ezra, *Literary Essays*, edited by T. S. Eliot. New York: New Directions, 1968.

———. *Ezra Pound and Music: The Complete Criticism*. Edited by R. Murray Schafer. New York: New Directions, 1977.

———. *"Ezra Pound Speaking": Radio Speeches of World War II*. Edited by Leonard W. Doob. Westport, Conn.: Greenwood Press, 1978.

———. "For T.S.E." p. 464. 1966. In Pound, Ezra, *Selected Prose, 1909–1965*, edited by William Cookson. New York: New Directions, 1973.

———. *Gaudier-Brzeska: A Memoir*. 1916. New York: New Directions, 1970.

———. *Guide to Kulchur*. 1938. New York: New Directions, 1970.

———. "Hell," pp. 201–13. 1934. In Pound, *Literary Essays*.

———. "The Jefferson-Adams Letters as a Shrine and a Monument," pp. 147–58. 1937–38. In Pound, *Selected Prose, 1909–1965*.

———. *Jefferson and/or Mussolini: L'idea Statale Fascism as I Have Seen It*. 1935. New York: Liveright, 1970.

———. "Letters to Woodward." *Paideuma* 15, no. 1 (1986): 105–20.

———. *Literary Essays*. Edited by T. S. Eliot. New York: New Directions, 1968.

———. "On Virtue." In "I Gather the Limbs of Osiris," pp. 29–31. 1911–1912. In Pound, *Selected Prose, 1909–1965*.

———. "Patria Mia," pp. 99–141. In *Selected Prose, 1909–1965*.

———. *Personae: The Collected Poems of Ezra Pound*. 1926. New York: New Directions, n.d.

———. *Pound/The Little Review: The Letters of Ezra Pound to Margaret Anderson: The Little Review Correspondence*. Edited by Thomas L. Scott, Melvin J. Friedman, and Jackson R. Bryer. New York: New Directions, 1988.

———. "The Renaissance," pp. 214–26. In Pound, *Literary Essays*.

———. *The Selected Letters of Ezra Pound, 1907–1941*. Edited by D. D. Paige. 1950. New York: New Directions, 1971.

———. *Selected Prose, 1909–1965*. Edited by William Cookson. New York: New Directions, 1973.

———. *The Spirit of Romance*. 1910. New York: New Directions, n.d.

———. *The Translations of Ezra Pound*. London: Faber and Faber, 1975.

Pound, Omar, and A. Walton Litz, eds. *Ezra Pound and Dorothy Shakespear, Their Letters: 1909–1914*. New York: New Directions, 1984.

Pound, Omar, and Robert Spoo, eds. *Ezra Pound and Margaret Cravens: A Tragic Friendship, 1910–1912*. Durham, N.C.: Duke University Press, 1988.

Praz, Mario. *The Flaming Heart: Essays on Crashaw, Machiavelli, and Other Studies in the Relations between Italian and English Literature from Chaucer to T. S. Eliot*. 1958. Gloucester, Mass.: Peter Smith, 1966.

Price, Alan. *Synge and Anglo-Irish Drama*. London: Methuen, 1961.

Prince, F. T. *The Italian Element in Milton's Verse*. Oxford: Clarendon Press, 1954.

Purcell, Sally, ed. *The Early Italian Poets*. Translated by Dante Gabriel Rossetti. Berkeley: University of California Press, 1981.

Pynchon, Thomas. *Gravity's Rainbow*. New York: Viking, 1973.

Quilligan, Maureen. "The Comedy of Female Authority in *The Faerie Queene*." *English Literary Renaissance* 17, no. 2 (1987): 156–71.

Rabaté, Jean-Michel. "Bruno No, Bruno Si: Note on a Contradiction in Joyce." *James Joyce Quarterly* 27, no. 1 (1989): 31–39.

Rainey, Lawrence. Review of James Longenbach, *Modernist Poetics of History*. *Modern Philology* 87, no. 1 (1989): 106–11.

Read, Forrest, ed. *Pound/Joyce: The Letter of Ezra Pound to James Joyce, with Pound's Essays on Joyce*. New York: New Directions, 1967.

Redman, Tim. "Pound's Library: A Preliminary Catalog." *Paideuma* 15, no. 2 and 3 (1986): 213–37.

Reynolds, Mary T. "The City in Vico, Dante, and Joyce." In *Vico and Joyce*, edited by Donald Phillip Verene, pp. 110–22. Albany, N.Y.: State University of New York Press, 1987.

———. *Joyce and Dante: The Shaping Imagination*. Princeton, N.J.: Princeton University Press, 1981.

Roche, Thomas P. *The Kindly Flame: A Study of the Third and Fourth Books of Spenser's* Faerie Queene. Princeton, N.J.: Princeton University Press, 1964.

Rollins, Hyder, ed. *Tottel's Miscellany*. 2 vols. Cambridge, Mass.: Harvard University Press, 1928.

Rosenthal, M. L., and Sally M. Gall. *The Modern Poetic Sequence: The Genius of Modern Poetry*. New York: Oxford University Press, 1983.

Rossetti, Dante Gabriel. *The Early Italian Poets, together with Dante's* Vita Nuova. 2d ed. London: J. M. Dent, 1908.

Ruthven, K. K. *A Guide to Ezra Pound's* Personae. Berkeley: University of California Press, 1969.

Said, Edward W. *Orientalism*. New York: Random House, 1979.

Salvadori, Corinna. *Yeats and Castiglione: Poet and Courtier*. Dublin: Allen Figgis, 1965.

Sanders, Frederick K., comp. *John Adams Speaking: Pound's Sources for the Adams Cantos*. Orono: University of Maine Press, 1975.

Schaar, Claes. *Marino and Crashaw: Sospeto d'Herode: A Commentary*. Lund: C.W.K. Gleerup, 1971.

Scott, Janet. *Les Sonnets Élisabéthains*. Paris: Champion, 1929.

———. "The Sources of Spenser's *Amoretti*." *Modern Language Review* 22 (1927): 189–95.

Sells, A. Lytton. *The Italian Influence in English Poetry: From Chaucer to Southwell*. Bloomington: Indiana University Press, 1955.

Sicari, Stephen. "Reading Pound's Politics: Ulysses as Fascist Hero." *Paideuma* 17, nos. 2 and 3 (1988): 145–68.

Singh, G. *Leopardi and the Theory of Poetry*. Lexington: University of Kentucky Press, 1964.

Skelton, Robin. *J. M. Synge and His World*. New York: Viking, 1971.

———. *The Writings of J. M. Synge*. Indianapolis: Bobbs-Merrill, 1971.

Smith, Hallett. "The Art of Sir Thomas Wyatt." *Huntington Library Quarterly* 9 (1946): 323–55.

Spenser, Edmund. *Poetical Works*. Edited by J. C. Smith and Ernest de Selincourt. 1912. London: Oxford University Press, 1970.

———. *The Works of Edmund Spenser: A Variorum Edition*. 9 vols. Edited by E. Greenlaw, C. G. Osgood, F. M. Padelford, and P. Heffner. Baltimore: Johns Hopkins University Press.

Spoo, Robert. "Pound's Cavalcanti and Cravens's Carducci." *Paideuma* 20 (1991): forthcoming.

Stock, Noel. *The Life of Ezra Pound*. 1970. Harmondsworth: Penguin, 1974.

Struever, Nancy. *The Language of History in the Renaissance*. Princeton, N.J.: Princeton University Press, 1970.

———. "Vico, Valla, and the Logic of Humanist Inquiry." In *Giambattista Vico's Science of Humanity*, edited by Giorgio Tagliacozzo and Donald Philip Verene, pp. 173–85. Baltimore: Johns Hopkins University Press, 1976.

Suitner, Franco. *Petrarca e la tradizione stilnovistica*. Florence: Leo S. Olschki Editore, 1977.

Surrey, Earl of, Henry Howard. *Poems*. Edited by Emrys Jones. Oxford: Clarendon Press, 1964.

Symonds, John Addington. *Renaissance in Italy*. 2 vols. New York: Modern Library, 1930.

Synge, J. M. *Plays: Book II*. Edited by Ann Saddlemeyer. Vol. 4 of *Collected Works*. London: Oxford University Press, 1968.

———. *Poems*. Edited by Robin Skelton. Vol. 1 of *Collected Works*. London: Oxford University Press, 1962.

———. *Prose*. Edited by Alan Price. Vol. 2 of *Collected Works*. London: Oxford University Press, 1966.

———. *Some Sonnets from "Laura in Death" after the Italian of Francesco Petrarch*. Dublin: Dolmen, 1971.

Tasso, Torquato. *Le rime de Torquato Tasso*. 3 vols. Edited by Paolo Solerti. Bologna, 1898–1902.

Theoharis, Theoharis Constantine. *Joyce's Ulysses: An Anatomy of the Soul*. Chapel Hill: University of North Carolina Press, 1988.

Thompson, William Irwin. *The Imagination of an Insurrection: Dublin, Easter, 1916*. New York: Harper and Row, 1972.

Thomson, Patricia. *Sir Thomas Wyatt and His Background*. Stanford, Calif.: Stanford University Press, 1964.

Thornton, Weldon. *Allusions in Ulysses*. New York: Simon and Schuster, 1973.

Timpanaro, Sebastiano. *Classicismo e illuminismo nell'Ottocento Italiano*. 2d ed. Pisa: Nistri-Lischi, 1969.

Toynbee, Paget. *Dante Alighieri: His Life and Works*. 4th ed. 1910. Edited by Charles S. Singleton. New York: Harper and Row, 1965.

Tuve, Rosemond. *Allegorical Imagery: Some Mediaeval Books and Their Posterity*. Princeton, N.J.: Princeton University Press, 1966.

Tytell, John. *Ezra Pound: The Solitary Volcano*. New York: Doubleday, 1987.

Valla, Lorenzo. *Lavrentii Valla Elegantiarum libri sex*. Venice: Aldi, 1536.

Varchi, Benedetto. *Storia fiorentina*. Augsburg: Paul Kuhzio, 1721.

Verene, Donald Phillip. "Vico as Reader of Joyce." In *Vico and Joyce*, edited by Donald Phillip Verene, pp. 222–31. Albany, N.Y.: State University of New York Press, 1987.

Verga, Giovanni. *Cavalleria Rusticana and Other Stories*. Translated by D. H. Lawrence. London: Cape, 1928.

―――. *Little Novels of Sicily*. Translated by D. H. Lawrence. New York: Seltzer, 1925.

―――. *Mastro-don Gesualdo*. Translated by D. H. Lawrence. New York: Seltzer, 1923.

Vickers, Brian. "Epideictic and Epic in the Renaissance." *New Literary History* 14, no. 3 (1983): 497–537.

Vickers, Nancy J. "Diana Described: Scattered Women and Scattered Rhyme." *Critical Inquiry* 8 (1981): 265–79.

Vico, Giambattista. *The Autobiography of Giambattista Vico*. Translated by Max Harold Fisch and Thomas Goddard Bergin. 1944. Ithaca, N.Y.: Cornell University Press, 1963.

―――. "Discovery of the True Dante." In *Discussions of* The Divine Comedy, edited by Irma Brandeis, pp. 11–12. Boston: D. C. Heath, 1961.

―――. *The New Science*. Translated by Max H. Fisch and T. G. Bergin. 3d ed. Ithaca, N.Y.: Cornell University Press, 1968.

―――. *Opere filosofiche*. Edited by Paolo Cristofolini. Florence: Sansoni, 1971.

―――. *Opere giuridiche*. Edited by Paolo Cristofolini. Florence: Sansoni, 1974.

Vinaver, Eugene. *The Rise of Romance*. New York: Oxford University Press. 1971.

Watson, George. *The English Petrarchans: A Critical Bibliography*. London: Warburg Institute Surveys, University of London, 1967.

Wells, Robin Headlam. *Spenser's* Faerie Queene *and the Cult of Elizabeth*. London: Croom Helm, 1983.

Weston, Jessie L. *The Legends of the Wagner Drama: Studies in Mythology and Romance*. New York: Charles Scribner's, 1896.

White, Hayden V. "What Is Living and What Is Dead in Croce's Criticism of Vico." In *Giambattista Vico: An International Symposium*, edited by Giorgio Tagliacozzo and Hayden V. White, pp. 379–89. Baltimore: Johns Hopkins University Press, 1969.

White, Patrick T. "James Joyce's *Ulysses* and Vico's 'Principles of Humanity.'" Ph.D. diss., University of Michigan, 1963.

Wilhelm, James J. *The American Roots of Ezra Pound*. New York: Garland, 1985.

―――. *Dante and Pound: The Epic of Judgement*. Orono: University of Maine Press, 1974.

―――. *The Later Cantos of Ezra Pound*. New York: Walker, 1977.

Wilkins, E. H. *The Making of the* Canzoniere *and Other Petrarchan Studies*. Rome: Edizioni di storia e letteratura, 1951.

Williams, Kathleen. *Spenser's World of Glass: A Reading of* The Faerie Queene. Berkeley: University of California Press, 1966.

Wills, Garry. *Cincinnatus: George Washington and the Englightenment*. Garden City, N.Y.: Doubleday, 1984.

―――. *Inventing America*. Garden City, N.Y.: Doubleday, 1978.

Witemeyer, Hugh. *The Poetry of Ezra Pound: Forms and Renewal, 1908–1920*. Berkeley: University of California Press, 1969.

Woodward, W. E. *George Washington, The Image and the Man*. New York: Boni and Liveright, 1926.

Wright, Louis B. *Middle-Class Culture in Elizabethan England*. Chapel Hill: University of North Carolina Press, 1935.

Wright, Natalia. *American Novelists in Italy, The Discoverers: Allston to James.* Philadelphia: University of Pennsylvania Press, 1965.

Wyatt, Thomas. *Collected Poems of Sir Thomas Wyatt.* Edited by Kenneth Muir and Patricia Thomson. Liverpool: Liverpool University Press, 1969.

Yates, Frances A. *Astraea: The Imperial Theme in the Sixteenth Century.* London: Routledge and Kegan Paul, 1975.

Yeats, W. B. *Autobiographies.* London: Macmillan, 1955.

——. *Explorations.* New York: Macmillan, 1962.

——. *The Poems.* Edited by Richard J. Finneran. Vol. 1 of *The Collected Works of William Butler Yeats.* New York: Macmillan, 1989.

Zapponi, Niccolò. *L'Italia di Ezra Pound.* Rome: Bulzoni, 1976.

Index

Reed Way Dasenbrock is associate professor of English at New Mexico State University, Las Cruces. He is the author of *The Literary Vorticism of Ezra Pound and Wyndham Lewis: Towards the Condition of Painting*, also available from Johns Hopkins.

Imitating the Italians

Designed by Ann Walston

Composed by G & S Typesetters, Inc.,
in Bembo text and display

Printed by The Maple Press Company
on 50-lb. MV Eggshell Offset
and bound in Holliston Aqualite

Lizzie's Story: A Slave Family's Journey to Freedom

By

Clarice Boswell

ISBN: 0-7596-9919-4 (e-book)
ISBN: 0-7596-9920-8 (Paperback)
ISBN: 1-4033-3290-8 (Hardcover)

This book is printed on acid free paper.

1st Books - rev. 02/04/05

Dedications:

Thanks to my husband, Henry, and children Constance, Claudia, Cathy, and Christopher, whose encouragement sustained me during the writing of this book, and for John and Frank, Jr., my two brothers, whose faith in me helped make the book a reality.

In loving memory of Mama Lizzie, my grandmother, and my parents, Frank Robert and Ora Belle Cannon.

iv

Acknowledgements

John M. Cannon, my younger brother in Seattle, Washington, for the endless hours he spent typing, critiquing and formatting the book for publication. Without his encouragement and patience, this journey would have been impossible. Henry A. Boswell, my soul mate since 1957, for his persistence and endless hours of carefully reading draft after draft of this book. Frank R. Cannon, Jr., my older brother, for his enthusiasm and willingness to help research the archives for pertinent history that enhanced the authenticity of this book. Constance L. (Boswell) Martin, Claudia L. (Boswell) Ellis, Cathy L. Boswell, and Christopher L. Boswell, my children, who followed the journey from its beginning. I leave them a legacy to cherish for generations to come. I am thankful for their support and willingness to help critique and enhance the contents of this book.

I would also like to acknowledge my debt to Hubert "Ruby" Boswell, my 97-year-old father-in-law, who has always been a source of support and inspiration to me. First cousins Horace Patrick and Joyce (Patrick) Morlin, they shared the stories that their mother told them about the family. Also Nancy Grider, retired English teacher from Joliet, for help on editing of this book.

Also Louise (Black) Poindexter and Mary L. Martin, my only two remaining aunts, will always be remembered for their encouraging words and support of this book. I am also indebted to my graphic artist Eric Hines for his time and talent in designing the cover. The pictures used to design the cover represent the authentic rocking chair,

the 1876 family Bible, and patch quilt quilted by Mama. There are numerous local residents that have encouraged me daily to complete the book. To those sources I owe a debt of thanks including the Sisters of the Joliet Area Alumni Chapter, Delta Sigma Theta Sorority, Inc., and the members of Grace United Methodist Church, Joliet, Illinois.

To those whose contributions I have neglected to mention, please accept my sincere apology. I owe all a great debt.

Table of Contents

Prologue

This is a story of an African family that arrived in America from West Africa on a slave merchant ship in the spring of 1850. Upon arriving in Maryland through the Chesapeake Bay they were placed in a holding stockade in Annapolis, which was among the smallest auction markets for slaves destined for the states of Kentucky, Tennessee, and Alabama. The family had survived the three-month Middle Passage journey across the Atlantic Ocean only to be auctioned to the highest plantation slave broker bid. The family consisted of mother, father, and two children ages five and seven.

Although the families are fact, some of the names and background information are fictional. Most of the factual information was gathered from family members, the 1876 family Bible, and information from many documented family pictures dating back to 1854. The old family Bible and photo albums enabled the writer to connect and envision the spirit of a family that encountered undue hardship, and physical and mental treatment that was harsh and cruel.

In creating the background for the story, the writer drew on much of the first-person dialogue to document actual accounts of events that the family encountered upon arriving in America in 1850.

As late as 1850 in some coastal areas along the Atlantic, the slave laws continued to be enforced as the need for free labor proved economically profitable. Federal laws, restricting slavery seemed

useless, as they were ignored by white masters, politicians, and others who were slave owners.

Slave brokers, acting as sellers in the north and buyers in the south, were licensed traders who bought and sold slaves on speculation. Delcy's parents, Eli and Leah Brent, and her two brothers, Josh and Reuben, were all auctioned and imprisoned in a stockade storage in Annapolis, Maryland. It is, however, a known fact that they arrived at the market house in Annapolis Harbor, Maryland as a family destined for slavery. This was a relatively small holding port because foreign slave trade had been greatly reduced since most states were purchasing slaves from the domestic market.

Slaves who were purchased for Kentucky plantations made an overland trip on foot across the mountains to reach their destination. Often at night they would sleep in jails, churches or warehouses. To ensure safe arrival, the human cargo was always chained and shackled.

Lizzie Brent Sheff Davis Cannon, born December 25, 1870, was the mother of eight children and one foster daughter, Katherine Louise Black, whom she raised from the age of five. At Lizzie's death on September 8, 1965, at the age of 94, she had nine grand children and four children living that lovingly called her Mama.

The map follows the route the Brent family traveled from Maryland to Kentucky. Eli and Leah Brent and their two sons, Josh and Reuben, landed on the shore of America in the spring of 1850. They were auctioned from the slave-holding pens at Annapolis, Maryland to a tobacco plantation master in Kentucky. With the aid of a slave broker representing Master Sheff, the difficult journey by foot

from Maryland into West Virginia and finally into Kentucky took about seven weeks. They were chained together and allowed to rest only a few times a day at which time they shared a few pieces of bread and drink of water. At night they slept in abandoned buildings or jails that provided rooms for traveling slaves. The journey ended in Leesburg, Kentucky at the plantation of Lloyd and Sarah Sheff, who would prove to be ruthless and cruel owners.

CHAPTER 1—1850: FROM AFRICA TO MARYLAND, THE LONGEST JOURNEY

The year 1850 was filled with devastating slave laws that tightened the screws of bondage on the institution of slavery in America. The Fugitive Slave Law of 1850 allowed bounty hunters to capture slaves in any state of the Union regardless of their status as a fugitive or free person and return them to their owners or re-sell them into slavery. Because the slaves were in a majority in most states, the labor market for illegally transporting Africans across the Atlantic to be auctioned and sold into slavery was no longer necessary.

When the Eli and Leah Brent family was captured from Africa and forced on the slave ship bound for America, they were among the last Africans to illegally cross the Atlantic. The 3-month journey was terrifying and very difficult. There was fear, hatred, and confusion among the slaves. Shackled to the floor, the slaves were beaten and denied food and water by the slave brokers. Many slave taskmasters used a dialect unfamiliar to the slaves, thus increasing an even greater fear for the Africans.

Many Africans did not survive the seemingly endless journey because of cruelty, starvation, and disease. Even though the slave brokers always chose the strongest and healthiest slaves they thought would survive the journey, they did not consider the possibility of the slaves contracting illnesses that were common in America but fatal in their African homeland. Nor did they count on having very strong

willed, rebellious Africans who would rather jump ship and drown than become a slave.

Eli and Leah watched with horror throughout the entire journey many deaths and suicides. They tried to keep Josh and Reuben's eyes away from such terrifying deaths, but they couldn't protect their children from all of the nightmares. On this particular voyage more than a fourth of the cargo did not arrive at its final destination. The slave brokers were not happy with the fact that so many died on the voyage, for they lost money.

The Brent family huddled tightly in a corner of the hold of the ship (bottom, where the rats were) and prayed they would make it safely to their destination. Little did they know the hardships of disease, pain, and death that awaited their arrival in America. Upon landing in Annapolis, Maryland the Brent family was removed from the ship's cargo bay and placed in a holding stockade. Here they would remain until it was time for them to be placed on the auction block and sold to the highest bidder.

Eli attempted to comfort his family as he spoke softly to his wife Leah,

"Leah, everything is going to be all right, you hear? You just hold on to me and the boys real tight. We're going to be all right."

The two sons, Reuben, age 7, and Josh, age 5, trembled with fear as they clung to their parents. Their greatest fear was being separated and never seeing Mama Leah and Papa Eli again. Eli drew his family close to his body. He knew they were cold from the damp floor in the holding pen. He was a big, strong man standing over six feet tall, with

deep, piercing eyes and high cheekbones. His rich brown complexion was representative of the native African arriving in America.

Leah and Eli comforted each other and the two boys as the family was harshly steered toward the auction steps. They witnessed other families weeping and clinging to each other as they were separated and sold to the highest bidder. Eli whispered to Leah,

"For some reason, they are keeping us together as a family." Leah breathed a sigh of relief.

Prior to the start of the auction, Zac Wallace, the slave broker, had an opportunity to discuss with the auctioneer his intent to purchase a family unit for Lloyd Sheff's tobacco plantation. Because Zac was a frequent buyer for the southern slave owners, he felt that the auctioneer would attempt to honor his request.

The auctioneer started the bid at $500 for the family. Eli felt humiliated when they stripped him of his clothes and examined his body for form and physical stature. Leah was spared the fate of many younger women whom she observed being stripped and humiliated.

Zac Wallace watched the bidders around him shouting out bids on Eli, while mostly ignoring Leah and the two boys. Zac could see the family being split by individual bids. Lloyd Sheff had given strict orders for Zac to purchase a complete family of slaves of good health and robust stature to work on his tobacco plantation in Leesburg, Ky. Zac became fearful of losing the opportunity to secure the family as the bidding continued to climb on Eli.

Suddenly, the bid was fifteen hundred dollars for Eli with only a few meager bids for Leah and the two boys. Zac could see the deal

slipping away. Lloyd Sheff had entrusted him with three thousand dollars to bid on a family. Suddenly Zac yelled out,

"I bid twenty eight hundred dollars on the whole family."

Immediately, a murmur came over the crowd but no other bids were forthcoming. A few tense moments elapsed and the auctioneer shouted, "Going once, going twice, sold to the gentleman from Kentucky!" The auctioneer instructed the recorder of sales to document the purchase of the Brent family consisting of one male named Eli, age 26, one female named Leah, age 24, and two small boys, Reuben, age 7, and Josh, age 5.

Eli loved his family and in his own way, he quietly expressed thankfulness that his family was not separated. After the sale was recorded, not much time lapsed before Zac prepared the family for the journey to the Sheff's tobacco plantation. Eli, Leah, Reuben, and Josh were huddled together awaiting instructions from Zac. They were poorly dressed for the cold long journey. Zac rode his prancing stallion as the family struggled to keep up on foot. The children tired more quickly since there was very little food and water to spare during the long journey.

At one point, Josh began to cry, as it was hard for him to keep pace. Reuben picked Josh up and put him on his back.

"Don't cry, Josh." Reuben consoled.

"You ain't heavy. Wrap yo' legs around me and hol' on tight."

Josh was also getting hungry, but he didn't dare ask for anything. Zac had a terrible temper that scared the boys. When they had trouble keeping up, Zac would harshly scold them. Once he even snapped his

whip as a warning for everyone to keep up. Eli and Leah were chained together and the boys walked beside them. The journey was rugged and the terrain up and down the hills was difficult for everyone. Leah would gently nudge the boys when she noticed they were lagging behind. Zac had a deadline to deliver the Brent family to Lloyd by the last of May in time to start planting tobacco.

Reuben and Josh often spoke quietly to each other. They were so afraid of what might happen to them. Josh confided in Reuben,

"Reuben, do you think they will take us away from Mama and Papa?"

"I don't think so Josh, but if they wanted to, they would have done that when Papa was standing on the steps and everyone was looking at him."

"Reuben?"

"Yeah Josh?"

"Mama looked so scared."

"Yeah, Josh."

"The other children were crying. It made me cry."

"Reuben?"

"Yeah, Josh."

"Where are we going?"

"I ain't sure, Josh, it's a long way from home." "Reuben? I miss home. Will we ever get to go back?"

"I ain't sure Josh."

"Reuben, I'm thirsty and I know Mama and Papa must be too."

The sun was beginning to go down and the evening's cool was causing Eli, Leah, and the two boys to shiver. All of them were extremely tired as they wearily moved forward, hoping that they would soon stop. Zac seemed to sense the exhaustion of the family and soon stopped at a nearby jail where food and shelter were provided the family. Day after day passed, seemingly endless: Maryland, West Virginia, and finally into Kentucky. Tired, weary, with blisters on their feet, and clothes tattered, they pushed forward on their journey.

The need for slave labor on the tobacco plantations was crucial during the 1850's. The demand for exporting tobacco made very profitable business. Cotton in the South, along with sugar, rice, and hemp, was expanding the demand for slave labor. The closer the family got to the plantation, the harder Zac drove them. However, during the last few days of the journey, he made certain they had an ample portion of food and water. It was essential that Zac Wallace deliver the family in good physical condition. After more than six weeks, the Brent family arrived on the plantation in Leesburg, Ky, where Master Lloyd and Miss Sarah impatiently awaited their delivery.

The slave taskmaster, Boss Calhoun, showed the family to their living quarters. The old, run-down log cabin located closer to the fields than to the master's house was in serious need of repair. Inside the one-room cabin was a potbellied stove, a pecan wood rocking chair, a bed, a table and four chairs, and a kerosene lamp. This was all very strange to the Brent family, because in Africa, not only were the

structure and furnishings different, but the village style of living where everyone supported each other as neighbors no longer existed. In Africa, the huts were made of bamboo and mud. Inside, covering the ground, were decorative and durable rugs that served as beds for the family. The tribal style of living was open and uninhibited. Men, women, and children were free to move about in social gatherings. Meals were prepared outside of the hut by the women in the village. The meal was a time for family unity and celebrating the collaborative efforts of the village people to have food as well as friendship.

As the Brent family huddled in their new home in America, fear rushed over them. They were in a strange land, with a strange language, and no familiar faces. Josh and Reuben were curious about the children who stared at them, saying nothing. Pearlie, their neighbor next door, was just as curious. Now she knew why Master Lloyd had sold the Weaver family in the log cabin next to her. It was to make room for a younger family.

After a few hours, Pearlie, the neighbor next door, gently knocked on the Brent's door. She was well groomed in a long gray dress and crisp starched apron that covered her shoes. The family stared with fear not knowing what to expect. The journey for the Brent family had been long and tiring, and no one had shown any acts of kindness toward them. Suddenly, Pearlie's face broke into a big smile and she extended a hand to Eli and Leah. She had prepared a pot of stew to welcome them to the life of slavery. She motioned for the family to sit down while she found a few things upon which to serve the food. The family was very hungry, especially the children.

Pearlie made many visits to the new family next door. During these visits, she began to develop various hand and body gestures accompanied by words as a means of communicating with the family, especially Leah. They began to bond as they walked to and from work. Several months later, as the family began to understand and relate to Pearlie, she told them about overhearing Master Lloyd negotiating with Zac Wallace to ride out to Annapolis, Maryland and bid on a family that he had an inside track on that was arriving on a merchant ship in April 1850. Pearlie knew she could use the help in the Master's house. After all, the Sheff children and the whims of Miss Sarah were a full time morning-till-night job and often overwhelming.

It was late May when the Sheff plantation owner took delivery of the Brent family. Pearlie was beginning to put together the idea of what Master Lloyd and Miss Sarah were thinking when they sold the Weaver family in the end cabin. Clifton and Bernice Weaver had been on the plantation for nearly twenty years. Fannie, their 17-year old daughter, had a rough time working in the fields. She wanted so much to work in the main house, but she knew that as long as Pearlie was there she would always be a field hand. Two of their sons, Morie, age 19, and James, age 21, had fled through the Underground Railroad and Master Lloyd knew it was only a matter of time before their third son Ralph, age 23, would join his brothers. Master Lloyd wanted a younger family that could grow up on the plantation as the Weaver family had.

8

Pearlie valued the Brent family, and in her spare time she let them know that the life of a slave was harsh and bitter. She told them how to stay out of the way of the overseer's whip, and what to expect from Miss Sarah. The family listened carefully as they slowly adjusted to the life of a slave with no rights or privileges that they once had in their homeland of Africa.

Leah was assigned to work in the main house with Pearlie. Miss Sarah was very impatient and resented showing Leah more than once how to do her job. Leah soon felt the harsh treatment of Miss Sarah. Leah did not have a good understanding of the English language, which made it even more difficult to adhere to Miss Sarah's demands. This lack of communication resulted in undue whipping and face slapping. Leah was very careful not to agitate or provoke Miss Sarah. She listened more carefully and soon began to understand more and more of what was expected of her. Quietly, she did her job, which consisted of cooking the meals, washing, ironing, making the beds, cleaning, and caring for Master Lloyd, Miss Sarah, and their three children. Pearlie comforted Leah when she returned home from the long day at Master Lloyd's house. Pearlie knew it was difficult to work for Miss Sarah. It was hard for Leah to keep up with the many demands of her own family as well.

Eli and the two boys were assigned to the tobacco fields under the supervision of Boss Calhoun, a very brutal man. Eli and the boys watched carefully the jobs of other slaves and soon became familiar with the tasks expected of slaves who worked the tobacco fields. Other slaves owned by Master Lloyd had huge scars on their backs

which frightened Eli and the boys. They had never seen anything like those deep scars. No one on the plantation said much to each other. Head down with a strap over the shoulders harnessing a team of mules, they plowed and later planted from sunup to sundown. Afterward there was wood to cut and split and animals to care for.

After a few months with the help of Pearlie, Leah began to understand Miss Sarah better and especially to understand what was expected of slaves who worked in the master's house. For example, she learned how to please Miss Sarah when serving tea as well as presenting her with a new dress or a beautiful patch quilt made from scraps of fabric given her. Leah took no chances of feeling comfortable in Miss Sarah's presence. She could be just as ruthless as kind. Leah stayed on task and did her job well.

After a twelve or fourteen-hour day in the fields for Eli, Reuben and Josh, and a busy day at Master Lloyd's house for Leah, there were many things to do at the old broken down cabin. Seemingly, something always needed fixing. Eli remembered when the old roof was leaking on the mud floor. It made such a mess trying to dry out the beds. He had to put fresh straw on the floor to soak up the water. It was near fall before the old roof was fixed. He had to stuff mud between the logs to keep out the winter wind and snow.

After a long day at the Master's house, Leah had a meal to fix and sometimes water to carry from the well for her family. Leah would often do the mending and quilting after the two boys were asleep. On occasion, she would simply enjoy sitting in the old pecan rocking

chair after she had carefully patched and mended the worn-out clothes. Most of the time the clothes had patches over patches.

Leah was always thinking about the family and trying to make life a bit more pleasant and comfortable. Sometimes she would surprise them with fresh straw mattresses or replace the worn out quilts with new ones made from discarded clothes from Master Lloyd's house.

Josh and Reuben were learning the routine of the plantation and took on more responsibilities. For example, every morning they had to hang the quilts on the fence to dry as a result of the dampness from the mud floor. Each day, they went to the fields with Eli and helped weed the crops as well as tend to the farm animals. Their evening chores were to make certain there was fresh water for the master's house. The boys hurried to finish the evening tasks so they could eat supper. They looked forward to Eli and Leah telling them stories about their life in Africa and the good old days, a life that they would never see again.

The daily demands on the Brent family seemed endless. They often talked about being free and wondered when freedom would become a reality. One day Eli asked another slave about the route to freedom and was told to never mention that again. The slave pointed to the scars on his back as a reminder of what to expect when slaves talked about freedom or the Northern Star. Eli became afraid for Leah, Reuben and Josh and warned them to never mention freedom to anyone. Eli believed that someday they would have a better life and be free, but had not yet allowed himself to make plans to improve their condition.

Eli and Leah sensed the tension on the plantation when Master Lloyd entertained visitors for dinner. Often Leah overheard the master talking about slaves running away and the awful things he threatened to do if he ever caught them on his plantation. Leah was often afraid for the fugitives who crossed the plantation late at night headed north. She cautiously gave them food and water and quickly sent them away.

As Leah sat in the old rocking chair, she often thought about the boys, now seven and nine years old. Each day the boys went to the tobacco field with Eli to help with the crops. Some days they were expected to pick vegetables from the garden and care for the farm animals. In the evening, they always made certain Leah had plenty wood for the fire that heated the water in the two big black pots in which she washed clothes. Reuben and Josh were obedient and well-behaved boys who did whatever was asked of them.

The boys loved the days when Leah sat in the rocking chair and Eli sat at the table smoking his corn cob pipe. He told them stories of life in their motherland of Africa. They liked to hear about the older boys in their village hunting and playing games where they could pretend to be great warriors. Sometimes the boys would look sad while longing for Africa where they were free to roam the countryside.

Eli always ended his stories,

"Those times all gone."

"Life will never be the same. Someday, if I live long enough, we shall be free."

Leah really missed her life in the village where activities were centered around families doing things together for the betterment of everyone. The village agricultural and trade market was the center of life for the family. The women would care for the gardens, weave the cloth, and tend the children. The older women would tell stories to the younger girls on the importance of the family, which formed the village. The women had a special way of preparing the girls for womanhood. They taught the young girls to work and instructed them about being a good mother. Leah remembered all they had said, and tried to practice the many things she had learned in her village.

Leah and Eli began to notice a number of runaway slaves crossing the fields down by the creek. They became very anxious for the boys. Boss Calhoun had warned all the slaves that they would get severe lashings with the whip if they were caught trying to escape. Eli wanted to protect the boys from escaping slaves who might try to persuade them to leave the plantation. The year was 1852, the demand for tobacco from the American and European market was at its highest for field workers. Adults and children worked from sun up until sun down.

Once when Master Lloyd was caught up on his work for a few days in the tobacco fields he decided to lease Eli out to another farmer. Other farmers were just as difficult to work for and often disallowed them the bare necessities, such as a drink of water. It was this type of cruelty that made slaves think about running for freedom. Eli thought, "where would he go? What would happen to him if he were caught? "Eli tried not to get too involved with the fugitive

13

slaves. However, he longed to know what freedom would be like in America. Eli became afraid for himself and the boys. Reuben and Josh were warned to be careful when they saw escaping slaves. They always watched for Boss Calhoun and Master Lloyd. Eli realized that the boys could be sold for a high price at their age. The last thing Eli wanted was for his family to be sold as punishment for helping escaping slaves or talking about freedom.

CHAPTER 2—1854: PEARLIE

Pearlie was one of the most trusted slaves owned by Master Lloyd and Miss Sarah. She had arrived in America from the west coastal shore of Africa, having crossed the Atlantic on a merchant ship with her father, mother, and younger sister, all destined for Charleston, South Carolina in the year 1845. She had endured the harsh journey to America to be sold into a harsher situation. She saw many Africans die enroute to America. Often the stench and foul air in the hold of the ship was unbearable. There was barely room to turn and no room to sit or stand.

When Pearlie disembarked the merchant ship, she was placed in a holding pen along with her family and hundreds of other Africans waiting their turn to be stripped of their dignity, examined and auctioned like cattle to the highest bidder. She remembered well that hot, muggy day in Charleston when she was sexually fondled and stripped of her clothes and paraded up and down in front of the bidders for their approval.

Pearlie's father, mother, and younger sister were sold separately. Pearlie never saw them again. She often wondered what happened to them. Pearlie was auctioned to a tobacco plantation owner in Tennessee. She did not know the journey from Charleston to Tennessee would take six weeks on foot. She and two other slaves were purchased for the Shelby plantation. Pearlie was frequently sexually abused by the master and other white overseers from the moment she arrived on the Shelby plantation. One day she

hemorrhaged so badly from the sexual assaults that she nearly died. After recovering, she found that she could never have children; thus, Pearlie was no longer a profitable slave. A barren slave was often useless, for slave owners expected pregnancies to ensure future slaves for profit.

Pearlie was put on the market again to be sold along with several other slaves from the Shelby plantation. Pearlie, now twenty, scared and helpless, was once again paraded in front of prospective buyers for a price. A slave broker representing Master Lloyd and Miss Sarah Sheff bid for her. Master Lloyd needed someone to help with the children. Pearlie was not worth as much as a barren slave woman but she would serve his household needs and she sold relatively cheap.

Miss Sarah took Pearlie into the master house and gave her the task of nurse and midwife for the family. Pearlie took her herbs and salves and nursed the Sheff family and nursed the slaves that had been whipped by the overseers for not pulling their weight on the plantation. Pearlie knew how to birth babies and care for the personal needs of Miss Sarah. When Miss Sarah was pregnant with her second baby, Pearlie was there to help with the delivery. Pearlie was by far Miss Sarah's most trusted house slave. After a few months, Master Lloyd provided a log cabin for Pearlie on the edge of the tobacco fields and she moved from the master's house. There were three cabins and an outhouse near the slave quarters. She liked that because she could see what was going on with the families that lived on either side. Periodically, the slave family on the other side of Pearlie would get together in the cabins and talk about freedom. Sometimes the

women would swap stories about Master Lloyd and Miss Sarah. Pearlie would laugh about how she would listen to their stories and pretend not to understand. She said,

"I learned how to play along, always listening to their business."

Five years after Pearlie's arrival on the Sheff plantation, the Brent family moved into the cabin next to her. She would miss the Weaver family since they were working the tobacco fields when she was bought by Master Lloyd. Pearlie had watched the Weaver children grow up and escape from the plantation. Now, a younger family had taken their place.

Leah and Eli were grateful for the help of Pearlie. She was highly respected by the slaves for her status with the Sheff family. There were certain unspoken codes of discrimination based on the color of one's skin imposed on the slaves. Slaves that were assigned to work in the master's house had a higher status often causing resentment by those slaves assigned to work the fields. Pearlie was able to help the Brent family understand what was expected of them and how to survive the demands of the master and the social culture within the slave community.

CHAPTER 3—1854: DELCY

Four years after Leah, Eli, Josh and Reuben arrived in Leesburg, Kentucky, Leah reflected on the struggle that the family had gone through since arriving on the Sheff tobacco plantation. Reuben turned eleven in the fall and Josh, now nine, wanted more than anything to learn how to read and write. They would listen to the Sheff children read as Miss Sarah taught them daily. However, there was no alloted time for schooling of slaves on the plantation. In fact, the boys did not know any slaves that could read and write.

One day Eli had to take a trip off the plantation for Master Lloyd. He hooked up the team of mules to the old farm wagon and called to Reuben to hop on the seat beside him. Reuben was excited, for it was his first time ever off the plantation. Eli explained to him that they were going to the plantation down the road to pick up some seed for planting. Reuben had always wondered what was beyond the plantation. On the journey, he saw many beautiful horses and large mansions like Master Lloyd's. He also saw other slaves all dressed up with big top hats and red coats with bright shiny buttons driving carriages taking the master's mistress to and from town.

Eli warned Reuben to keep his head down so as not to imply anything between him and the beautiful mistresses all dressed up in silks and satins with beautiful hats and umbrellas. Reuben noticed that the fancily dressed slaves hopped off the carriage and opened the door to carefully help each passenger down. Those white women seemed happy. Their skin was pale and their hair was neatly curled with

18

ribbons and bows. They were like nothing he had ever seen in his life. Eli saw the excitement in Reuben's eyes; he knew how much trouble a young, black, male slave could cause by looking at a white woman in a curious way.

Eli took this time to talk to Reuben. He told him how some slaves were punished, by either whipping or hanging, for just looking at a white woman. Reuben acknowledged everything Papa Eli told him. Getting in trouble was the last thing he wanted. Eli told him that he had heard of a young boy just like him being sold away from his mama and papa just for glancing at a mistress. Reuben stayed in the wagon while Eli loaded the seed in the back. Eli quickly stepped up on the wagon and gave the mules a snap as they hurriedly bumped their way back to the plantation. Reuben talked all the way home about the things he saw that day outside the plantation. He could hardly wait to tell Josh about his trip. Josh was full of questions and anxious to hear about everything that Reuben had seen.

Josh and Reuben were beginning to ask questions about the life of other people beyond the plantation. Their curiosity grew more each day as they saw the runaway slaves in the evenings after all the field bosses were gone. They became brave and discretely asked a few slaves which way they were headed. They knew they were seeking freedom because Papa and Mama Leah had slipped the fugitive slaves food through the kitchen window and sent them on their way. The boys eventually put together bits and pieces of information and started to understand that thing called, "The Underground Railroad," would take them North toward freedom. Leah decided it was the right time

19

to talk to the boys about the things she had heard from Pearlie. The Master's guests talked about the escaping slaves and the Underground Railroad. Seemingly, the Masters did not know how so many slaves were finding their way North.

Pearlie had observed the same curiosity and desire for freedom in Josh and Reuben as she did in the Weaver boys. They escaped the Sheff plantation prior to the arrival of the Brent family. Pearlie became increasingly concerned for the safety of the boys and decided to share with Leah the secret codes of the quilts used by the fugitive slaves to make their journey north.

Although Pearlie had seen many fugitive slaves crossing the Sheff plantation, she did not share her knowledge of the codes, patterns, and hidden secrets of the quilts. She knew that information would let the slaves know where they could stop for food and shelter on "The Liberty Trail," later known as the Underground Railroad. She explained to Leah that the Underground Railroad was a secret group of people who cared about freeing slaves by helping them escape; by letting them use their homes for shelter, fixing them food, giving them clothes and medicines, and even showing them the way to the next safe place. Some of the secret people were called abolitionists. They helped hide and direct the slaves by developing the carefully selected patterns in the quilts that contained the messages and maps.

The abolitionists would visit the different plantations pretending to be merchants peddling house wares, tax collectors or census takers. They knew the blacksmith was the trusted servant in many instances. Pearlie knew Pete, the blacksmith, from the Shelby plantation in

Tennessee. She knew Pete had contact with almost everyone entering the Shelby plantation. Knowing that Pearlie was a quilter, he asked her to make several quilts using the special patterns that had been shown to him by the abolitionists.

Pearlie had witnessed slaves severely punished by her past master. She knew Master Lloyd would deal out the same punishment to his slaves who offered help to fugitives crossing his plantation. It was with the greatest of confidence and promise of secrecy that Pete shared the messages with Pearlie which she now shared with Leah.

She continued to explain to Leah that the simple quilt was one item that was common to both the master's and the slave's household.

Leah learned from Pearlie that the grandmother's flower garden quilt indicated that there was a root cellar or shed with a false floor to hide under behind the flower garden. This really impressed Leah. Pearlie told Leah how she was entrusted with the quilt codes while working on the Shelby plantation.

Leah carefully explained to her sons how secret codes were hidden in the quilts as a message to help the runaway slaves find safe houses on their way north to freedom. The Sheff plantation was not a safe stop for runaway slaves. However, every chance Leah got, she would share a piece of bread or drink of water, always hoping she would not get caught.

Leah really wanted the boys to know the danger of escaping, the danger of not knowing what to expect beyond the plantation, and most of all, danger of not knowing who could be trusted. There were many dangers in escaping, especially alone. The Masters had well-

trained dogs that would hunt a slave down. If the slave did not know which direction to go, they could be easily tracked, found, and re-sold. Being sold away from one's parents was just one of the punishments for running. The boys thought long and hard about the possibility of being separated from Papa and Mama Leah.

One night when all was quiet and the old fire in the cooking stove was cooling down there was a tap at the kitchen window. It scared everyone. Papa Eli asked the family to stay quiet. He moved slowly toward the door and asked,

"Who is it?" A soft, quiet voice spoke,

"A friend, who just wants a little food and a drink of water."

Leah moved quietly around the cabin, filling a small cloth sack with a few leftover biscuits and a piece of salt pork meat. The voice nervously thanked her and disappeared in the night. Josh and Reuben were not allowed to say anything. Papa Eli warned the boys to never say a word about what they saw.

Eli told the boys about the Northern star and watching for moss growing on the north side of the trees down by the creek. Someday, they would understand why the slaves would run away so they would be free. There were several patches of trees that offered refuge and directions to the fleeing slaves.

One morning Eli found a young boy about the age of Reuben hiding among the tobacco leaves. The leaves were so broad that the little fellow could not be seen from a distance. They scared each other. Eli asked him his name and where was he coming from. He said,

"My name is Joplin, but they call me 'Jop'. I come from Massa Nash's plantation. I been runnin' three days looking fo' my folks. They was sold last week and I was left behind."

Eli offered him his lunch, which he gladly accepted, and took off running into the thick grove of trees which led to the creek heading North.

About a month later, Eli had another chance to talk briefly to a fugitive slave. It was almost daybreak and Eli was preparing to take one of his trips to pick up supplies for Master Lloyd. This particular morning, as he was busily hooking up the mules to the wagon, a tall, thin, very frightened, runaway slave suddenly stepped out of the barn and begged him not to call for help. He explained,

"I 'scaped from massa Owen's place in Tennessee. I'm on ma way north where I can cross the Ohio River and make it ta' Canada. I have a brother that 'scaped some months back and I'm hopin' to join him soon."

Eli, being a big man, was really not afraid of the slave as much as being caught talking to him. Eli in no way wanted to risk the punishment of having his family sold or separated from the children. Eli asked if he had a name. He said,

"They call me Jobe."

Since it was so early in the morning, there was not much traffic on the main path. Eli asked Jobe to stay in the barn while he filled and spread the straw over the bottom of the wagon. Then Jobe got in and lay very flat while Eli covered him up. Jobe was very grateful and careful not to move. As Eli hooked up the mules and started out, he

23

took a little side trip down by the creek near the thick trees and pretended to let the mules drink while Jobe slid from under the straw. He quickly moved into the water and headed north toward Ohio. Eli's heart was beating so hard he could literally feel it pounding through his raggedy shirt. Eli feared being caught. After he picked up his supplies, he tried to dismiss what had happened, but somehow the young man had made an impression upon him. He sighed deeply and whispered,

"One day, dear Lord, one day."

He gave the mules a 'giddy-up' and headed back to the plantation.

As the hot summer months turned to the cool days of fall, it was time to harvest the fields of dried tobacco, as well as tend to the last of the vegetables left in the garden. Most of the vegetables, turnips, potatoes, and squash were either canned or stored in a cool root cellar under the Master's house. All the fruit was picked from the trees and neatly placed in the cellar before the first signs of winter.

Leah had waited until she was getting bigger and bigger and it was getting harder to conceal that she was pregnant. She finally told Josh and Reuben that she was expecting a baby sometime in November. Miss Sarah already suspected something, but had not openly asked Leah if she was pregnant. Pearlie knew because Leah had confided in her as they walked to work daily. Pearlie assured Leah that she would be there to help her with the delivery of her new baby. Leah took a few minutes from her busy household chores to let Miss Sarah know that she was expecting in the late fall. Miss Sarah showed some compassion toward Leah who was faithful to her and

the family. She offered her a few things that her children no longer needed and told her she had clothes and items for the baby. Leah thanked her, being somewhat surprised, at her rare generosity.

As the fall days passed, Leah routinely entered the cabin after a long days work; she always looked forward to relaxing with her sewing and quilting sitting in the old rocking chair. She would wait for Eli and the boys to come home from their chores in the field and finish work around the cabin. The boys were good about bringing in the wood to make the fire. Eli would sometimes help make the meal. Once in a while, Miss Sarah would offer her families' leftovers to Leah. This was always appreciated since Leah was nearing time to deliver. She was frequently exhausted after a days work at the mansion. Her feet were beginning to swell and the walk to and from the log cabin was getting harder each day.

Leah began to sense a change in the weather and realized her time to deliver was drawing near. Pearlie was keeping an eye on Leah and noticed how tired she became at the end of each day. On a cold night when the full moon was bright, Eli went next door and got Pearlie to come stay with Leah. He did not know the first thing to do to help Leah, nor did he know much about birthing babies, only birthing the farm animals. The boys made a big fire in the cooking stove and filled the pots full of water. They sat quietly waiting for Pearlie to tell them what to do. Pearlie prepared her usual herbs and drugs to help with the pain of childbirth. Leah was ready for delivery. Minutes before midnight on November 28, 1854, Leah gave birth to a healthy baby girl. There was great excitement and joy when the baby cried

immediately. Josh and Reuben were excited to have a sister. Eli danced and cried as he held the new baby girl in his arms. He raised her to the heavens and gave thanks to God. They decided to name her Delcy, after an aunt who lived in Africa. They knew they would never be able to return to their homeland. Naming her Delcy acknowledged their African heritage as they continued to extend their family in America.

CHAPTER 4—1854-LEAH REMINISCES

After the birth of Delcy, the family provided her with loving attention. Josh and Reuben adored her and Papa Eli spent time helping Leah care for her. Since she was born during the fall, chores around the Master's house were far less demanding than the daily grind of tending crops from sunup to sundown. Eli and the boys stayed busy repairing worn equipment and tending the livestock. Sometimes twice a day they would split wood for both their cabin and the master's house. In the morning they would make certain all the animals were fed and the cows milked. Leah did most of the sewing and quilting during the cold fall and winter days. She especially enjoyed quilting the beautiful patterns shared by Pearlie. Delcy was always by her side well wrapped in quilts to keep her warm.

When Delcy was barely two weeks old, Leah returned to the Master's house and resumed her usual household chores. At least she didn't have to take Delcy out in the cold the first two weeks. Josh and Reuben cut and stacked firewood so the little log cabin was always warm and cozy. Before the cold weather set in, Eli had packed mud into the cracks around the window and door which helped to keep the drafts of the howling winds from entering during the winter.

Delcy was a happy baby. She had facial features similar to Eli. She had big piercing eyes and high cheekbones that set her apart from Leah's features. Leah had a gentle look about her face. She was a very slim and petite woman, weighing a little more than 120 pounds. Eli was over six feet tall and topped the scale at 210 pounds. Reuben was

a lot like Eli and Josh resembled Leah. Josh was sensitive to the harsh treatment of Master Lloyd and often cried, unlike Reuben, who was often angry about the treatment of slaves. Even though Josh was small for his age, he had a husky body and was very strong.

Sometimes at night Leah would reflect back to Africa where she longed for the life they had before word spread throughout the villages that Africans were being captured and taken from their homeland. The bearded white men ran through their villages grabbing men, women and children, chaining them together. Those captured were made to walk across the hot earth to several holding cells, then placed on big slave ships. Leah had lived in fear of this day. The European slave catchers were ruthless and cruel. They were paid well to catch as many Africans as a merchant's ship could hold. The captives were chained together while they were prepared for the long, torturous voyage across the Atlantic to America.

When Leah, Eli and the two boys were captured, everyone in the small village was chained together except for the old, sick, and weak. She could not forget the panic and shock during the long walk to the ship. They had never been that far from their village, so everything was very strange and frightening.

As Leah looked at Delcy sleeping quietly in her little box beside the potbellied stove that warmed the cabin, she wondered what Delcy's future would be. Delcy had a disposition that was restless, unlike the boys. Oh, how Leah wished for Africa and freedom for her family. Most of all, she longed for a better life for the children. Josh and Reuben would never have the chance to play with the other boys

or follow the men to the wooded areas to collect firewood and bamboo that was used to make baskets and mats. Growing up in Africa as a young man meant leaving early in the morning on hunting trips and returning late in the evening with fresh meat. The whole village shared the kill and celebrated with song and dance. Leah missed the children's laughter and comfort of the older women in the village.

Leah did not have much time to reminisce about her family in Africa. She always intended to tell the boys about life in their native country. Now that Delcy had arrived, Leah made a vow to share as many of the stories with the children as she and Eli could remember. She wanted her children to be able to pass the stories on to their children for generations to come.

Leah looked around the cabin and everyone was asleep. She quietly tucked the children in and sat for a while in the rocker and drifted off to sleep watching Delcy sleep peacefully.

The next morning was routine, except she prepared to take Delcy to work with her. Because the weather was cold, Leah carefully bundled Delcy in warm quilts before placing her in a sling over her shoulders to make the trip to Master Lloyd's house. Leah would have to carry Delcy with her as she did her chores, since there was no convenient place to lay her down in order to keep an eye on her.

Miss Sarah did not make it convenient for Leah to care for Delcy. She even made the remark that Delcy was one more mouth to feed. Leah resented the comment and quickly clutched Delcy closely to her body as a gesture to Miss Sarah that she was more than just another

29

slave. Leah had a way of letting Miss Sarah know that her comment was hurtful. Leah responded by letting Miss Sarah know that Delcy was special to her and her family. She did not have to worry about Leah slacking on her household tasks. Leah was even more careful by attempting to avoid Miss Sarah as she went about doing her job. Leah knew Miss Sarah quite well and knew how hurtful and sharp-tongued she could be. Leah knew the winter months were long and contact was unavoidable. She didn't mind carrying Delcy around. She could nurse her and talk to her whenever she was awake. Delcy slept quietly the first few months, waking only when it was time to nurse and have her diaper changed.

Leah was a good cook. One of her special meals for the Sheff family was boiled turnips, and stewed apples from the cellar and roast pork shoulder from the smoke house. With every meal she served a fresh loaf of bread with sweet churned butter. This was Master Lloyd's favorite, especially the fresh buttermilk from the churn. Once a week all the beds were changed and the mattresses and pillows were fluffed and fresh linen was put on every bed. Strangely, there was one room that Leah never serviced. Most of the children's rooms were on the second floor of the mansion except for the one on the third floor near the attic. Miss Sarah showed Leah the room when she first arrived four years ago but asked her not to service the room.

Washing and ironing became difficult for Leah during the winter months. The fire in the big old stove in the wash house kept the building fairly warm. Once the water was hot, Leah would toss a bar of lye soap made from fat meat into the tub. The soap would begin to

melt and make large lathering suds when Leah would scrub the clothes on the old washboard. Every piece of clothing was spotless. Leah would then use the second tub for rinsing. Afterward, she would wring out by hand all the extra water and hang the clothes to dry. Sometimes the clothes would freeze before drying. It was an amusing sight to see Master Lloyd's 'long johns' hanging on the clothesline as stiff as a board. Leah hated the idea of bringing in the frozen clothes and hanging them in the wash- house to dry. After everything dried Leah would start ironing, which would take the greatest part of the day. Everything was ironed. She would make a big fire in the cook stove and set two or three cast irons on the stove to heat at once and begin pressing the sheets and pillowcases. It took more time to press the ruffled petticoats and dresses than it did to iron the men's work and dress clothes. Leah was a beautiful laundress. She hoped someday to teach Delcy how to properly iron clothes. There was money to be made if a free person were asked to do other people's laundry.

CHAPTER 5—ANNA, THE HIDDEN CHILD OF MASTER LLOYD AND MISS SARAH

Anna was born shortly after Pearlie arrived on the Sheff plantation. Pearlie remembered how sick Miss Sarah was during her pregnancy. Master Lloyd gave Pearlie strict orders to never leave Miss Sarah alone. Pearlie had a room next to Miss Sarah so she could care for her night and day. Miss Sarah would always shout orders,

"Pearlie, bring me a cup of tea."

"Pearlie, fix my pillow."

Sometimes Pearlie could not sleep for Miss Sarah calling her all the time. Then, one morning, Miss Sarah went into labor when her water broke. Pearlie began to prepare her special herbs to help ease the pain of birth as she had done many times before. She prepared the bed for giving birth so Miss Sarah would be comfortable.

After a long day of labor, now going into the evening, Miss Sarah had not delivered. Pearlie called for Master Lloyd to get on his horse and ride to Georgetown, a little village about thirty miles away, to get the only doctor in the area. Seemingly, hours had passed before he returned and it was now nearing twelve hours since Miss Sarah's water had broken. A little after noon the next day, Pearlie and old Doc Beckins helped Miss Sarah deliver her second child, a baby girl they named Anna. She was born breech birth with the umbilical cord wrapped around her neck. She was a very sick baby. No one expected her to live.

After a few months, Anna was found to be blind and non-responsive to Pearlie and Miss Sarah. She was unable to hold her head up or move her arms and legs. Pearlie knew there was something very wrong with Anna. After six months, Miss Sarah refused to nurse or care for Anna. The attic room on the third floor was prepared as a nursery. This locked room was where Anna would spend the rest of her life. Pearlie was ordered to keep the door locked, but make certain Anna had what she needed. The tiny baby was underweight and difficult to feed. Miss Sarah rarely visited Anna, therefore, she began to bond with Pearlie. Leah knew never to get into a discussion with Miss Sarah about the child, because this angered her to have to talk about Anna. Leah avoided saying anything to anyone about the hidden child.

CHAPTER 6—1855: WINTER TURNS TO SPRING

As winter gradually turned to spring, Delcy became more active and less willing to stay strapped to Leah. She was gaining weight and getting too heavy for Leah to carry around while she continued to work. Delcy seemed to want attention when her mother was the busiest. All the same, Leah was a very fussy mother and always attempted to address the needs of Delcy as much as possible.

It appeared as though all the chores centered around planting and caring for the crops. As spring turned into summer, most of the farm animals had babies and Josh and Reuben especially enjoyed playing with the small animals.

Delcy was beginning to notice her brothers as they played in the cabin. Josh and Reuben adored her and spent much of their free time playing with her. She laughed out loud and had a big smile that covered her little round face. By the time Delcy was two, she was very independent and curious about many things on the plantation. Josh and Reuben took good care of her when Mama Leah was unable to take her to work. Sometimes Delcy would cry to follow Mama Leah to work. Leah was very careful not to bring Delcy to work with her when special events were planned. When Miss Sarah was having guests, and using her best china and silver, it was not a good idea for a curious baby to be around.

Mama Leah realized that the boys were now young men and it was becoming more difficult to convince them that the plantation would be their life's work. Josh and Reuben were beginning to

challenge Eli and Leah about their own freedom. Why did they aid so many fugitive slaves and still live under the rules of Master Lloyd? They saw several run-away slaves a week seeking food and a place to rest overnight. The boys knew the perfect place in the barn behind the stable where the slaves could hide. Often at night they would slip food out to the barn to the young fugitives. Josh and Ruben were becoming less fearful about the consequences for aiding the slaves. Their willingness to take risks was becoming a great concern to their parents. Eli and Leah knew it was a matter of time before their own sons would want to take their freedom into their own hands. On the plantation Eli and Leah sensed a feeling of unrest among the other young slaves.

One morning when Leah and Delcy were preparing to go to Master Lloyd's house to start breakfast, Leah noticed two strangers standing beside their horses talking to Master Lloyd. She felt as though she knew one of the strangers but was not sure. As Leah drew closer to the house, she recognized one of the men as Zac Wallace, the slave broker that had bought them six years ago from the auction steps in Annapolis, Maryland. How could she ever forget that scrubby face and deceitful personality? Her heart began to race with fear. Why would he be visiting Master Lloyd if it were not to sell off the slaves? After all, that was his business: selling and purchasing slaves. All day Leah worked in fear. She could hardly wait to get home to share what she saw with Eli. The first thing that crossed her mind was that Master Lloyd was planning on selling the boys. She had overheard a group of plantation owners talking about the hard times on their

plantations because the slaves were escaping in large numbers and there were hardly any dependable ones left to plant and tend the crops.

At other times the men talked about the possibility of a Civil War. They wanted the South to become their own nation, and the North would become independent of the South. Leah was beginning to tie everything together. She worried about the safety of the boys if they were sold to another plantation far away. She feared they would run for freedom and perhaps be caught or killed.

As the year 1860 approached and a new President was campaigning for office, the talk on the plantations was both frightful and hopeful. There was news about a possible war between the states that might eventually set the slaves free. Leah became vigilant and clung onto every word that was spoken at the dinner table. Delcy, now six, was big enough to be helpful, but also curious enough to ask questions about the visitors. Leah tried to keep her busy and away from the Master's house.

Delcy would take water to Papa Eli, Josh, and Reuben as they worked in the fields. Also, she would feed the chickens and ducks in the morning and evening. She would rattle the corn in her little tin bucket and the ducks and chickens would follow her to the feeding trough. She even attempted to milk the cow with one hand. Eli would let her try even though he was not sure she was big enough to handle milking. Sometimes the old cow would kick the bucket over and Eli feared Delcy could get hurt.

During the fall of 1860, there was a feeling of restlessness among the Sheff family and the servants. The fugitive slaves that would cross the plantation were talking about freedom and the war that was brewing in the South over slavery. Master Lloyd began to fear the loss of Josh and Reuben. There was always the possibility of selling them before they had a chance to run. The thought of selling the boys terrified Eli and Leah. Master Lloyd made every effort to keep the news of escaping slaves and the tension between the North and South from the slaves, but to no avail. Leah listened to the visitors talk to Master Lloyd about the economic loss to the plantations if the slaves were set free. Josh, now 15, and Reuben, 17, were aware of the forthcoming war and it was hard to convince them to stay on the plantation. They knew if they left, it would create a hardship for Papa Eli, but the options to stay were not good either. Leah and Eli discussed with the boys the dangers of war and the hopeful desire for their freedom.

The Confederate Army recruiters were already scouring the country in the South, enlisting white soldiers for the war. At the beginning of the war in 1861, it was general knowledge that the white officers and recruits did not trust the slaves to carry weapons. The soldiers feared not only for their lives, but also repercussions and revenge on their families. Retaliation against the masters by the slaves was one of the greatest fears of the South in arming slaves to fight on the side of the Confederates.

Josh and Reuben stayed on the plantation during the winter of 1861, but in the spring of 1862 and the war casualties were mounting

on both sides, Josh and Reuben quietly bid Eli, Leah and Delcy goodbye. They headed on horseback toward Ohio, going north to join the Union Army. Under pressure from both black and white antislavery leaders, the first African-American regiment was formed. Josh and Reuben joined the segregated army fighting on the side of the Union. No one ever heard from them again. If they survived the war, they never returned to the Sheff plantation. They possibly went on to freedom in another part of the country, or they died in battle as did so many other blacks. During the war, the labor in the fields rested on the shoulders of Eli, Benjamin and Minnie Paine, two faithful servants who were left behind.

CHAPTER 7—1861-1865: THE CIVIL WAR DAYS

Life on the plantation during the Civil War between 1861 and 1865 was unbearable. There was fear everywhere of Yankee soldiers invading the homes and destroying everything. In most instances, the women and children were the only ones left to keep the plantations going. The few slaves that remained were either too old to leave the plantation or had no place to go. Most of the able bodied slaves had long fled the fields and work places in large numbers. Some of the younger slaves were forced to join the Confederate Army. Many defected north to fight on the side of the Union. There was the promise of freedom if the North defeated the South. As the war progressed, the word of freedom was spreading rapidly throughout the South and North. Slaves were beginning to rebel against the harsh treatment of the slave masters. Many masters tried to prohibit the slaves from escaping but to no avail. Many slaves left the plows in the fields and ran for freedom. There was not enough money in the South to finance the war. With few slaves to tend the crops, the war was using up a large portion of the economic gains generated from the sale of crops. The South was slowly becoming economically devastated. The free labor of slavery was rapidly dwindling and no one was sure when it would all end.

The year 1863 at the height of the Civil War, Josh and Reuben had not made contact with their family. Delcy had just turned nine and the workload on the Sheff plantation was more demanding of her, Eli, and Leah. The household and field work were endless for Eli who

39

worked from sunup until sundown. The job of hauling water, splitting the wood, and caring for the work animals was left for Eli, Leah, and Delcy. Because of the advancing age of their neighbors, Benjamin and Minnie Paine, they were only capable of sharing some of the less strenuous farm activities such as caring for the pigs and chickens, collecting eggs, and doing various other odd jobs as required by Master Lloyd and Miss Sarah.

Master Lloyd had cut the tobacco crop by half since he no longer had the help or the resources to harvest the usual acreage. Pearlie continued to work in the master's house. Most of her time was spent taking care of Anna since the other Sheff children were gone from the plantation. Miss Sarah rarely said much about how long Pearlie took to do her work.

Both Master Lloyd and Miss Sarah were concerned about the accumulated debt that they had from borrowing money against the plantation in order to meet the farming expenses. Help was short and they could not count on free slave labor anymore. Slaves enroute to the North frequently passed the Sheff plantation seeking food, shelter, and medicine. Most would hide out in the corncrib or tobacco barn, seeking a few hours of rest and sleep before continuing their journey north. Eli and Leah remained cautious in offering help to the fleeing slaves. Delcy was willing to risk the harsh punishment from Master Lloyd if he caught her helping the slaves. Delcy would slip the fleeing slaves food and clothing. One day she was caught taking clothes off the clothes line to give to a fleeing family. Master Lloyd was so angry with Delcy that he gave her a severe whipping. She was so strong

willed that Leah and Eli knew that the life ahead for Delcy would be a difficult one without their care and guidance.

Delcy was very unhappy on the plantation. Seemingly, she could do nothing right, at least not to satisfy Master Lloyd. She was very bitter and resented the day-to-day struggle imposed on her family. At times, the struggle to keep the crops cultivated and the garden and animals tended seemed endless. The lack of help was a problem on nearly every plantation. One day Master Lloyd made a deal with another plantation master to hire out Eli for a day. Eli was very hesitant in going to some one else's plantation to work. He had done that once before and found the workload was so hard that he was sick for several days afterward from heat exhaustion. Delcy could see the stress taking its toll on her father. He was the type of person who rarely complained to the master. Because he was somewhat slow in making the journey, Delcy spoke abruptly and sarcastically to Master Lloyd in defense of Eli. Master Lloyd slapped Delcy so hard she spun around and hit the ground. Eli became so angry he picked up Delcy and walked toward the cabin as though the day was over. Master Lloyd did not pursue Eli. For the first time Eli truly felt like running away and taking his family. Perhaps Master Lloyd thought the same thing, because he never approached Eli again about working for another master.

After the experience with Delcy, Eli hoped there would be some changes for the better. The old plantation was gradually falling into disarray as the war continued. The crops were less profitable and extra help was no longer available. There was no money to buy

lumber to fix fences or repair the house. The old cooking stove had seen better days and the few animals left would graze the pastures that were becoming stripped of their hay and barley. Eli and Leah were weary and unable to keep up with the demands on them. Each did the best they could to prepare the meals and tend to the farming chores.

As Delcy became even more rebellious and sassy to Master Lloyd, her treatment became more harsh and severe. Tensions mounted between Master Lloyd and Eli and Leah over the treatment of Delcy. One morning when everyone arose for the task assignments for the day, Delcy was gone. She had slipped out of the cabin during the night. Her parents' fear was intense because they worried about how a young slave girl could survive the wilderness, and if she could by chance meet someone traveling the Underground Railroad. Before daybreak, Delcy returned, exhausted. She had been unable to continue the escape because she had never been off the plantation in her life, so she was unfamiliar with the surroundings. Leah and Eli were extremely happy to see her and glad that she had returned safely. Fortunately, Master Lloyd never learned of her attempt to escape.

One year later, 1864, the Civil War, in its third year, continued to drag on. The Sheff plantation was falling deeper and deeper in debt. Theirs was not the only plantation the local banks had foreclosed on. The plantations were in debt for seed, supplies, and parts to repair equipment. Still unable to purchase seed for spring planting and to repair the worn out equipment, Master Lloyd made one more plea to the bank for an extension on his loan but to no avail. Master Lloyd had one option: that was to sell Eli and Leah so he could at least buy

food and needed household items to support the family. Word of selling Eli and Leah outraged Delcy to the extent that her thoughts of retaliation intensified against Master Lloyd. After fourteen long toiling and faithful years of sweat and tears, Eli and Leah would be sold. The Sheff's decided Delcy would remain on the plantation because she was young, strong and healthy and could be useful in the house and in the fields. Despite her many good qualities, Delcy was known for her fiery temper. The Sheff's tolerated Delcy's outbursts because she was was a valuable asset to their plantation.

One Monday morning when Leah and Delcy were on their way to the Master's house to do the washing as they did every Monday morning, they saw from a distance Master Lloyd talking to Zac Wallace. He always brought bad news. Leah and Delcy became afraid. Everyone knew that Master Lloyd was so broke that he didn't know where his next piece of bread was coming from. Master Lloyd waited until Eli came to the house to fill the wash tubs with water and help build the fire under the big tubs as he usually did, since Josh and Reuben were gone. While standing near the laundry tubs, Master Lloyd broke the news to Eli and Leah that he would have to sell them because he needed the money. Delcy, now ten, was devastated. Miss Sarah showed great remorse at the selling of Leah. At least the sale was private and they did not have to stand on an auction step as they had fourteen years ago when Zac purchased them for Master Lloyd. Eli was a faithful and good worker. He always did as he was told. Eli and Leah sobbed as they clung to each other.

Zac borrowed a wagon from Master Lloyd so Eli and Leah could pack a few personal things that they wanted to take. There was not much from which to choose. Most of the household items were in poor condition, like everything else on the plantation. Leah decided to leave the rocking chair and other items for Delcy since she would remain there under the supervision of Pearlie. As the wagon pulled up in front of the cabin Leah and Eli hugged Delcy with all their strength and vowed to see each other again. Delcy cried uncontrollably. She believed her parents were going a long way. Zac tied his horse to the back of the wagon and once again chained Eli and Leah to the wagon and climbed into the seat, gave the mules a crack and the long journey to the Jenkins plantation in Tennessee became a reality.

Master Jenkins had offered Master Lloyd a good price for the two. He had a smaller tobacco plantation and the workload would not be as heavy for Eli and Leah.

As the wagon pulled onto the dusty road leading from the plantation, Delcy ran behind the wagon until she was too tired to keep up, then she fell to the ground sobbing as she watched the wagon carrying Mama Leah and Papa Eli disappear into the dust. As she pulled herself off the ground and slowly walked toward the empty cabin that sat on the edge of the tobacco field, Pearlie was there to comfort her. She explained that Master Lloyd was facing hard times, and it was hard to let them go. This made no sense to Delcy. She asked Pearlie,

"Why didn't they sell us as a family? Why was I left alone?"

Pearlie had seen families sold and separated many times before but she did not have answers for Delcy. As she pulled away from Pearlie and entered the empty cabin she stared at the rocking chair that had the same old straw stuffed cushion that Mama Leah had made many years ago. She remembered how the old rocker had been used to rock her when she was small and how Mama Leah would mend and quilt way into the night sitting by the lamplight. Delcy sat gently in the old rocker and began to sing the song Leah had sung to her when she was a baby.

"Sweet little baby girl, born in the cold of night, nobody knows about you. Sweet little baby girl, so quiet as you sleep, nobody knows what lies ahead, so sleep, gently, sleep." Delcy wept for hours and finally fell asleep in the wee hours of the morning.

Delcy was certainly in no mood to walk to Master Lloyd's house. After all, she had rarely made the trip alone. Mama Leah had always been beside her. That was their time to laugh and talk. This day was different from any other day in her life. Pearlie made her way to the house without Delcy. Delcy thought about running away again and working in the war camps that she had heard about but she didn't know her way. She had mixed feelings about how to get even with Master Lloyd for selling Mama and Papa.

CHAPTER 8—1865: DELCY ALONE

Delcy returned to the Master's house several days later. Miss Sarah showed no compassion toward Delcy and displayed her usual abrupt and curt disposition. Delcy had become accustomed to her behavior. But she could not help thinking about the law that was signed by President Lincoln declaring that slavery no longer existed, and that all slaves were to be set free.

"What kind of freedom were the slaves promised?"

Delcy certainly did not see much freedom on the plantation. Master Lloyd ignored the Proclamation setting slaves free. He tried to say that slavery was good.

He even talked about how good he had been to Leah and Eli.

"It only made me mad to know that he thought I would fall for something like that," Delcy told Pearlie.

Delcy began to listen carefully to the conversations and questions that Master Lloyd would be discussing with other plantation owners. She heard all about the war and how the slaves continued to fight to set themselves free. She really wanted to hear more about freedom. Mama Leah and Papa Eli had always promised her that someday she would be free.

As the months passed, Pearlie was always there for Delcy when she felt lonely or when there was tension building between her and Master Lloyd. Pearlie could sense that Delcy was bitter and angry a great deal of the time. She often broke things or omitted doing a certain task that was required of the house help, and when she was

corrected, she displayed a hostile disposition that often got her into a great deal of trouble. One time Master Lloyd requested a fresh glass of buttermilk from the cellar. When Delcy brought him the milk it was spoiled. After questioning Delcy, he discovered that she had left the top off the buttermilk and the flies had spoiled the milk. To punish her, he made her drink the spoiled milk. Delcy became very sick. She vomited for hours, after which he proceeded to beat her with a buggy whip until large welts appeared all over her back and shoulders. Delcy was treated and comforted by Pearlie. After that whipping, Delcy made a vow that Master Lloyd would never beat her again. She often plotted his death in the most severe way and wished the most awful things would happen to him. Her thoughts were filled with ways to destroy Master Lloyd for all the hurt and pain he had brought upon her and her family.

In the year 1865, a year after the sale of Eli and Leah, the Civil war ended. There was even more talk about the slaves being free, especially in the North. Many free blacks chose not to return to the harsh southern plantation life. Those that did return found working conditions had not changed much. Most plantations were in ruin and the crops that once flourished at the hands of slave labor were gone. Delcy noticed freed blacks crossing the tobacco plantation headed north to find their families or to find a better life. Some free blacks and their families began the move westward where jobs or land were, they hoped, more available. All Delcy could think of was how trapped she felt on Master Lloyd's plantation with no place to go. As she settled back into her routine of cleaning and helping with the farm

chores, she heard talk of really bad things happening to free blacks who tried to leave the South. She did not have a clear idea of everything that was said as she eaves-dropped on the dinner conversation between Miss Sarah and Master Lloyd. Certainly she did not want to be caught by any roaming white vigilante group looking to do harm to runaway free blacks. Her fears forced her to remain on the Sheff plantation.

As Delcy was fast approaching her fifteenth birthday, she began reflecting often about the family that she once loved and counted on to always be there for her. She thought that everything good was gone. She missed Mama Leah and Papa Eli. She wondered if they were free, and if they would they keep their promise to come back to get her. At every opportunity, Delcy displayed a rebellious attitude toward Master Lloyd. One afternoon during supper, Delcy spilled a pot of hot tea that landed on Master Lloyd. Before she could move and clean up the spill, Master Lloyd beat and abused her. Seemingly, all his anger for the many things he once tolerated from her was now directed toward her behavior and attitude toward him. Delcy tried to defend herself against Master Lloyd by abruptly leaving the house. She was frightened, for she had never physically stood up to Master Lloyd. This time somehow seemed different.

"If I am free, why do I feel more like a slave than ever before?"

Delcy ran all the way to the cabin and rocked nervously while trying to find comfort. Master Lloyd had been angry with her before, but never like this. Pearlie helped clean up the supper dishes and hurriedly made her way down the dusty path to see about Delcy.

Pearlie tried to comfort her by hugging her and wiping away her tears. Pearlie understood the harshness of plantation life as she spoke gently to Delcy about her own life as a young girl and how to avoid the wrath of Master Lloyd. Delcy didn't see any way out. After several hours of talking to Pearlie, Delcy prepared for bed and Pearlie went to her little cabin next door.

During the night, Delcy was awakened by a rattle at the door. She was terrified. She could not imagine who it was. Before she could sit up in bed, Master Lloyd broke down the cabin door. She tried to fight him off, but he ripped off her clothes. He raped her although she continued to struggle to free herself. Master Lloyd shouted at her, trying to humiliate her, so she would feel less than the strong human being she grew to be. In his perverted way, he was trying to "teach her" that she was nothing without him and what he could provide for her.

The brutal attack left Delcy distraught and afraid. Pearlie came over to check on Delcy and found her huddled in the corner of the room with her face buried in her hands, clothes ripped off, and the cabin in disarray. Delcy tried to pull herself together to explain to Pearlie what had happened to her in the middle of the night. Pearlie comforted Delcy and tended to the wounds and bruises left on her body and face as a result of the assault.

Delcy became extremely depressed and found it difficult to get up in the morning and go to the Sheff house. She tried to avoid Master Lloyd by working outside and tending to the animals and garden. Because the Sheff's could not afford to hire more help, it became an

almost impossible task for Pearlie to keep up the household and care for Anna. After the small garden was harvested, and the work outside diminished, Delcy returned inside to the Master's house, carefully avoiding Master Lloyd.

Several months after the sexual assault, Delcy realized that she was expecting a child. The fear of being pregnant overwhelmed her. Miss Sarah asked prying questions of her. They were all directed toward her gaining weight and the noticeable change in the clothes that Delcy chose to wear in order to conceal her pregnancy. Delcy often chose to ignore the questions and quickly proceeded to prepare the meals and do required housework. The more noticeable Delcy's pregnancy became, the more curious Miss Sarah became. Also, Delcy became more withdrawn and depressed. Miss Sarah knew Delcy was pregnant. She even implied that Delcy had been with someone that stopped by the plantation looking for work.

As fall set in on the plantation, Delcy collected small scraps of fabric and other used pieces of linen and old clothes given to her by Miss Sarah to prepare for the baby. The first thing she made was a small patch quilt that had many old familiar pieces left behind by Mama Leah and Papa Eli. Pearlie was cautious when talking to Delcy about the baby. She knew how sensitive and depressed Delcy would become. However, Delcy knew that Pearlie would be there for her. Delcy continued to be cautious around Master Lloyd. She was afraid he might decide to beat her and cause her to lose the baby. Therefore, she tried to avoid any confrontations of any kind with him. All Delcy could think of at this point, was the life she wanted for her child, and

just how protective she would have to be. As winter approached, her pregnancy was more obvious and she became even more withdrawn. Master Lloyd was very nervous around Delcy and at one point commented,

"I didn't mean you no harm, I just wanted to teach you a lesson."

Delcy turned sixteen in November. She had made a few small gowns and prepared a box that she kept under the bed with fresh scraps of white linen. As the winter snow began to fall and the Christmas season was nearing, Miss Sarah decorated the Sheff home. In the meantime, Delcy became increasingly tired and less able to do what was required of her. As Christmas Eve approached, Delcy felt differently and knew her time was near.

Late Christmas Eve, after fixing dinner for the Sheff family, Delcy went into labor. She hurriedly finished her work and headed home. She reached the cabin before dark. She filled the wooden bin with fire logs and all the extra pots and pans with snow and ice before resting for a minute. Delcy knew Pearlie was home because she could see her footprints in the snow leading to her door. She was trying to decide when to call Pearlie. She knew she moved around much slower now and it would take her a little more time to get through the snow to reach the cabin. Delcy was tired and decided to wait a while before knocking on Pearlie's door. Wearily, she sat quietly in the rocker and reminisced about how things used to be.

CHAPTER 9—1870: DELCY GIVES BIRTH TO LIZZIE

Christmas Eve 1870 was one of the most chilling days of winter. The wind sliced through the cracks of the cabin. Snow had been falling all day and now it was knee high between the cabin and the woodpile, which was at least fifty feet from the front door. The old cabin was one of three still standing on the Sheff's tobacco plantation in Leesburg, Kentucky.

As Delcy sat alone in the cabin, her mind wandered. "Where did the time go?" she thought. "The days of laughter from the slave children playing in the late evenings after tending to the master's farm chores, all gone. The bright green burly tobacco leaves glistening from the morning dew, just about all gone. Only a few acres here lately to tend." She remembered how they used to stand on the edge of the fields where the cabins were, straining their eyes to see as far as they could see. It seemed as though they could look for miles and see the beautiful pink blossoms that draped the top of each stalk of tobacco as harvest time drew near. The rows between the plants were so straight they could see each little leaf that grew on the tobacco stalk.

Behind the cabins on their walk to the Master's house, they would pass the barnyard. The farm animals were well cared for because Delcy and her family made sure they always had plenty of food and water. Sometimes, she thought, the animals often fared better than the people did. The chore of feeding the animals was mostly the job of

the children. Now the children were all gone. "All grown, I suppose," she sighed out loud. "Don't know why no one would bother coming back here visiting. Most don't care if you are alive or dead. The few cows left in the barnyard give just enough milk for Master Lloyd and the few of us still living in the log cabins. Only three free blacks left. Pearlie next door is the friendliest. She is beginning to have health problems. She must be past forty." Delcy noticed Pearlie prayed a lot as well as talked a lot about life as it used to be. She supposed Pearlie knew more about that than anybody else on the plantation. She had been around, it seemed, forever. She was the one who was birthing babies; people and animals. Pearlie was faithful to Anna. She sighed, "Poor thing, never gets out of that room."

Delcy thought about the times she had to feed the farm animals. Everywhere she looked, there were chickens and ducks. Red ones, speckled ones, white ones with rosy red head cones. They were always pecking and walking in the clean water. Master Lloyd was always yelling to change the water. Those nasty ducks were always making a mess. Every fall they would help kill the older fat ducks. "We would pluck their feathers, especially the soft fuzzy down feathers. We used them to stuff the pillows and bed mattresses for the Master's house. We were thankful to get fresh straw and hay once a year to fill our own home made pillows and bed mats." Now, there were only a few animals left. Most of the animals, except for the two teams of mules, were all gone. "Just like the men folks that kept the plantation going, all gone. Master Lloyd and Miss Sarah don't have any more money. All they talk about is how it used to be. The tobacco

crops get smaller and smaller because nobody is around to plant and chop the weeds." Delcy remembered having barely enough food to keep them going. "Times ain't getting any better. Ain't got no help," Delcy huffed out loud. "Master Lloyd and Miss Sarah are treating us like we ain't free." Delcy would see free folks crossing the fields all the time on their way up north looking for their families and work along the way. She couldn't help wondering about what it was truly like to be free.

As Delcy shivered from the cold, she looked around the cabin. It had barely enough furnishings. Against the wall facing east was a wooden bed with a big thick mattress stuffed with fresh straw. It looked lumpy because of a big scrap quilt made from old clothes that covered the bed from side to side. Under the bed was a wooden storage box that held extra clothing, bedding material and scraps of cloth used for mending and quilting. Delcy's mama, Leah, had a gift for sewing and quilting that kept the family with clothes and bedding.

In the middle of the floor was a big wooden table that nearly filled the entire room. Hanging from the ceiling on a big rusty nail was an old kerosene lamp that would sway when the wind whistled. Mama's handmade curtains covered the only window in the cabin. There were two Bentwood chairs at the table and two straight back chairs, hand made by Papa Eli, that were placed near the potbellied stove that was used for cooking and heating the cabin. In one corner the rocking chair made from pecan wood had a well-used woven bottom that looked like a wooden basket made from hand stripped hickory tree

bark. The rocker used to belong to Master Lloyd and Miss Sarah, just like most of the furniture.

She remembered watching Mama Leah heat the old iron on the top of the stove. Delcy learned how to press each little scrap of material before neatly shaping it into a little patch for the quilt. Delcy was very handy around the house. Not only was she good at making quilts, but she was also a very good cook. Leah had taught her how to cook, iron, and sew. She thought about how the women would often mend clothes and swap stories and quilt pieces. During the days of plenty, the women would sit around the fire and invent new recipes for fixing the small rations of salt pork, smoked fish, and cornmeal that were issued weekly by the Master. Once in a while, leftover garden vegetables, milk, and cheese were shared for Sunday dinner. Sometimes on Sunday, the other slave families would put all their food rations together and boil up a big supper feast. Everyone would sing and dance. The children especially liked to celebrate birthdays. Little did they know the hardships that lay ahead of them.

As her baby moved inside, she felt warm and sick at the same time. She gently rubbed her tight belly. "This is not the time to be alone" she thought, as she began to tremble with fear at the thought of giving birth. As she rocked from side to side, the birth pains began to come closer and closer. The unborn baby seemed to sense her mother's fear of being alone. Delcy had been alone a lot lately—five years to be exact. Except for Pearlie, life was very sad and dreary. Delcy would have left the Sheff's plantation by now but she knew

absolutely no one beyond the fields. What would she do? Where would she go? She felt trapped. She was trapped.

In the silence of the cold night, Delcy could sometimes hear the crackle from the potbellied stove where the fire was beginning to burn out. Sitting in the old rocking chair, the sixteen-year old, ex-slave girl was quickly approaching her time to deliver her first child.

Delcy suddenly felt a sharp pain in her back. She cried as a wave of pain gradually moved through her body. She thought about the presence of Mama Leah and how wise she'd always been in providing words of comfort and advice in difficult times. This had to be the worst Christmas Eve ever. In the past, Christmas had been a merry time for the Brent family. Once again, Delcy reflected on old times. Mama Leah would always make sure that Christmas was special. Delcy remembered Mama Leah making her a doll out of corn shucks and dressing it in a tiny print bandanna and skirt. "I carried it everywhere. I remember how, one day, I left it at old Master Lloyd's house and the next day it was gone. Miss Sarah made like she never saw it, but I knew she was lying. She was so mean; she probably burned it up. I never trusted her anyhow. I cried for hours over my doll. Mama Leah knew how sad I was. One day when my two brothers, Josh and Reuben, finished shucking the corn in the crib for the cattle and the chickens and ducks, they brought home a big hand full of corn shucks. Mama Leah spent nearly all evening making me another doll. After that, she reminded me to always leave my doll at home because Miss Sarah did not love the doll as much as I did. From that time on I never forgot what Mama said about love."

Delcy felt her breathing get harder and she began to sweat. With all the strength she could muster, she made her way through the knee-high snow to the cabin next door where Pearlie lived. Even though Pearlie had no children of her own, she had delivered more babies than she could count on her hands and toes.

Frantically, Delcy called,

"Miss Pearlie, you in there? Miss Pearlie, my baby is coming!"

Miss Pearlie answered Delcy with a calm tone in her voice,

"Delcy, can you make it back to the cabin?"

"Yes," said Delcy.

"The fire is getting low and I am afraid the water got cold."

Pearlie assured Delcy that she would be there as soon as she dressed and put some things in her birthin' bag. She also told Delcy to put another log in the stove and put the ice and snow on the stove to melt before she got there.

As Delcy made her way back to the cabin she tried to remember what she had seen Mama Leah do in times like these. She did what Pearlie told her to do. She removed the neatly folded clean linen from the large wooden box under the bed and placed it on the straight back chair by the stove. She had previously filled the small wooden box from the barn with fresh straw to use as a cradle.

Time was moving quickly. Delcy sat in the rocker and rocked impatiently. She cradled her arms around her belly wondering what was keeping Miss Pearlie from coming through the door. She glanced at the old clock ticking on the wall; it was a little past midnight. It was Christmas.

Suddenly, without knocking, Pearlie rushed through the door with a large bag full of prepared homemade remedies. Pearlie had learned from her mother and grandmother which herbs and roots to use and how to mix them to help a woman through birthing. She always wore a neatly pressed white apron and a long gray dress that swept the floor. She hustled around the tiny cabin making preparations for the delivery. Excitingly, Delcy gave out a loud cry. She felt her baby move closer and closer to the birthing position. As Delcy lay in the birthing position, she knew it would not be long before she needed to push. Delcy began to feel the pain of childbirth. Pearlie held her hand and Delcy squeezed with all her strength. With one big push, Delcy delivered her child.

Pearlie carefully washed the baby with warm water, wrapped her in the linen and the little quilt, and placed her in Delcy's arms. The patch quilt that Delcy had made from scraps of material was just the right size. Pearlie leaned close to Delcy and spoke softly wishing her,

"Merry Christmas. You have been given the greatest gift on this special day."

Delcy asked Pearlie to name the baby girl. She thought this would be the greatest gift for Pearlie. She had never been asked to name a baby. She thought long and hard and decided on Lizzie. This name really pleased Delcy. As she rested with Lizzie snuggled warmly in her arms, she sang softly to her,

"Sweet Little baby girl, beautiful in my sight; nobody knows your name, like the Holy One born on this Night. Sweet little baby girl, so

quiet and as you sleep; no one knows what lies ahead, so sleep gently, sleep."

Delcy lay exhausted. It wasn't long before she drifted off to sleep. The long darkness of the night gradually turned to day. The snow finally ended and the sky cleared. The sun's rays on the snow caused it to sparkle like diamonds. When Delcy awoke, she noticed Pearlie moving about quietly adding wood to the fire that had burned low during the night. She had fixed breakfast for Delcy and made sure Lizzie was snug and warm. As Pearlie opened the door, snow fell inside. She quickly swept away the snow in order to make a path to the woodpile. She would not go home until she was sure that Delcy and Lizzie would be okay.

Delcy began to stir around in the room, fussing over Lizzie and making sure the cold weather would not take her child. She knew that many babies died due to the cold and she was not about to let that happen to Lizzie. She tucked her warmly in her little box and moved it closer to the potbellied stove. After Pearlie fed Delcy, she left to prepare the Christmas meal for Master Lloyd and Miss Sarah's family.

Delcy stared into the fire and her thoughts brought her back to when Mama Leah would fix Christmas dinner for the family. It wasn't like the Sheff's but it was a blessing. The slaves that worked in the house had to work on Christmas Day due to all the company the Sheff's would have. The visitors would pull up to the big house in their fancy buggies with the women clothed in their finest dresses and the men in their best suits and hats. They would bring gifts and food

sometimes. After the white folks were fed and started dancing and singing, the slaves were allowed to go back to their cabins. The leftovers were always plentiful and divided among those helping in the kitchen. When Mama Leah cooked the leftovers, she would take the hog parts and make the best hog headcheese and sausage. She boiled the feet, ears, and tail and made a pig stew. She added potatoes, turnips, and onions from the cellar. Mama Leah shared her holiday secrets of food preparation with Delcy, who would one day teach Lizzie these traditional recipes.

CHAPTER 10—1871: DELCY GETS MARRIED

Lizzie, born out of violence, was comforted and protected by Delcy. As Delcy told Pearlie the story of how Master Lloyd had raped her, Pearlie listened with compassion. Afterward, Delcy wept bitterly. She wanted so much more for Lizzie than the harshness of life on the Sheff tobacco plantation. Somehow life on the plantation didn't seem much different for the few sharecroppers that now worked the tobacco fields. Even though the slaves were free, Delcy felt trapped on the farm. She often became controlled by fear of violent retaliation against her.

When Lizzie's birth was recorded in the old 1876 family Bible, it read "Born December 25, 1870, Lizzie Brent Sheff." This was Delcy's chance to document history in a way that Lloyd Sheff would never forget the violent act of rape that resulted in the birth of beloved Lizzie.

Delcy soon turned her attention to Lizzie, gently cradling her in her arms as she began to move back and forth in the rocking chair, softly humming the tune she remembered from her mother. Delcy sang the little tune over and over as she nestled her to her breast,

"Sweet baby girl born on Christmas day, no one knows about you. Sweet little baby girl, born to bring joy and peace on this day. Sleep baby Lizzie on this special day."

As time passed and the harsh winter of 1870 gradually turned to spring of 1871, Lizzie was growing healthy and strong. She seemed to have a significant place in Miss Sarah's life as a special child, since

she bore some resemblance to Master Lloyd. Miss Sarah had no doubt that Lizzie was a mulatto child fathered by Master Lloyd. However, she never discussed it with Delcy or Master Lloyd. This delicate circumstance was quite common on most plantations in the south.

As Miss Sarah aged, she had not changed much in demeanor; she was still outspoken and demanding. As she grew more feeble from a stroke that left her partially paralyzed on the left side, she continued to give commands for service. All the plantation children were gone and the Sheff children rarely returned to the plantation except for Christmas.

Now that Pearlie was unable to spend much time with Anna, Delcy had to help both Miss Sarah and Anna. Miss Sarah was now frequently left alone; just like Anna locked in the attic room. The Sheff grandchildren rarely saw Miss Sarah and Master Lloyd. Sometimes Miss Sarah talked about missing the children, but then she dismissed the thought and prepared to sit in a big overstuffed chair looking out the dining room window thinking of what used to be. Most of the beauty of the plantation, which included white fences and beautifully maintained flowers and trees, was all gone. Now the fences needed fixing and the flower gardens were all full of weeds.

As the time for spring planting of the tobacco grew near, Master Lloyd found himself in a predicament: a crop to be planted and no help. In order to plant the tobacco before the spring rain, he would need a new sharecropper. After the war, it was common for free blacks to leave the south headed north looking for work. They often

wandered from one plantation to another inquiring about sharecropping or other odd jobs.

Over the past few weeks, several ex-slaves had stopped at the Sheff plantation and inquired about work. After a few days they moved on. Master Lloyd was getting older and unable to manage the tobacco planting. He thought about asking the neighboring farmer about sharing field hands, but the neighbor had no one to share. As he leaned on the hitching post in front of the mansion, he thought about the abundance of help and wealth he had access to in the "good old days." He looked around at all the work that needed to be done. He squinted his eyes as he strained to identify the figure walking down the old dusty road leading to the plantation. As the figure drew closer, he moved from the hitching post to greet the man approaching.

The time could not have been better for Neut Smith, a tall ex-slave from Georgia, very robust in stature, looking for work. Master Lloyd offered Neut the opportunity to sharecrop the tobacco, and in return, he would receive a portion of money when the crop was sold.

Delcy could see Neut from the window. She hoped with all her heart that Master Lloyd had hired him. She watched as Master Lloyd showed Neut his living quarters, and then walked him to the fields where the crops would be planted. Neut seemed pleased to have a job and was very polite in accepting the working conditions set forth by Master Lloyd.

Delcy felt that Neut was someone special when she first saw him. She made a point of introducing herself to Neut as she prepared supper for him in the Sheff's kitchen. Neut was very hungry after

traveling for days looking for work. Most of his time was spent on the move, walking for miles and eating whenever an act of kindness was shown to him by free blacks. He was pleased to finally get a good hot cooked meal.

Delcy observed that Neut was very kind and gentle. She made small talk with him as she watched him eat. He talked about the cotton plantation in Georgia where he worked as a slave and how he did not want to return to Georgia. Delcy told him about her life as a slave girl on the tobacco plantation and baby Lizzie, who was barely four months old. She wanted someone to share her desire for freedom. She saw in Neut, her chance to leave the plantation so they would have a better life. As Neut finished his dinner, Master Lloyd came to the kitchen and reminded Neut that the breakfast bell rang at six o'clock and he was expected to be ready for work. Neut had much to learn about tobacco. He had always worked in the cotton fields. To him there appeared not to be much difference; he understood that all farming required planting, plowing and harvesting.

As Delcy continued her chores for Miss Sarah, she looked forward to preparing supper for Neut. Supper time was their chance to get to know each other and talk about old times. Neut and Delcy began to establish a special friendship that had prospects of growing into a promising future.

Delcy had never had anyone treat her as kindly as Neut. He was different; he seemed to know how to treat a lady.

Neut Smith had spent the early years of his life on the Murphy plantation working the cotton fields as a boy and later as a blacksmith.

He worked in the stables in the evening caring for the horses after picking cotton all day. At the age of sixteen he began to help the blacksmith shoe the horses as well as repair the harnesses. After the war ended in 1865, Neut had no desire to stay on the Murphy plantation. He worked at a number of odd jobs for the first few years after the war before stopping at the Sheff plantation looking for work. Neut was a man of few words. Although he could recognize some words and math numbers, he could not read and write. He was hard working and honest. If he gave a person his word that something would be done, one could count on it being done.

After a six-month courtship, Neut asked Delcy to marry him. He hoped that he had proved to her that he could be trusted, and promised to love and care for both her and Lizzie as though Lizzie were his own.

Soon after Delcy turned eighteen, Neut and Delcy were married. Delcy got all dressed up in her very best cotton dress. Master Lloyd was relieved because he felt that Delcy wound remain on the plantation if Neut stayed. He knew if she left, he would have no one to care for Sarah and Anna. Little did Lloyd Sheff know the thoughts of leaving the plantation were more frequent.

When Lizzie was two, Delcy gave birth to her second child, a baby boy, on March 4, 1872. They named him Charley. Lizzie was so excited to have a baby brother and was eager to help Mama Delcy care for him.

Neut and Delcy continued to work as sharecroppers on the Sheff plantation. As sharecroppers, they were given a minimal salary at the

end of each tobacco season for their work. As Charlie and Lizzie bonded as brother and sister, Lizzie began to assume more and more responsibility. She helped with the farm animals by feeding the chickens and ducks, churning the milk to make butter, and carrying water to the field for Neut and the other workers that would move from farm to farm often working a different plantation every two or three days. There were a large number of day workers because farm work was seasonal. In these lean economic times, most plantation owners could not afford to hire more than one or two full time sharecroppers.

In the spring of 1875, Pearlie became sick and no longer was able to work. Delcy would look in on her daily and make sure she had her meals and fresh water. Delcy and Neut, with two active children, spent as much time as possible with Lizzie and Charlie. Lizzie was a smart little girl. She wanted to learn to read and write like Master Lloyd and Miss Sarah's grandchildren. She became friends with Lucy Bell, Master Lloyd's oldest granddaughter. Lucy Bell would pretend to play school and Lizzie would be her student. Lizzie soon learned to read, write and do simple math problems.

In the fall of 1875, Delcy and Neut had another baby, but it did not live very long. Delcy and her family were all grief stricken when the baby died. In 1877, when Lizzie was seven, Delcy gave birth to their third child, a girl whom they named Mary. Once again, Lizzie helped with the new baby along with her barnyard and household chores. It seemed that with each baby, Lizzie had more and more responsibility.

Mary was a fussy baby and Delcy often had to spend more time nursing and caring for her. It was becoming increasingly difficult to take care of two households. Both Miss Sarah and Pearlie were failing in health and having problems with mobility. Delcy continued to care for Anna and Miss Sarah, but the farm chores were the duty of Neut and the children. Taking the children to work with her, Delcy did all the washing, cooking and cleaning. Charlie followed Lizzie around as she helped with the laundry, hanging clothes on the line to dry, and filling the water tubs. She also carried small pieces of wood and dried corncobs to keep the fire going.

Delcy took good care of Pearlie, as her health continued to decline. In the fall of 1877, Pearlie died at the age of 51. She was buried in the graveyard for slaves on the Sheff plantation. Delcy and her family felt the loss of a dear and devoted friend.

Lizzie was beginning to learn how to quilt, knit, crochet, and cook by watching Mama Delcy. Neut remained in the field for long hours. His time with the family was mainly spent doing chores. After helping Master Lloyd, who was aging, and Miss Sarah who was chronically complaining, Neut managed to provide for the needs of both households. He always split and stacked the wood and kept the water barrels and buckets filled with fresh water from the well.

As months turned to years, 1879 found Delcy, Neut, and the children getting older with seemingly little hope of leaving the Sheff plantation. Lizzie, now nine, remained small for her age while Charlie seven was large for his age. Mary, now two, was relatively happy and required little additional care from Lizzie or Charlie.

During the summer of 1879, Lizzie assumed much more of the plantation duties. When the animals would see her coming with her little buckets of grain and water, they followed her until she fed and watered them. Lizzie was often tired from helping Miss Sarah and the children.

One day Lizzie noticed Mama Delcy was expecting another baby. She did not show her pregnancy until almost time to deliver because she wore large over-the-shoulder aprons that hid her figure. Delcy gave birth to her fourth child on November 18, 1879. It was a baby girl that she named Martha.

Delcy felt the hard times of often not having enough food to feed everybody. Most of the clothes her children wore were handed down from the Sheff grandchildren and patched in many places. Lizzie hardly remembered what it was like to have a new dress made out of flour sacks by Mama Delcy.

As Lizzie celebrated her ninth birthday, Delcy sensed the struggle for Master Lloyd and Miss Sarah to provide for the sharecroppers and their families as they once did. Delcy and Neut needed more space to care for a growing family.

Later that year, in the early spring while Neut was planting the tobacco crop, Master Lloyd suffered a heart attack and nearly died. The tobacco barn was in need of repairs and the crops were demanding much of Neut's time. Due to the death of Pearlie, Delcy helped more with Anna, Master Lloyd and Miss Sarah. Lizzie was often left alone to care for her younger brother and sisters.

In the spring of 1880, Master Lloyd and Miss Sarah were both in poor health and most of the buildings, including the master house, were in poor condition. Since Master Lloyd and Miss Sarah's children showed little interest in the property, there were serious decisions to be made regarding the future of the plantation. Delcy and Neut were expecting again in November, so this was a serious time in their lives to make decisions that would be in the best interest of their family.

CHAPTER 11—1880: THE YEAR OF CHANGE AND DECISION

The year 1880 began with Delcy, Neut, Lizzie, Charlie, Mary, and Martha all living in the little one room log cabin. The curtains hanging from the one window in the kitchen were always freshly starched and crisp. A patch quilt hanging from the ceiling beam served as a room divider, separating the sleeping quarters of Delcy and Neut from that of the four children. Lizzie, Mary and Martha shared one big mattress on the floor near the potbellied stove. The overstuffed straw mattress always had colorful quilts made from scraps that Miss Sarah had passed on to Delcy. Charlie had his own mattress. He did not mind sleeping alone since Martha, the youngest of the children, often wet the bed.

Every morning Delcy would hang the quilts out to dry. Neut made his way to the fields and Lizzie helped the children get dressed and prepared breakfast. Chores were done around the log cabin before leaving for the Sheff house. One spring morning, Delcy was hesitant about attending to her chores at the masters' house. She was "free"; no longer a slave, yet she still acted and felt like one. She was no further ahead in her life at age 26 than she was at age 16 when she met Neut ten years ago. She always wanted her own home, a place where her children could truly be free of the ways of slavery. She thought long and hard how she still addressed Lloyd Sheff as "Master Lloyd" and Sarah Sheff as "Miss Sarah". Her children deserved more than the continued struggle and mental anguish of slavery. Delcy

thought about how it could be if she were allowed to make her own decisions.

Despite occasional failures and feelings of despair, she knew that she and Neut could make it on their own. She could see the gradual decline of Master Lloyd and Miss Sarah. She knew time was closing in on their life and their ability to maintain the plantation. For the remainder of the day, all Delcy could think about was a way off the plantation. If they were ever to make a move, it was now, right after the crops were planted. Charlie was growing larger and stronger every day. Delcy knew he would soon be old enough to work the fields behind a team of mules. She certainly did not want to see him working for Master Lloyd.

The time seemed right for Delcy to look beyond the plantation. Lizzie was tiring of the household routine of cleaning and feeding Anna, who was still locked in the third floor room. It was hard for Lizzie to help Delcy care for Mary and Martha, look after the farm animals, help with the family meals, and occasionally tend to old Miss Sarah. Delcy was definitely getting impatient with caring for everyone but herself.

The year 1880 did indeed prove to be a time of decisions. Delcy could hardly wait for Neut to return home from the fields so she could vent her frustrations about living on the plantation. She was ready to put her foot down and let him know that it was time to move on. She reminded Neut that he was doing the work of two or three people. When he would return to the cabin after a long day of work, he was so tired that often he would rely on Charlie and Lizzie to do more of the

hauling of water and splitting the wood for the old worn-out cook stove at the Sheff's house, as well as for their family. In the past, when field help was living on the plantation, chores were often divided, but now the free blacks did not return to Master Lloyd's fields. They left looking for the promise of land, seed, and a mule. However, Delcy doubted if they ever found that dream, but she was not looking for a dream, she only wanted a chance to earn wages for her work.

She was a beautiful laundress, and on several occasions she had done laundry for other plantation owners. Some lived as far as Georgetown, a little village about 30 miles from the Sheff plantation. She could place three irons on a hot stove at once and turn out a beautiful load of clothes. Delcy was also a good cook and there wasn't much she couldn't fix. She remembered how Mama Leah could always seemingly make a little bit go a long way. She could make the best fried apple pies and bread pudding from leftover bread. Because sewing was another of her skills, she often mended Neut's overalls over several sets of patches. They held up so well, they lasted another season. The children didn't have much in terms of clothes, but they were always neat and clean.

Delcy wondered about her parents and two brothers, Reuben and Josh. She imagined if they were still alive, and if so, how they looked.

When Neut returned from the fields and his evening chores were done, Delcy had prepared a special meal that included leftovers from Master Lloyd and Miss Sarah's supper. The children were playing outside the cabin, unaware that Mama Delcy had a verbal surprise for

Neut. When Neut came in for supper, Delcy did not hesitate in telling him that she was prepared to leave the plantation "right now!." Neut was taken by the sudden and firm voice of Delcy. He listened carefully as Delcy put forth her best argument.

"Neut," she said,

"You still act like a slave." "Yes sir Master this and yes sir Master that, you are so beholding to Master Lloyd."

Neut knew Delcy was serious. She snapped her eyes and put her hands on her hips in exhibiting a temper that Neut had not seen in her for a long time. She was making her point, that it was time to begin their move off the plantation into a land where free people could earn money for their labor. Master Lloyd's tobacco crop was so small that he barely made enough to keep food on his table, which meant even less for Neut and his family.

She discussed with Neut the possibility of getting hired as a sharecropper on another farm where the crops were being planted. All day Neut thought about the outburst of Delcy. He knew she would accept no excuse to stay. Several days later, Neut decided to take a trip to look for another sharecropping job and a better place to move his family. The plans to leave the plantation were finally in motion. He hooked the team of mules to the wagon and sat squarely on the wood wagon seat as he had done many times. He dared not look back for fear he would change his mind. After all, there were other free blacks seeking jobs and Neut feared that he would not be hired.

After several weeks of promises and looking for a piece of land and a house he could fix up for his family, he met Mr. Walters, a

tobacco farmer near Georgetown. Neut was inquiring about work at the general store in Georgetown when Les Snider, the store owner, told him he knew a farmer named Stewart Walters who was looking for help to sharecrop on his tobacco farm. He gave Neut the directions to Mr. Walters' farm that was about five miles from Georgetown. Neut thanked Mr. Snider and boarded his wagon headed for the Walters' farm. As he entered the farm from the main road, Mr. Walters was fixing a gate near the entrance to the farm. He greeted Neut with a pleasant handshake and said,

"Could I help you?"

Neut mentioned that Mr. Snider, the general store owner, had told him that he might find work on his farm. Mr. Walters welcomed Neut and invited him to get off the wagon and join him on the porch where they could talk. Neut was hopeful that Mr. Walters would hire him. Neut could tell the farm had been kept up and everything was neat and trimmed.

Mr. Walters was glad to hire a strong honest worker. He promised Neut that he would sell him one acre of land at the far north corner of the farm that had an abandoned log cabin on it as well as an out house and a fenced in chicken coop for fifty dollars, if he would work for him for five years. This sounded like a fair deal to Neut.

The two rode on the wagon to see the land and the old log cabin. Even though it was in bad condition, it could be repaired over time. The promising thing about the old log cabin was that it could be enlarged so the children could have room for beds, and they would not have to sleep on the floor, especially during the cold, harsh winter

months. Mr. Walters told Neut that he could have the wood from an old corncrib that had been torn down to make room for a new barn. Because Neut was handy around the farm, he was always fixing things for Master Lloyd and Miss Sarah, so he was confident he could make the cabin larger for his family. Neut and Mr. Walters shook hands and Neut got back on the wagon, gave the mules a snap of the reins and drove the thirty miles back to the Sheff plantation. He was so excited that he could hardly wait to tell Delcy the good news. All the way back he thought about adding a little cooking area for Delcy, and maybe a washing house next to the cabin; and raising chickens, and planting a garden. The children would be free to run and play and help with the garden and care for the animals. Delcy could take in laundry just like she planned in order to earn extra money to help with the children. As he approached the Sheff plantation, he urged the mules to move a little faster. He knew that Delcy would be very happy to hear of his successful trip.

Once home, Delcy ran to meet Neut as he stepped of the wagon. Delcy asked,

"Good news, I hope?"

When Neut told Delcy the story of moving to a new farm with the dream of a home and an acre of land, Delcy danced and sang for joy. The children huddled around as Delcy and Neut started praising God and jumping up and down. Martha, the youngest, was turning five months old, and Lizzie, now ten, always paid attention to Mary and Charlie so they would not get into trouble. They were too young, of course, to understand the meaning of what was happening. Lizzie

understood somewhat, but seemed confused and uncertain. That evening, the news of moving and having a home of their own was overwhelming. The happy event called for a special celebration. Delcy fixed one of her special suppers. She had saved vegetables and meat from the Sheff's cellar and smoke house for just such an occasion.

Delcy noticed that Lizzie appeared sad. Charlie and Mary were singing and dancing along with Neut and Delcy while Lizzie held baby Martha gently comforting her during the excitement and celebration. Mama Delcy sat in the rocker and pulled Lizzie up on her knee and explained to her what she felt it would be like to be free. She explained that as long as they stayed on Master Lloyd and Miss Sarah's plantation, they would never be free. They would always be treated as slaves, beholding to the Sheff's whims and needs with no dignity or respect. Lizzie was thinking about the friendship with Lucy, the Sheff's oldest granddaughter. She was her only friend. When Lucy would visit Grandma and Grandpa Sheff she would always play school with Lizzie and bring her a book to read. Lizzie was always excited to see Lucy and hear about her school in Georgetown. Lizzie believed that someday she would be able to go to school. It was a good thought but one Lizzie knew was far in the distance and a journey all in itself. Caring for the children and helping Mama Delcy came before anything.

Charlie had mixed feelings about moving. This was the only place he had ever known. In fact, he had only been off the plantation twice in his life, and that was when Neut took him to a neighboring

plantation to pick up grain for the animals. Charlie did not have much time to play like most eight-year-old boys. He often got to ride the mules home from the field to the Master's house. He enjoyed talking to them as he was giving them food and water. Sometimes he played with the three Sheff grandsons. He didn't care much for Jebb who was somewhat of a bully. He often teased Charlie about how black his color was, and how white Lizzie was. One time Jebb made a remark about Lizzie being half white and that Grandpa Sheff was her "pappy." Charlie got so mad he hit Jebb with all his might and they rolled and tumbled on the dusty ground until Charlie pinned him down. He gave Jebb a good licking and made him say "Uncle" and also promise to never say anything like that again. Delcy made Charlie go home and scolded Jebb for starting the fight. She had explained to Lizzie why her color was different from that of Charlie, Mary and Martha. Lizzie accepted Master Lloyd as her father, but not in the loving and compassionate way she accepted Neut. After all, Delcy had married Neut when Lizzie was barely a year old. Neut was the only father Lizzie knew and loved.

After the planting of the spring tobacco crop in late May, Neut and Delcy broke the news to Master Lloyd and Miss Sarah that they would be moving to their own land and home in Georgetown where Mr. Walters, a tobacco farmer, had sold them an acre of land. They were looking forward to the promise of a better life for their family. Master Lloyd, Miss Sarah, and Anna would have to turn to their children for help. Master Lloyd was very ill and slowly dying from internal bleeding. Neut had made an agreement with Mr. Walters that

they would prepare to move in about a month, giving the Sheff children time to make arrangements for the care of their parents and Anna.

CHAPTER 12—1880: TRAGEDY ON THE PLANTATION

Neut, Delcy, and the children began to make plans to leave the Sheff plantation within the next few weeks. In the meanwhile, after a long and agonizing illness of the "flux", which resulted in bleeding of the bowels, Master Lloyd died. Poor old Miss Sarah, partially paralyzed, was as "nutty as a fruitcake" and could not be left alone. She could not be trusted to do anything without someone watching or helping her. At the death of master Lloyd, Delcy figured the Sheff children would move quickly to bury him in the family cemetery located on the plantation. The children also had to decide what to do with Miss Sarah and Anna. As Delcy and Neut attended the burial of master Lloyd, the Sheff family was apparently anxious to settle the estate and put Miss Sarah in a "feeble minded" institution where she could live the rest of her life. Anna was the most difficult to decide the best placement for. After all, she had never been beyond the walls of the Sheff house. Since she was blind and unable to move about, her care was more demanding than Miss Sarah. The Sheff children had very little time to make decisions for their family before Neut, Delcy, and the children would be moving.

None of the children or grandchildren showed any interest in the tobacco plantation. As a gesture of good will and loyalty, the children offered Neut and Delcy the team of mules and wagon along with their belongings in the cabin. Neut inquired about taking some of the food in the cellar and smoke house and a small assortment of tools that

would help him fix up his new home. All the Sheff children agreed that Neut and Delcy were indeed deserving, and offered to share other small items from the Sheff's house. Neut and Delcy quickly removed the items offered them and returned to the log cabin.

As the Sheff children prepared to pack the necessary clothes and personal items for Miss Sarah and Anna, they noticed smoke coming from the kitchen area of the house. The children scurried around trying to locate the smell of smoke. It didn't take long to discover that the old kitchen stove had burning cinders falling on the wooden floor under the stove. The flames had already spread under the sink and had set fire to the icebox sitting in the corner. Without warning, the kitchen curtains went up in flames. The curtains and wallpaper began to burn fiercely. The most anyone could do was save their lives and that of Miss Sarah and Anna.

The children began frantically to try to reach Anna on the third floor as the flames roared from room to room. No one could find the key to unlock the door and the smoke and heat was so intense that the locked door could not be approached to save Anna.

As the family ran from the burning house, Neut, Delcy and the children could see the masters' house burning from a distance. By the time they returnd to the Sheff home it was fully engulfed in flames. Everything was lost. Anna never had a chance. Miss Sarah began to mumble about Anna in the locked room. She had tried to enter the burning house but the children restrained her. After the flames died down, Anna's charred body was removed from the house and buried next to master Lloyd. As the children were preparing Miss Sarah to

leave, the key to the attic was found in a little pocket purse that she kept in her dress pocket. The family grieved openly at the tragic death of Anna.

Neut and Delcy felt mixed emotions at the burning of what was once a grand home for the Sheff family. Neut's feelings were far more sympathetic than Delcy's. Her sadness was tempered by a feeling of relief, and a sense of justice for all the harsh treatment, pain, and injustice the Sheff's had wrought upon her. The Sheff children led Miss Sarah to the wagon where some of her belongings were packed in an old trunk that had been stored in the barn. As the Sheff family yelled a "giddy-up" to the team of horses pulling the wagon, Miss Sarah looked back and began to weep quietly, knowing that she would never return to the plantation life and lifestyle to which she had become accustomed. But mostly she felt the horror of Anna's death that would haunt her forever.

Neut, Delcy and the children watched as the wagon carrying Miss Sarah left the plantation. They were saddened by the horrible death of Anna but excited to have a place to move to that would belong to them. Finally, a place they could call home. As the children helped with the final packing of the furniture in the cabin and collecting the tools, there was barely enough room for them. Neut and Delcy rearranged some of the things on the wagon to make room for the final item in the cabin, the old pecan wood rocking chair. The old chair was needed to rock the next baby that Neut and Delcy were expecting.

Lizzie sighed as she squeezed between the furniture, holding Martha in her lap to keep her from bouncing around. Delcy and Neut sat proudly together on the wooden bench attached to the wagon. Neut gave the mules a snap of the whip and moved toward the path that led past the burned home and onto the open road that led to Georgetown. As the wagon rolled past familiar things on the plantation, such as the duck and chicken pen, and the stall where the old red cow was milked, Lizzie began to softly cry.

Delcy sat quietly on the wooden wagon bench reflecting on her life of abuse, punishment, the selling of her parents, the loss of her brothers, the birth of Lizzie, and finally the marriage to Neut. From the time of her birth in 1854 to the present time of June 1, 1880 was an experience in life that she never wanted her children to have to suffer through. She explained to Lizzie that she never wanted her to experience not having a loving mother and father, and always being at the mercy of a brutal and sexually abusive master. Lizzie listened and tried to understand. She asked Mama Delcy to tell her about where they were going. Delcy told her it was a better place and someday they would understand how much it meant to have something that's ours. Lizzie asked about going to school, and if there would be friends to play with. Delcy promised her that she would be able to go to school, maybe not every day, but she would continue to learn to read and write, so she could teach Charlie and the other children.

As the wagon rolled out into the open space of the fields and trees, the children became more thrilled. They had only been off the plantation once or twice in their lives. As the view of the property

grew smaller and smaller in a haze of dust kicked up by the rolling wobbly wagon wheels, Lizzie waved her little hand to the land in the distance. The journey was beginning; it was a point of no return. Neut snapped the reins of the mules; their new home was just a few miles away.

CHAPTER 13—1880: THE SUMMER - A NEW DESTINY

Traveling from the Sheff plantation to the farm of Mister Walters near Georgetown was a distance of about thirty miles. Leaving the Sheff's place was a cross roads in their lives; they were shaking off the mental and physical shackles of slavery and taking on a new life of freedom. Delcy's dream of freedom was finally a reality. She could hardly wait to attend a real African Methodist Church and make friends and listen to a preacher talk about freedom and read the Bible. She knew there was a school in Georgetown for African American children. They called it the Freedom School. She did not know much about city living. The only time she ever left the plantation was to attend a funeral with Miss Sarah on an adjoining plantation. She hoped so much that Charlie, Lizzie and Mary could go to school regularly. She dreamed of loading the children in the wagon and driving the five miles to Georgetown where she could look at pretty clothes in the store windows. If she could earn enough money from her washing and ironing, she could buy material to make the children's clothes and perhaps new curtains. Most of all, she wanted the children to have new shoes that fit. She knew that very soon she would be truly free, and nobody would ever treat her like a slave or take her joy of freedom. She wondered what Neut was thinking. Once she saw him looking back as though he was afraid of what lay ahead. She gently placed her hand on his sturdy shoulder and assured him

that the journey to their new home would be their first step of hope for a better life.

Lizzie held on to Martha as the wagon bumped and squeaked along the road across the miles to the new farm. As the evening sun began to set, the wagon loaded with all their belongings rolled onto the Walters farm. Even though the trip had taken all day, the children were excited and full of energy. They wanted to see as much of the new farm as possible before the sun set. As the wagon stopped in front of Mr. Walters' home, he came out to meet Neut, Delcy, and the children. He directed them toward the acre of land that housed the log cabin, long ago abandoned by the slaves. Neut guided the wagon down the rutted path for the last quarter mile to what would be their new home.

As Neut halted the wagon in front of the cabin, Delcy and the children anxiously hopped off the wagon, eager to examine their new home. As Delcy pushed open the door, she and the children slowly entered the log cabin expecting the worst. It was empty except for a cooking stove Mr. Walters had moved into the cabin. He also had left a few cooking utensils on the kitchen sink along with an old oil lamp full of oil.

Delcy was excited. As Neut and the children started unloading the wagon, Delcy made a fire in the stove, using wood from a small pile outside. She prepared some of the food that was given her from the cellar of the Sheff plantation. The children were allowed to run and play. They were so tired that they barely ate the stewed vegetables and salt pork Delcy had prepared. After supper, Lizzie and Charlie set

up the mattresses and covered them with big fluffy quilts. As they prepared to bed down for the night, Neut offered a prayer of thanksgiving for their new home and a new start as a truly free family.

The next day Mr. Walters rode his mare down to the cabin and offered other small household items to the family. Delcy was very thankful and asked Mr. Walters about working in the house and what was expected of her and the children. She did not hesitate to let him know that she was expecting another child in the spring of 1881, and that she would like some type of wage for her service. She felt good about letting him know right up front that she was a free woman.

She asked him about taking in washing and ironing and having Sunday off so she and the family could go to church. She was also concerned that Lizzie should have some kind of schooling so she could teach the other children to read and write. He told Delcy that there was a school for "colored" children in Georgetown, and he was sure she could have Sunday off. In fact, he thought that taking in washing and ironing would be helpful for her to earn extra money.

Delcy had never been listened to with so much understanding and compassion. She glanced at Neut with a seriousness that took him by surprise. Delcy seemed certain of what she wanted that Mr. Walters could only agree that it was the right thing to do.

Mr. Walters told Delcy about his family and what he expected of her in the house. He admitted to Delcy that he needed someone to help with the care of his wife, who had been sick for several years. She was bed-ridden and unable to care for herself. Delcy assured him that she would clean and prepare the meals and take daily care of his

wife. Mr. Walters told her that their children helped out on Sundays and she would be able to have time with her family. That suited her just fine. So far, Mr. Walters had granted Delcy what she wanted.

After getting settled in the cabin the next day, Charlie cut wood for the stove and help Papa Neut with the farm chores while Lizzie cared for the children and dreamed of making new friends. Lizzie did not see any children her age that she could play with or help her with her reading and writing. She became quiet and appeared unsure about the new home. Delcy told Lizzie that she would be busy for a while getting adjusted to the new farm, and she was certain there would be children her age at church. Later that day, Delcy and the children made their way to the Walters' house and met Miss Liza, Mr. Walters' wife. Miss Liza seemed glad to meet Delcy and the children. Delcy could see that they would get along from the start. She was nothing like Miss Sarah.

Miss Liza was a well-schooled lady and her room was filled with books and various pictures and ornaments. As the children entered the house, they were very quiet and amazed at all the beautiful things sitting around on heavily starched doilies and table covers. Lizzie was excited about seeing all the books and beautiful pictures. She asked Miss Liza for permission to see some of her books. She modestly told Miss Liza that she could read and write a little. Miss Liza offered to teach Lizzie to read and write. She was very pleased that Lizzie could already read somewhat. Miss Liza loved having children around her. Lizzie was very polite and appreciated her kind offer to teach her. Miss Liza had become the friend that Lizzie needed to care about her.

She would be glad to help Mama Delcy at the house while Charlie watched the children so she could learn from Miss Liza. Before Lizzie left the house for the day, Miss Liza offered her a small primer book to take home. Later, that night after supper, Lizzie began to read the little book to Charlie and the family. She was extremely happy.

On Sunday, Neut and Delcy loaded all the children in the wagon and headed for church out in the country. The little African Methodist church was about ten miles from the farm. In fact, the church was located about halfway between Leesburg and Georgetown. What a joy for Delcy, Neut, and the children to be able to experience real singing and preaching. There were many children to play with. Delcy and Neut found everyone very friendly. The preacher talked about God and His son Jesus and how he wanted us to be free. After all the singing and preaching they took up a collection for the preacher. They didn't have anything to give but they believed they soon would. Excitingly, Neut and Delcy looked forward to the Sunday when they could give an offering. After church the preacher stood at the door thanking them for coming, and as he shook everyone's hand, he invited them back next Sunday. They sang all the way home. Delcy was beginning to enjoy freedom in a way that was hard to express. She spent a considerable time shouting and praising God for setting her and the family free.

In the meanwhile, Mr. Walters told several families in Georgetown about Delcy taking in washing and ironing. She had gotten permission from Mr. Walters to borrow the wagon to go into town once a week to pick up laundry, and she would return the

finished clothes on the weekend. The first week, Mr. Walters lined up two families that wanted her services. At last she was earning a little money. She earned about two dollars and twenty-six cents for her first week's work. Soon the word got around that Delcy was a good laundress and all her customers were pleased. Delcy began to teach Lizzie how to iron, and soon they had enough ironing to keep them both busy.

When Lizzie would go with Delcy to work in the Walters' house, Miss Liza was always glad to see her and willingly helped her to read and write and do simple math. One day Miss Liza offered Lizzie a big storybook to take home. Lizzie could hardly finish her chores. She wanted to read the new book given to her by Miss Liza. Delcy, Neut and the children were thankful to Mr. Walters and Miss Liza for helping them with their family, and for allowing Delcy to take in ironing, and for teaching Lizzie to read and write. Neut was glad they moved to the Walters farm. He promised Delcy he would fix up the cabin before winter, and they would have a joyous celebration when the tobacco crop sold in the fall. Mr. Walters had proved to be an honest person, and Neut assured him he would honor the handshake agreement to work for five years to pay off the fifty dollars debt on the one-acre of farmland and the cabin.

As Delcy became more comfortable caring for Miss Liza, they began to confide in each other about their families. Delcy found out that Miss Liza was partially paralyzed from a previous stroke she had several years ago. Because Delcy and Lizzie were very patient with

Miss Liza, Mr. Walters often rewarded them by giving them a little extra money for her care and for their work around the house.

Charlie, Mary and Martha were very careful not to touch any of the beautiful dishes and pictures in the main house. Delcy had instructed them to never touch things that did not belong to them. The children were very attentive to Miss Liza and only entered her room when she invited them. Delcy was grateful that she could bring the children with her to work. When Charlie worked the tobacco fields with Neut, and Lizzie helped Delcy with the housework at Miss Liza's, Mary and Martha had to come along.

Lizzie continued to make progress with her studies. She had read several books and her writing and math skills were improving. Charlie, Delcy and Neut were also learning to read the Bible. Lizzie would sit in the rocker and teach Mama and Papa to read and write along with Charlie.

There was not much extra time around the farm, so right after supper, everyone would help clean the kitchen so they could have reading time. Everyone would sit around the potbellied stove to keep warm while Lizzie would read stories. Neut and Charlie were often busy with the fall harvest of the tobacco and gathering the last vegetables from the garden, thus they would sometimes work after supper and miss hearing Lizzie read.

Delcy's days were busy preparing food for storage in the cellar which included dried beans, sweet potatoes, turnips, apples and red potatoes. Delcy and Lizzie were also busy with washing and ironing

which consisted of making the trip to town to pick up and drop off freshly pressed clothes for other families.

Delcy was beginning to show with her fifth child. She had been through childbirth enough times that she knew exactly what to do. Lizzie was hoping that the new baby would be a boy. She also knew that she would have to help with another baby. Lizzie wanted to continue her reading and writing lessons so that Miss Liza would let her bring more books home to read to the family. Lizzie hoped another baby would not interfere with her friendship with Miss Liza.

On Sundays, Delcy, Neut and the children were getting to know more sharecroppers from other farms. Attending church was an important time for Delcy, Neut, and the children to socialize with other families. They enjoyed going to church for the sermon and staying for the basket dinners after church. Everyone would bring a dish of their best "fixings". There would be pecan pies, fried chicken, sweet potatoes, green beans and salads. The women would spread the food from their baskets on benches and tables sometimes inside the church or outside if the weather was nice, and everyone would eat from each other's pots and pans. Delcy's favorite food to fix was fried apple pies. She knew to soak the dried apples until they were plump and juicy. She would add butter, sugar, and spices, then spread the mixture on little circles of a flaky pie crust. Then she would fry them in a big black cast iron skillet until golden brown. The fried pies were enjoyed by everyone and always seemed to be one of the most popular desserts.

As the fall winds blew and the shorter days of winter began, Neut and Charlie were busy cutting and stacking the wood beside the cabin and the air holes in the cabin were filled with mud to keep out the wind. It was another cold winter and the children were kept busy tending the animals as well as making certain Mr. Walters and Miss Liza were warm and comfortable.

Because the winter was so cold and the children were small, Delcy, Neut and the children were often unable to make the ten-mile trip to church. They really missed going to church. Most of all, they missed their friends. But with Delcy approaching her seventh month of pregnancy, it was too risky to leave during the bitterly cold months. The roads were often closed due to snowdrifts and if they could not make it home there would be little or no help on the road. This was the first winter the family had in their own home. Delcy and Neut made certain the children had a warm cozy home and, most of all, beds to sleep in rather than sleeping on the damp mud floor.

As the season changed from winter to spring, on March 18, 1881, Delcy gave birth to a son. She named him Nace. Charlie was glad to have a brother. The little sisters pitched in to help. Lizzie began her usual care of the new baby rocking him to sleep in the rocking chair. She was a good big sister, very loving and patient when caring for the children. As the early spring season neared, life for Neut, Delcy and the children was never better. They had survived the long cold winter with plenty food and a warm cabin. The little log cabin was filled with laughter and singing. Neut and Mr. Walters walked around the

farm to make plans for the spring planting. Neut was counting the time until he would own his acre of land- only four more years to go.

As Neut, Charlie and Mr. Walters prepared the tobacco fields, Neut made certain the equipment was in good shape and the mules ready to go. Between the years 1881 and 1883 the family was able to earn more than enough money to pay Mr. Walters the fifty dollars for the one acre of farmland. In fact, they had saved enough to remodel the old log cabin. Another bedroom was added, the washroom was enlarged and a porch was built on the front. Delcy would soon need the space. She had given birth to her seventh child September 19, 1883 – a boy she named Benjamin. The farm prospered and Mr. Walters always paid Neut his fair share of the tobacco crop when it was sold on the market. Neut and Mr. Walters had a gentleman's agreement that made them more than boss and sharecropper – they respected each other as friends.

In the spring of 1886 Miss Liza's health began to fail and she became less able to help Lizzie with her studies. Lizzie had a good start that enabled her to teach her brothers and sisters how to read and write. One Sunday morning in May 1886 Miss Liza died in her sleep. Mr. Walters was now alone. His life seemed empty. Life was not the same with Miss Liza gone. Shortly after the funeral on May 17, 1886 Delcy gave birth to her eighth child, a boy, John Eli. She called him Eli after her father.

Mr. Walters, Neut and the children continued to work the farm for many years. The Walter's children and grand children continued to visit their father on Sunday and they too established a friendship with

the Smith family. Mr. Walters died in 1892 after a short illness. His elder son, Jacob, continued to run the farm after the death of his father.

CHAPTER 14—1885: LIZZIE'S JOURNEY

Lizzie, now fifteen, was interested in meeting friends at the Leesburg Methodist Church and maybe even going to a candy 'taffy pull' or a Saturday night social occasionally. Neut agreed to take her and Charlie on some Saturday evenings after all the chores were done. It was during one of the church socials that she met a young man named James (Jim) Davis. Lizzie knew she was too young to be serious about a young man, but she did enjoy his company. Lizzie thought about marriage, but she knew she was needed to help care for the small children as well as help with the household chores at the Walters home.

Lizzie and Jim started seeing each other more often. Two years later, when Lizzie turned seventeen, Jim asked her to marry him and move to Georgetown where he lived and sharecropped on another farm. The idea of marriage literally swept Lizzie off her feet. First, this was a way out of an overcrowded cabin where the family was steadily growing and space was scarce. Also, the idea of living in Georgetown really appealed to her. Lizzie had only left the farm to go with Delcy to pick up laundry and to church at Leesburg. Jim asked Neut and Delcy for Lizzie's hand in marriage and in 1887, Lizzie and Jim Davis were married in a simple ceremony at the Leesburg Methodist Church. There was no honeymoon. Lizzie packed up a few things from the family cabin and moved from the farm to a little house in Georgetown adjoining the farm where Jim was a sharecropper. Lizzie was very excited to have her own little house.

She fixed up the house and made it home for Jim and herself. She knew several people in Georgetown, since over the past seven years they had done laundry for many families. Lizzie made her way around the town looking for other people interested in hiring her to do their laundry. Over a period of several months, Lizzie had a half dozen customers that she laundered for every week. She earned enough to keep the household going and put a few dollars away for the baby she was expecting the next year in July. Jim and Lizzie were excited about the new baby.

Lizzie could hardly wait to see Mama Delcy, Papa Neut, and the children on Sunday at church so she could tell them the good news. Lizzie worked up until the time she gave birth to her first son, William Aaron, born, July 31, 1889. Lizzie was a loving and caring mother to her baby son. After all, Lizzie was accustomed to caring for babies. She had practically raised the first seven babies that Delcy and Neut had. As soon as Lizzie got her strength back, she worked in the home taking in laundry, baking pastries, and doing alterations on clothes. Lizzie even sold vegetables from the little garden that she had planted at the back of the house. She did a variety of things to keep the family going financially.

Two years after the birth of Will, Lizzie gave birth to a baby girl whom she named Leah, after Delcy's mother, the grandmother she never knew. Lizzie found that two babies were a handful. It was becoming a problem for Lizzie that Jim was not home very often. She spent an increasing amount of time alone with the children. One Sunday, while attending church, Lizzie overheard the ladies talking

about Jim and some of the things he was doing. This caused Lizzie to become suspicious about his absence from the home. As the year ended and the tobacco crop was sold, Lizzie noticed that Jim was unwilling to share his profit from the sale of tobacco with her and the children. As time passed, their marriage became strained. Lizzie tried to keep the marriage and family together. Feeling very distraught, Lizzie was pregnant with their third child.

The year 1893, Lizzie gave birth to a son she named Charlie, after her beloved brother. Lizzie was beginning to suffer from hard times, both financially and spiritually. It was hard to keep up with her many odd jobs and manage three small children. Lizzie soon realized that Jim was no longer faithful to her and the children. Her dilemma was what to do. She knew she could not go back home to Delcy and Neut, because there were now nine children in the Smith home and space was not adequate to bring three more babies to an already overcrowded home.

As winter approached, Lizzie formally divorced Jim Davis in the year 1895. There she was with three small children: Will, six, Leah, four, and Charlie, barely two. Lizzie pondered her situation. She knew she had to leave the little house she had worked so hard to fix up, but she needed a safe place for the children. She had become acquainted with many people in Georgetown and she knew there had to be a family that would take them in for labor and minimal wages. She knew Mrs. Opel Smothers was a good and kindhearted person who had a servant's home that was not in use. Lizzie recalled that once when she was about fifteen, Mrs. Smothers had asked her if she

wanted to live in her home and work for her. At that time, Lizzie could not because she was needed at home to help Mama Delcy with the children and attend to the farm. Now, more than ever she needed to know if the offer still stood.

Lizzie and the three children bundled up and walked the short distance to Mrs. Smothers home to inquire about working for her and staying in the servant's house. Mrs. Smothers, who knew that Lizzie was an honest, hard-working woman, agreed that Lizzie and the family could move in as soon as the house could be cleaned since it had not been used for several years. The next few days Lizzie and the children returned to clean the little house. The day before Thanksgiving, they moved in and Lizzie began work for the Smothers family. Mrs. Smothers was very generous to Lizzie and the children. They always had plenty food, milk, bread and fresh churned butter. Lizzie felt very blessed to have such a safe place to live. Lizzie was given scraps of fabric to make clothes for the children and quilts for their beds. Once a month Mrs. Smothers would allow Lizzie to use the family wagon and horse to visit her family in Georgetown and go to church. She was always glad to see Mama Delcy and Papa Neut. She always marveled at how her brothers and sisters had grown and how excited they were to see her.

Lizzie worked for the Smothers family for three years before meeting her second husband, Simon Cannon, who was a widower with an infant daughter. His wife had died as a result of giving birth to their daughter, Annie Bell, born February 22, 1896. Lizzie was very cautious in accepting Simon's attention. She was hesitant about

keeping company with any man, and certainly had not contemplated re-marrying so soon. Simon asked Lizzie if she would consider helping with the care of his infant daughter Annie Bell. Lizzie agreed to help with her care while working for the Smothers family. Annie Bell was no problem to care for, and her daughter, Leah, was excited to have a baby in the house. Mrs. Smothers did not mind Lizzie adding one more child to the family. Lizzie eventually got to know Simon as an honest and caring person, and a relationship began that would eventually lead to marriage.

Simon was a very successful farmer who sharecropped on a big tobacco farm outside Georgetown. He was offered a chance to sharecrop and become the overseer of a larger tobacco farm in Jessamine County, Kentucky. Sharecropping a larger farm would enable Simon to make more money, and it would also give Lizzie's three children a chance to work the fields to earn money. On the farm in Jessamine County there was a little house on the property that was once used as a trolley car station for passengers going between Nicholasville and Lexington, Kentucky. The little station was called the tollgate house. Even though it was small, it was in good condition and could easily be converted to a home for Lizzie and the children. After two years of courtship, Lizzie consented to marry Simon on November 12, 1898. Lizzie, Annie Bell, Will, Leah, and Charlie packed up their belongings from the Smothers house and moved to their new home located near the side of the road in Nicholasville, Kentucky. The old tollgate house was now a home for the Simon Cannon family.

Once again Lizzie and the children fixed up the little place and added fresh curtains and new fluffy quilts to the beds, which made it home. It was not hard to find work in Nicholasville. Lizzie quickly got out the word that she would take in laundry and was available to clean houses. Many residents from Nicholasville would drive by the house and drop off their laundry and alterations. Lizzie and Leah were in business. Everyone helped with the field crops as well as the household chores. Simon was a good stepfather to Lizzie's three children as well as a good father to Annie Bell. He truly adored his new wife Lizzie, and was always concerned about her well-being. What a change from her first marriage to Jim Davis. Lizzie had to learn to trust all over again. Because she had waited three years before accepting Simon's hand in marriage, she had an appreciation of what marriage and family life should be. After settling into their home and getting to know people in the little community of Nicholasville, Simon and Lizzie moved their church membership from the Leesburg Methodist Church to Bethel African Methodist Episcopal Church in Nicholasville. Lizzie, Simon and the children became active members in the Sunday school. Simon joined the Board of Trustees and Lizzie became a member of the Missionary society of the church. The little church on the corner of York Avenue was in need of repair and expansion to accommodate the increasing membership. Simon was a very active financial member and was one of several trustees to sign a loan to help remodel and expand the church. After several months of marriage, Lizzie and Simon began their family.

The year 1900, May 15, Lizzie gave birth to a son named Elmer. Elmer was a difficult birth and was born with serious health problems. He lived a little more than four months. He died October 4, 1900 from pneumonia. The death of Elmer was devastating to the mental health of Lizzie. In despair, she confided in Mama Delcy and found strength in her support. Also, in the year 1900, at the age of forty-six, Delcy gave birth to her thirteenth and last child. Delcy reminded Lizzie that she had four children to die before age three. She knew how heart breaking it was to see one's babies die so young. Lizzie found comfort in the fact that she had a family that supported her during this difficult time. Lizzie was a woman of great faith and she relied on her spiritual strength to sustain her.

She soon began helping out in the fields, working in her garden, and caring for the farm animals that Simon had purchased. Their little farm consisted of chickens, ducks, pigs, cows and several teams of mules. Every fall Simon would butcher a hog so the family would have meat for the winter. He would share the meat with Delcy and Neut when they would visit each other in Georgetown.

Two years after the death of Elmer, Lizzie was expecting another child. On January 13, 1902, Lizzie gave birth to a son they named Joe. He was a healthy baby that the family loved from the first sight. Leah, now eleven, was an affectionate big sister and was very helpful with the baby. She also was a big help to Lizzie, working in the garden and milking the cows.

Will, now thirteen was working in the fields beside Simon. Charlie, now nine, would tag along to care for the animals and haul

water for the tobacco workers. After a long day of working in the tobacco fields, the children all pitched in to split wood and haul water from the spring so Lizzie and the family could have fresh drinking water everyday.

On July 30, 1904, Lizzie gave birth to another son, named Roy. Once again, this was a difficult delivery for Lizzie. When Roy was born, he had problems breathing and appeared to have seizures (probably epilepsy) that caused him to collapse and shake uncontrollably. After a constant battle of poor health, Roy died at the age of two in 1906. His death had an even greater effect, both physically and mentally, on Lizzie and Simon. Lizzie became very despondent and required a great deal of understanding and patience from her family. It was seven years before Lizzie would give birth to another child.

On March 10, 1911, Lizzie gave birth to her first daughter by Simon. They named her Mary Antionette. What a joy to give birth to a healthy baby girl. Everyone was excited. With Annie Bell now fifteen, Joe nine, and Leah, Will, and Charlie grown, the attention Mary Antionette received was constant.

Leah was now dating Frank Strauss, a much sought after gentleman and a very successful farmer in Jessamine County. He owned his own home and farm on the Shun Road in Nicholasville, Kentucky. He took a great deal of time in selecting the right woman to marry. Leah always hoped that someday she would marry Frank. However, she was very reserved and responsible as they planned their

future together. She was pleased when Frank presented her with an engagement ring that properly announced his intentions to marry her.

The year 1913 was a year of joy for the family. Charlie met his wife Celia Sanders in Nicholasville, and on February 5, 1913 they were married. A few months later, Annie Bell met Willie Howard. They were married on April 16, 1913. This meant that within a few months, two of Lizzie and Simon's children moved from the home. However, Leah and Will, still single, continued to work with Simon in the tobacco fields.

Later that year, Lizzie gave birth to her last child, a son, born August 8, 1913. She named him Frank Robert. He was a real delight to older sister Mary Antionette, now two, who loved him from the first moment he was born. Leah became a second mother to the two young children while Lizzie continued to work the fields and tend to the garden and livestock. Between Leah and Lizzie, the children were always under good care.

The following year, tragedy struck the family again. In March 1914, Annie Bell died giving birth to her first child. The baby died a few days later causing great pain to the family. Simon had lost his first daughter along with his first grandchild. It seemed that death was a frequent and painful part of life. Surely, times would get better as they moved into the year 1915.

But this was not the case. Early in the spring of 1915, Joe became ill with uncontrollable coughing spells, and later began to cough up blood. He was diagnosed with tuberculosis and after a few months, he

died on September 17, 1915. With his death, Lizzie had lost her first three sons by Simon.

Leah was there to support her mother. She helped with Mary Antionette and Frank Robert as though they were her own children. Lizzie had endured so much pain and loss. She continued to draw upon her strong faith and belief in God, which helped her through the difficult times.

Lizzie continued to visit her family in Georgetown as often as possible. With the crops and farm work, it was difficult to travel long distances for more than a day. On Lizzie's most recent visit to the family in Georgetown, Neut had not been feeling well. He complained of being short of breath and Lizzie noticed that his feet and hands were swollen.

In the months that followed, Neut's health continued to decline. One evening while sitting in the old pecan rocking chair, Neut had a massive heart failure and died October 30, 1916. Delcy felt a great loss in her life. Neut had been responsible for making her dream of freedom and owing a home a reality. With young children in the home, Delcy was able to continue living on the farm until the children were grown and on their own. Mary, one of the older daughters remained on the farm with Delcy.

The year 1916 was a financially bountiful year for the Cannon family. Will, Charlie, and Simon each earned nearly five hundred dollars from the sale of their tobacco crop. One more year and they would be able to purchase the farm for sale about four miles north of their home that had thirty-six acres. The property also had an old log

cabin that once served as a halfway house for slaves and masters as they journeyed from the north to the south. The masters would stop there for rest and chain the slaves in a holding pen that was directly behind the cabin until such time as the master's pleasures were met, and then they moved on. Also on the farm, was an underground root cellar used to store vegetables, ice, and perishable foods such as milk and butter. The asking price for the farm was nine thousand dollars. Simon did not have enough money saved to buy the entire thirty-six acres, so he, Charlie, and Will made an agreement to purchase the farm as equal partners. They would split the farm into three plots so they each could have an equal share to raise their own tobacco crops.

In the year 1917, Leah and Frank Strauss married and Leah moved from the home to live with Frank on a farm that he owned south of Nicholasville on Shun Road. Lizzie missed her terribly. They were not only mother and daughter, but also best friends. After the marriage of Leah, Will and Charlie continued sharecropping with their stepfather, Simon, and saving their money for a down payment on the farm.

The year 1917 was another good year financially for Simon, Will, and Charlie, with the tobacco selling at a record price. With their share of the sale of the crop, they each had the necessary money to buy their twelve acres. Charlie, who was now married to Celia and living in Nicholasville, offered his twelve acres to Leah and Frank Strauss. Leah wanted to be closer to Lizzie so she could help with the family. She persuaded Frank Strauss to sell the farm on Shun Road and reinvest in the thirty-six acres with Simon and Will. It was a good

buy for Leah and Frank because the farm on Shun road only had four acres.

Simon wanted the twelve acres adjoining a farm to the North of Leah and Frank. Since Leah and Frank had the largest investment to put down on their share, they chose the strip of land with the log cabin, root cellar, and tobacco barn with the understanding that Lizzie and Simon, along with Will, Mary Antionette, and Frank Robert, could live with them until the big house on the hill was finished. The big house on the hill was the home that Simon had promised to build for Lizzie and the children. Will chose to live with Simon and Lizzie and did not build a home on his property. Will was satisfied with the end strip that had an old corncrib on it that was used to store corn and hay for the cattle.

When the family moved from the old tollgate house to their new farm, the move was a boost to Lizzie's mental and emotional health. The land had several ponds and a fresh water spring that provided water for the family. A deep well was located on Leah and Frank's property that had the coldest, purest water one could imagine. In the spring of 1918, after Simon finished the home, Lizzie and the children excitedly moved in.

Simon, Will, Frank, and Leah began to purchase livestock for milk and butter, and chickens and ducks for eggs and meat. They continued to slaughter several hogs every winter, and made their own sausage and smoked their own meat in a smoke house that was built behind the big house on the hill. Lizzie and Simon began to prosper. Leah and Lizzie worked hard taking in laundry along with picking

and canning vegetables from the garden. They had become a team, as they sold butter, cream, eggs, and vegetables to the stores in Nicholasville. They also participated in an open vegetable market in Nicholasville during the summer. Between working in the fields and looking after the children, they had a full day.

As the years passed, Lizzie continued to stay in touch with her family in Georgetown. She and her brother Charlie visited each other on occasion, and once a year they would have a big family reunion where all the brothers and sisters would come together and share stories about their lives and families.

By the year 1926, Delcy, now seventy-two, was beginning to fail. She had severe arthritis and she was in constant pain. Her life was gradually slowing to the extent that some days she hardly had the energy to get out of bed. All of Delcy's children were gone except for her daughter Mary. She and Delcy remained in the original cabin located on the Walters farm until Delcy's death on April 6, 1926. Lizzie and the family attended the funeral that was held at the Leesburg Methodist Church where she and Neut and the children were members. Delcy was laid to rest in the church cemetery next to Neut.

Mary remained in the old home less than a year. It was in need of repair and more than Mary could care for by herself. Mary offered to divide the few belongings in the cabin among the brothers and sisters. All Lizzie wanted was the old pecan rocking chair that was part of the original furniture when her grand parents, Leah and Eli, moved into the log cabin on the Sheff plantation in 1850, and the family Bible

dating back to 1876. Granny Delcy, as she was affectionately called, would have wanted Lizzie, her first born, to have the old rocking chair and the Bible as a memento of the past life that once existed on the plantation.

Lizzie placed the pecan rocker in a special place in the big house on the hill. It was in need of repair, but the spirit of those from the past remained alive in the old chair. With the death of both parents, Lizzie felt blessed to have a home, a loving husband and five living children; Will, Leah, Charlie, Mary Antionette, and Frank Robert.

Lizzie turned her attention to providing an education for Mary Antionette and Frank Robert. They had been attending a small rural "colored" school called Little Zion that housed the first through eighth grade. Contrary to the customary educational goals for most blacks at the time, Lizzie had bigger plans for their continued education past the eighth grade. She visited the school in Nicholasville for "colored" children and met Professor Caldwell who was eager to enroll them in a high school program. Throughout Jessamine County there were several rural schools that offered the "colored" children an opportunity to learn to read and write, though most only went through the eighth grade. However, most "colored" children were occupied with working the tobacco fields, and school was not a high priority for many farm children. This was not the case with Lizzie. She knew how hard she had struggled and begged Delcy for a chance to read and write. Education for Mary Antionette and Frank Robert became an obsession with Lizzie. She had taught Frank

Robert and Mary Antionette as much as she could with the limited education she was able to acquire from Miss Liza.

Frank Robert and Mary Antionette were very bright students. They both were able to read, write and do math when they entered school. Every morning Lizzie would hook up the team of mules to the wagon and drive the four miles to Nicholasville for Frank Robert and Mary Antionette to go to school. At the appropriate time Mary Antoinette graduated from high school and enrolled in Kentucky State Teachers College, Frankfort, Kentucky, a Land Grant College for "colored" students. The program offered a two-year certificate in teaching. Frank Robert followed behind two years later and enrolled in a teacher education program with an interest in History. Mary Antionette graduated with her two-year certificate in 1934. She was hired to teach at Little Zion, the country school she had once attended as a child in Jessamine County.

It was during her tenure as a teacher that she met a tiny little girl named Katherine Louise Black who she befriended. Louise would come to Little Zion with her brother Robert so she would not be left alone while her mother and father worked as sharecroppers on a nearby farm. Louise was often alone and Mary Antionette knew this. One cold snowy day, Mary Antionette asked Katie, Louise's mother, permission for Louise to come and live with them. Katie gave permission for Louise to be in the loving care of Lizzie. It was easy for her to serve as a foster mother to Louise.

When Mary Antionette left Kentucky and moved to Hampton, Virginia to complete her four years of college, she met her husband

109

Richard Patrick and never returned to Kentucky to live. Louise remained in the loving care of Lizzie and Simon. Frank Robert continued his education at Kentucky State Teachers College where he met his wife Ora Belle Hamilton. After graduating with a certificate in History, Frank Robert and Ora Belle were married in May 1936. After the marriage of Frank Robert and Ora Belle they moved to Nicholasville and assumed residence with Lizzie and Simon.

Frank Robert began his teaching career at the Jessamine County School for Colored Children under the principalship of Professor Julius Caesar Caldwell, where he once attended as a boy.

Lizzie was very wise, and yet soft and gentle, loved, and gave so much love. She quietly died in her sleep at the age of ninety-four on September 8, 1965.

EPILOGUE

In the summer of 1938, June 27, I began my journey with Mama, my grandmother, Lizzie. No, there was no slave ship on the shores of West Africa waiting at anchor to begin its voyage to America. There was no slave master waiting to auction my body to the highest bidder, nor divide the family into separate pieces of property so one's roots could never be connected again. I am humbled by the past stories that were told to Mama by her mother Delcy. It is a privilege to walk in the footprints of Mama as she revealed her stories to me, her granddaughter.

Mama was a tiny grandmother, barely five feet tall and weighing less than one hundred pounds. She had long white hair that was worn in a small bun on the back of her head and a wave of hair that draped her forehead. Her voice was soft, warm and tender. I rarely ever heard her raise her voice even to laugh out loud. I never remember Mama being young. When I was born, Mama was sixty-eight years old. She began sharing her stories and life struggles with me when she was in her seventies. I vividly remember her little round wire rim glasses and false teeth that she would take out every night and put in a case on the night stand beside her bed. Mama always wore long cotton print dresses and aprons made from feed sacks. Her underclothes were all homemade from bleached white feed sacks. Her petticoat was as long as her dress and her underwear, called teddies, were simple and accommodating. Mama always wore brown or black cotton stockings and brown, laced shoes representing the simplicity of her life.

Many of the stories she told reflected the spiritual and religious values that she instilled in her children and grandchildren. If one listened closely while she was washing clothes or preparing dinner, one would hear her singing her favorite hymn from the old brown covered Gospel Pearl Songbook, published by the Sunday School Evangelistic Meeting Convention, Nashville, Tennessee, 1921.

"Marching homeward day by day, To a land that's free from weeping. Singing all along the way, Of the Savior and His love. Trusting in Him day and night, Sweetly resting in his keeping and for right we will fight, Till we're safe with Him above."

The more she sang the song, the more I would be drawn into the words and what they must have meant to her through her journey to freedom. As I grew older, the songs Mama used to sing and the stories she told took on a new meaning and substance.

We shared a bedroom for eighteen years before I left home to enter college at what is now Kentucky State University in Frankfort, Kentucky. Our tiny bedroom included two windows in the room, one facing east and one facing south, that gave Mama and me a beautiful view of the farm. When the weather was clear the two of us could see for miles. On the wall were two family pictures going back to the days of slavery. One was a very large framed picture of Mama's mother, Delcy, and the other was a smaller framed picture of her mother's sister, Mary Brent. The pictures had very stern facial expressions with deep piercing eyes. Sometimes their expressions were so frightening that I would hide under the cover to keep from

looking at them. One time I asked Mama why they looked so angry. Mama replied,

"They didn't have much to smile about, being a slave working from sunup until sundown. They never knew from day to day if they would have enough food to eat or if they would be sold and separated from their children, family and friends".

I cherished sleeping in the little twin bed next to Mama. There was a sense of security when the storms would rage outside with the winds and rain dashing against the window. Mama would gently pat her hand on the side of the bed beckoning for me to crawl into her bed, where she would gently cradle me in her arms and sing the old spiritual, Stand By Me.

"When the storms of life are raging, stand by me. When the world is tossing me like a ship upon the sea, Thou who rules wind and water, stand by me."

Mama's bed was always comforting and neatly adorned with fluffy hand pieced quilts. One night I asked her to tell me about the beautiful star quilt on her bed. As she told the story about the Northern Star Quilt, she said,

"The star was designed to guide the escaping slaves into the northern cities on their way to Canada. Some called the quilt the Ohio Star because Ohio was a free state, and many escaping slaves were sometimes guided by the star quilt to reach the free state of Ohio. So when the Northern Star quilt was displayed in Ohio on rail fences or near a safe house that protected fugitive slaves, the fleeing slaves knew they were headed north."

The story fascinated me so much that I asked about the quilt on my bed. It was heavy and warm. Mama explained that it was a nine patch square quilt made from the scraps of many old dresses, shirts and aprons that had a few good spots left in them. She explained how the nine patches were used to write the names of family members who no longer worked or lived on the same plantation. Their names and sometimes birth dates were scribbled on the square and saved as a record of family members. Mama said that the families always hoped that they would meet again someday, and the quilt would be a reminder of who was born and was once a part of the family. Unfortunately, many families that were separated during slavery, as well as during the Civil War, never returned to the plantations to join their loved ones.

I was always curious about the old rusty round top trunk that was in a dark corner of the attic. Sometimes I would sneak into the attic searching for old memories that were a part of the past. Most of the time I was scared to enter the dark room because I could hardly find my way due to a lot of junk things. I wondered if there were other old quilts stored in the trunk that had history pertinent to the Underground Railroad in Kentucky. With that in mind, I began to search from room to room in the big house looking for all kinds of quilt patterns. All the family members that lived in the big house had quilts on their beds.

The flying geese quilt was one of Mama's favorites. From time to time I asked Mama about the quilts in the trunk. I really wanted Mama to tell me about her favorite quilt. She began one afternoon to tell me her story as the seasons were beginning to change from

summer to fall, and the air had a certain chill that was a reminder that cold weather was near. As Mama and I sat outside on the old rusty swing that hung from the ceiling beams of the front porch, Mama was very quiet. We sat together on the swing many times talking and folding clothes or quilting and sometimes visiting with family and friends. This particular afternoon was different because Mama wanted me to listen and be quiet. I asked her,

"What were we listening for?"

She replied, "The sounds of fall."

Way up in the sky we could hear the Canadian Geese "honking" as they flew in a perfect V over the house. What a strange sound. The geese were flying south for the fall and winter where they would find food and water. In the spring they would return north when the rivers and streams would be thawed from the cold winter months. Finally, the beautiful quilt story was revealed. Mama really cherished the special flying geese quilt. She said that most slaves escaping north relied on the hidden messages in certain quilts to alert them that the Underground Railroad that followed the rivers and lakes north was now open.

I looked on all the beds for the flying geese quilt. I could not find it on any of the eight beds occupied by the family members. I asked Mama to show me the flying geese quilt that was in the attic in the big trunk. I really wanted to know why it was so important to Mama and the family. After a few days, Mama decided it was time to share what was in the old trunk. She got an old oil lamp and carefully lit it. She beckoned for me to follow her up stairs to the dark attic for a look in

the old trunk. It was dark in there. We would hear the sound of mice scurrying across the floor trying to hide behind some of the old boxes and clothes that cluttered the attic. I was not afraid as long as Mama was ahead of me with the old lamp. She cautioned me to never try to bring a lighted candle or lamp into the attic because I could cause a fire and that would destroy the home and others may get hurt. I never will forget the lesson on safety as we entered the dark attic room.

After opening the old trunk in the attic, there was the flying geese quilt neatly folded among other beautiful quilts and lace edged sheets and hand embroidered pillowcases. I thought every thing in the old trunk was absolutely beautiful. Mama gently opened the quilt and looked at all the beautiful pieces that were lined up side-by-side forming a perfect "V". When I asked about other quilts in the trunk, Mama assured me that some were her mother's and others were family favorites. I asked Mama how she knew so much about the quilts and their patterns. She replied, "Delcy, your great grandmother, told me the secrets of the quilts that her mother, my grandmother Leah, had told her."

The secrets of the quilt patterns were entrusted to the family members as a legacy to the freedom of slaves as they traveled the Underground Railroad. Mama replied that she had given as a wedding gift some of the family quilts to her daughter Mary Antionette who lived in Lynchburg, Virginia.

The family home on Nicholasville road, about six miles south of Lexington, was a friendly place for many people. It was located on US Highway 27 and was convenient for friends to drop in for a visit.

Visitors were always welcomed with open arms and offered something to eat. For example, the old Watkins salesman was always peddling his ointments, salves, vanilla and spices to the farmers in the area. Apparently, he managed to time his visit with Mama when the family was having breakfast. He always started out by telling Mama how good everything smelled. I often wondered if he actually smelled the bacon and sausage cooking as he pulled in the drive in his horse drawn buggy, or if he just felt welcome sitting at the family table eating breakfast. Whichever the case, Mama would have never turned him away. Like the Watkins salesman, there were numerous hobos who would stop for milk and bread. There always seemed to be plenty to go around for the family and to share with others. One of the sweet spirits of Mama was her willingness to share. She would say,

"It makes my heart sing with joy, and sing I must do for Christ's sake. He is the one that gives me all I have and I know how easy it is to lose all you have."

Mama continued to give and share with others and trust that God would always supply her needs; He truly did.

During the summer, I was very busy helping Mama pick the fruit from the orchard and gather the vegetables from the garden. Summer was a big time on the farm. Sometimes Mama would can over a thousand jars of fruits and vegetables in preparation for the winter months. Mama would kill the oldest ducks and chickens for meat, and my job was to help pluck the feathers, especially from the ducks, to be used to stuff fresh pillows and mattresses for the winter. Those old

feather-tic mattresses were big and lumpy and hard to make up in the morning before going to school.

Among Mama's prized possessions was the big old family Bible that was once her mother's. I was always curious about the large family Bible dating back to 1876. There was a special place in the living room that one could always find the Bible. The children were not allowed to play in the living room. It was set aside for guests and visitors. There were French doors that separated the living room from the family room where I spent most of my younger days. On special occasions, and with permission, Mama would share the beautiful pictures of her family and the history of all the births, deaths, and marriages of the Brent, Smith, and Cannon families. So many had died young. Mama would talk about the family and the hardship of seeing the children die at a young age. On the wall in the living room were two very special pictures of family members. I thought it was strange that no other pictures were displayed in that room.

One day, I asked Mama to tell me about the pictures. She told me that one picture was of her three sons by Simon; the other, was his portrait. She spoke of her sorrow at the death of the three sons and how Simon was special. Because of his love for her and the children, he provided them a home for life.

Sometimes Mama would tell stories about the lives of her family as they struggled through slavery. She often recalled the hardships of her family as they journeyed toward freedom. Once Mama told me to,

"Get a good education and study hard."

She never forgot how difficult it was for her to learn to read and write while helping with the chores on the plantation. She always stressed getting an education and studying. I can remember her faithfully reading the Bible and a daily prayer guide called "The Upper Room." Mama was a dedicated Church member, both financially and spiritually, and she made sure everyone in the family went to church every Sunday. She was very faithful in preparing the unleavened bread for the Communion Sunday service. She would carefully make the salt-free pastry and lightly bake the bread. Afterward, she would prepare the grape juice that was poured into little tiny communion cups and placed in shiny silver trays. I looked forward to the first Sunday in each month when Mama would help the preacher serve communion to the congregation. After the service, Mama would allow all the children to eat the left over bread and empty the little glass communion cups. The memory of the things that Mama did for me made a great impression on my life.

I vividly remember the times when Mama would visit her brothers and sisters who resided in Leesburg, Kentucky. The family gatherings were celebrated at the Methodist Church in Leesburg where Mama's parents, brothers, and sisters are buried. The little country church was surrounded by thick brush, weeds, and an out door toilet. I was always afraid of finding field mice and especially snakes in the churchyard. Whatever the fear may have been, there were no excuses to not attend the basket meeting at the church. Each family member would bring covered dishes of food to serve and share with the others. This celebration called "basket meeting" was held once a year usually in

July. It was always hot and there were plenty ants, bugs, and mosquitoes. I was always glad when the family gathering was over, because I had severe allergies and the weeds and chiggers made for a miserable day. However, I knew this was a special time for Mama to be with her family, and as a result, I tried to never show any displeasure in going to the reunion out of respect for Mama.

Among the fondest memories I have of Mama are the old fashioned recipes she used to prepare for the family. Her white bean soup with ham and cornbread was something worth waiting for. Mama taught me to cook most of the foods for the family by watching and helping her. Another one of Mama's favorite recipes was fried fruit pie. This recipe was never written down, but I know her mother passed it on to her. Mama would use fruit from the orchard that was dried by slicing it into quarters and spreading it on top of an old tin roof that covered the chicken house to dry. My job was to spread the apples, peaches, and apricots on the hot tin roof in the morning, then gather them all up in the evening before sunset. If the evening dew were to dampen the fruit, this would cause it to mold and spoil. The drying process took about a week. After the fruit was thoroughly dry, Mama would put it in clean feed sacks to be stored in a cool place until she was ready to make her special fried fruit pies.

Mama was also an expert at making "home brewed beer". In the cellar of the house was a dark, dead end room that was used for storing the special "home brew beer". I was never given the recipe but as much as my memory serves, the ingredients included: yeast, malt, sugar, water and hops. Mama would mix all the ingredients in a big

crock jug, covering it tightly to allow the brew to ferment and turn into beer. After a designated time, she would pour the beer into dark colored bottles, tightly pressing corks in the top of each and placing them in the dark room. After a few weeks, when the house was very quiet, one could hear the corks popping and the beer spewing everywhere. This meant that the home brew was ready to be served.

Mama would say to the children,

"Stay out of the cellar, there's a big black snake hiding under the steps."

She knew it was tempting to the grandchildren to sneak down stairs to taste the "home brew beer." Mama would always invite grown-folks to have a bottle of the special brew. Visitors and friends of Mama seemed to come back year after year waiting for her to invite them to have a bottle or two.

One Sunday, the preacher was invited to dinner with the family. After eating, the preacher asked Mama if he could have a little of that special brew. Mama replied,

"I suppose so, a little never hurt anyone."

We watched the preacher drink one, then two, and then three bottles. When he got ready to get out of his chair to leave he was as "drunk as a skunk" as we would say in the south. I laughed and laughed. Poor old Reverend, he tried to walk but his legs were like rubber. All he could do was sink back in the chair and laugh too.

We soon found out just how sick the "home brew" would make us feel. Once my younger brother decided to sneak a few bottles out of the basement without Mama's knowledge. He drank the warm brew

"like a man." Sure enough, after about an hour, my little brother was crawling in the house "sick as a dog." I knew that the home brew had done a number on him.

Now I know why Mama always told the children it would make us sick if we drank it. I used to shake the bottle, then pop the cork and sip the rich white foam as it ran down the bottle. I wished I had never tried the warm bottle of brew. "Too much, too late."

I'm sure everyone has a homemade remedy story. Mama's mother, Delcy, shared her recipe as far back as 1885. Mama would cook a special root tea in the spring of the year that everyone in the family had to drink including the children. The tea was made from roots that she would gather from the field and around tree trunks. She would combine the roots in a big pot filled with water and place it on the back of the wood burning stove. It would seemingly simmer for days. It smelled terrible. When the water would boil low, Mama would add a little more and continue steaming the roots. When it was ready, it was as dark as bark on a tree. Mama would line up all the children and give each one a big cup to drink. It tasted terrible, even after you added lots of sugar. When I asked Mama,

"Why do we have to drink the dark root tea?" Mama replied,

"It will kill all the winter germs and make you healthy for the summer."

Mama had a reason and answer for everything. After our share, the adults would have some. No one ever dared not to drink their share, and there was always more where that came from. In retrospect, we were really healthy and rarely had bad colds. I never

knew the ingredients used in this tea and cannot imagine finding the right combination of herbs to duplicate the recipe.

I inherited the old pecan rocking chair that dates back to 1850 when Mama's grandparents, Eli and Leah Brent, were sold into slavery to work on the Sheff tobacco plantation in Leesburg, Kentucky. The rocker was one of a few pieces of furniture found in the old log cabin placed there by Master Lloyd. I have since had the old rocker restored to its original pattern. One childhood memory of the old chair was that it had little short rockers and was very low to the floor. If one rocked back too far, it would tip over. Today, it sits in my bedroom alongside the original dresser that Mama and I shared in the big farmhouse on the hill. Mama shared her final stories at the age of 94. She commented that,

"God left me here for a reason. I was the first child born to Delcy in 1870 and I will be the last child to die. I have lived a long time, a life full of sorrow and joy. Love each other as I have loved each of you."

Over the years there was one story that Mama never shared with me, but my father, Frank Robert, did. Before his death May 8,1988, my father shared the story of how Delcy, Mama's mother, was brutally beaten and raped by Lloyd Sheff for "sassy" and intolerable behavior. Delcy never forgave him for the harsh treatment. Before leaving the plantation, Delcy crushed broken glass so fine that it looked like powder and daily stirred a few teaspoons of the glass into Lloyd Sheff's buttermilk. Over a period of a few months, Lloyd began to bleed from the bowels. The disease was diagnosed as the "flux".

Little did the Sheff family know at that time that Delcy was keeping her vow that Lloyd Sheff would never beat or violate her sexually again. Lloyd Sheff died in the year 1880 prior to the family leaving the plantation. Delcy never forgave nor forgot the rape she encountered at the hands of Lloyd Sheff that resulted in her pregnancy and the birth of Mama Lizzie. Although Mama was conceived of violence, her life exemplified love that she demonstrated in many ways throughout her life.

Mama died in her sleep on September 8, 1965.

Chronology of Events

1850	Eli, Leah, Reuben and Josh arrive in America at the Annapolis, Maryland slave market.
1854	Delcy Brent, daughter of Eli and Leah Brent, is born November 18, 1854; died April 6, 1926
1854	Neut Smith, sharecropper on Lloyd Sheff plantation, born September 10, 1854; died October 30, 1916
1870	Lizzie Brent Sheff, daughter of Delcy and Master Lloyd Sheff, born December 25, 1870
1871	Neut and Delcy marry in the spring of 1871. To this union 13 children are born.
1870 – 1880	Lizzie lives on Sheff plantation with Mama Delcy, Neut, and siblings.
1880	Lizzie leaves the plantation with parents and siblings and moves to the Walter's farm in Georgetown, Kentucky.
1887	Lizzie meets Jim Davis at a church gathering in Leesburg, Kentucky. They are married in the spring of 1887. Three children are born to this union: William Aaron (July 26, 1888), Leah Ann (March 1, 1891) and Charlie (June 8, 1893).
1895	Jim and Lizzie divorce
1898	Lizzie marries Simon Cannon, November 12, 1898. To this union five children are born: Elmer (May 15, 1900), Joe (January 13, 1902), Roy (July 30, 1904),

Mary Antionette (March 10, 1911), and Frank Robert (August 8, 1913). Two other children complete the family: Annie Bell (March 1, 1896), Simon's daughter by a previous marriage, and Katherine Louise Black (January 21, 1926), Lizzie's foster daughter.

1936	Frank Robert marries Ora Belle Hamilton. To this union three children are born: Frank Robert, Jr. (February 10, 1937), Mary Clarice (June 27, 1938) and John Merrell (May 17, 1939).
1965	Lizzie Brent Sheff Davis Cannon dies.
1988	Frank Robert, Sr. dies.
2001	Mary Clarice Cannon Boswell writes the story of her family's history from slavery to freedom.

Author Information

Dr. Clarice Boswell has resided in the Joliet, Illinois vicinity with her husband Hank since 1959. She is the mother of four children and has seven grandchildren. Dr. Boswell received her early training in Nicholasville, Kentucky where her father was principal of the colored school. She attended Kentucky State College, a land grant historically black college, where she received a bachelor degree in nutrition and home economics education and met her husband, Hank.

After moving to Joliet, Illinois in 1959, Mrs. Boswell worked as a dietitian at Silver Cross Hospital before being employed at Joliet East High School as a home economics teacher. In 1962 Mrs. Boswell entered Northern Illinois University where she earned a master's degree in education while simultaneously working on a second master's degree from Illinois State University in counseling with an emphasis on pupil personnel services.

In the fall of 1968, Mrs. Boswell was assigned to the counseling department at Joliet East High School where she served until it closed in 1984. She transferred to Joliet West High School as a counselor and career education advisor. In the fall of 1988, Mrs. Boswell re-entered Northern Illinois University to pursue a doctorate degree in adult continuing education with a focus on leadership, education, policies and service. Dr. Boswell graduated in May 1991 with her Ed. D degree. In the fall of 1990, Dr. Boswell was selected to chair the department of pupil personnel services at Joliet Central High School where she served for five years before retiring in June of 1995.

Dr. Boswell was so impressed with the historical research defining the struggle of historically black institutions that she continued her research to include the origin, struggle and journey of her family.

Delcy Brent Smith, born, November 18, 1854 to Leah and Eli Brent. Married Neut Smith, Spring 1871. To this union thirteen children were born. Delcy died April 6, 1926 in Leesburg, Kentucky.

Lizzie Brent Sheff Davis, age 28.

Lizzie Brent Sheff Davis Cannon, born December 25, 1870, was the mother of eight children and one foster daughter, Katherine Louise Black, whom she raised from the age of five. At Lizzie's death on September 8, 1965, at the age of 94, she had nine grandchildren and four children living that lovingly called her Mama.

Simon Cannon, born, March 1, 1872. The second husband of Lizzie and the father of Anna Bell and five children with Lizzie.

Neut Smith, born September 10, 1854, Moved to Kentucky looking for work in 1870. He stopped at the Sheff plantation where he was hired as a tobacco sharecropper for the Lloyd Sheff family. There he met Delcy (and baby Lizzie) who worked for the Sheff family. After a short courtship, Delcy and Neut were married in the spring of 1871. To this union, thirteen children were born.

House on the hill in Nicholasville, Kentucky that Simon Cannon built for his wife Lizzie and their children in 1917. Remodeled porch and siding added.

The tobacco fields of Kentucky were rich and fertile. The crops of Burley tobacco were tended by slaves with overseers that were often harsh and cruel. Sometimes food and water were withheld from the slaves as a punishment for not working as fast as the Master thought they should.

The old log cabin on the farm purchased by Simon Cannon, Leah and Frank Strauss, and Charlie Davis. Later, in 1935, Frank Cannon inherited Simon's share; William Davis bought out his brother Charlie, and Leah and Frank Strauss lived in the old log cabin. It still remains on the farm owned by the Cannon family. 2001.

African Methodist Church-

Leesburg, Kentucky

1927

Printed in the United States
94248LV00002B/7-105/A